THE ORGANIZATIONAL PSYCHOLOGY OF SPORT

This ground-breaking book is the first to provide an intergrated overview of how organizational psychology can be used to understand and improve performance in elite sport. Using recent theoretical advances from this burgeoning area of research, each chapter offers key conceptual issues and practical insights across a range of topics.

The book is organized into four constituent parts:

- Attitudes and emotions in sports organizations
- Stress and well-being in sports organizations
- Behaviors in sports organizations
- Environments in sports organizations

Covering key areas such as attitudes to employment, conflict and change management, leadership, and relationships with the mass media, the book shines a spotlight on how organizational issues play a fundamental role in the experience of individuals and teams.

In an era of ever-increasing professionalism in sport, the book provides an invaluable new perspective on performance at the elite level. Including contributions from an international range of academics and practitioners, it will be essential reading for any student or practitioner within sport and exercise psychology.

Christopher R. D. Wagstaff is a principal lecturer and the discipline director for sport and exercise psychology at the University of Portsmouth, UK. He acts as a consultant to organizations operating in high pressure environments, both in sport and beyond.

THE ORGANIZATIONAL PSYCHOLOGY OF SPORT

Key issues and practical applications

Edited by Christopher R. D. Wagstaff

LONDON AND NEW YORK

First published 2017
by Routledge
2 Park Square, Milton Park, Abingdon, Oxon, OX14 4RN

and by Routledge
711 Third Avenue, New York, NY 10017

Routledge is an imprint of the Taylor & Francis Group, an informa business

© 2017 selection and editorial matter, Christopher R. D. Wagstaff; individual chapters, the contributors

The right of the editor to be identified as the author of the editorial material, and of the authors for their individual chapters, has been asserted in accordance with sections 77 and 78 of the Copyright, Designs and Patents Act 1988.

All rights reserved. No part of this book may be reprinted or reproduced or utilised in any form or by any electronic, mechanical, or other means, now known or hereafter invented, including photocopying and recording, or in any information storage or retrieval system, without permission in writing from the publishers.

Trademark notice: Product or corporate names may be trademarks or registered trademarks, and are used only for identification and explanation without intent to infringe.

British Library Cataloguing in Publication Data
A catalogue record for this book is available from the British Library

Library of Congress Cataloging in Publication Data
Names: Wagstaff, Christopher R.D., editor.
Title: The organizational psychology of sport : key issues and practical applications / edited by Christopher R. D. Wagstaff, PhD.
Description: Milton Park, Abingdon, Oxon ; New York, NY : Routledge, 2016. | Includes index.
Identifiers: LCCN 2016010492| ISBN 9781138955172 (hardcover : alk. paper) | ISBN 1138955175 (hardcover : alk. paper) | ISBN 9781138955196 (pbk. : alk. paper) | ISBN 1138955191 (pbk. : alk. paper) | ISBN 1315666537 (ebook)
Subjects: LCSH: Sports – Psychological aspects. | Sports administration. | Organizational behavior.
Classification: LCC GV706.4 .O66 2016 | DDC 796.01/9–dc23
LC record available at http://lccn.loc.gov/2016010492

ISBN: 978-1-138-95517-2 (hbk)
ISBN: 978-1-138-95519-6 (pbk)
ISBN: 978-1-315-66653-2 (ebk)

Typeset in Bembo
by HWA Text and Data Management, London

CONTENTS

Figures and tables vii
About the editor viii
List of contributors ix
Preface xii
Acknowledgements xvii

1 Organizational psychology in sport: an introduction 1
   Christopher R. D. Wagstaff

PART I
Attitudes and emotions in sport organizations 9

2 Commitment in sport and exercise: implications for individual, group, and organizational functioning 11
   Ben Jackson, Daniel F. Gucciardi, Ken Hodge, and James A. Dimmock

3 Emotions in sport organizations 33
   Christopher R. D. Wagstaff and Sheldon Hanton

4 Attitudes to employment in sport organizations 62
   Sarah Gilmore

PART II
Stress and well-being in sport organizations 81

5 Stress in sport: the role of the organizational environment 83
   David Fletcher and Rachel Arnold

6 Well-being in sport organizations 101
   Rich Neil, Helen M. McFarlane, and Andrew P. Smith

7 Resilience in sport: a critical review of psychological
   processes, sociocultural influences, and organizational
   dynamics 120
   *Christopher R. D. Wagstaff, Mustafa Sarkar, Claire L. Davidson, and
   David Fletcher*

PART III
Behaviors in sport organizations 151

8 Leadership in sport organizations 153
   Calum A. Arthur, Christopher R. D. Wagstaff, and Lew Hardy

9 Prosocial and antisocial behaviors in sport organizations 176
   Maria Kavussanu and Nicholas Stanger

10 Media behavior in sport 193
    Elsa Kristiansen, Frank E. Abrahamsen, and Paul M. Pedersen

PART IV
Environments in sport organizations 215

11 The social environment in sport organizations 217
    Luc Martin, Mark Eys, and Kevin Spink

12 Optimal environments for team functioning in sport
    organizations 235
    *Katrien Fransen, Filip Boen, Jeroen Stouten, Stewart Cotterill, and
    Gert Vande Broek*

13 "We are in this together": a social identity perspective on
    change and conflict management 256
    Matthew J. Slater, Jamie B. Barker, and Stephen D. Mellalieu

Index 274

FIGURES AND TABLES

Figures

2.1	An illustration of the three-component model of commitment	16
3.1	An integrated model for emotion research in sport organizations	36
5.1	A simplified meta-model of stress, emotion, and performance	87
8.1	The Tripartite Model of Leadership (TML)	163
12.1	The four attributes that characterize resilient teams	246
12.2	A model of shared leadership, team identification, and team resilience as predictors of optimal team functioning and performance	250

Tables

10.1	Advice and examples for media interactions	200
10.2	Overview of behavior strategies to use with media	204

ABOUT THE EDITOR

Dr Christopher D. Wagstaff is a Chartered Psychologist and Associate Fellow of the British Psychological Society (BPS), registered Practitioner Psychologist with the Health and Care Professions Council (HCPC), British Association of Sport and Exercise Sciences (BASES) accredited Sport and Exercise Scientist, and Fellow of the Higher Education Academy.

He is a principal lecturer at University of Portsmouth, UK, where he is discipline director for sport and exercise psychology. Dr Wagstaff has published widely in the area of organizational psychology in sport, with projects spanning the areas of employee emotions and attitudes, stress and well-being, organizational behavior, and high performance environments. He is an associate editor for the *Journal of Applied Sport Psychology* and *Journal of Applied Case Studies in Sport and Exercise Sciences* and a member of the editorial board of *Case Studies in Sport and Exercise Psychology*.

As a practitioner psychologist, his consultancy work spans a diverse range of clients including international, Olympic and Paralympic athletes, coaches and support staff, business executives, government agencies, FTSE 100 companies, senior military officers in the British Army, Navy and Air Force, emergency service personnel, politicians, and performing artists.

As a partner of the HCPC he advises on fitness to practice and registrant appeal panels. He also works in an advisory capacity as a Registration Assessor for BASES and HCPC and provides supervision to probationary practitioners undertaking supervised experience (BASES) and Stage II supervised practice (BPS) qualifications.

Born in Birmingham, England, Chris now lives in the South Downs National Park in Hampshire. When not working, he spends his time with his partner, son, and dog, and plays rugby in the national league and guitar in private.

LIST OF CONTRIBUTORS

Dr Frank E. Abrahamsen, Norwegian School of Sport Sciences, Norway.

Dr Rachel Arnold, Department for Health, University of Bath, United Kingdom.

Dr Calum A. Arthur, School of Sport, Stirling University, United Kingdom.

Dr Jamie B. Barker, School of Psychology, Sport and Exercise, Staffordshire University, United Kingdom.

Professor Filip Boen, Department of Kinesiology, University of Leuven, Belgium.

Professor Gert Vande Broek, Department of Kinesiology, University of Leuven, Belgium.

Dr Stewart Cotterill, Department of Sport and Exercise, Winchester University, United Kingdom.

Ms Claire L. Davidson, School of Sport, Exercise and Health Sciences, Loughborough University, United Kingdom.

Dr James A. Dimmock, School of Sport Science, Exercise and Health, University of Western Australia, Australia.

Professor Mark Eys, Department of Kinesiology and Physical Education, Wilfred Laurier University, Canada.

Dr David Fletcher, School of Sport, Exercise and Health Sciences, Loughborough University, United Kingdom.

Dr Katrien Fransen, Department of Kinesiology, University of Leuven, Belgium.

Dr Sarah Gilmore, University of Exeter Business School, University of Exeter, United Kingdom.

Dr Daniel F. Gucciardi, School of Physiotherapy and Exercise Science, Curtin University, Australia.

Professor Sheldon Hanton, Cardiff School of Sport, Cardiff Metropolitan University, United Kingdom.

Professor Lew Hardy, School of Sport, Health, and Exercise Sciences, Bangor University, United Kingdom.

Professor Ken Hodge, School of Physical Education, Sport and Exercise Sciences, University of Otago, New Zealand.

Dr Ben Jackson, School of Sport Science, Exercise and Health, University of Western Australia, Australia.

Dr Maria Kavussanu, School of Sport, Exercise and Rehabilitation Sciences, University of Birmingham, United Kingdom.

Dr Elsa Kristiansen, School of Business and Social Sciences, University College of Southeast Norway, Norway.

Dr Luc Martin, School of Kinesiology and Health Studies, Queens University, Canada.

Ms Helen M. McFarlane, Cardiff School of Sport, Cardiff Metropolitan University, United Kingdom.

Professor Stephen D. Mellalieu, Cardiff School of Sport, Cardiff Metropolitan University, United Kingdom.

Dr Rich Neil, Cardiff School of Sport, Cardiff Metropolitan University, United Kingdom.

Professor Paul M. Pedersen, School of Public Health, Indiana University, USA.

Dr Mustafa Sarkar, College of Arts and Science, School of Science & Technology, Nottingham Trent University, United Kingdom.

Dr Matthew J. Slater, School of Psychology, Sport and Exercise, Staffordshire University, United Kingdom.

Professor Andrew P. Smith, School of Psychology, Cardiff University, United Kingdom.

Professor Kevin Spink, College of Kinesiology, University of Saskatchewan, Canada.

Dr Nicholas Stanger, School of Sport, Leeds Beckett University, United Kingdom.

Professor Jeroen Stouten, Faculty of Psychology and Educational Sciences, University of Leuven, Belgium.

Dr Christopher R. D. Wagstaff, Department of Sport and Exercise Science, University of Portsmouth, United Kingdom.

PREFACE

This book is about how people in sport organizations experience them. It concerns the ways people interpret and understand their sport organization and the behaviors of those they transact with in such environments.

It has been fifteen years since the first research paper on organizational psychology in sport was published by Tim Woodman and Lew Hardy (2001). In concluding their study, Woodman and Hardy asked:

> Is a sport psychologist equipped with the necessary expertise to help a sporting organization… at the organizational level? Today, with most sport psychology courses biased heavily toward psychological skills training for athletes, we doubt it… However, there are a number of ways in which sport psychologists might be able to help the team at an organizational level.

In the intervening years since these sentiments were expressed there have been considerable developments in the area of organizational psychology in sport. Indeed, the domain has matured markedly from its early foundations in organizational stress to incorporate the study of a diverse range of phenomena from a variety of epistemological, ontological, and methodological perspectives. In the last half decade alone, a number of reviews have been published charting the emergence of lines of inquiry within organizational psychology in elite sport (Fletcher & Wagstaff, 2009), emphasizing the value of examining positive organizational phenomena (Wagstaff, Fletcher, & Hanton, 2012), and outlining a research agenda and organizing structure for future research in the area (Wagstaff & Larner, 2015). I would argue that the substantial research developments in this area increasingly support Woodman and Hardy's sentiment that, "there are a number of ways in which sport psychologists might help at organizational levels". Nevertheless, the bourgeoning body of literature on organizational psychology in sport is not the only illustration of the emergence of this domain. Leading applied practitioners have gone as far as stating that "organizational issues probably have the biggest impact [of any psychosocial factor] on performance" (Jones, 2002, p. 279). Additionally, while I would argue that most sport psychology courses continue to be "heavily biased toward psychological skills training for athletes", it gives me great pleasure that the topic of "organizational issues" was recently included in the British Psychological Society's curriculum standards for accredited Masters degrees in sport and exercise psychology. These program standards must be achieved by all accredited courses in the UK and the inclusion of "organizational issues" in curricula is indicative of the growing recognition of the educational, theoretical, and applied importance of organizational psychology in sport, exercise, and performance psychology.

This book comprises thirteen chapters showcasing the latest research advances within the domain of organizational psychology in sport. Chapter 1 provides an introduction to organizational psychology in sport and attempts to define, delimit, and demystify relevant concepts. Thereafter, the book is divided into four parts aligned with Wagstaff and Larner's (2015) organizing structure for research and application in the domain of organizational psychology in sport. To elaborate, Wagstaff and Larner proposed four dimensions which I have adopted as a backbone for this book: attitudes and emotions in sport organizations; stress and well-being in sport organizations; behaviors in sport organizations; and environments in sport organizations.

Attitudes and emotions in sport organizations

Due to their impact on a range of psychosocial variables associated with well-being and performance, perhaps the most promising dimension of organizational psychology in sport relates to the interrelated areas of affect, emotion, mood, and attitudes. Jackson, Gucciardi, Hodge, and Dimmock (Chapter 2) review the way in which commitment has traditionally been operationalized in sport and exercise, before outlining how knowledge of commitment might be informed and advanced by drawing from established frameworks within organizational and social psychology. In a review of emotions in sport organizations, Wagstaff and Hanton (Chapter 3) consider the various levels at which emotion phenomena exist and present a multilevel theory of emotions in sport organizations, extending across five levels, from the within-person level to the emotional climate and culture within organizations. In Chapter 4, Gilmore provides an overview of research examining scientists' and sport medics' attitudes towards employment within sport organizations. It is alarming that although the study of individuals' attitudes to their employment has been a significant focus of research for over sixty years within the management and organization studies, there remains a relative dearth of such foci within the sport psychology domain, despite evidence to suggest the centrality of employee attitudes and emotions to experiences of work sport science and sport medicine professions.

Stress and well-being in sport organizations

The highly complex social and organizational environments in elite sport impose numerous demands on the performers and personnel that function within them (i.e., preparation, expectations, interpersonal relationships), with advice frequently sought from psychologists on dealing with the pressures that accompany participation (Fletcher & Wagstaff, 2009). Indeed, the area of stress has received more research attention than any other dimension within organizational psychology in sport. Fletcher and Arnold (Chapter 5) take stock of the considerable momentum in organizational stress research in sport over the past decade and provide a timely updated review of the area. In doing so, the authors address a number of key issues relating to conceptualization, relationships with performance and well-being, and the optimization of athletes' stress experience. To provide a balance of issues in this part, Neil, McFarlane, and Smith (Chapter 6) focus on well-being in sport organizations through the lens of *wellness*, utilizing concepts from positive psychology. Specifically, Neil and colleagues consider the construct of well-being conceptually and empirically through the perspectives of hedonism and eudaemonism. They also offer a critical insight into well-being research relevant to sport organizations with directions for future research and potential intervention strategies to promote well-being within sport organizations. In the last chapter in this part, Wagstaff, Sarkar, Davidson, and Fletcher (Chapter 7) critically review the psychological processes underpinning the sociocultural influences on, and the organizational dynamics surrounding resilience in athletes and teams in sport. In doing so, the authors also propose a research agenda for the future study of resilience in sport organizations.

Behaviors in sport organizations

The third part of this book is dedicated to the research within organizational psychology that encompasses the diverse topics aligned with organizational behavior. Topics aligned with this dimension examine the impact of individual, group, and organization-wide behavior on well-being and performance. In the first chapter in this part, Arthur, Wagstaff, and Hardy (Chapter 8) highlight the need for sport psychology researchers to focus on what leaders *do* at different levels of sport organizations, by calling for leadership researchers to move beyond the coach–athlete relationship and turn their attention to leadership throughout the organizational structure. The authors discuss hierarchical structures and integrate leader distance theories into the sport organizational context, before outlining a behavioral taxonomy that is cognizant of leader distance and leadership *of* and *in* sport organizations. Next, Kavussanu and Stanger (Chapter 9) review the literature pertaining to prosocial and antisocial behaviors that might have important implications for the effective functioning of sport organizations. To elaborate, the authors discuss the antecedents and consequences of prosocial and antisocial behaviors, delineating moral and motivational variables, before evaluating the contribution of research on organizational citizenship behavior for advancing knowledge on psychological and physical welfare in sport organizations. In the last chapter in this part, Kristiansen, Abrahamsen, and Pedersen (Chapter 10) review the influence of the mass media – as well as social media – on the behavior of individuals in sport. The authors look closely at the growing research examining the media behavior of athletes, journalists, and organizations under the rubric of "media behavior". In doing so, Kristiansen and colleagues give practical advice for sport psychologists and organizations to better help their employees (e.g., athletes, managers, coaches) cope with media coverage and increase the effectiveness of their interactions with the media.

Environments in sport organizations

Sport organizations are characterized by multiple stakeholder groups (e.g., departments, teams) that must share resources in the pursuit of individual, team, and organizational goals. The environments in which such work is done are likely to impact its effectiveness. It follows that a greater understanding of such environment-related factors will benefit functioning at various organizational levels. In the first chapter in this part, Martin, Eys, and Spink (Chapter 11) outline a case for examining an aspect of the social environment within sport organizations that typically receives little attention – the group(s) within the group – in an attempt to better acknowledge and discuss the presence and interrelatedness of various subgroups and more fully understand the social environment in sport organizations. The authors use recent research to illustrate the importance of accounting for different subgroups, the identification of key groups, and the interrelatedness of various subgroups. Next, Fransen, Boen, Stouten, Cotterill, and Vande Broek (Chapter 12) outline how leaders can create optimal environments for team functioning as facilitators of shared leadership using the lens of social identity theory. Specifically, they argue that coaches can facilitate performance by acting as a facilitator of shared leadership, an identity manager, and a conflict manager. Slater, Barker, and Mellalieu (Chapter 13) also draw from a social identity perspective in an attempt to develop our understanding of the growing issue of change and conflict management within elite sport environments. Their narrative highlights the value of social identity approaches for such challenges and outlines two intervention frameworks through which effective change management may be facilitated with a view to optimizing organizational functioning.

Each chapter in this book provides a review of the most pertinent literature and a summary of the key messages for future research and/or applied practice. These elements were perceived as pivotal for the main purposes of this book

– to integrate and instigate. My primary goal for this book has been to offer an integrated text for students, neophytes, experienced practitioners, and the cognoscenti. While my aim has been to be integrative, no edited collection could claim to be comprehensive, yet I believe this collection offers a very broad coverage of both established themes and emerging lines of inquiry by the leading scholars in this domain. My secondary goal – to instigate – relates to my hope that new research ideas, applied insights, and collaborative networks will be initiated as a result of this book. The chapters herein certainly contain new research ideas as well as calls for the use of novel and under-represented methodologies and research designs. While it will require the passage of time to evaluate the extent to which this text generates applied insights regarding the competencies of applied practitioners, I am proud that the contributor list to this book includes a genuine international representation. I sincerely hope that the collaborations begun, maintained, and revived here provide the impetus for further work by the contributors and entice others to advance this exciting domain of research and practice toward new lines of inquiry and new ways of working.

References

Fletcher, D., & Wagstaff, C. R. D. (2009). Organizational psychology in elite sport: Its emergence, application and future. *Psychology of Sport and Exercise, 10*(4), 427–434. doi:10.1016/j.psychsport.2009.03.009

Jones, G. (2002). Performance excellence: A personal perspective on the link between sport and business. *Journal of Applied Sport Psychology, 14*(4), 268–281.

Wagstaff, C. R. D., Fletcher, D., & Hanton, S. (2012). Positive organizational psychology in sport. *International Review of Sport and Exercise Psychology, 5*(2), 87–103. doi:10.1080/1750984X.2011.634920.

Wagstaff, C. R. D., & Larner, R. J. (2015). Organisational psychology in sport: Recent developments and a research agenda. In S. D. Mellalieu and S. Hanton (Eds.) *Contemporary advances in sport psychology: A review* (pp. 91–119). London: Routledge.

Woodman, T., & Hardy, L. (2001). A case study of organizational stress in elite sport. *Journal of Applied Sport Psychology, 13*(2), 207–238.

ACKNOWLEDGEMENTS

I am very grateful to all the authors for their contributions to this book. Integrating contributions from individuals in nine countries across three continents was a challenging task, and I hope you are as pleased with the results as I am. My appreciation is also extended to the staff at Routledge Publishing, who were instrumental in instigating this process. Finally, I would like to express special thanks to my partner, family and friends for their ongoing love and support throughout the production of this book and my career in general.

1
ORGANIZATIONAL PSYCHOLOGY IN SPORT

An introduction

Christopher R. D. Wagstaff

In the latter part of the twentieth century, elite sport was host to substantial commercialization and globalization (see de Bosscher, Bingham, Shibli, van Bottenburg, & De Knop, 2008; Fletcher & Wagstaff, 2009; Houlihan & Green, 2008). Thus far, during the twenty-first century there has been little indication that these changes will slow or desist. Indeed, the future of elite sport is likely to be more complex, turbulent, and volatile. The implication of such changes has been a growing demand for the establishment of organizational systems that instantly and consistently deliver success. In response to such requirements, there has been an increasing technologicalization, medicalization, and scientization of elite sport performance environments as organizations seek a competitive edge (Wagstaff, Thelwell, & Gilmore, 2016). Such actions echo the observations of sport management scholars who have described the current state of unrest as a "global sporting arms race" (see de Bosscher et al., 2008), defined by the creation of isomorphic institutions characterized by coordinated policies and processes, hierarchically-structured bodies, with democratized authority and shared collective goals. Given the changing landscape of elite sport, scholars have increasingly emphasized the importance of exploring the organizational contexts in which elite sport performers operate (see, for reviews, Fletcher & Wagstaff, 2009; Wagstaff, Fletcher, & Hanton, 2012a; Wagstaff & Larner, 2015). Indeed, in view of the pivotal role of human performance for optimizing the functioning of these organizations (see Wagstaff, Fletcher, & Hanton, 2012b), the domain of organizational psychology has much to contribute to the changing face of elite sport (see Fletcher & Wagstaff, 2009).

What is organizational psychology in sport?

The foundations of organizational psychology lie with the confluence of industrial and organizational (I/O) and the changing landscape of elite sport environments. Wagstaff et al., (2012a) described I/O psychology as "a general practice specialty of professional psychology with a focus on scientifically-based solutions to human problems in work and other organizational settings. In these contexts, I/O psychologists assess and enhance the effectiveness of individuals, groups, and organizations" (American Psychological Association, 2011). I/O psychologists recognize the interdependence of individuals, organizations and society and consider problems such as employee turnover, absenteeism and productivity; succession planning and development of managers and executives; organizational restructuring; workplace stress and safety; and worker motivation and performance (Wagstaff et al., 2012a).

Scholars have typically distinguished between three concentrations of I/O psychology (e.g., Landy & Conte, 2009): personnel psychology, organizational psychology, and human engineering. Personnel psychology (often integrated within human resources in many workplaces) addresses issues such as recruitment, selection, training, performance appraisal, promotion, transfer, and termination. This work typically relates to the methods and principles used to select and evaluate potential employees and overlaps with talent identification and team composition procedures in sport organizations. Nevertheless, traditionally such roles have been performed by individuals responsible for the performance department (e.g., manager, performance director, director of sport), with input from scouts and performance analysts. The value of psychological input regarding these issues lies in the view that individuals have fluctuating work behaviors and attitudes and that information relating to these changes can help predict, maintain, and increase performance and satisfaction.

Organizational psychology integrates research foundations in social psychology and organizational behavior to address emotional and motivational aspects of organizational life. The main aim of this work is the evaluation of what motivates employees to have a successful, productive, satisfying work environment. Consequently, organizational psychologists commonly focus on topics such as attitudes, fairness, motivation, stress, leadership, teams, and broader aspects of organizational and work design. Given its emphasis on the reactions of people to work and their resultant action, tendencies and responses, both the organization and the people within its sphere of influence are of importance. Hence, organizational psychologists might also seek to achieve a fit between people, the work demands they might face and the organization's idiosyncratic characteristics. Therefore, the principal purpose of organizational psychology is to provide applied knowledge to help organizations function more effectively. Indeed, to reiterate the sentiments of Wagstaff et al. (2012a) in their call for a *positive* research agenda for organizational psychology in sport, "there appears to be scope for sport psychologists to better understand the key variables which improve the way in which operators work together to accomplish their tasks through the medium of organizational psychology" (p. 89). Moreover, Wagstaff and Larner (2015) proposed that organizational psychology principles could advance sport performance through two means: the development of optimally functioning sport organizations and via the enhancement of the quality of work life for those that operate with their sphere of influence.

Human engineering refers to the study of human limitations with respect to their organizational environment and relates to the design of products, technology, systems, and environments that optimize performance. Whilst personnel psychology aims to find the best individual for the work, and organizational psychology aims to match the best person to relevant roles, human engineering aims to develop environments and systems that are compatible with the characteristics of the worker. According to Landy and Conte (2009) the diverse environmental aspects of this work may include tools, work spaces, information display, shift work, work pace, machine controls, and safety. This approach integrates cognitive science, ergonomics, physiology, anatomy, and biomechanics. The role of human engineering psychologists in sport could incorporate the optimal understanding, functionality, and integration of medical, technological, and scientific advances by sport performers.

Although I perceive value in each of the three concentrations or sub-disciplines of general I/O psychology, it is my belief that the biggest potential benefit to sport organizations is the optimization of organizational psychology factors, under the rubric of positive organizational psychology in sport (POPS; Wagstaff et al., 2012a). Hence, the predominant focus of this book is on topics aligned with the second concentration outlined above. Nevertheless, to enable a full appreciation of the salience of this area, it is important to give further consideration to its value for elite sport performance.

Vacuums and the myth of individualism

Advocates of organizational psychology in sport (see, e.g., Fletcher & Wagstaff, 2009; Wagstaff & Larner, 2015) have frequently referred to an oft-quoted passage from Hardy, Jones, and Gould's (1996) early sport psychology text: borrowing from Shaw's work on social environments (1981) they concluded their book by noting that "elite athletes do not live in a vacuum; they function within a highly complex social and organizational environment, which exerts major influences on them and their performances" (pp. 239–240). Allied with Hardy et al.'s vacuum analogy of the environments in which elite sport performers prepare and perform, there are many dangers of what I would label a "myth of individualism". That is, a fallacy that sporting success or failure is wholly determined by individual effort or ability has prevailed for some time in society. The power of this myth lies in its promotion of a social fixation on talent and eliding of the salience of a wealth of interpersonal, group, and organizational factors that impact performance. This is not to say that elite sport performers do not require talent, or that this cannot be nurtured and supplemented with individual effort; indeed, such factors are pivotal for initial success and might be largely responsible for fugacious underdog triumphs. Nevertheless, *sustained* success in high performance domains is predicated on looking beyond a perspective that individualism or related ephemeral factors (e.g., talent, deliberate practice, religious dogma, effort, luck, physical prowess) alone can result in ongoing success. That is, recurrent success in elite sport is not solely dependent on the talent (i.e., embodied competence) of individual performers, but on how effectively these individuals build and maintain working relationships with a systematic collective of stakeholders (e.g., coaches, managers, performers), supports (e.g., scientific, medical, and technological expertise), networks (e.g., social support), and bodies (e.g., sport organizations, commercial sponsors) to optimize day-to-day productivity in preparation for and performance at major competitions (see Wagstaff et al., 2012b).

In addition to the importance of dispelling the myth of individualism for sporting success, there is also a need to view sport organizations as more than systematized collectives aimed at promoting success, but as a workplace that must ensure the well-being of its employees. That is, examining the psychological states of individuals during their engagement with organizations and at home (i.e., their work–life balance) might allow for a better understanding of the well-being of sport performers. Well-being considers a wide range of experiences including the demands (e.g., stressors) and functioning (e.g., success factors). Indeed, such concepts consider positive (e.g., enthusiasm) and negative (e.g., anxiety) affective states, outcomes such as work-related well-being (e.g., psychosomatic health, job satisfaction), as well as the processes (e.g., communication) that facilitate these ends. Hence, the value of organizational psychology in sport lies with its examination and facilitation of factors to debunk the erroneous belief that talent alone prevails and its acknowledgment that elite sport environments are places of work requiring considerations for sportspeople as employees with requisite rights, needs, and expectations.

In line with the growing acknowledgement of the importance of organizational issues in elite sport, three recent reviews have summarized the emergence, application, and potential futures for this domain. Specifically, in 2009 an article by Fletcher and Wagstaff was published in *Psychology of Sport and Exercise* that reviewed a (then) nascent body of research concerned with the emergence of organizational issues in elite sport. Fletcher and Wagstaff (2009) reviewed six lines of inquiry pointing to the salience of these issues: factors affecting Olympic performance; organizational stress; perceptions of roles; organizational success factors; performance environments in elite sport; and organizational citizenship behavior. Wagstaff et al. (2012a) reviewed the literature relating to the *positive* aspects of organizational psychology research in sport. Within their review, Wagstaff et al. defined and delimited relevant concepts, including organizational psychology and positive organizing, with a particular emphasis on extant research relating to organizational functioning in sport (i.e., positive environments, positive behaviors, and positive outcomes) and a call for attention to be paid to topics such as culture, climate and change, in addition to those aligned with positive organizational behavior and scholarship (see Wagstaff et al., 2012a). More recently, Wagstaff and Larner (2015) provided a review of the recent developments in the literature relating to organizational psychology in sport. In doing so, they delimited and demystified organizational psychology from similar concentrations of I/O psychology. Moreover, they provided an organizing structure to align extant and potential future lines of inquiry within organizational psychology in sport. It is this framework that provides the backbone of this text, which has parts dedicated to attitudes and emotions; stress and well-being; behaviors; and environments.

Conclusion

The changing landscape of elite sport environments has stimulated a burgeoning body of research examining organizational psychology in sport. Indeed, particular strengths within this domain relate to the elucidation of an understanding of emotion- and attitude-related phenomena, stress and well-being in athletes, coaches, support staff, and parents, key behaviors associated with optimal functioning, and environments which facilitate elite performance. Indeed, the chapters in this text review some of the excellent work that has begun to provide insights into the predictors of sustained organizational performance in sport that might be controlled and influenced through empirically grounded interventions. Despite these fruitful endeavors, there remains much to be understood regarding organizational psychology in sport and further research is required to expand extant and incorporate new lines of inquiry.

A salient point for consideration as you read this book relates to the complexity of organizational dynamics, and the apparent intertwined nature of the core dimensions and topics they encompass (Wagstaff & Larner, 2015). For example, the chapters included here highlight many variables of interest that appear to transcend dimensions through level of analysis or influence (e.g., stress, leadership). Hence, an important obligation for researchers in this domain is to provide conceptual clarity to demystify the hierarchical, correlational or causal nature of their variables of interest others of relevance. Therefore, and in line with the suggestions of Wagstaff et al. (2013), researchers must be cognizant of levels of analysis (i.e., individual, dyadic, team, organizational) within organizational psychology.

In this book, much of the focus is on research aligned with organizational psychology. Nevertheless, as alluded to in my introductory sentiments, this reflects just one of three general I/O psychology concentrations with limited space dedicated to a discourse on the importance of personnel psychology or human engineering factors. Research on such concentrations includes employment practices within sport organizations and their implications for the performance and well-being of employees (see Chapter 4). Such research might benefit by using techniques commonly associated with personnel psychology, including the use of exit interviews when seeking to make improvements in organizational functioning. Human engineering research within sport organizations might prove the most problematic of the three, given the advanced development of sport biomechanics and technology and the work of practitioners to enhance the interface between individuals in organizations and these supports. Nevertheless, it is possible that psychologists can optimize the understanding and integration of such supports if they are afforded such a role by organizations.

Finally, it is important to note that despite the nascent state of some of the areas of inquiry within this domain, much of the research reviewed here has used inductive research designs, grounded in the sport context to examine phenomena with divergent origins. Indeed, the recent use of ecologically valid and representative designs to examine organizational psychology concepts in sport such as ethnography (e.g., Wagstaff et al., 2012b), action research (e.g., Wagstaff et al., 2013), and case studies (Cruickshank, Collins, & Minten, 2013) are highly suitable for research in its infancy. Moreover, it is reassuring to observe that researchers have begun to develop sport specific measures of organizational-related variables (e.g., Arnold, Fletcher & Daniels, 2013; Jackson, Gucciardi & Dimmock, 2014) as these lines of inquiry have blossomed. I hope future research in this domain will continue these good practices of scientific study.

References

American Psychological Association. (2011). *Defining the practice of sport and performance psychology*. Washington DC: Division 47, Exercise and Sport Psychology, Practice Committee.

Arnold, R., Fletcher, D., & Daniels, K. (2013). Development and validation of the organizational stressor indicator for sport performers (OSI-SP). *Journal of Sport and Exercise Psychology, 35*, 180–196

Cruickshank, A., Collins, D., & Minten, S. (2013). Culture change in a professional sports team: Shaping environmental contexts and regulating power. *International Journal of Sports Science and Coaching, 8*(2), 271–290.

De Bosscher, V., Bingham, J., Shibli, S., Van Bottenburg, M., & De Knop, P. (2008). *The global sporting arms race. An international comparative study on sports policy factors leading to international sporting success*. Aachen: Meyer & Meyer.

Fletcher, D., & Wagstaff, C. R. D. (2009). Organizational psychology in elite sport: Its emergence, application and future. *Psychology of Sport and Exercise, 10*(4), 427–434. doi:10.1016/j.psychsport.2009.03.009

Hardy, L. J., Jones, G., & Gould, D. (1996). *Understanding psychological preparation for sport: Theory and practice of elite performers*. Hoboken, NJ: John Wiley & Sons.

Houlihan, B., & Green, M. (2008). *Comparative elite sport development. Systems structures and public policy*. London: Elsevier.

Jackson, B., Gucciardi, D. F., & Dimmock, J. A. (2014). Toward a multidimensional model of athletes' commitment to coach-athlete relationships and interdependent sport teams: A substantive-methodological synergy. *Journal of Sport & Exercise Psychology, 36*, 52–68.

Landy, F. J., & Conte, J. M. (2009). *Work in the 21st century: An introduction to industrial and organizational psychology*. Hoboken, NJ: John Wiley & Sons.

Shaw, M. E. (1981). *Group dynamics: The psychology of small group behavior*. New York: McGraw-Hill.
Wagstaff, C. R. D., Fletcher, D., & Hanton, S. (2012a). Positive organizational psychology in sport. *International Review of Sport and Exercise Psychology, 5*(2), 87–103. doi:10.1080/1750984X.2011.634920.
Wagstaff, C. R. D., Fletcher, D., & Hanton, S. (2012b). Positive organizational psychology in sport: An ethnography of organizational functioning in a national sport organization. *Journal of Applied Sport Psychology, 24*(1), 26–47. doi:10.1080/10413200.2011.589423.
Wagstaff, C. R. D., Hanton, S., & Fletcher, D. (2013). Developing emotion abilities and regulation strategies in a sport organization: An action research intervention. *Psychology of Sport and Exercise, 14*(4), 476–487. doi:10.1016/j.psychsport.2013.01.006.
Wagstaff, C. R. D., & Larner, R. J. (2015). Organisational psychology in sport: Recent developments and a research agenda. In S. D. Mellalieu and S. Hanton (Eds.) *Contemporary advances in sport psychology: A review* (pp. 91–119). London: Routledge.
Wagstaff, C. R. D., Thelwell, R. C., & Gilmore, S. (2016). Sport medicine and sport science practitioners' experiences of organizational change. *Scandinavian Journal of Medicine and Science in Sport, 25*(5), 685–698.

PART I
Attitudes and emotions in sport organizations

2

COMMITMENT IN SPORT AND EXERCISE

Implications for individual, group, and organizational functioning

Ben Jackson, Daniel F. Gucciardi, Ken Hodge, and James A. Dimmock

> Individual commitment to a group effort – that is what makes a team work, a company work, a society work, a civilization work.
> Vince Lombardi, American Football coach, NFL Hall of Fame Member
> (Lombardi, 2003, p. 105)

Introduction

Whether listening to athletes explaining their achievements, employees describing their reasons for staying with an organization, or people discussing the longevity of their romantic relationship, we commonly hear individuals talk of their "commitment" to the activity, entity, or person in question. Due in part to the frequency with which we encounter this concept in daily life, sustained empirical attention has been directed toward understanding the nature, origins, and implications of "commitment". Indeed, within social (see Cropanzano & Mitchell, 2005; Johnson, 1991; Rusbult, Martz, & Agnew, 1998), organizational (see Meyer, 2009; Meyer & Maltin, 2010), educational (see Jenkins, 1995), and athletic (see Weiss & Amorose, 2008) contexts, individuals' persistence, well-being, and performance have all been examined through a "commitment" lens. In this chapter, we review the way in which commitment has traditionally been operationalized in sport and exercise, before outlining how our knowledge of commitment might be informed and advanced by drawing from established frameworks within organizational and social psychology.

Prior to examining the commitment literature in sport and exercise, though, it is important to provide a working definition of the construct, which we use as a scaffold throughout the material that follows. This task is not a straightforward one, given that scholars are yet to arrive at any single and universally-endorsed definition of the construct (for different perspectives, see Meyer & Herscovitch, 2001; Solinger, van Olffen, & Roe, 2008). Most conceptualizations of commitment, however, emphasize that it represents a "force that binds an individual to a course of action of relevance to one or more targets" (Meyer & Herscovitch, 2001, p. 301). That is, commitment refers to a *psychological* desire, or drive, that helps direct individuals' behavior. Importantly, central to most definitions is the notion that individuals direct their "commitment" toward one or more entities or foci (for a detailed discussion, see Meyer & Herscovitch, 2001). In sport, for instance, the entity or focus might take the form of (an athlete's commitment to) a playing partner, a coach, a team, a subgroup within one's team, an organization, and/or a sport itself. Similarly, in relation to exercise, a relevant entity or focus might include one's exercise partner or group, a delivery organization (e.g., a fitness company), an instructor, and/or an exercise modality. In the following section, we chart the development of commitment research in sport and exercise; our aim is to provide a broad overview of the way in which commitment has been (and is) typically studied within sport and exercise contexts.

Commitment in sport and exercise: an overview

Guided by the extensive literature that had developed outside of sport and exercise (e.g., Becker, 1960; Kelley, 1983; Rusbult, 1980), a focus on commitment in athletic settings emerged during the late 1980s and early 1990s. Initially, commitment was considered largely as an explanatory mechanism for understanding athletic burnout and attrition (see Gould & Petlichkoff, 1988; Smith, 1986). Schmidt and Stein (1991), however, provided the impetus for concentrated research in this area by presenting a framework in which they positioned commitment as the focal construct. In particular, having articulated a range of antecedent factors (e.g., enjoyment, perceived benefits, perceived costs, available alternatives), these authors posited that individuals might experience different forms of commitment based on the relative profile of those antecedents. Schmidt and Stein contended that athletes may experience a relatively adaptive form of "enjoyment-based" commitment under a given set of antecedent conditions (e.g., high enjoyment and perceived benefits, allied with low perceived costs regarding one's sport involvement), but alternatively, might experience a less desirable form of commitment when antecedent conditions encouraged feelings of entrapment (e.g., low enjoyment and benefits alongside high perceived costs and few alternatives). Although Schmidt and Stein did not test these proposals, Scanlan and her colleagues built on their work, and, in 1993, presented a series of studies in the *Journal of Sport & Exercise Psychology* (Carpenter, Scanlan, Simons, & Lobel, 1993; Scanlan, Carpenter, Schmidt, Simons, & Keeler, 1993; Scanlan, Simons, Carpenter, Schmidt, & Keeler, 1993), in which they articulated, operationalized, and demonstrated empirical support for a formalized model of sport commitment. In doing so, Scanlan and colleagues outlined that commitment represented a psychological desire that may determine one's persistence in an activity, and forwarded a model of sport commitment that would become the platform for much of the research that was to emerge in this area over the ensuing 20 years.

Scanlan and colleagues (Scanlan, Carpenter, et al., 1993) defined sport commitment as "the desire and resolve to continue participation in a sport over time" (p. 18). Guided by the assertion that strong feelings of sport commitment would contribute to behavioral perseverance (i.e., retention to one's sport), these authors drew from theory (e.g., Rusbult, 1980) and articulated that commitment was likely to be strengthened in response to a number of antecedent factors, namely when:

- *Enjoyment* levels were high (i.e., athletes enjoy playing their sport).
- *Involvement opportunities* were high (i.e., athletes anticipate or accrue benefits from their sport involvement, including friendships, skill, mastery, fitness, etc.). Note: this antecedent has also latterly been referred to as "valuable opportunities".
- *Personal investments* (such as time, effort, and money) in one's sport were high.
- *Social constraints* were high (i.e., expectations or norms regarding significant others that engender feelings of obligation to continue one's involvement).
- *Involvement alternatives* were low (i.e., attractive alternatives that compete with one's sport participation). Note: this antecedent has also latterly been referred to as "other priorities".
- *Social support* was high (i.e., feeling supported and encouraged to continue one's sport participation by significant others), and athletes' *desire to excel* – defined using personal, task, or normative criteria – was high. Note: these antecedent themes were added to the sport commitment model following subsequent work conducted after the original model was presented (see Scanlan, Russell, Beals, & Scanlan, 2003; Scanlan, Russell, Magyar, & Scanlan, 2009; Scanlan, Russell, Scanlan, Klunchoo, & Chow, 2013; Scanlan, Russell, Wilson, & Scanlan, 2003).

In the years since the development of the model, there has been a consistent focus in the literature on testing these proposed antecedents (for an overview, see Weiss & Amorose, 2008). With the exception of somewhat equivocal findings regarding the role of the social constraints construct (for coverage, see Scanlan et al., 2013), there appears to be (at least some) empirical support for each of the variables proposed to predict sport commitment (see Weiss & Amorose, 2008). The evidence that enjoyment acts as a support for commitment is particularly compelling (e.g., Carpenter & Coleman, 1998). Indeed, some authors have even demonstrated that the effects of the other predictor variables on commitment might occur through (i.e., be mediated by) enjoyment (e.g., Weiss, Kimmel, & Smith, 2001; Weiss & Weiss, 2006), although it is important to note that this perspective is not unanimously endorsed (see Scanlan et al., 2009). Despite most attention being directed toward the determinants of commitment, the implications of this construct with respect to behavioral persistence (e.g., continued involvement, training frequency) have also been documented using both qualitative (e.g., Scanlan, Russell, et al., 2003b) and quantitative (e.g., Casper, Gray, & Stellino, 2007; Santi, Bruton, Pietrantoni, & Mellalieu, 2014; Vallerand & Young, 2014; Weiss & Weiss, 2006) approaches. Researchers in this area have also made conceptual advancements by considering how age and competitive level might moderate the effects of theorized determinants (e.g., Casper & Andrew, 2008; Weiss, 2014; Weiss & Weiss, 2007), as well as offering contextual diversity by focusing on athletic populations with varied geographical (e.g., Choosakul, Vongjaturapat, Li, & Harmer, 2009), developmental (e.g., Young & Medic, 2011), and skill-level (e.g., Scanlan et al., 2009) backgrounds.

Although the literature reviewed above is not exhaustive, it nonetheless demonstrates the continued effort that investigators have exerted in studying commitment over the last three decades. Nevertheless, there are important ways in which we might build upon our understanding of how commitment operates in sport and exercise settings. First, although Scanlan and colleagues (Scanlan, Carpenter, et al., 1993) asserted that commitment might be examined at different "levels of analysis" (i.e., in relation to different focal entities or actions), researchers in sport and exercise have yet to fully explore this notion. That is not to say that no attention has been directed toward varied entities or targets. For instance, limited work has been conducted with the aim of examining coach commitment and burnout (Raedeke, 2004; Raedeke, Granzyk, & Warren, 2000), exploring athletes' commitment to their sport team (e.g., Scanlan et al., 2009), and investigating relations between exercise commitment and exercise participation (Wilson et al., 2004). However, the majority of published commitment research has considered *athletes' commitment to their sport*, at the expense of the many other potential "targets" toward which athletes might direct their commitment. One way in which we might begin to understand more about the development and implications of commitment, therefore, is to study athlete commitment as it applies to a broader array of targets/foci (e.g., commitment to one's playing partner, coach, team, organization). Moreover, although the focus on athlete commitment is understandable given the importance of retention and persistence, there remains much to discover regarding the role of commitment among the various non-athlete cohorts that exist in sport and exercise (e.g., coaches/managers, administrators, exercise class attendees, performance directors). Later in this chapter, we provide a range of suggestions for future research that are rooted in these considerations.

Second, despite sport and exercise psychologists acknowledging for some time that commitment may take different forms (see Scanlan, Carpenter, et al., 1993; Schmidt & Stein, 1991), a multidimensional approach to the study of commitment is yet to become fully established in sport and exercise research. Raedeke (1997) demonstrated that individuals might be committed to their sport for different reasons, and a number of other sport- (e.g., Santi et al., 2014; Scanlan, Chow, Sousa, Scanlan, & Knifsend, 2016; Scanlan et al., 2013; Weiss & Weiss, 2006; Young & Medic, 2011) and exercise-based (Wilson et al., 2004) investigations have provided support for the notion that individuals might experience qualitatively different types of commitment. Despite these findings, much of the commitment work that exists in the sport and exercise literature has treated commitment as a *unidimensional* construct. In the material that follows, we: (a) describe multidimensional commitment frameworks that exist in organizational and social contexts; (b) identify the limited number of sport- and exercise-related studies that have utilized these (and other multidimensional) frameworks; and (c) consider the ways in which these frameworks might be used to advance our understanding of commitment and associated outcomes (e.g., retention, participation) in sport and exercise.

Multidimensional commitment perspectives

> In anything we do, any endeavor, it's not what you do, it's why you do it.
> Howard Schultz, Starbucks Chairman and Chief Executive Officer
> (Schultz & Yang, 1997, p. 18)

Social and organizational psychologists have long recognized that commitment is best understood (and measured) as a multidimensional construct (see Becker, 1960; Johnson, 1973). Although a number of different multidimensional models have been developed, there is some degree of commonality across prominent social (see Johnson, Caughlin, & Huston, 1999) and organizational (see Meyer, Stanley, Herscovitch, & Topolnytsky, 2002) frameworks in terms of the types of commitment that are theorized to exist. In particular, a three-component view of commitment is relatively well-entrenched within close relationship (Johnson, 1991) and workplace (Meyer & Allen, 1991) settings, and this conceptualization may be of value for the study of commitment to one's relationships, groups, teams, and organizations in sport and exercise. According to these frameworks, individuals may be committed to staying in/with a relationship, team, group, or organization due to their identification with, and emotional attachment to, that target. This dimension is often referred to as *affective* commitment in the organizational literature, and *personal* commitment in the relational literature (example measurement item, "this organization has a great deal of personal meaning for me"). A second commitment type reflects the notion that individuals may desire to remain in/with their relationship, team, group, or organization due to a sense of obligation, or moral attachment, to that target; this dimension has been termed *normative* (or *moral*) commitment (example measurement item, "I owe a great deal to my organization"). Finally, individuals might continue their involvement in/with their relationship, team, group, or organization as a result of feeling "locked in" due to the perceived costs associated with withdrawal and a lack of available alternatives; this dimension has been termed *continuance* (or *structural*) commitment (example measurement item, "I feel that I have too few other options to consider leaving this organization"). Throughout the remainder of this chapter we refer to these dimensions according to the terms used in the organizational literature, as it is these terms that have been utilized in the multidimensional commitment research that has recently begun to emerge in sport.

Meyer and colleagues (Meyer, Allen, & Smith, 1993) distinguished between the three factors by noting that individuals "with a strong affective commitment remain… because they *want* to, those with a strong continuance commitment remain because they *need* to, and those with a strong normative commitment remain because they feel they *ought* to" (p. 539, emphasis added). In outlining their three-component framework (see Figure 2.1), they also asserted that affective, normative, and continuance commitment are not mutually exclusive (Meyer & Allen, 1991), and that an individual can experience all three dimensions to varying degrees at any point in time. In sport, for instance, an athlete could report a strong affective (i.e., emotional attachment and identification) and normative (i.e., moral obligation) desire to remain with a coach, team, or organization, while simultaneously feeling "locked in" to that coach, team, or organization in light of investments made and limited available alternatives (i.e., strong continuance commitment).

In addition to accounting for the multidimensionality of commitment, the practical value of the three-component framework lies in the antecedents, correlates, and consequences that are theorized to align with the focal constructs, and how these processes might vary across commitment dimensions (Meyer et

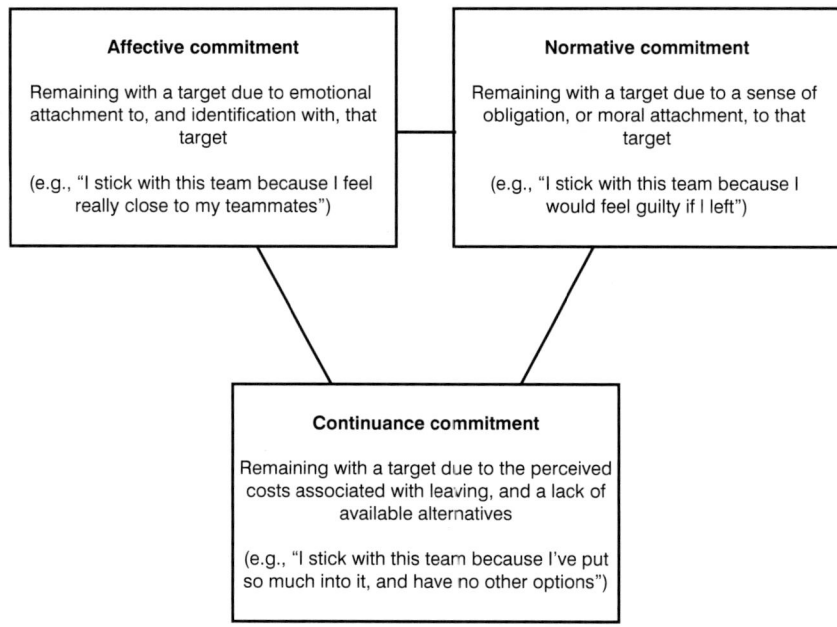

FIGURE 2.1 An illustration of the three-component model of commitment

al., 1993). Given the abundance of research attention that this framework has received in workplace settings, a comprehensive review of the three-component literature is beyond the scope of this chapter (for reviews, see Meyer, 2009; Meyer et al., 2002). It is important, however, that we briefly chart the determinants and consequences that are theorized (and have been shown) to align with the different commitment dimensions in non-sport and exercise organizational research, in order to demonstrate the potential relevance of these constructs for participation, performance, behavior, and well-being in sport and exercise.

Correlates and outcomes of affective, normative, and continuance commitment

The three-component model was built on the premise that all three forms of commitment are likely to support retention, and meta-analytic evidence demonstrates that scores on each of the types of commitment correlate negatively with turnover and withdrawal cognitions (Meyer et al., 2002). Beyond turnover and retention, however, Meyer and colleagues (Meyer & Allen, 1991) contended that there was likely to be a somewhat divergent pattern of consequences for affective, normative, and continuance commitment. Affective commitment is considered to be the most adaptive of the three dimensions, and is theorized to align most strongly with favorable behavioral outcomes, in the form of attendance, performance, organizational citizenship behavior (i.e., voluntary, positive, constructive, and prosocial behavior at work), and reduced absenteeism. These behavioral consequences have often been considered in terms of their economic benefit at the organizational level (e.g., enhanced productivity, reduced loss-to-absenteeism); however, the three-component model may also hold relevance for understanding individual health and well-being. Affective commitment is proposed to alleviate stress and work-related conflict, and correlate positively with satisfaction, involvement, and commitment toward other related targets (e.g., toward one's occupation). Normative commitment – which typically correlates positively and strongly with affective commitment (see Bergman, 2006; Meyer et al., 2002) – is also proposed to align with these desirable organizational and individual outcomes, albeit at a weaker magnitude than the patterns observed for affective commitment. Finally, in light of the pressure and lack of alternatives reported by those who score highly on continuance commitment, it is posited that this dimension may be negatively related, or unrelated, to those adaptive outcomes discussed above (for a review, see Meyer & Maltin, 2010).

There is empirical support for these assertions; Gagné and colleagues (Gagné, Chemolli, Forest, & Koestner, 2008), for example, revealed positive relations between employees' affective commitment and autonomous motivation. Similarly, in their meta-analysis, Meyer et al. (2002) demonstrated that stronger affective commitment was associated with more favorable scores on absenteeism, performance, organizational citizenship behavior, job satisfaction, job involvement, occupational commitment, stress, and work–family conflict (see also Meyer, 2009; Park & Rainey, 2007). Normative commitment displayed relations with these variables that were relatively consistent in terms of direction, but tended to be weaker in magnitude than those observed for affective commitment (see also Gagné et al., 2008; Park & Rainey, 2007). Continuance commitment, meanwhile, displayed a pattern of associations that appeared to (at least in part) substantiate the contention that this form of commitment may be detrimental for individuals and organizations. Strong continuance commitment was associated with lower satisfaction, performance, and perceptions of support, as well as greater stress and work–family conflict (see also Park & Rainey, 2007). The evidence indicates, therefore, that the endorsement of affective and normative commitment might be desirable for both individual well-being and organizational productivity, but that continuance commitment might be accompanied in some cases by deleterious personal and group-level outcomes.

Antecedents of affective, normative, and continuance commitment

Having discussed the implications of the three-component model, we now turn our attention to the factors that underpin the respective dimensions. Meyer and Allen (1991) outlined that affective commitment would be strengthened through the receipt of support from one's organization and supervisor, and meta-analytic results have substantiated these assertions. Meyer et al. (2002) concluded that employees reported greater emotional attachment and identification with their organization when they felt that they received strong organizational support (see also Aubé, Rousseau, & Morin, 2007; Rhoades, Eisenberger, & Armeli, 2001), and when they believed that their superior displayed transformational leadership characteristics. Affective commitment was also stronger when individuals reported lower levels of role ambiguity and role conflict, and when they held favorable perceptions of organizational justice in terms of fairness relating to work outcomes, processes, treatment, and information-provision (see also Park & Rainey, 2007). There is also evidence that individual difference variables are associated with the strength of one's affective commitment. For example, the big five personality traits (in particular agreeableness), self-efficacy, and autonomous (i.e., self-determined) motivation all appear to align positively with the affective dimension of commitment (see Choi, Oh, & Colbert, 2015; Gagné et al., 2008; Meyer et al., 2002).

Normative commitment reflects a strong moral obligation that one "ought to" persist with a given target. Meyer et al. (2002) reported correlations for this dimension that were consistent in terms of direction with those observed for affective commitment (i.e., self-efficacy, organizational support, transformational leadership, role ambiguity/conflict, organizational justice), but that were, for the most part, weaker in magnitude (see also Aubé et al., 2007; Park & Rainey, 2007). Interestingly, investigators have also demonstrated that normative commitment is associated with greater introjected motives for participation (i.e., participation due to internal pressures such as guilt; Gagné et al., 2008), who hold collectivist (as opposed to individualist) values, who conform to high power distance values, and who adopt a long-term orientation (Meyer et al., 2012b). Finally, the evidence regarding theorized antecedents of continuance commitment is mixed. Meyer et al. (2002) concluded that continuance commitment – the feeling of being "locked in" to remaining with a target – was positively associated with tenure, and was associated with a number of organizational factors in the opposite direction to the relationships that were observed for affective and normative commitment. Specifically, strong continuance commitment – which is often unrelated or negatively related to a number of desirable workplace outcomes – was associated with low perceptions of organizational support, transformational leadership, organizational justice, and strong feelings of role ambiguity and role conflict.

In summarizing the nature of the three-component model, it may be worthwhile to contrast the multidimensionality of that approach with the unitary perspective that has often been adopted in sport-based work. Although recent advancements have been made in the measurement of sport commitment (see Scanlan et al., 2016, and coverage in the following section), much of the sport-focused work conducted to date has assessed commitment with items such as "How hard would it be for you to quit playing [on your team]?" It might be possible to infer the reason for a given rating on this item on the basis of responses provided on the antecedent constructs (e.g., enjoyment, personal investments, other priorities); however, when viewing this item (in isolation) through a multidimensional lens, we cannot detect with any certainty which type (or types) of commitment the respondent is experiencing. That is, it is difficult to determine whether the respondent might find it hard to quit their team because: (a) they love the team (i.e., affective commitment); (b) they feel obliged to continue with the team (i.e., normative commitment); (c) they feel that they have no other options available but to stay with that team (i.e., continuance commitment); or (d) some combination of all the above. Particularly in light of the distinct consequences with which these dimensions align in organizational contexts, it appears important that we account not only for the *quantity* of a person's commitment in sport and exercise, but also the *quality* (i.e., type) of that commitment.

To this point, we have presented some broad (and differing) perspectives regarding the conceptualization and measurement of commitment, and have demonstrated that a three-component approach to the study of commitment – which is not fully established in sport and exercise – might have merit in understanding individual and group functioning. We have yet to consider in detail, however, the range of potential implications associated with the three-component model in sport and exercise contexts, and it is this issue on which we focus our attention for the remainder of the chapter.

Applications in sport and exercise

The sport commitment model has generated sustained research attention since its inception, and continues to help shape our understanding of commitment in sport and exercise. In discussing the merits of the three-component framework, therefore, we are not advocating that researchers abandon what has been done in sport; rather, that they attempt to integrate a multidimensional perspective within studies exploring the determinants and outcomes of sport commitment (see, for example, Santi et al., 2014; Wilson et al., 2004; Young & Medic, 2011). In line with this suggestion, Scanlan and colleagues (Scanlan et al., 2016) very recently presented a novel two-component measurement approach, which accompanied a revised sport commitment model and accounted for different commitment dimensions (as well as theorized predictors of those dimensions in line with the antecedents described previously). In their article, Scanlan et al. (2016) provided an operational definition of *"enthusiastic commitment"* (e.g., "I am dedicated to keep playing this sport"), representing individuals' resolve and desire to persist in their sport, as well as *"constrained commitment"* (e.g., "staying in this sport is more of a necessity than a desire"), relating to individuals' feelings of obligation to continue their sport involvement (for more information on initial validity evidence for these measures, see Scanlan et al., 2016).

Consistent with Scanlan et al.'s (2016) proposals, the use of a multidimensional assessment approach – whether defined using a two- or three-factor perspective – may allow researchers to capture a more nuanced view of the development of commitment, and the role that this construct plays with respect to persistence, well-being, and functional outcomes. The three-component model, for example, holds relevance for investigating commitment-based differences across a range of personal (e.g., stress), relational (e.g., relationship longevity), team-level (e.g., cohesion), and organizational (e.g., turnover) outcomes. Meanwhile, devising how to foster adaptive forms of commitment (e.g., affective or enthusiastic commitment) might be valuable within recreational sport and exercise settings that are characterized by high levels of dropout, and an understanding of the development of continuance (or constrained) commitment could enable researchers and practitioners to detect elite performers at risk of burnout, reduced performance, and withdrawal.

Many of the proposals such as those relating to the three-component model above are yet to be tested in an empirical sense in sport or exercise. That is not to say, however, that there is no evidence to support Meyer and colleagues' (see Meyer, 2009; Meyer et al., 2002) multidimensional perspective in these contexts. For example, investigators have explored affective and normative commitment perceptions among volunteers in sport clubs and organizations. Volunteering plays a crucial role in the administration of recreational sport (Engelberg, Zakus, & Skinner, 2007), and commitment among this cohort has received scrutiny in light of diminishing volunteer numbers (see Engelberg, Zakus, Skinner, & Campbell, 2012). Using a sample of volunteers from athletics centers, Engelberg et al. (2012) presented an instrument development study in which they assessed affective and normative commitment to three different "targets", namely one's athletic center, one's volunteer team, and the volunteering role itself. The authors demonstrated evidence for the distinguishability of commitment perceptions relating to different targets, and provided some initial validity evidence pertaining to their measures (particularly for affective commitment measures). Other work that has focused on sport volunteers has considered only the affective dimension of the three-component model; for instance, Bang, Ross, and Reio (2013) demonstrated positive associations between affective commitment and job satisfaction among volunteers at non-profit sport organizations. There is also evidence that strong affective commitment toward one's sport organization is associated with greater affective commitment to one's volunteering role, more effective role performance, and adaptive turnover outcomes (e.g., Cuskelly & Boag, 2001; Engelberg, Skinner, & Zakus, 2011). Although these investigators did not examine the three-component model in its entirety (i.e., did not account for all possible dimensions), the literature on volunteers in sport is a useful illustration of how different commitment dimensions have previously been considered in athletic contexts.

The majority of sport-related studies that have drawn from Meyer and colleagues' three-component model have been directed toward volunteering; however, formative work on coach commitment has also taken place. In one such study, Engelberg-Moston and colleagues (Engelberg-Moston, Stipis, Kippin, Spillman, & Burbidge, 2009) measured coaches' affective, normative, and continuance commitment to their club, with participants drawn from various sports including field hockey, rugby, basketball, soccer, and athletics. Analyses revealed positive associations between affective and normative dimensions, and that these commitment perceptions were negatively associated with coach burnout indices (continuance commitment was dropped from analyses in this investigation due to poor internal consistency estimates). In another investigation, Turner and Chelladurai (2005) assessed coaches' affective, normative, and continuance commitment in relation to their sport organization and (separately) their occupation. Correlation analyses showed that affective and normative commitment to the organization and occupation were negatively related to coaches' intentions to leave their organization and occupation, respectively. Moreover, the authors also reported that strong affective commitment to the organization on the part of coaches (i.e., coaches who were emotionally attached to, and identified strongly with, their organization) was associated with desirable team performance outcomes, as measured by the team's finishing position in its athletic conference.

The remaining group of studies that have drawn from the three-component commitment framework within the sport literature have explored athletes' affective, normative, and/or continuance commitment. Research with collegiate athletes, for instance, has shown support for a multifaceted approach to the study of commitment to one's university, team, and head coach (Turner & Pack, 2007), and demonstrated that commitment perceptions may align with important personal (i.e., intentions to leave) and group-related (i.e., team cohesion) outcomes (Ha & Ha, 2015; Turner & Pack, 2007). Finally, Jackson, Gucciardi, and Dimmock (2014) were guided by the three-component model in seeking to explore the validity of instruments designed to measure: (a) individual-sport athletes' commitment to their relationship with their coach; and (b) team-sport athletes' commitment to their team. Jackson and colleagues adapted Meyer et al.'s (1993) workplace instrument to assess affective (example item, "My relationship with this coach/being part of this team has a great deal of personal meaning for me"), normative (example item, "I would feel guilty if I left this coach/team now"), and continuance (example item, "Right now, staying with this coach/team is a matter of necessity as much as desire") commitment in these two contexts.

In addition to providing support for structural aspects of validity for the measures (i.e., dimensionality, internal consistency), Jackson and colleagues (2014) reported a series of correlations that were consistent with theoretical assertions. That is, athletes who reported strong affective and normative commitment to their coach also reported stronger satisfaction with the coach, greater confidence in their coach's ability, and more positive intentions to remain with their coach and in their sport. Similarly, those who scored highly on affective and normative commitment to their team responded more positively in terms of their satisfaction with the team, perceptions of task and social cohesion, and intentions to continue with the team and the sport. Interestingly, consistent with the findings that have emerged for continuance commitment in the organizational literature, athletes who felt "locked into" their relationship or team actually reported weaker intentions to remain with that coach/team (if given the choice about whether to remain or not). To this point, therefore, there appears to be preliminary evidence for the utility of multidimensional commitment models in sport (including Scanlan and colleagues' (2016) recent two-component conceptualization); however, there is a very limited number of studies that have examined the development and implications of different commitment dimensions. In the following section, we present a range of theory-derived suggestions for research on sport commitment, as well as considering potential applications for the study of multidimensional commitment in exercise contexts.

Future directions

Prior to offering suggestions for future research, it is worth cautioning that the three-component model is not the *only* framework that may be fit-for-purpose in terms of examining the multidimensionality of commitment in sport and exercise. There are clear parallels between aspects of the three-component model and Scanlan and colleagues' (2016) two-dimensional approach, for example, and research that considers the merits and applicability of both frameworks in diverse sport settings is encouraged. There are also a number of other alternative perspectives to the study of commitment that warrant consideration (see Meyer & Herscovitch, 2001), and there is some conjecture in the organizational literature regarding a number of aspects of the three-component model (interested readers should see Bergman, 2006; Solinger et al., 2008). Accordingly, below we outline a number of broad conceptual issues relating to the three-component model about which sport and exercise psychologists should be cognizant when pursuing research in this area. Following our coverage of those issues, we consider some sport- and/or exercise-specific recommendations for future work.

Relations with motivation

An important issue that has received attention in the organizational sphere is the matter of redundancy/overlap between commitment (as defined and operationalized in the three-component model) and motivational processes (see Meyer, Becker, & Vandenberghe, 2004). As defined within self-determination theory (SDT; Deci & Ryan, 2000), individuals may pursue a course of action according to one or more motives, ranging from those that are more autonomous (i.e., pursued for reasons such as enjoyment, interest, and due to consistency with one's identity and values) to those that are more controlled (i.e., pursued due to internal or external pressures) in nature. There are clear parallels between some of the motivational regulations outlined within SDT and the components within the three-component commitment model. Affective (or enthusiastic) commitment, for example, is closely related to the SDT principle that individuals might participate in an activity due to the value it holds and the inherent pleasure they derive from it (i.e., autonomous motivation), whereas normative (or constrained) commitment, in part, resembles the feelings of obligation and guilt that accompany introjected regulation. Finally, continuance commitment, which is associated with external pressures and contingencies, aligns to a degree with the concept of external regulation outlined in SDT.

Researchers have recognized the commonality that exists between SDT regulations and the three-component model (see Gagné et al., 2008; Gagné & Deci, 2005; Meyer et al., 2004); however, Gagné et al. (2008, p. 223) delineated between motivation and commitment by noting that "the target of commitment is an entity (e.g., organization, person or event), whereas the target of motivation is a course of action (for which movement is necessary)". We acknowledge that this may be somewhat at odds with some of the existing sport commitment research, in which individuals' commitment *to a sport* (i.e., which could be considered a "course of action") has been assessed. Nonetheless, by applying Gagné et al.'s principle to sport (2008), motivation might be measured in relation to participation in one's sport, with commitment assessed in relation to remaining with the relationship, team, and/or organization within which one's sport participation is couched. On the basis of this distinction, Gagné et al. (2008) contended that different motivational orientations might precede the development of different commitment responses in the work domain. Using cross-lagged analyses, they subsequently presented evidence that motivational variables (i.e., reflecting motivation for one's job) were, on the whole, a better predictor of commitment (i.e., reflecting commitment to one's organization) than organizational commitment variables were of job motivation.

Researchers are encouraged to address the potential for similar relationships within sport and exercise. For example, it would be interesting to explore how motivational regulations relating to one's exercise participation (e.g., "I participate in circuit training exercise because it is fun and enjoyable…") might orient individuals toward certain types of commitment to the gymnasium they attend (e.g., "…and I want to keep exercising here because I feel really attached to this gym"). Alternatively, it would be enlightening to examine whether dissonance and maladaptive outcomes result in cases where there is conflict between one's motivation for sport (e.g., "I play soccer because I love it…") and one's commitment toward a team or relationship (e.g., "…but I'm only with this coach/team because I'm stuck here"); that is, if such perceptions can co-exist. Irrespective of the shared/unique conceptual "space" that exists between motivation and commitment constructs, though, it is also necessary from a practical standpoint to test whether SDT and commitment constructs, when assessed together, have independent meaning in terms of shaping behavior in sport and exercise. Moreover, we encourage that, in cases where the referent of respective motivational and multidimensional commitment assessments may overlap (e.g., studying relations between motivation for one's sport and commitment to one's sport), investigators provide a clear conceptual rationale for the inclusion of both measures.

Dimensionality and relevance of continuance commitment

There has been persistent debate within the organizational literature as to whether continuance commitment is best defined and measured as a single-factor or bi-dimensional construct (for a review, see Jaros & Culpepper, 2014). Proponents of the bifurcated approach contend that continuance commitment comprises two distinct components, one reflecting a perception that an individual has too few alternatives to consider leaving an organization (often termed "LoAlt"), and another reflecting the sacrifice of personal investments (e.g., social, economic investments) that would occur were one to leave the organization (often termed "HiSac"). Although the potential for sub-dimensions within continuance commitment has been acknowledged for some 20 years (Meyer & Allen, 1997), evidence for this approach is somewhat equivocal, and researchers often still rely on a unidimensional definition when assessing commitment. Indeed, in the limited work that has taken place in sport to date, both the unidimensional (Jackson et al., 2014) and bi-dimensional (Turner & Chelladurai, 2005) approaches to measuring continuance perceptions have been employed.

Recent work outside sport has demonstrated that continuance commitment may in fact be unidimensional, and is best represented by the "HiSac" component only (Jaros & Culpepper, 2014). Although individuals make significant investments into their sport and exercise endeavors (e.g., time, financial, social), they may also develop the feeling that there are limited alternatives to their current position. In sport, for example, coaches may feel that there are limited alternative roles for them in comparable organizations, whereas athletes may feel that there are a lack of other teams or partners with which they could feasibly compete. Similarly, in terms of exercise participation, individuals may come to believe that there are no other suitable facilities or trainers that could adequately satisfy their needs. With this in mind, prior to examining correlates and outcomes, it may be worthwhile to conduct exploratory work that seeks to understand the nature of continuance commitment in sport and exercise contexts. Given the voluntary nature of recreational sport and exercise, it might also be beneficial for researchers to chart the extent to which continuance commitment (i.e., the feeling of being "locked in") is actually manifest in these contexts, as well as the conditions under which, and the persons for whom, it may (or may not) develop.

Relations between affective and normative commitment

Meta-analytic evidence indicates that affective and normative commitment are strongly and positively correlated, and that these two dimensions often align in the same direction with behavioral and perceptual outcomes (Meyer et al., 2002). That being the case, at least at an empirical level, the distinction (or lack thereof) between these two concepts has received attention in the literature (see Bergman, 2006). Considering the links discussed previously between commitment dimensions and SDT motivational regulations (see Gagné et al., 2008; Meyer & Maltin, 2010), those with a background in SDT might be somewhat surprised by the close relations that are observed between affective and normative commitment, and the consistency in terms of the nomological net associated with these two dimensions. Affective commitment closely resembles the notion of autonomous motivation outlined in SDT, which is self-determined in nature and aligns positively and consistently with well-being and persistence-related outcomes (see Deci & Ryan, 2000). Normative commitment, meanwhile, is characterized by moral obligation, and most closely relates to the introjected regulation concept within SDT, which is considered a less adaptive (and more controlled) form of motivation and does not typically display the same relationships with correlates as autonomous motivation. With this issue in mind, we encourage researchers in sport and exercise to draw from Bergman's (2006) recommendations for distinguishing between affective and normative commitment, and encouraging unique associations with related concepts. These recommendations include methodological (e.g., assessing the cross-lagged relations between affective and normative perceptions), analytical (e.g., computing partial correlations between affective and normative perceptions that account for potential shared antecedents) and conceptual (e.g., reexamining the meaning of "obligation") strategies, and implementing one or more of these approaches may be worthwhile as researchers consider the unique contribution of normative commitment among athletic populations.

Broadening the scope of commitment research in sport and exercise

Earlier in this chapter, we noted that athlete commitment might be directed toward an array of targets, and that a more complete understanding of commitment may result if researchers were to diversify the focus of their work. The multidimensional framework might be used to examine varied targets among athlete cohorts, including their commitment toward a playing partner or coach, their subgroup within a team (e.g., their offensive teammates), their team as a whole, and/or their broader organization. Indeed, a comprehensive assessment that incorporated multiple targets might provide fascinating insight into the potential for target-dependent discrepancies within one's commitment perceptions. Similarly, an investigation into exercisers' commitment regarding their trainer, classmates/training partner, and facility might provide novel information regarding the way in which exercise experiences shape distinct commitment responses, and how commitment to different targets may contribute in different ways to maintenance/dropout.

In addition to diversifying the targets of individuals' perceptions, commitment researchers in sport and exercise might draw from the two- or three-component models to explore outcomes of commitment beyond retention/turnover. In the organizational literature, implications for a host of personal and group-level outcomes have been demonstrated, and in sport, it would be worthwhile to consider how athlete commitment relates to well-being (e.g., coping, stress), behavior (e.g., performance, effort, attendance at training), and interpersonal processes (e.g., cohesion, prosocial behavior, conflict). Aside from the implications of commitment, there is also significant scope to explore the role of environmental influences (i.e., antecedents) on the formation of different commitment perceptions in sport and exercise (see Scanlan et al., 2016); examining the role of need-supportive (versus need-thwarting) instructional practices represents one such avenue.

Finally, there is already evidence to support the utility of the three-component model among the important non-athlete cohorts that exist in sport (e.g., coaches, volunteers; Engelberg et al., 2012; Turner & Chelladurai, 2005). That being the case, there is a strong rationale to extend the study of commitment to other populations. Interesting focal populations might include the support, executive, and administration staff at professional sport organizations, given their role in facilitating the day-to-day activities of athletic personnel. Similarly, there may be value in exploring the commitment perceptions of parents in relation to the sporting organizations in which their children participate, with an emphasis on the implications for parent behavior and support for their child's involvement. From an exercise and physical activity perspective, one can also readily envisage how trainers or physical education teachers might instruct in markedly different ways as a function of their different commitment profiles. In such scenarios, it might be important to explore whether strong continuance commitment (i.e., feeling locked into one's role) among trainers/teachers might lead to a degree of apathy and suboptimal instructional methods, causing those under their instruction to experience detrimental outcomes. Support staff, parents, teachers, and trainers are just a selection of the populations to which a multidimensional commitment lens may be applied, and there appears to be a range of interesting cohorts that are ripe for investigation outside of athlete-based samples.

Consider synergistic approaches

Although there is merit in investigating commitment perceptions using variable-centered methods, researchers in organizational settings have also applied person-centered approaches to attempt to understand the naturally-occurring patterns that may exist across commitment dimensions. Using analytic techniques such as cluster analysis and latent profile analysis, it is possible to not only determine the prominent patterns of affective, normative, and continuance (or enthusiastic and constrained) commitment that individuals display, but also to examine the correlates of those patterns (see, for example, Meyer, Stanley, & Parfyonova, 2012; Somers, 2009; Wasti, 2005). In sport, these exploratory techniques would allow researchers to consider the prevalence of different commitment profiles, and how environmental (e.g., need support, transformational leadership) and personal (e.g., stress, engagement, performance) factors might coincide with a particular pattern of commitment. In addition, one interesting line of enquiry in this area would be to consider the potential for contagion or consensus effects among group members' commitment profiles. Within teams, exercise classes, or organizations, it would be intriguing to test whether particular types of commitment might generalize or spread across group members, and whether common profiles might emerge through communication and interaction styles. Such a study would also allow for investigation of the way in which differences in individuals' commitment profiles might have implications for interpersonal relations. In sum, there are a range of possibilities for future multidimensional commitment research that include, but are not limited to:

- studying relations between commitment dimensions and motivational regulations;
- exploring the dimensionality and relevance of continuance commitment;
- delineating the relations between affective and normative commitment;
- broadening the scope of commitment research in terms of foci, populations, and outcomes;
- considering synergistic (e.g., cluster, profile analysis) commitment issues, as well as potential contagion effects within team contexts.

Conclusion

For over 20 years, researchers have studied the development of athlete, coach, and exerciser commitment, and have explored how this concept might support behavioral persistence. In this chapter, we presented an overview of the framework that has most commonly been used in these investigations (i.e., the sport commitment model), before considering how commitment research in sport and exercise might be informed by drawing from perspectives that are widely used by organizational and social psychologists. In particular, we focused our attention primarily on the three-component framework, which specifies that individuals might experience qualitatively different types of commitment, and that these commitment dimensions may develop in distinct ways and have unique implications for individual and group-related outcomes. Formative work has been conducted using this model (and using a related two-component model) in sport; to date, however, there has been no sustained attempt to test the main tenets of the (two- or) three-component model among sport or exercise cohorts. Accordingly, we presented a selection of interesting opportunities for researchers studying sport and exercise commitment, and called for a research agenda that examines a new generation of targets, populations, and processes. A number of important conceptual issues require attention in order to provide a working model for researchers in this area; however, embracing a multidimensional commitment perspective may help researchers, practitioners, and participants better understand the forces that drive behavior in sport and exercise.

References

Aubé, C., Rousseau, V., & Morin, E. M. (2007). Perceived organizational support and organizational commitment: The moderating effect of locus of control and work autonomy. *Journal of Managerial Psychology, 22*, 479–495.

Bang, H., Ross, S., & Reio, Jr., T. G. (2013). From motivation to organizational commitment of volunteers in non-profit sport organizations: The role of job satisfaction. *Journal of Management Development, 32*, 96–112.

Becker, H. S. (1960). Notes on the concept of commitment. *American Journal of Sociology, 66*, 32–40.

Bergman, M. E. (2006). The relationship between affective and normative commitment: Review and research agenda. *Journal of Organizational Behavior, 27*, 645–663.

Carpenter, P. J., & Coleman, R. (1998). A longitudinal study of elite cricketers' commitment. *International Journal of Sport Psychology, 29*, 195–210.

Carpenter, P. J., Scanlan, T. K., Simons, J. P., & Lobel, M. (1993). A test of the sport commitment model using structural equation modeling. *Journal of Sport & Exercise Psychology, 15*, 119–133.

Casper, J. M., & Andrew, D. P. S. (2008). Sport commitment differences among tennis players on the basis of participation outlet and skill level. *Journal of Sport Behavior, 31*, 201–219.

Casper, J. M., Gray, D. P., & Stellino, M. B. (2007). A sport commitment model perspective on adult tennis players' participation frequency and purchase intention. *Sport Management Review, 10*, 253–278.

Choi, D., Oh, I.-S., & Colbert, A. E. (2015). Understanding organizational commitment: A meta-analytic examination of the roles of the five-factor model of personality and culture. *Journal of Applied Psychology, 100*(5), 1542–1567. Advance online publication.

Choosakul, C., Vongjaturapat, N., Li, F., & Harmer, P. (2009). The sport commitment model: An investigation of structural relationships with Thai youth athlete populations. *Measurement in Physical Education and Exercise Science, 13*, 123–139.

Cropanzano, R., & Mitchell, M. S. (2005). Social exchange theory: An interdisciplinary review. *Journal of Management, 31*, 874–900.

Cuskelly, G., & Boag, A. (2001). Organizational commitment as a predictor of committee member turnover among volunteer sport administrators: Results of a time-lagged study. *Sport Management Review, 4*, 65–86.

Deci, E., & Ryan, R. (2000). The "what" and "why" of goal pursuits: Human needs and the self-determination of behavior. *Psychological Inquiry, 11*, 227–268.

Engelberg, T., Skinner, J. L., & Zakus, D. H. (2011). Exploring the relationship between commitment, experience, and self-assessed performance in youth sport organizations. *Sport Management Review, 14*, 117–125.

Engelberg, T., Zakus, D. H., & Skinner, J. L. (2007). Organizational commitment: Implications for voluntary sport organizations. *Australian Journal on Volunteering, 12*, 26–34.

Engelberg, T., Zakus, D. H., Skinner, J. L., & Campbell, A. (2012). Defining and measuring dimensionality and targets of the commitment of sport volunteers. *Journal of Sport Management, 26*, 192–205.

Engelberg-Moston, T., Stipis, C., Kippin, B., Spillman, S., & Burbidge, K. (2009). Organisational and occupational commitment as predictors of volunteer coaches' burnout. *Australian Journal on Volunteering, 14*, 1–9.

Gagné, M., Chemolli, E., Forest, J., & Koestner, R. (2008). The temporal relations between work motivation and organizational commitment. *Psychologica Belgica, 48*, 219–241.

Gagné, M., & Deci, E. L. (2005). Self-determination theory and work motivation. *Journal of Organizational Behavior, 26*, 331–362.

Gould, D., & Petlichkoff, L. (1988). Participation motivation and attrition in young athletes. In F. L. Smoll, R. A. Magill, & M. J. Ash (Eds.), *Children in sport* (pp. 161–178). Champaign, IL: Human Kinetics.

Ha, J.-P., & Ha, J. (2015). Organizational justice-affective commitment relationship in a team sport setting: The moderating effect of group cohesion. *Journal of Management & Organization, 21*, 107–124.

Jackson, B., Gucciardi, D. F., & Dimmock, J. A. (2014). Toward a multidimensional model of athletes' commitment to coach-athlete relationships and interdependent sport teams: A substantive-methodological synergy. *Journal of Sport & Exercise Psychology, 36*, 52–68.

Jaros, S., & Culpepper, R. A. (2014). An analysis of Meyer and Allen's continuance commitment construct. *Journal of Management & Organization, 20*, 79–99.

Jenkins, P. H. (1995). School delinquency and school commitment. *Sociology of Education, 68*, 221–232.

Johnson, M. P. (1973). Commitment: A conceptual structure and empirical application. *The Sociological Quarterly, 14*, 395–406.

Johnson, M. P. (1991). Commitment to personal relationships. In W. H. Jones & D. W. Perlman (Eds.), *Advances in personal relationships* (Vol. 3, pp. 117–143). London: Jessica Kingsley.

Johnson, M. P., Caughlin, J. P., & Huston, T. L. (1999). The tripartite nature of marital commitment: Personal, moral, and structural reasons to stay married. *Journal of Marriage and Family, 61*, 160–177.

Kelley, H. H. (1983). Love and commitment. In H. H. Kelley, E. Berscheid, A. Christensen, J. H. Harvey, T. L. Huston, G. Levinger, E. McClintock, L. A. Peplau, & D. R. Petersen (Eds.), *Close relationships* (pp. 265–314). New York: W. H. Freeman and Company.

Lombardi, V., Jr. (2003). *What it takes to be #1: Vince Lombardi on leadership.* New York: McGraw-Hill.

Meyer, J. P. (2009). Commitment in a changing world of work. In H. J. Klein, T. E. Becker, & J. P. Meyer (Eds.), *Commitment in organizations: Accumulated wisdom and new directions* (pp. 37–68). New York: Routledge

Meyer, J. P., & Allen, N. J. (1991). A three-component conceptualization of organizational commitment. *Human Resource Management Review, 1*, 61–89.

Meyer, J. P., & Allen, N. J. (1997). *Commitment in the workplace: Theory, research and application.* Newbury Park, CA: Sage.

Meyer, J. P., Allen, N. J., & Smith, C. A. (1993). Commitment to organizations and occupations: Extension and test of a three-component conceptualization. *Journal of Applied Psychology, 78*, 538–551.

Meyer, J. P., Becker, T. E., & Vandenberghe, C. (2004). Employee motivation and commitment: A conceptual analysis and integrative model. *Journal of Applied Psychology, 89*, 991–1007.

Meyer, J. P., & Herscovitch, L. (2001). Commitment in the workplace: Toward a general model. *Human Resource Management Review, 11*, 299–326.

Meyer, J. P., & Maltin, E. R. (2010). Employee commitment and well-being: A critical review, theoretical framework and research agenda. *Journal of Vocational Behavior, 77*, 323–337.

Meyer, J. P., Stanley, D. J., Herscovitch, L., & Topolnytsky, L. (2002). Affective, continuance and normative commitment to the organization: A meta-analysis of antecedents, correlates and consequences. *Journal of Vocational Behavior, 61*, 20–52.

Meyer, J. P., Stanley, D. J., Jackson, T. A., McInnis, K. J., Maltin, E. R., & Sheppard, L. (2012a). Affective, normative and continuance commitment levels across cultures: A meta-analysis. *Journal of Vocational Behavior, 80*, 225–245.

Meyer, J. P., Stanley, L. J., & Parfyonova, N. M. (2012b). Employee commitment in context: The nature and implications of commitment profiles. *Journal of Vocational Behavior, 80*, 1–16.

Park, S. M., & Rainey, H. G. (2007). Antecedents, mediators, and consequences of affective, normative, and continuance commitment: Empirical tests of commitment effects in federal agencies. *Review of Public Personnel Administration, 27*, 197–226.

Raedeke, T. D. (1997). Is athlete burnout more than just stress? A sport commitment perspective. *Journal of Sport & Exercise Psychology, 19*, 396–417.

Raedeke, T. D. (2004). Coach commitment and burnout: A one year follow-up. *Journal of Applied Sport Psychology, 16*, 333–349.

Raedeke, T. D., Granzyk, T. L., & Warren, A. (2000). Why coaches experience burnout: A commitment perspective. *Journal of Sport & Exercise Psychology, 22*, 85–105.

Rhoades, L., Eisenberger, R., & Armeli, S. (2001). Affective commitment to the organization: The contribution of perceived organizational support. *Journal of Applied Psychology, 86*, 825–836.

Rusbult, C. E. (1980). Commitment and satisfaction in romantic associations: A test of the investment model. *Journal of Experimental Social Psychology, 16*, 172–186.

Rusbult, C. E., Martz, J. M., & Agnew, C. R. (1998). The investment model scale: Measuring commitment level, satisfaction level, quality of alternatives, and investment size. *Personal Relationships, 5*, 357–391.

Santi, G., Bruton, A., Pietrantoni, L., & Mellalieu, S. (2014). Sport commitment and participation in Masters swimmers: The influence of coach and teammates. *European Journal of Sport Science, 14*, 852–860.

Scanlan, T. K., Carpenter, P. J., Schmidt, G. W., Simons, J. P., & Keeler, B. (1993). An introduction to the sport commitment model. *Journal of Sport & Exercise Psychology, 15*, 1–15.

Scanlan, T. K., Chow, G. M., Sousa, C., Scanlan, L. A., & Knifsend, C. A. (2016). The development of the Sport Commitment Questionnaire-2 (English version). *Psychology of Sport and Exercise, 22*, 233–246.

Scanlan, T. K., Russell, D. G., Beals, K. & Scanlan, L. A. (2003a). Project on Elite Athlete Commitment (PEAK): II. A direct test and expansion of the sport commitment model with elite amateur sportsmen. *Journal of Sport & Exercise Psychology, 25*, 377–401.

Scanlan, T. K., Russell, D. G., Magyar, M., & Scanlan, L. A. (2009). Project on Elite Athlete Commitment (PEAK): III. An examination of the external validity across gender, and the expansion and clarification of the sport commitment model. *Journal of Sport & Exercise Psychology, 31*, 685–705.

Scanlan, T. K., Russell, D. G, Scanlan, L. A., Klunchoo, T., & Chow, G. (2013b). Project on Elite Athlete Commitment (PEAK): IV. Identification of new candidate commitment sources in the sport commitment model. *Journal of Sport & Exercise Psychology, 35*, 525–535.

Scanlan, T. K., Russell, D. G., Wilson, N. C., & Scanlan, L. A. (2003b). Project on Elite Athlete Commitment (PEAK): I. Introduction and methodology. *Journal of Sport & Exercise Psychology, 25*, 360–376.

Scanlan, T. K., Simons, J. P., Carpenter, P. J., Schmidt, G. W., & Keeler, B. (1993). The sport commitment model: Measurement development for the youth-sport domain. *Journal of Sport & Exercise Psychology, 15*, 16–38.

Schmidt, G. W., & Stein, G. L. (1991). Sport commitment: A model integrating enjoyment, dropout, and burnout. *Journal of Sport & Exercise Psychology, 8*, 254–265.

Schultz, H., & Yang, D. J. (1997). *Pour your heart into it: How Starbucks built a company one cup at a time.* New York: Hachette Books.

Smith, R. (1986). Toward a cognitive-affective model of athletic burnout. *Journal of Sport Psychology, 8*, 36–50.

Solinger, O. N., van Olffen, W., & Roe, R. A. (2008). Beyond the three-component model of organizational commitment. *Journal of Applied Psychology, 93*, 70–83.

Somers, M. J. (2009). The combined influence of affective, continuance and normative commitment on employee withdraw. *Journal of Vocational Behavior, 74*, 75–81.

Turner, B. A., & Chelladurai, P. (2005). Organizational and occupational commitment, intention to leave and perceived performance of intercollegiate coaches. *Journal of Sport Management, 19*, 193–211.

Turner, B. A., & Pack, S. (2007). Multidimensional commitment of intercollegiate student-athletes: Its effects on intention to leave and satisfaction. *Journal for the Study of Sports and Athletes in Education, 1*, 141–156.

Vallerand, J., & Young, B. (2014). Are adult sportspersons and exercisers that different? Exploring how motives predict commitment and lapses. *International Journal of Sport and Exercise Psychology, 12*, 339–356.

Wasti, S. A. (2005). Commitment profiles: Combinations of organization commitment forms and job outcomes. *Journal of Vocational Behavior, 67*, 290–308.

Weiss, M. R., & Amorose, A. J. (2008). Motivational orientations and sport behavior. In T. S. Horn (Ed.), *Advances in sport psychology* (3rd ed., pp. 115–155). Champaign, IL: Human Kinetics.

Weiss, M. R., Kimmel, L. A., & Smith, A. L. (2001). Determinants of sport commitment among junior tennis players: Enjoyment as a mediating variable. *Pediatric Exercise Science, 13*, 131–144.

Weiss, W. (2014). Competitive-level differences on sport commitment among high school and collegiate-level athletes. *International Journal of Sport and Exercise Psychology. 13*(3), 286–303. Advance online publication.

Weiss, W. M., & Weiss, M. R. (2006). A longitudinal analysis of commitment among competitive female gymnasts. *Psychology of Sport & Exercise, 7*, 309–323.

Weiss, W. M., & Weiss, M. R. (2007). Sport commitment among competitive female gymnasts: A developmental perspective. *Research Quarterly for Exercise and Sport, 78,* 90–102.

Wilson, P. M., Rodgers, W. M., Carpenter, P. J., Hall, C., Hardy, J., & Fraser, S. N. (2004). The relationship between commitment and exercise behavior. *Psychology of Sport and Exercise, 5,* 405–421.

Young, B. W., & Medic, N. (2011). Examining social influences on the sport commitment of Masters swimmers. *Psychology of Sport and Exercise, 12,* 168–175.

3

EMOTIONS IN SPORT ORGANIZATIONS

Christopher R. D. Wagstaff and Sheldon Hanton

Introduction

We all tend to think we know emotion when we see it, yet researchers have for some time proposed a wide variety of definitions and still there is no global consensus. The most widely held view is that emotions are adaptive responses to the demands of the environment (Ekman, 1992; Scherer, 1984; Smith & Ellsworth, 1985), which have a range of possible consequences (Frijda, 1988). Whereas emotions typically refer to discrete and intense but short-lived experiences, moods are experiences that are longer and more diffuse, and lack awareness of the eliciting stimulus. Moods can be created by stimuli of relatively low intensity, or can be supplanted by emotions that fade so that the initial antecedent is no longer salient (e.g., Cropanzano, Weiss, Hale, & Reb, 2003; Schwarz, 1990). Affect is an umbrella term encompassing mood and emotion (Forgas, 1995). In this chapter we focus on the emotion phenomena.

Most theorizing and research on emotion in sport has focused on the personal experience and intrapersonal consequences of emotions in athletic samples. That is, in sport, emotion is typically studied as a within-person, one-direction, non-repetitive phenomenon; focus has traditionally been on how one individual feels in reaction to various stimuli at a certain point in time. While we do not dispute the value of such research foci for enhancing our understanding of individual performance, we believe this somewhat narrow focus does not allow for a full appreciation of emotion phenomena in sport organizations. We would argue that people recognize – and inevitably react emotionally and otherwise – to expressions of emotion of other people in their day-to-day transactions with others in sport. Consequently, dyads, groups, teams, and organizations are witness to instances of individual influence through emotion experience and expression. One's emotions influence the thoughts and behaviors of others; others' reactions can then influence their future interactions with the individual expressing the original emotion, as well as that individual's future emotions and behaviors. People can mimic the emotions of others, thereby extending the social presence of a specific emotion, but can also respond to others' emotions, extending the range of emotions present. People can also draw attributions and extract meanings from others' emotions and these processes are sensitive to various moderating factors, including demographic variables (e.g., gender or race) and situational variables (e.g., relative power of participants). In observing the complex and occasionally chaotic sport milieu in which individuals operate, Wagstaff, Fletcher, and Hanton (2012a) labelled sport organizations "emotional cauldrons" (p. 32). In this chapter we consider the multiple levels at which emotion phenomena exist in these sport organizations.

Emotions at multiple levels of analysis in sport organizations

Imagine yourself at a team meeting ahead of a major performance in which tactics are being discussed. You don't have a strong opinion concerning the tactics – it doesn't relate too much to your role – but as the coach explains why they think one tactical approach should be adopted, one of your teammates, a senior player, belligerently accuses the coach of trying to force through their opinion. The coach responds in kind, and an angry exchange evolves and escalates. Others present – coaches and players – try to calm things down, but you feel embarrassed. Eventually the coach apologizes, but your angry teammate does not acknowledge the apology, and the discussion continues in an unpleasant atmosphere until decisions are made and the meeting ends. The coach and your teammate do not talk to each other from that point on, and the atmosphere in the squad becomes tense. Other people – the manger and performance director – who were not present at the meeting but heard about it have become involved by asking for an explanation of the incident, as they have come to develop anxiety about future meetings, the coach's leadership, and the performance of the team. Moreover, the tabloid media have heard about the spat and have broadcast the issue to the global media, casting a magnifying glass over the team in the days leading up to the big performance. No one knows how the media were notified, but seeds of distrust have been sown between the players, coaches, and management.

It is likely that most applied sport psychologists have encountered situations where expressions of emotion by one individual shape the emotions, thoughts, and behaviors of others. Yet these situations are poorly captured by the prevailing research on emotion in sport, which has generally maintained a *within-person* view, focusing primarily on the antecedents and consequences of an individual's own affective reactions. For example, a wealth of research in sport psychology has been dedicated to the study of competitive anxiety (see, for a comprehensive review, Wagstaff, Neil, Mellalieu, & Hanton, 2012). The collective conceptualization of this research is that emotions are experienced by an *individual* prior to, or during, a sport performance performed by the same *individual*. Indeed, the support for such a conceptualization has been substantial, with over 100 full-length research articles dedicated to competitive anxiety alone, making this concept one of the most prolifically studied within the field of sport psychology (see Wagstaff, Neil, et al., 2012). This body of work has also been fruitful; it has illustrated the importance of appraisal in the anxiety response process and distinguished a significant number of antecedent and mechanistic variables that influence the anxiety–performance relationship. Nevertheless, our goal in this chapter is to stimulate greater research attention on the reciprocal and multilevel influence of emotions in sport organizations (see also Wagstaff, Fletcher, & Hanton, 2012b). This is not intended to detract from the study of emotion phenomena at the intrapersonal level, quite the contrary, but research and theory must better reflect reality in that athletes, coaches, managers, scientists, and medics operating in sport organizations do not just experience their emotions privately, they also express them to others, triggering divergent emotional ripple effects.

Throughout this review we draw from the emotion literature in sport, organizational, and general psychology, across which there has been a similar confluence of ideas. Indeed, the idea that emotions have interpersonal consequences is not new. A healthy number of authors have argued that emotions play a regulating role in social interaction, influencing not only the behavior of the "emoter" but also that of others in the social environment (e.g., Ashkanasy, 2003; Coté, 2005; Elfenbein, 2007; Frijda & Mesquita, 1994; Hareli & Rafaeli, 2008; Keltner & Haidt, 1999; Parkinson, 1996; Parkinson, Fischer, & Manstead, 2005; Rafaeli & Sutton, 1989; Van Kleef, 2009). We support this extant work and hope to stimulate research in the unique sport context that adds veracity to the proposition that one person›s emotion has the potential to shape the behaviors, thoughts, and emotions of multiple people through a process of reciprocal influence over time. Our arguments are also predicated on the notion that emotions are manifested through facial, vocal, postural, or verbal behavior, and so can be perceived by (and therefore can affect) others (Ekman, 1992; Ekman & Friesen, 1976; Fridlund, 1994; Izard, 1971; Keltner, Ekman, Gonzaga, & Beer, 2003; Rimé, Mesquita, Boca, & Philippot, 1991). We also build on the premise developed elsewhere that people react to and draw inferences from others' emotions (Baumeister, Stillwell, & Heatherton, 1995; Clark, Pataki, & Carver, 1996; Coté, 2005; Rafaeli & Sutton, 1987, 1989), and that emotions may affect not only the person at whom the emotion was directed (e.g., the coach in our scenario previously), but also third parties who observe an agent's emotion (e.g., you, as a relatively uninvolved participant in the meeting). Specifically, this chapter presents a multilevel theory of emotions in sport organizations, extending across five levels, from the within-person level to the emotional climate and culture within organizations. The first level in this model is *within*-person, and involves the temporal variations in mood

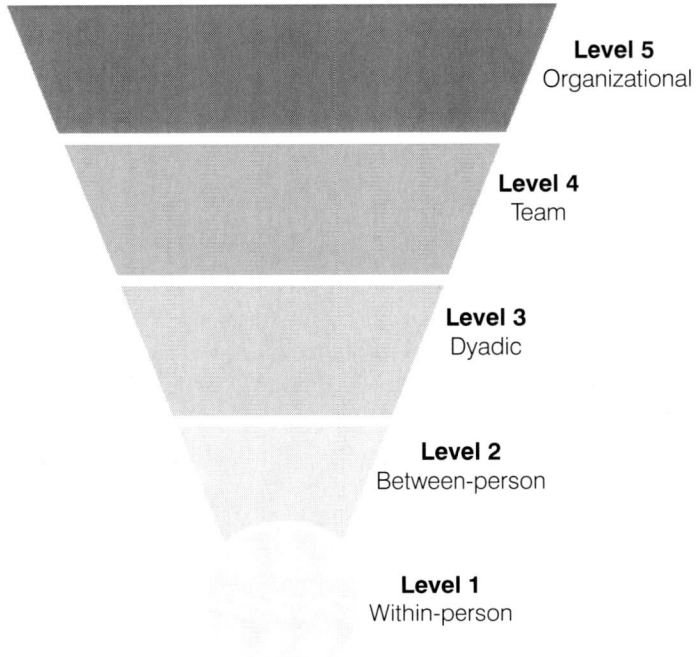

FIGURE 3.1 An integrated model for emotion research in sport organizations

and emotion that people experience in their daily operation within their sport organization. The remaining levels in the model proceed through the individual level, to interpersonal relationships and groups, and then to organizations. The five levels are illustrated in Figure 3.1, showing the potentially salient topics at each level. While few models are complete, we hope this model will help to articulate the value in moving away from the prevailing examination of emotion phenomena at the individual level in sport, and toward an inclusive, multilevel model that spans micro (i.e., individual), meso (e.g., dyadic, team), and macro (i.e., organizational, cultural) dimensions.

Level 1: emotion at the within-person level of analysis

What makes emotions a unique and challenging variable to study in sport is their dynamic nature; they change rapidly from day to day, and even from moment to moment. Hence, scholars seeking to conceptualize and study emotions at the within-person level have widely highlighted the present challenges facing the field, not least regarding when and how to best measure emotions. Before we turn our attention to the fluctuating within-person emotional experience, it is important to acknowledge the diverse theoretical perspectives that exist at this level of analysis.

The substantial research dedicated to emotional experience at the within-person level in sport has prompted the development of numerous associated models. For instance, general approaches to the emotion–performance relationship at the within-person level in sport have been developed, including *inter alia*: cognitive-motivational-relational theory (CMR; Lazarus, 2000), individual zone of optimal functioning (IZOF; Hanin, 2000), and the meta-model of stress, emotions, and performance (Fletcher & Fletcher, 2005). There have also been numerous accounts of anxiety–performance specifically including, for example: multidimensional anxiety theory (see Martens, Burton, Vealey, Bump, Smith, 1990), Jones's (1995) control model, catastrophe model (see Hardy, 1990), theory of reinvestment (see Masters, 1992), attentional control theory (see Eysenck & Calvo, 1992), biopsychosocial model of challenge and threat (see Blascovich, Seery, Mugridge, Norris, & Weisbuch, 2004), and the theory of challenge and threat states in athletes (see Jones, Meijen, McCarthy, & Sheffield, 2009). While a review of each of these and their allied research is beyond the scope of this chapter, the number is perhaps indicative of the extent of research dedicated to the examination of emotional experience in sport performers.

As alluded to above, and in light of the variety of theoretical approaches adopted to examine intrapersonal emotion experience in sport, a breadth of research exists which illuminates a wide spectrum of emotions (e.g., anxiety) with different designs (e.g., Jones & Uphill, 2011; Mullen & Hardy, 2000; Robazza & Bortoli, 2007; Séve, Ria, Poizat, Saury, & Durand, 2007; Woodman et al., 2009). Nevertheless, emotion has primarily been the emotion of interest to sport psychologists (see Wagstaff, Neil, et al., 2012), with researchers mostly highlighting the negative impact of anxiety on sport performance (e.g., Woodman & Hardy, 2003). Indeed, there is substantial evidence that anxiety can impair performance in soccer penalty kicks (e.g., Jordet, 2009; Wilson, Wood, & Vine, 2009), table tennis (e.g., Williams, Vickers, & Rodrigues, 2002), golf putting (e.g., Vine, Moore, & Wilson, 2011), and rock climbing (e.g., Nieuwenhuys, Pijpers, Oudejans, & Bakker, 2008). In addition, Nibbeling, Daanen, Gerritsma, Hofland, and Oudejans (2012) found several indications that efficiency in running in an aerobic task was reduced by anxiety. In contrast to these results, there also exists a body of research that has found anxiety to be associated with positive outcomes. Specifically, substantial research has been dedicated to examining whether anxiety symptoms can be perceived as either facilitative or debilitative to performance; that is, when an individual reports experiencing cognitive or somatic anxiety symptoms, whether they believe that these feelings will be helpful or harmful to their performance. Numerous studies have found that when the directional scale is considered, the variance predicted by anxiety increased; that is, scores on the directional scale appear to be effective predictors of performance (see, for reviews, Jones, 1995; Raglin & Hanin, 2000; Wagstaff, Neil, et al., 2012).

While the study of performers' emotional experience has firmly established its place in sport psychology, almost all of this research has focused on the examination of negative emotions in competitive environments, such as anxiety. Indeed, there is a relative dearth of research examining the daily affective experiences of sport performers within their dyads, teams, and organizations or the value of emotion-based interventions to improve psychological well-being and organizational performance. McCarthy (2011) recently argued that the benefits of positive emotions have hitherto not been wholly realized in sport, especially in their capacity to result in greater self-efficacy, motivation, attention, problem-solving, and coping with adversity.

Although most of the research on the emotion–performance relationship at the within-person level has centered on negative emotions, more recently there have been calls to redress the imbalance of research attention toward negative emotions and their impact on physical performance (see McCarthy, 2011). Indeed, a body of research has begun to emerge examining the role of a range of discrete emotional experiences on sport performance. For instance, Rathschlag and Memmert (2015) examined the effects of self-generated emotions on sprinting times, with performance significantly better in conditions when participants recalled personal happiness emotional episodes before sprinting than in anxiety or emotion-neutral conditions. Baron, Guilloux, Begue, and Uriac (2015) measured emotional responses during sprint intervals performed on level, down, and up surfaces. Participants' self-selected speeds were correlated with the rating of perceived exertion, the affective balance, the desire to stop, and the resources needed for the task in all conditions, whereas the pleasure, the desire to continue, and the capacity to realize the task were correlated with speeds only during level and uphill running. Mean values of emotional parameters were significantly different during running on a flat surface, downhill, and uphill. Lane et al. (2015) recently asked fifteen participants to report emotional states associated with their best, worst, and ideal performance. Results indicated that a best and ideal emotional state for performance composed of feeling happy, calm, energetic, and moderately anxious whereas the worst emotional state for performance composed of feeling downhearted, sluggish, and highly anxious. In a second stage of their study, Lane et al. (2015) developed online emotion regulation interventions aimed at increasing the intensity of unpleasant emotions (e.g., feel more angry and anxious) or reducing the intensity of unpleasant emotions (e.g., feel less angry and anxious). Using a repeated measures design, participants used each intervention before running a 1600 m time trial and data were compared with a no-treatment control condition. The intervention designed to increase the intensity of unpleasant emotions resulted in higher anxiety and lower calmness scores but no significant effects on 1600 m running time. The intervention designed to reduce the intensity of unpleasant emotions was associated with significantly slower times for the first 400 m. The authors suggested that future research should investigate emotion regulation, emotion, and performance using quasi-experimental methods with performance measures that are meaningful to participants.

While the examples above illustrate a recent research shift to adopt a more holistic research agenda for within-person emotion experience in sport, there remains much to be examined at this level relevant to sport performance. For example, with some notable exceptions (e.g., Hanton, Thomas, & Maynard, 2004; Thomas, Hanton & Maynard, 2007), little within-person emotion research has considered the daily fluctuations of emotional experiences' influence on attitudes, motivation, well-being, and performance. Ironically, while performance anxiety remains comparably under-examined in non-sport organizations, the daily fluctuations of emotions in the workplace has for a long time been of interest to organizational psychologists. Much of the research on within-person emotion experience in non-sport organizations has drawn from the affective events theory (AET; Weiss & Cropanzano, 1996) to articulate the cause and effect nature of emotions in the daily lives of individuals operating within organizations. AET emerged from the field of organizational behavior in the mid-1990s. It is predicated on the proposition that individuals' behavior and performance in their role (notionally, at work) are not so much determined by attitudes and personality, but rather by moment-by-moment variations in the way they feel (see Weiss, Nicholas, & Daus, 1999). Weiss and Cropanzano (1996) argued that events and conditions in one's environment constitute "affective events," and that it is these events that ultimately determine moods and emotions. The experience of such moods and emotions might lead to the formation of long-term attitudes (e.g., changes in commitment and identity) or behaviors (e.g., performance, burnout) (see Wright, Bonnett, & Sweeney, 1993; Wright & Cropanzano, 1998). The seminal contribution of AET in the organizational domain was that, for the first time, an attempt was made to tackle the ongoing, temporally varying processes that underlie behavior in organizations. Indeed, AET considers the multilevel nature of emotions itself. At the between-person level (and as we discuss below), personal dispositional variables such as trait affectivity (Watson & Tellegen, 1985) affect the formation of positive and negative emotions. At the organizational level, the model in its present configuration (viz., Weiss & Cropanzano, 1996) takes into account aspects of the work environment, including role characteristics, organizational stressors, and requirements for emotional labor (discussed later in this chapter).

Level 2: emotion at the between-person level of analysis

Although the experience of emotion is largely idiosyncratic, dynamic, and ephemeral, there are both aspects and effects of emotions that can be studied at the between-person level. That is, there are certain variables, derived from within-person processes, that appear as a multitude of personal outcomes. These might include, for example, satisfaction, turnover, prosocial behaviors (see Chapter 9, this volume), commitment (see Chapter 2, this volume), identity, engagement, and performance. Indeed, of these variables, commitment, engagement, identity, and burnout reflect emotionally-driven liking and attachment (or lack thereof) to one's sport organization. In addition to these variables, other aspects of emotions at the individual level are describable in terms of traits. Examples of these individual differences include trait affect (see Ntoumanis & Jones, 1998) and emotional intelligence (EI; see Meyer & Fletcher, 2007).

EI has received growing interest in the field of sport psychology (see, for reviews, Laborde, Dosseville, & Allen, 2015; Latimer, Rench, & Brackett, 2007; Meyer & Fletcher, 2007). Laborde et al. recently reviewed some of the EI literature in sport, focusing principally on research that has examined EI as a trait or mixed model, as opposed to an ability (see, for a review, Meyer & Fletcher, 2007). The authors' literature search identified thirty studies that had targeted EI in the context of sport performance, with varied samples of sport performers, coaches, and spectators, and broadly examined associations between individual athletic performance (e.g., Crombie, Lombard, & Noakes, 2009; Kajbafnezhad, Ahadi, Heidarie, Askari, & Enayati, 2011; Laborde, Dosseville, Guillén, & Chávez, 2014; Perlini & Halverson, 2006; Zizzi, Deaner, & Hirschhorn, 2003), sex differences (Costarelli & Stamou, 2009; Dunn, Brackett, Ashton-James, Schneiderman, & Salovey, 2007; Laborde et al., 2014), competition day emotions (Lane et al., 2010; Lane & Wilson, 2011; Lu, Li, Hsu, & Williams, 2010), physiological stress responses (e.g., Laborde, Brüll, Weber, & Anders, 2011), psychological skill usage (Kajbafnezhad et al., 2012; Lane et al., 2009), and organizational functioning (e.g., Wagstaff, Hanton, & Fletcher, 2013). Collectively, the extant findings generally support the existence of a positive relationship between EI and athletic performance, with females generally scoring higher than males, and higher EI being related to more positive competition day emotions, and greater psychological skill usage and organizational functioning. Laborde et al. (2015) speculated that high trait EI athletes might perform better because they appraise competitions as a challenge and use more effective coping strategies in response to competition stress. Nevertheless, somewhat contradictory findings have emerged where trait EI has not differentiated between performance levels (e.g., Laborde, Lautenbach, Allen, Herbert, Achtzehn, 2014) and with trait EI being related to isometric maximal voluntary contractions, both in the presence and absence of a mental stressor (Tok, Binboğa, Guven, Çatikkas, & Dane, 2013). Laborde et al. (2015) concluded their review by stating that there is currently a limited conceptual foundation for associations between trait EI and movement parameters and more research is needed to ascertain whether EI is related to athlete strength and movement variations under pressure. Beyond the potential salience of EI in athletes, there is growing evidence that EI is also important for effective coach functioning. In order to help their athletes achieve optimal performance, and in order to foster adaptive coach–athlete relationships, coaches require effective leadership skills and these are contingent on understanding and adapting to the emotional needs of the athlete (Chan & Mallett, 2011; Thelwell, Lane, Weston, & Greenlees, 2008).

Although EI has been widely viewed as an individual's *ability* to identify, understand, use, and regulate emotion in everyday life (see, Meyer & Fletcher, 2007; Zeidner, Matthews, & Roberts, 2009), Laborde et al. (2015) observed that much of the research on EI in sport has conceptualized EI as a trait using no less than seven assessment tools with varying conceptual underpinnings, an issue the authors state reflects the conceptual and methodological confusion that accompanies EI. The use of trait and mixed-model approaches to EI have been widely criticized (see, for review, Zeidner et al., 2009) for including a composite of mental abilities (e.g., emotional self-awareness, empathy, problem-solving, impulse control) and self-reported personality characteristics (e.g., empathy, impulsivity, and assertiveness), thus confusing the common conceptualization of intelligence as a distinct capacity, as it is defined by the pure "ability" model of Salovey and Mayer (see, for a review, Mayer, Salovey, & Caruso, 2008). The lack of conceptual consensus reflects the early challenges allied with the early development of EI and could – perhaps should – have been avoided. Researchers should reflect carefully about the scale (and corresponding EI conceptualization) they adopt, as this decision will no doubt inform subsequent decisions and current practices (Laborde et al., 2015). Once conceptual consensus is achieved, it is likely that EI will be better integrated as a salient between-person emotion variable in sport. Indeed, emotion-related individual difference research has much to offer our understanding of the emotion process, and might offer areas for overlap with other important individual differences studied in sport, which also contain emotion-related dimensions, such as mental toughness (see Gucciardi, Hanton, Gordon, Mallett, & Temby, 2015) and resilience (see Chapter 7, this volume). It follows that research is required to further elucidate relationships between these personal dispositional variables and personal outcome variables. Nevertheless, given the focus of this chapter on emotions as a multilevel dynamic phenomena, it is the next level of analysis – interpersonal interactions – that is potentially a more novel contribution to extant theory.

Examining emotions in sport dyads, teams, and organizations

Within this integrative model of emotion, levels 3, 4, and 5 relate to the perception and communication of emotions in dyads, groups and teams, and organizations. This chapter has hitherto provided a treatment of what might be considered relatively well-established lines of inquiry relating to emotion in sport at levels 1 and 2. In order to better locate the additional levels in the present model, we provide a rationale for examining emotions at social levels. Friesen et al. (2013) argued that sport is fundamentally a social activity as athletes interact with teammates, coaching staff, opponents, officials, family, fans, and sport administrators. In this context, the social functions and interpersonal regulation of emotions need to be considered when addressing emotions in sport. In turn, researchers have recognized the importance of social influences on emotions and some studies have been conducted exploring the social aspects of emotion phenomena in sport. The examination of emotion at the interpersonal level aligns with recent conceptual developments regarding emotions as social information (see Van Kleef, Homan, & Cheshin, 2012) within the general emotion research domain. That is, we propose that sport psychologists can build on the emerging work outside of sport, to better understand the way by which emotions not only influence those who experience them, but also those who observe them (e.g., Coté, 2005; Elfenbein, 2007; Van Kleef, 2009). For example, an athlete's competitive anxiety might be influenced by the emotions they perceive in their teammates; a coach's half-time talk might be shaped by the expressions of their athletes. Clearly then, and as alluded to in the introduction to this chapter, there is much more to emotion than the private experience of a given emotion as emotional expressions are a potential source of influence (Van Kleef, Van Doorn, Heerdink, & Koning, 2011). Given this observation, it is surprising that little research attention has been devoted to interpersonal emotion dynamics, or the consequences of interpersonal expressions in sport. Before a consideration of a number of potential variables of interest at the interpersonal level, it is important to provide an overview of social-functional perspectives on emotion.

Parkinson (1996) argued that the emotion process is principally a social process, given that the main causes, consequences, and functions of emotions are often situated within transactions between two or more people. Indeed, Parkinson theorized that the primary purpose of expressing emotion is to achieve indirect interpersonal effects and thereby mediate the social transaction between to agents; people express their emotions to communicate to a real or imagined "other" about the meaning they derive from their current situation or environment. For instance, emotional expressions convey information about the expresser's inner feelings (Ekman, 1992), social motives (Fridlund, 1994), and orientation toward other people (Hess, Blairy, & Kleck, 2000; Knutson, 1996). In addition, emotional expressions inform observers about the expresser's appraisal of the situation (Manstead & Fischer, 2001). Van Kleef's (2009, 2010) Emotions as social information (EASI) model is rooted in the early social-functional perspectives on emotion (e.g., Fischer & Manstead, 2008; Frijda & Mesquita, 1994; Keltner & Haidt, 1999; Parkinson, 1996). According to Van Kleef (2010), interpersonal emotional influence occurs through two channels: affective reactions and inferential processes. To elaborate, emotional expressions often evoke affective reactions in observers through the transfer from expresser to observer via emotional contagion processes, involving mirror neuron activity, mimicry, and afferent feedback (e.g., Hatfield, Cacioppo, & Rapson, 1994). Emotional expression can also influence impressions and interpersonal liking. For instance, numerous studies across different domains of social interaction (personal relations, team work, leader–follower relations, dispute resolution, negotiation, and coalition formation) converge in demonstrating that the effects of one person's emotional expressions on another's behavior are often driven by affective reactions (see Van Kleef, 2010). Expressions of happiness elicit reciprocal feelings of happiness and positive impressions, which are conducive to constructive interpersonal interactions and cooperation. Conversely, expressions of anger elicit reciprocal anger and negative impressions, which undermine cooperative social exchange.

Emotional expressions can also wield interpersonal influence by triggering inferential processes in observers (Van Kleef, 2009) such that observers may infer information about the expresser's feelings, attitudes, relational orientation, and behavioral intentions (Keltner & Haidt, 1999), which in turn influence the observer's behavior. The implications of an emotional display covary with the context, but the basic informational value of discrete emotions generalizes across situations (Van Kleef, 2009). To illustrate, a rugby player who shows up late for a team meeting with a strength and conditioning coach might infer from his anger that he is not amused and that he should make more effort to be on time in the future.

In short, the premise of the EASI model is that emotional expressions can influence observers' behavior by the distinct but mutually influential processes of eliciting affective reactions and triggering inferential processes (Van Kleef, 2009). In some cases inferences and affective reactions lead to the same behavior. For example, the distress of an athlete after a loss might signal for a manager that help is required (inference) but also triggers negative feelings in the manager (affective reaction), both of which foster supportive behavior. Nevertheless, According to Van Kleef (2009), the extent to which either process occurs is moderated by two factors: the observer's information processing ability and motivation and social-relational factors. For instance, when faced with an aggressive act from an opponent in competition, one's own reciprocal aggression might drive competition, but one's inference that the other's aggression is beyond the bounds or laws of acceptable behavior might encourage a retaliatory aggressive act.

Building on the idea that emotional expressions provide information about the expresser, the EASI model posits that the interpersonal effects of emotional expressions depend on the observer's motivation and ability to process the information conveyed by these expressions. Specifically, the deeper the information processing, the stronger the relative predictive power of inferences. Conversely, the shallower the information processing, the stronger the relative predictive power of affective reactions (Van Kleef, 2009). This idea is supported by several studies. In a series of negotiation experiments (Van Kleef, De Dreu, & Manstead, 2004), participants conceded more to an angry counterpart than to a happy one when they had low need for cognitive closure, time pressure was low, or they had low power (circumstances that heighten information processing motivation), but not when they had high need for closure, time pressure was high, or they had high power (circumstances that lower information processing motivation). When participants were motivated to engage in thorough information processing they inferred from their counterpart's anger that they had ambitious limits and from happiness that they were lenient and easy to get (see also Sinaceur & Tiedens, 2006). When participants were not motivated to process information deeply they did not draw such inferences, and their behavior was unaffected by the counterpart's emotional expressions. A similar moderating role of information processing was demonstrated in the study on leadership and team performance described earlier (Van Kleef 2009). Followers with high dispositional information processing motivation (as measured prior to the interaction) performed better when their leader displayed anger rather than happiness, because in the case of anger they inferred that their performance was suboptimal and that they needed to work harder, whereas in the case of happiness they inferred that they had done a good job and that no further effort was needed. Followers with low information processing motivation, in contrast, performed better when the leader displayed happiness rather than anger, because the leader's happiness put them in a good mood and made them like the leader, whereas the leader's anger annoyed them and made them dislike the leader. Comparable findings were also obtained in a study of engagement on a creativity task (Van Kleef, Anastasopoulou, & Nijstad, 2010) and the motivation to respond to a partner's suffering in an emotionally adaptive way (Van Kleef, Oveis, Van der Löwe, LuoKogan, Goetz, & Keltner, 2008).

Level 3: emotion at the interpersonal level of analysis

Although sport-specific research is required, the emerging findings testing the EASI model have some potential implications for emotions in sport. Indeed, given the nature of many sports precludes athletes from paying substantial attention to the facial expressions of their coaches and teammates (Friesen et al., 2013), capitalizing on opportunities for effective and efficient emotion communication would appear to be an imperative for successful coaching. In support of this hypothesis, Hanin (2003) demonstrated that ice hockey coaches were successfully able to describe the behavioral cues that indicated the emotional state of their hockey players. Yet despite such observations, Hanin (2007) proposed that research on interpersonal behavioral indicators within sport is rare. Therefore, there is a need to develop ecologically valid methods for measuring the extent to which athletes, coaches, sport scientists and medics, and performance directors are able to discern the emotions of those they interact with in the pursuit of performance enhancement.

Returning to the potential value of the EASI mode, the relative predictive power of inferences and affective reactions in sport will also likely depend on social-contextual factors. One such factor concerns the interdependence structure of the situation (e.g., cliques, subgroups, cohesion, motivational climate). An extensive review of research on the interpersonal effects of emotions in cooperative and competitive settings (Van Kleef et al., 2010) revealed that although affective reactions and inferential processes occur in both types of settings, inferential processes are relatively more important in competitive situations, which are characterized by lower trust. In such situations, emotional expressions provide important strategic information that helps observers better understand their counterpart's intentions and determine an adaptive course of action. Similarly, Gross, Richards and John (2006) suggested that the type of emotion regulation strategy chosen will often influence the strength of the dyadic relationship. In sum, the EASI model provides a potentially useful model for guiding emotion research at the interpersonal level of analysis given its acknowledgement of the consequences of emotion expression, thus complementing existing models that focus on the *intra*personal effects of emotions on cognitions and behavior.

In the sport context, cultural norms distinct to each sport have surfaced in both research and applied contexts. Gallmeier (1987) highlighted how teammates, fans, and coaches influenced the emotions of ice hockey players, who then altered their expressions and behaviors to respond in appropriate accordance with the expected norms of hockey culture. Galvan and Ward (1998) described an intervention intended to change the aggressive behaviors of players that were perceived to be in violation of tennis display rules by posting descriptions of the athletes' outbursts for the public to see. Research has also demonstrated the importance of expressing emotion in an appropriate manner in order to achieve desired effects. Breakey, Jones, Cunningham, and Holt (2009) examined female ice hockey players' perceptions of their coach's mid-game speeches. They found that the amount of emotion the coach himself exuded, the length and content of his speeches (i.e. whether they were short and meaningful, and referenced team values), the timing of his speech, whether or not his perceptions agreed with the athletes', and whether he left out expected pieces of information were perceived as the determining factors as to whether or not the speech was positively or negatively received. Similarly, Boardley, Kavussanu, and Ring (2008) found that athletes' perceptions of their coach's ability to motivate them were linked to the coach's emotional expressions of effort, commitment, and enjoyment. Together, this suggests that the outcomes of interpersonal emotion regulation strategies rely not only on the strategies themselves but also on the manner in which they are delivered. Similar research has reported that the competitive situation will also affect how receptive athletes are to the emotional content of their coaches' speeches. For example, Vargas-Tonsing and Guan (2007) reported that athletes had a desire to hear greater amounts of emotional content as opposed to informative content specifically before a championship game, when the team was considered an underdog and when competing against an opponent ranked higher in the standings (Friesen et al., 2013).

At the dyadic level, emotions can assist the organization of transactions between two individuals. That is, emotional expression assists one's partner to understand one's feelings, beliefs, attitudes, and behavioral intentions, and serve to coordinate complementarity and reciprocity during social situations. Indeed, research in sport psychology has also suggested that inferential processing influences the emotions and behaviors of others, not least within the coach–athlete relationship (Jowett & Poczwardowski, 2007; Mageau & Vallerand, 2003). For example, Vargas-Tonsing, Myers, and Feltz (2004) found that when coaches acted confidently themselves, their athletes experienced increased self-efficacy, because an athlete observing a confident coach appraised their chances for success as good. Other studies have shown that coaches who share their appraisals of performance and give feedback with high informational value enhance the confidence and self-efficacy of their athletes (Amorose & Weiss, 1998; Vargas-Tonsing, 2009). This might be attributed to the coaches giving their athletes more opportunity to process their appraisals of the situation and bring their own emotions in line.

In other coach–athlete research, Lafrenière, Jowett, Vallerand, Donahue, and Lorimer (2008) examined the role of passion in the quality of the coach–athlete relationship. Distinguishing between two types of passion (viz. harmonious and obsessive) revealed that harmonious passion positively predicted a high-quality coach–athlete relationship, whereas obsessive passion was largely unrelated to such relationships. Furthermore, these effects were fully mediated by positive emotions. Finally, the quality of the coach–athlete relationship positively predicted coaches' subjective well-being. These findings highlight passion as a salient factor to consider when trying to predict the quality of coach–athlete relationships, yet future research is needed to more firmly establish when each type of passion may affect the coach–athlete relationship, and identify the nature of the psychological processes mediating such effects. Other dyadic research in sport has focused on children's and adolescents' relationships with peers and parents. In Weiss, Smith, and Theeboom's (1996) work with children and adolescents, a number of distinct dimensions emerged that help us to understand young people's friendship experiences in sport. Children and adolescents experienced a number of positive aspects of friendship from their involvement in sport, including companionship, self-esteem enhancement, intimacy, emotional support, and assistance in conflict resolution. More recently, Carr and colleagues (Carr, 2009; Carr & Fitzpatrick, 2011) have examined young people's attachment relationships with parents as a potential predictor of their friendship quality, generally highlighting that adolescent perceptions of dyadic sporting friendships are constructed as a consequence of both actor and partner attachment characteristics. That is, adolescents' perceptions of the quality of friendship are not dependent on only one's own attachment characteristics, but also on the attachment characteristics of one's friend. In other dyad research, Sève, Poizat, Saury, and Durand (2006) noted that emotional expression exchange between table tennis players was deliberately managed to facilitate impressions of confidence in one another.

Level 4: emotion at the group and team level of analysis

At the group level, emotions serve the purpose of defining social norms, roles, and status, creating boundaries, and reflecting team identity. Indeed, Keltner and Haidt (1999) proposed that emotions help interacting groups with shared identity and purpose to meet collective goals. For example, researchers have explored the effects of personal-disclosure and mutual-sharing (PDMS) on a range of outcomes including cohesion and communications, confidence and trust in teammates, greater understanding and awareness of themselves, increased closeness to teammates, and greater motivation to play for their team and each other (see Dunn & Holt, 2004; Holt & Dunn, 2006). More recently, Evans, Slater, Turner, and Barker (2014) highlighted the effects of PDMS to enhance group functioning in a football academy setting. That is, data indicated an improvement in social identity, collective efficacy, and team performance after a single bout of PDMS focused on sharing personal stories with teammates. Although little is known about the precise mechanisms underpinning PDMS, Holt and Dunn (2006) suggested that the observed benefits might be explained by the emotional intensity, the variety of emotions experienced when disclosing previously unknown personal information to fellow team members. Further, discovering information that would otherwise remain private might facilitate empathy, shared understanding, and common experiences of problems and issues that serve to promote socio-emotional bonds between teammates (see Dunn & Holt, 2004; Evans et al., 2014; Hardy & Crace, 1997).

In a recent systematic review of the team contact sport literature (e.g., rugby, football, ice hockey), Campo, Mellalieu, Ferrand, Martinent, and Rosnet (2012) provided a taxonomy of team sport athletes' emotions, as well as antecedents, coping responses, and moderators of athletes' emotional experiences. The results highlighted the importance of social influences on athletes' emotional experiences, as the influence of others (e.g., negative relationships, criticism, teammates' behaviors) was identified as an antecedent of athletes' negative emotions in over 58 percent of the studies they reviewed, whereas athletes' own errors (e.g., physical or mental errors) were reported as antecedents of negative emotions in 52.9 percent of the reviewed studies. Researchers have also acknowledged the role of group membership on emotional experience. For instance, Uphill and Jones (2007) provided evidence that athletes' sense of belonging to an "elite" group was associated with their emotional experience of pride. Surprisingly, despite several reviews highlighting the potential value (e.g., Friesen et al., 2013; Tamminen & Crocker, 2013) and scarcity (e.g., Campo et al., 2012) of group and team emotion and regulation, few studies have emerged exploring how athletes' emotional experience, regulation, and expression impacts others and how the same processes within others function within a team context. Nevertheless, several lines of research have emerged examining affective concepts for teams (e.g. Moll, Jordet, & Pepping, 2010; O'Neill, 2008; Tamminen & Crocker, 2013; Totterdell, 2000). To elaborate, there is some evidence of the influence of group or team environment on the emotions of actors within that team. Totterdell (2000) examined emotional contagion among professional cricket players and reported that athletes' positive, happy moods were linked to the collective happy mood of their teammates, which was also associated with players' subjective performances. Players who were older, more committed to the team, and more susceptible to emotional contagion showed greater associations between their own mood and that of their teammates. Totterdell suggested that associations between individual-team moods may be related to athletes' emotional expressiveness and affective communication via deliberate and non-deliberate facial, verbal, and behavioral expressions.

Moll et al. (2010) examined emotional contagion through video analysis of soccer players' celebratory behaviors following penalty kicks. Athletes' behaviors associated with the display of pride after a successful penalty kick were associated with the team's eventual success, and findings highlighted the importance of social interactions between teammates during competitions. Similarly, Ronglan (2007) reported that players deliberately expressed excessive joy and enthusiasm after successful performances in order to increase opponents' feelings of defeat. Additional studies examining intimidation in football and ice hockey have highlighted the intention in athletes to induce unpleasant feeling states in their counterparts (Kerr & Grange, 2009; Shapcott, Bloom, & Loughead, 2007). These findings support research suggesting that body language and non-verbal communication is important for interactions between athletes and their teammates, opponents, and coaches (LeCouteur & Feo, 2011; Manley et al., 2008). For example, Buscombe, Greenlees, Holder, Thelwell, and Rimmer (2006) revealed that the inferences tennis players made about their opponents' body language and clothing influenced their perceptions of the dispositional traits of their opponent and their perceived anticipated match outcome. Specifically, when opponents displayed confident body language, tennis players felt less likely to succeed against them and inferred that their opponents' confidence was due to their anticipation of victory.

Tamminen and Crocker (2013) recently examined emotional self-regulation and interpersonal emotion regulation within a team of competitive curlers. Data collection involved multiple semi-structured interviews with all four members of a female high-performance curling team, as well as observation of team meetings, practices, and games over a full season. The findings indicated the use of a number of emotional self-regulation (body language and self-censorship) and interpersonal emotional regulation (providing positive and/or technical feedback, humour, cueing teammates about their emotions, prosocial actions, and indirect actions) strategies. Further, the findings suggested that performers were aware of and considered social and contextual factors (e.g., social norms and role on team) when regulating emotions in team meetings, practices, and games toward the achievement of multiple goals (e.g., positive performances, positive social relationships).

In addition to emotion regulation, sport psychologists have increasingly noted the importance of emotional labor in sport organizations (e.g., Wagstaff et al., 2012a, 2012c). Morris and Feldman (1996) defined emotional labor as "the effort, planning and control needed to express organizationally desired emotions during interpersonal interactions" (p. 987). It is possible that the efforts associated with engaging in emotional labor might have intrapersonal or interpersonal costs for sport performers. Indeed, a recent study by Wagstaff and Weston (2015) examined the interplay between emotional experience and regulation and psychosocial and task outcomes in a performance team. Specifically, in a study with a military team during a two-month Antarctic mountaineering expedition, Wagstaff and Weston found maladaptive emotion regulation strategies (e.g., suppression) to be rated as effective despite their use being correlated with negative intrapersonal (e.g., mental fatigue) and interpersonal (e.g., cohesion) outcomes. The authors concluded that the demanding expedition environment influenced participants' perceptions of emotion regulation requirements, regulation strategy selection, and effectiveness, which, in turn, were associated with greater levels of mental fatigue, instances of conflict, and decreased team performance. Together, the findings from Tamminen and Crocker (2013) and Wagstaff and Weston (2015) offer an excellent insight into self and interpersonal emotional regulation in teams and it is hoped that future research continues to build in these nascent findings.

Level 5: emotion at the organizational level of analysis

In addition to the emerging exploration of emotion contagion and regulation in sport teams, scholars have also acknowledged the importance of regulating emotions in sport organizations (e.g. Lane et al., 2012; Wagstaff et al., 2012a, 2012c). For example, Wagstaff et al. (2012a) conducted a nine-month ethnography in an Olympic national sport organization (NSO), highlighting the development and maintenance of interpersonal relationships to be the critical building blocks for optimal organizational functioning. Moreover, individuals better able to monitor and manage their emotions were more likely to forge and maintain successful relationships. That is, participants used emotion-related abilities for managing conflict, communicating emotion, and managing and expressing emotion to maintain the psychological contract, engaging in contagious emotion regulation, and emotion regulation to aid the building and maintenance of relationships. The use of these emotion abilities and regulation strategies increased what Wagstaff et al. (2012a) termed "psychosocial capital" (i.e., enhanced levels of engagement and social relationships) and displays of prosocial behavior within the organization. Conversely, the absence of such abilities appeared to put a strain on interpersonal relationships, reduced individuals' social standing, and gave way to power struggles. In an attempt to extend the ethnographic work of Wagstaff et al. (2012a), Wagstaff et al. (2012c) used a semi-structured interview approach to identify key emotion abilities (i.e., identifying, processing and comprehending, and managing emotions) associated with the use of specific experience and expression regulation strategies (e.g. forward-tracking, back-tracking, reappraisal, suppression, and impulse control). To elaborate, Wagstaff et al. (2012c) found emotion abilities to influence regulation strategy selection through sociocultural norms present within organizations. For example, participants reported that adhering to expectations and norms relating to emotional expression to be a major contributing factor in regulation strategy selection. Based on these findings, Wagstaff et al. proposed a socio-cognitive model of emotion regulation in organizations to explain the antecedents to and consequences of emotion regulation.

Initial support has emerged for Wagstaff et al.'s (2012c) socio-cognitive model of emotion regulation in organizations (e.g., Friesen et al., 2013; Tamminen and Crocker, 2013; Wagstaff et al., 2013). For example, using a two-phase action research intervention, Wagstaff et al. (2013) found emotion regulation and ability workshops improved the practice of participants, their emotional regulation strategy use, and perceptions of relationship quality and closeness. Moreover, participants receiving an extended one-to-one coaching intervention showed improvement in EI ability scores in addition to the benefits demonstrated via workshops. The findings indicated that short-term generic interventions to promote the use of adaptive emotion regulation strategies might be effective in sport organizations, but the purposive development of EI might require more longitudinal and idiographic approaches. In light of the fruitful body of work reviewed above, it would appear that the requirement for emotion regulation and EI abilities have been underestimated in sport and reflect a pervasive necessity of organizational life (Wagstaff & Larner, 2015).

Perhaps the most recent development regarding emotions at the organizational level relate to sport medics' and scientists' experiences of organizational change (e.g., Wagstaff, Gilmore, & Thelwell, 2015; Wagstaff, Thelwell, & Gilmore, 2016). To illustrate, Wagstaff et al. (2015a) explored sport medicine and science practitioners' experiences of organizational change using a longitudinal design over a two-year period. Specifically, data were collected in three temporally defined phases via forty-nine semi-structured interviews with twenty sport medics and scientists (SMSs) employed by three organizations competing in the top tiers of English football and cricket. The findings indicated that change occurred over four distinct stages: anticipation and uncertainty, upheaval and realization, integration and experimentation, normalization and learning. Moreover, the data highlighted salient emotional, behavioral, and attitudinal experiences of medics and scientists following organizational change. With regards to job attitudes, Wagstaff et al. (2015) asserted that the transition from one stage to another appeared to be dependent on appraisals of a number of factors including practitioner resilience and that SMSs who had experienced repeated cycles of change had become more resilient in their response to change. Moreover, the authors noted that the learning opportunities in the fourth and final stage of change was essential for promoting resilience among employees. The longitudinal design adopted by Wagstaff et al. allowed the authors to capture SMSs experiences of the change process as it occurred and influenced their thoughts, behaviors, and practice over time. Perhaps most significantly, the findings highlight the extent to which sport medics and scientists professionals were vulnerable to the continual change processes within professional sport.

Responding to calls for the investigation of employees' responses to recurrent change events, Wagstaff et al. (2016) recently studied employees' experiences of repeated organizational change. Data were gathered via twenty semi-structured interviews with ten employees from two organizations competing in English football's Barclays Premier League. The results indicated that employees responded to recurring organizational change in positive and negative emotional, behavioral, and attitudinal ways. One of the main positive response themes related to resilience. Specifically, although participants generally reported a largely negative experience of change, many of the participants who had experienced repeated change recognized resilience as an inherent characteristic of working in high-performance domains. That is, although participants commonly reported a largely negative perception of change events, they stated that they were developing more positive responses to subsequent change events than their first experience of such change. In summarizing the emerging organizational change in sport research, it would appear that when change is initiated by owners and strategic-level managers, those that the change is aimed at influencing (i.e., those tasked with implementing and coping with the change) generally report a declining emotional attachment to the organization over repeated iterations of change. Moreover, such experiences are perceived to influence one's behavior during that process, and thus play a significant role. Notably, such findings have implications for research and practice, which are presented in the next section along with considerations from the broader themes covered in this chapter.

Future research directions

In this review we have called for the integration of numerous extant and well-established theories and models into an overarching multilevel schema of emotion phenomena research in sport organizations. Nevertheless, substantial research efforts over many years would be required to examine the holistic model in full. Hence, we suggest that the intergrative model of emotion in sport organizations outlined here be used as an initial exploratory framework for orienting research endeavors. In this manner the potential usefulness of this model lies in guiding research design rather than stimulating specific research questions.

While we hope to stimulate a variety of research lines of inquiry with this review, several methodological considerations are worthy of mention. Much of the extant research reviewed in this chapter has adopted cross-sectional questionnaire or longitudinal interview and observation data collection techniques. While such techniques have many benefits, they are variously vulnerable to either retrospective recall bias or are dependent on the researcher being an effective conduit for presenting narratives for the reader. One solution to this problem is the use of forms of data collection variously labelled ecological momentary analysis, diary, and experience sampling method (ESM) (e.g., Conner Christensen et al., 2003). We focus on the latter here. ESM typically entails participants receiving randomized signals (e.g., text messages, smartphone app alerts) during a period of data collection, at which time they complete questions administered via an electronic diary or app about their present or latest experience. One advantage of ESM is that it permits researchers to study personal events as they unfold in their natural and spontaneous context. Another advantage is that ESM facilitates repeated measurements over time, to allow the observation of patterns of given phenomenon (e.g., at a specific time of the day or part of the sport schedule). When frequency estimates of specific emotions are needed, ESM may yield more reliable data than the aggregated, retrospective, and cognitively biased data obtained in questionnaire studies (Ready, Weinberger, & Jones, 2007). Moreover, ESM is consistent with Brunswick's (1956) notion of *representative design*, which involves randomly sampling stimuli from the environment, so that environmental properties are preserved.

Although the consideration of emotion phenomena at multiple levels of analysis in sport organizations is relatively nascent, researchers (e.g., Wagstaff, Hanton, & Fletcher, 2013) have noted the importance of considering issues of level of measurement and focus or what Rousseau (1985) labelled as issues of aggregation bias, which can occur in two ways. The first is the cross-level fallacy, where the same functional relationship is assumed to exist at two levels. To elaborate, scholars conducting organizational research risk a cross-level fallacy unless they can logically assume that concepts have a functional equivalence across levels (Rousseau, 1985). For example, Wagstaff et al. (2013) attempted to avoid the assumption that changes measured at the between-person level (i.e., emotion abilities) necessarily led to changes at the organizational level (i.e., organizational functioning). Nevertheless, issues of measurement level are easier to theorize about than to apply in practice and researchers might need to exercise both patience and pragmatism until ecologically valid measurement tools can be developed. The second manifestation of aggregation bias is referred to as the contextual fallacy. This issue arises when researchers neglect to specify the different contextual factors that affect relationships at each level of the study. For example, it would be fallacious to generalize relationships developed at one level of the model to another without including the moderating effect of context that exists at each level. Given the nuanced sociocultural characteristics of sport dyads, teams, and organizations (and perhaps beyond to national cultures and sport types), researchers must consider how such contextual factors (e.g., culture, climate, change, leadership) moderate or mediate proposed findings. Given these observations, it is important for researchers examining emotions at multiple levels in sport organizations to acknowledge and account for the clustered nature of data.

Conclusion

To conclude, we return to reflect on the present status of emotion research in sport. We would argue that the study of emotion in sport is generally viewed as a mature research area and one that represents a ubiquitous area of applied sport psychology practice with individuals, dyads, teams, and organizations. Yet, we are both surprised and excited to highlight in this review how much remains to be systematically examined within this domain. Given leading emotion theorists (e.g., Van Kleef, 2010) have specifically identified the sport domain as one of great potential for research, and that sport organizations offer a vibrant context for studying the influence of multilevel variables and human performance, it is clear that those of us engaged in researching such phenomena have not fully seized the opportunities available to us. We finish by reiterating key messages for future research and applied practice.

Key messages for future research

- In sport, emotion has typically been studied as a within-person, one-direction, non-repetitive phenomenon, which is a somewhat narrow focus and does not allow for a full appreciation of emotion phenomena in sport organizations.
- Much stands to be gained from moving away from the prevailing examination of emotion phenomena at the individual level in sport, and toward an inclusive, multilevel model that spans micro (i.e., individual), meso (e.g., dyadic, team), and macro (i.e., organizational, cultural) dimensions.
- Dyads, groups, teams, and organizations are witness to instances of individual influence through emotion experience and expression.
- Sociocultural norms distinct to each sport are evident in both research and applied contexts within sport psychology. Further research is required to further illuminate the dynamics surrounding self and interpersonal emotional regulation in teams.
- Research is required to examine the multilevel model of emotion in sport organizations outlined here and might benefit from the use of ecological momentary analysis, diary, and experience sampling methods while also attempting to address issues of aggregation across levels of analysis.

Key messages for applied practice

- Individuals fulfilling a variety of roles within sport organizations (i.e., athletes, coaches, managers, support staff) are vulnerable to and influence the emotions of those they transact with, therefore sport psychologists must better prepare for working with individuals and circumstances that transcend multiple levels of the organizational hierarchy.
- The requirement for emotion regulation and emotional intelligence abilities have been underestimated in sport and reflect a pervasive necessity of organizational life. It would be valuable for sport psychologists to incorporate the ability to develop such competencies into their skillset.
- Although reported as a necessary emotion regulation strategy within sport organizations, suppressing ones emotional expression appears to have undesirable implications for relationships and sport performance.
- Emotional expressiveness and affective communication via deliberate facial, verbal, and behavioral expressions might have utility in sport environments during both competition and everyday life.
- Discovering information that would otherwise remain private might facilitate empathy, shared understanding, and common experiences of problems and issues that serve to promote socio-emotional bonds between teammates.

References

Amorose, A. J., & Weiss, M. R. (1998). Coaching feedback as a source of information about perceptions of ability: A developmental examination. *Journal of Sport and Exercise Psychology, 20*, 395–420.

Ashkanasy, N. M. (2003). Emotions in organizations: A multilevel perspective. *Research in Multi-level Issues, 2*, 9–54.

Baron, B., Guilloux, B., Begue, M., & Uriac, S. (2015). Emotional responses during repeated sprint intervals performed on level, downhill and uphill surfaces. *Journal of Sports Sciences, 33*(5), 476–486.

Baumeister, R. F., Stillwell, A. M., & Heatherton, T. F. (1995). Personal narratives about guilt: Role in action control and interpersonal relationships. *Basic and Applied Social Psychology, 17*, 173–198.

Blascovich, J., Seery, M. D., Mugridge, C. A., Norris, R. K., & Weisbuch, M. D. (2004). Predicting athletic performance from cardiovascular indexes of challenge and threat. *Journal of Experimental Social Psychology, 40*, 683–688.

Boardley, I. D., Kavussanu, M., & Ring, C. M. (2008). Athletes' perceptions of coaching effectiveness and athlete-related outcomes in rugby union: An investigation based on the coaching efficacy model. *Sport Psychologist, 22*(3), 269–287.

Breakey, C., Jones, M., Cunningham, C. T., & Holt, N. (2009). Female athletes' perceptions of a coach's speeches. *International Journal of Sports Science and Coaching, 4*(4), 489–504.

Brunswick, E. (1956). *Perception and the representative design of psychological experiments*. Berkeley, CA: University of California Press.

Buscombe, R., Greenlees, I., Holder, T., Thelwell, R., & Rimmer, M. (2006). Expectancy effects in tennis: The impact of opponents' pre-match non-verbal behaviour on male tennis players. *Journal of Sports Sciences, 24*(12), 1265–1272.

Campo, M., Mellalieu, S., Ferrand, C., Martinent, G., & Rosnet, E. (2012). Emotions in team contact sports: A systematic review. *Sport Psychologist, 26*(1), 62–97.

Carr, S. (2009). Adolescent–parent attachment characteristics and quality of youth sport friendship. *Psychology of Sport and Exercise, 10*(6), 653–661.

Carr, S., & Fitzpatrick, N. (2011). Experiences of dyadic sport friendships as a function of self and partner attachment characteristics. *Psychology of Sport and Exercise, 12*(4), 383–391.

Chan, J., & Mallett, C. (2011). The value of emotional intelligence for high performance coaching. *International Journal of Sports Science and Coaching, 6*(3), 315–328.

Christensen, T. C., Barrett, L. F., Bliss-Moreau, E., Lebo, K., & Kaschub, C. (2003). A practical guide to experience-sampling procedures. *Journal of Happiness Studies, 4*(1), 53–78.

Clark, M. S., Pataki, S. P., & Carver, V. H. (1996). Some thoughts and findings on self-presentation of emotions in relationships. In G. J. O. Fletcher & J. Fitness (Eds.), *Knowledge structures in close relationships: A social psychological approach* (pp. 247–274). Mahwah, NJ: Erlbaum.

Costarelli, V., & Stamou, D. (2009). Emotional intelligence, body image and disordered eating attitudes in combat sport athletes. *Journal of Exercise Science & Fitness, 7*(2), 104–111.

Coté, S. (2005). A social interaction model of the effects of emotion regulation on work strain. *Academy of Management Review, 30*(3), 509–530.

Crombie, D., Lombard, C., &Noakes, T. D. (2009). Emotional intelligence scores predict team sports performance in a national cricket competition. *International Journal of Sports Science and Coaching, 4*, 209–224.

Cropanzano, R., Weiss, H. M., Hale, J. M., & Reb, J. (2003). The structure of affect: Reconsidering the relationship between negative and positive affectivity. *Journal of Management, 29*(6), 831–857.

Dunn, J. G., & Holt, N. L. (2004). Toward a grounded theory of the psychosocial competencies and environmental conditions associated with soccer success. *Journal of Applied Sport Psychology, 16*(3), 199–219.

Dunn, E. W., Brackett, M. A., Ashton-James, C., Schneiderman, E., & Salovey, P. (2007). On emotionally intelligent time travel: Individual differences in affective forecasting ability. *Personality and Social Psychology Bulletin, 33*(1), 85–93.

Ekman, P. (1992). An argument for basic emotions. *Cognition and Emotion, 6*(3–4), 169–200.

Ekman, P., & Friesen, W. V. (1976). Measuring facial movement. *Environmental Psychology and Nonverbal Behavior, 1*(1), 56–75.

Elfenbein, H. A. (2007). Emotion in organizations: A review and theoretical integration. *The Academy of Management Annals, 1*(1), 315–386.

Eysenck, M. W., & Calvo, M. G. (1992). Anxiety and performance: The processing efficiency theory. *Cognition and Emotion, 6*(6), 409–434.

Fischer, A. H., & Manstead, A. S. R. (2008). The social functions of emotion. In M. Lewis, J. Haviland-Jones, & L. F. Barrett (Eds.), *Handbook of emotions* (3rd ed.) (pp. 456–468). New York: Guilford Press.

Fletcher, D., & Fletcher, J. (2005). A meta-model of stress, emotions and performance: Conceptual foundations, theoretical framework, and research directions. *Journal of Sports Sciences, 23*(2), 157–158.

Forgas, J. P. (1995). Mood and judgment: The affect infusion model (AIM). *Psychological Bulletin, 117*(1), 39–66.

Fridlund, A. J. (1994). *Human facial expression: An evolutionary view.* San Diego, CA: Academic Press.

Friesen, A. P., Lane, A. M., Devonport, T. J., Sellars, C. N., Stanley, D. N., & Beedie, C. J. (2013). Emotion in sport: Considering interpersonal regulation strategies. *International Review of Sport and Exercise Psychology, 6*(1), 139–154.

Frijda, N. H. (1988). The laws of emotion. *American Psychologist, 43*(5), 349–358.

Frijda, N. H., & Mesquita, B. (1994). The social roles and functions of emotions. In S. Kitayama & H. R. Markus (Eds.), *Emotion and culture: Empirical studies of mutual influence* (pp. 51–87). Washington, DC: American Psychological Association.

Gallmeier, C. P. (1987). Putting on the game face: The staging of emotions in professional hockey. *Sociology of Sport Journal, 4*(4), 347–362.

Galvan, Z. J., & Ward, P. (1998). Effects of public posting on inappropriate on-court behaviors by collegiate tennis players. *The Sport Psychologist, 12*, 419–426.

Gross, J. J., Richards, J. M., & John, O. P. (2006). Emotion regulation in everyday life. In D. K. Snyder, J. A. Simpson, & J. N. Hughes (Eds.), *Emotion regulation in couples and families: Pathways to dysfunction and health* (pp. 13–35). Washington, DC: American Psychological Association.

Gucciardi, D. F., Hanton, S., Gordon, S., Mallett, C. J., & Temby, P. (2015). The concept of mental toughness: Tests of dimensionality, nomological network, and traitness. *Journal of Personality, 83*(1), 26–44.

Hanin, Y. L. (2000). Individual zones of optimal functioning (IZOF) model: Emotion-performance relationships in sport. In Y. L. Hanin (Ed.), *Emotions in sport* (pp. 65–89). Champaign, IL: Human Kinetics.

Hanin, Y. L. (2003). Performance related emotional states in sport: A qualitative analysis. *Qualitative Social Research, 4*(1), Article 5.

Hanin, Y. L. (2007). Emotions in sport: Current issues and perspectives. In G. Tenenbaum, & R. Eklund (Eds.), *Handbook of sport psychology* (3rd ed.) (pp. 31–58). New York: Wiley & Sons.

Hanton, S., Thomas, O., & Maynard, I. (2004). Competitive anxiety responses in the week leading up to competition: The role of intensity, direction and frequency dimensions. *Psychology of Sport and Exercise, 5*(2), 169–181.

Hardy, L. (1990). A catastrophe model of performance in sport. In G. Jones & L. Hardy (Eds.), *Stress and performance in sport* (pp. 81–106). Chichester: John Wiley & Sons.

Hardy, C. J., & Crace, R. K. (1997). Foundations of team building: Introduction to the team building primer. *Journal of Applied Sport Psychology, 9*(1), 1–10.

Hareli, S., & Rafaeli, A. (2008). Emotion cycles: On the social influence of emotion in organizations. *Research in Organizational Behavior, 28*, 35–59.

Hatfield, E., Cacioppo, J. T., & Rapson, R. L. (1994). *Emotional contagion.* New York: Cambridge University Press.

Hess, U., Blairy, S., & Kleck, R. E. (2000). The influence of facial emotion displays, gender, and ethnicity on judgments of dominance and affiliation. *Journal of Nonverbal Behavior, 24*(4), 265–283.

Holt, N. L., & Dunn, J. G. (2006). Guidelines for delivering personal-disclosure mutual-sharing team building interventions. *Sport Psychologist, 20*(3), 348–367.

Izard, C. E. (1971). *The face of emotion.* New York: Appleton-Century-Crofts.

Jones, G. (1995). More than just a game: Research developments and issues in competitive anxiety in sport. *British Journal of Psychology, 86*, 449–478.

Jones, M. V., & Uphill, M. (2011). Emotion in sport: Antecedents and performance consequences. In J. Thatcher, M. V. Jones, & D. Lavallee (Eds.), *Coping and emotion in sport* (2nd ed.) (pp. 33–61). Hove: Routledge.

Jones, M., Meijen, C., McCarthy, P. J., & Sheffield, D. (2009). A theory of challenge and threat states in athletes. *International Review of Sport and Exercise Psychology, 2*(2), 161–180.

Jordet, G. (2009). Why do English players fail in soccer penalty shootouts? A study of team status, self-regulation, and choking under pressure. *Journal of Sports Sciences, 27*(2), 97–106.

Jowett, S., & Poczwardowski, A. (2007). Understanding the coach-athlete relationship. In S. Jowett and D. Lavallee (Eds.), *Social psychology in sport* (pp. 3–14). Champaign, IL: Human Kinetics.

Kajbafnezhad, H., Ahadi, H., Heidarie, A. R., Askari, P., & Enayati, M. (2011). Difference between team and individual sports with respect to psychological skills, overall emotional intelligence and athletic success motivation in Shiraz city athletes. *Journal of Basic and Applied Scientific Research, 1*(11), 1904–1909.

Kajbafnezhad, H., Ahadi, H., Heidarie, A., Askari, P., & Enayati, M. (2012). Predicting athletic success motivation using mental skin and emotional intelligence and its components in male athletes. *The Journal of Sports Medicine and Physical Fitness, 52(5),* 551–557.

Keltner, D., & Haidt, J. (1999). Social functions of emotions at four levels of analysis. *Cognition and Emotion, 13*(5), 505–521.

Keltner, D., Ekman, P., Gonzaga, G. C., & Beer, J. (2003). Facial expression of emotion. In R. J. Davidson & H. H. Goldsmith (Eds.), *Handbook of affective sciences* (pp. 415–432). London: Oxford University Press.

Kerr, J. H., & Grange, P. (2009). Athlete-to-athlete verbal aggression: A case study of interpersonal communication among elite Australian footballers. *International Journal of Sport Communication, 2*(3), 360–372.

Knutson, B. (1996). Facial expressions of emotion influence interpersonal trait inferences. *Journal of Nonverbal Behavior, 20*(3), 165–182.

Laborde, S., Brüll, A., Weber, J., & Anders, L. S. (2011). Trait emotional intelligence in sports: A protective role against stress through heart rate variability? *Personality and Individual Differences, 51*(1), 23–27.

Laborde, S., Dosseville, F., Guillén, F., & Chávez, E. (2014b). Validity of the trait emotional intelligence questionnaire in sports and its links with performance satisfaction. *Psychology of Sport and Exercise, 15*(5), 481–490.

Laborde, S., Lautenbach, F., Allen, M. S., Herbert, C., & Achtzehn, S. (2014b). The role of trait emotional intelligence in emotion regulation and performance under pressure. *Personality and Individual Differences, 57*, 43-47

Laborde, S., Dosseville, F., & Allen, M. S. (2015). Emotional intelligence in sport and exercise: A systematic review. *Scandinavian Journal of Medicine & Science in Sports. 26*(8), 862–874 doi: 10.1111/sms.12510

Lafrenière, M. A. K., Jowett, S., Vallerand, R. J., Donahue, E. G., & Lorimer, R. (2008). Passion in sport: On the quality of the coach-athlete relationship. *Journal of Sport & Exercise Psychology, 30*(5), 541–560.

Lane, A. M., & Wilson, M. (2011). Emotions and trait emotional intelligence among ultra-endurance runners. *Journal of Science and Medicine in Sport, 14*(4), 358–362.

Lane, A. M., Thelwell, R. C., Lowther, J., & Devonport, T. J. (2009). Emotional intelligence and psychological skills use among athletes. *Social Behavior and Personality: An International Journal, 37*(2), 195–201.

Lane, A. M., Devonport, T. J., Soos, I., Karsai, I., Leibinger, E., & Hamar, P. (2010). Emotional intelligence and emotions associated with optimal and dysfunctional athletic performance. *Journal of Sports Science and Medicine, 9*(3), 388–392.

Lane, A. M., Beedie, C. J., Jones, M. V., Uphill, M., & Devonport, T. J. (2012). The BASES expert statement on emotion regulation in sport. *Journal of Sports Sciences, 30*(11), 1189–1195.

Lane, A. M., Devonport, T. J., Friesen, A. P., Beedie, C. J., Fullerton, C. L., & Stanley, D. M. (2015). How should I regulate my emotions if I want to run faster? *European Journal of Sport Science, 11*, 1–8.

Latimer, A. E., Rench, T. A., & Brackett, M. A. (2007). Emotional intelligence: A framework for examining emotions in sport and exercise groups. In M. Beauchamp & M. Eys (Eds.), *Group dynamics advances in sport and exercise psychology: Contemporary themes* (pp. 3–22). New York: Routledge.

Lazarus, R. S. (2000). How emotions influence performance in competitive sports. *The Sport Psychologist, 14*, 229–252.

LeCouteur, A., & Feo, R. (2011). Real-time communication during play: Analysis of team-mates' talk and interaction. *Psychology of Sport and Exercise, 12*(2), 124–134.

Lu, F. J., Li, G. S. F., Hsu, E. Y. W., & Williams, L. (2010). Relationship between athletes' emotional intelligence and precompetitive anxiety. *Perceptual and Motor Skills, 110*(1), 323–338.

Mageau, G. A., & Vallerand, R. J. (2003). The coach–athlete relationship: A motivational model. *Journal of Sports Science, 21*(11), 883–904.

Manley, A., Greenlees, I., Graydon, J., Thelwell, R., Filby, W. C. D., & Smith, M. J. (2008). Athletes' perceived use of information sources when forming initial impressions and expectancies of a coach: An explorative study. *The Sport Psychologist, 22*, 73–89.

Manstead, A. S. R., & Fischer, A. H. (2001). Social appraisal: The social world as object of and influence on appraisal processes. In K. R. Scherer & A. Schorr (Eds.) *Appraisal processes in emotion: Theory, methods, research* (pp. 221–232). New York: Oxford University Press.

Martens, R., Burton, D., Vealey, R. S., Bump, L. A., & Smith, D. E. (1990). Development and validation of the Competitive State Anxiety Inventory-2. In R. Martens, R. S. Vealey, & D. Burton (Eds.), *Competitive anxiety in sport* (pp. 117–190). Champaign, IL: Human Kinetics.

Masters, R. S. (1992). Knowledge, knerves and know-how: The role of explicit versus implicit knowledge in the breakdown of a complex motor skill under pressure. *British Journal of Psychology, 83*(3), 343–358.

Mayer, J. D., Salovey, P., & Caruso, D. R. (2008). Emotional intelligence: New ability or eclectic traits? *American Psychologist, 63*(6), 503–517.

McCarthy, P. J. (2011). Positive emotion in sport performance: Current status and future directions. *International Review of Sport and Exercise Psychology, 4*(1), 50–69.

Meyer, B. B., & Fletcher, T. B. (2007). Emotional intelligence: A theoretical overview and implications for research and professional practice in sport psychology. *Journal of Applied Sport Psychology, 19*(1), 1–15.

Moll, T., Jordet, G., & Pepping, G. J. (2010). Emotional contagion in soccer penalty shootouts: Celebration of individual success is associated with ultimate team success. *Journal of Sports Sciences, 28*(9), 983–992.

Morris, J. A., & Feldman, D. C. (1996). The dimensions, antecedents, and consequences of emotional labor. *Academy of Management Review, 21*(4), 986–1010.

Mullen, R., & Hardy, L. (2000). State anxiety and motor performance: Testing the conscious processing hypothesis. *Journal of Sports Sciences, 18*, 785–799

Nibbeling, N., Daanen, H. A., Gerritsma, R. M., Hofland, R. M., & Oudejans, R. R. (2012). Effects of anxiety on running with and without an aiming task. *Journal of Sports Sciences, 30*(1), 11–19.

Nieuwenhuys, A., Pijpers, J. R., Oudejans, R. R., & Bakker, F. C. (2008). The influence of anxiety on visual attention in climbing. *Journal of Sport & Exercise Psychology, 30*(2), 171–185.

Ntoumanis, N., & Jones, G. (1998). Interpretation of competitive trait anxiety symptoms as a function of locus of control beliefs. *International Journal of Sport Psychology, 29*, 99–114.

O'Neill, D. (2008). Injury contagion in alpine ski racing: The effect of injury on teammates' performance. *Journal of Clinical Sport Psychology, 2*(3), 278–292.

Parkinson, B. (1996). Emotions are social. *British Journal of Psychology, 87*(4), 663–684.

Parkinson, B., Fischer, A. H., & Manstead, A. S. R. (2005). *Emotion in social relations: Cultural, group, and interpersonal processes*. New York: Psychology Press.

Perlini, A. H., & Halverson, T. R. (2006). Emotional intelligence in the National Hockey League. *Canadian Journal of Behavioural Science, 38*(2), 109–119.

Rafaeli, A., & Sutton, R. I. (1987). Expression of emotion as part of the work role. *Academy of Management Review, 12*(1), 23–37.

Rafaeli, A., & Sutton, R. I. (1989). The expression of emotion in organizational life. *Research in Organizational Behavior, 11*(1), 1–42.

Raglin, J. S., & Hanin, Y. L. (2000). Competitive anxiety. In Y. L. Hanin (Ed.), *Emotions in sport* (pp. 93–111). Champaign, IL: Human Kinetics.

Rathschlag, M., & Memmert, D. (2015). Self-generated emotions and their influence on sprint performance: An investigation of happiness and anxiety. *Journal of Applied Sport Psychology, 27*(2), 186–199.

Ready, R. E., Weinberger, M. I., & Jones, K. M. (2007). How happy have you felt lately? Two diary studies of emotion recall in older and younger adults. *Cognition and Emotion, 21*(4), 728–757.

Rimé, B., Mesquita, B., Boca, S., & Philippot, P. (1991). Beyond the emotional event: Six studies on the social sharing of emotion. *Cognition and Emotion, 5*(5–6), 435–465.

Robazza, C., & Bortoli, L. (2007). Perceived impact of anger and anxiety on sporting performance in rugby players. *Psychology of Sport and Exercise, 8*(6), 875–896.

Ronglan, L. T. (2007). Building and communicating collective efficacy: A season-long in-depth study of an elite sport team. *Sport Psychologist, 21*(1), 78.

Rousseau, D. M. (1985). Issues of level in organizational research: Multi-level and cross-level perspectives. *Research in Organizational Behavior, 7*(1), 1–37.

Scherer, K. R. (1984). Emotion as a multicomponent process: A model and some cross-cultural data. In P. Shaver (Ed.), *Review of personality and social psychology* (5th ed.) (pp. 37–63). Beverly Hills, CA: Sage.

Schwarz, N. (1990). *Feelings as information: Informational and motivational functions of affective states.* New York: Guilford Press.

Sève, C., Poizat, G., Saury, J., & Durand, M. (2006). A grounded theory of elite male table tennis players' activity during matches. *Sport Psychologist, 20*(1), 58–73.

Sève, C., Ria, L., Poizat, G., Saury, J., & Durand, M. (2007). Performance-induced emotions experienced during high-stakes table tennis matches. *Psychology of Sport and Exercise, 8*(1), 25–46.

Shapcott, K. M., Bloom, G. A., & Loughead, T. M. (2007). An initial exploration of the factors influencing aggressive and assertive intentions of women ice hockey players. *International Journal of Sport Psychology, 38*(2), 145–162.

Sinaceur, M., & Tiedens, L. Z. (2006). Get mad and get more than even: When and why anger expression is effective in negotiations. *Journal of Experimental Social Psychology, 42*(3), 314–322.

Smith, C. A., & Ellsworth, P. C. (1985). Patterns of cognitive appraisal in emotion. *Journal of Personality and Social Psychology, 48*(4), 813–838.

Tamminen, K. A., & Crocker, P. R. (2013). "I control my own emotions for the sake of the team": Emotional self-regulation and interpersonal emotion regulation among female high-performance curlers. *Psychology of Sport and Exercise, 14*(5), 737–747.

Thelwell, R. C., Lane, A. M., Weston, N. J., & Greenlees, I. A. (2008). Examining relationships between emotional intelligence and coaching efficacy. *International Journal of Sport and Exercise Psychology, 6*(2), 224–235.

Thomas, O., Hanton, S., & Maynard, I. (2007). Anxiety responses and psychological skill use during the time leading up to competition: Theory to practice I. *Journal of Applied Sport Psychology, 19*(4), 379–397.

Tok, S., Binboğa, E., Guven, S., Çatıkkas, F., & Dane, S. (2013). Trait emotional intelligence, the Big Five personality traits and isometric maximal voluntary contraction level under stress in athletes. *Neurology, Psychiatry and Brain Research*, 19(3), 133–138.

Totterdell, P. (2000). Catching moods and hitting runs: Mood linkage and subjective performance in professional sport teams. *Journal of Applied Psychology, 85*(6), 848–859.

Turner, M. J., Slater, M. J., & Barker, J. B. (2014). Not the end of the world: The effects of rational-emotive behavior therapy (REBT) on irrational beliefs in elite soccer academy athletes. *Journal of Applied Sport Psychology, 26*(2), 144–156

Uphill, M. A., & Jones, M. V. (2007). Antecedents of emotions in elite athletes: A cognitive motivational relational theory perspective. *Research Quarterly for Exercise and Sport, 78*(2), 79–89.

Van Kleef, G. A. (2009). How emotions regulate social life the emotions as social information (EASI) model. *Current Directions in Psychological Science, 18*(3), 184–188.

Van Kleef, G. A. (2010). The emerging view of emotion as social information. *Social and Personality Psychology Compass, 4*(5), 331–343.

Van Kleef, G. A., De Dreu, C. K., & Manstead, A. S. (2004). The interpersonal effects of anger and happiness in negotiations. *Journal of Personality and Social Psychology, 86*(1), 57–76.

Van Kleef, G. A., Oveis, C., Van der Löwe, I., LuoKogan, A., Goetz, J., & Keltner, D. (2008). Power, distress and compassion turning a blind eye to the suffering of others. *Psychological Science, 19*(12), 1315–1322.

Van Kleef, G. A., Anastasopoulou, C., & Nijstad, B. A. (2010). Can expressions of anger enhance creativity? A test of the emotions as social information (EASI) model. *Journal of Experimental Social Psychology, 46(6)*, 1042–1048.

Van Kleef, G. A., Van Doorn, E. A., Heerdink, M. W., & Koning, L. F. (2011) Emotion is for influence. *European Review of Social Psychology, 22*(1), 114–163.

Van Kleef, G. A., Homan, A. C., & Cheshin, A. (2012). Emotional influence at work: Take it EASI. *Organizational Psychology Review, 2*(4), 311–339.

Vargas-Tonsing, T. M. (2009). An exploratory examination of the effects of coaches' pre-game speeches on athletes' perceptions of self-efficacy and emotion. *Journal of Sport Behavior, 32*(1), 92–111.

Vargas-Tonsing, T., & Guan, J. (2007). Athletes' preferences for informational and emotional pre-game speech content. *International Journal of Sports Science and Coaching, 2*(2), 171–180.

Vargas-Tonsing, T. M., Myers, N. D., & Feltz, D. L. (2004). Coaches' and athletes' perceptions of efficacy enhancing techniques. *Sport Psychologist, 18*(4), 397–414.

Vine, S. J., Moore, L. J., & Wilson, M. R. (2011). Quiet eye training facilitates competitive putting performance in elite golfers. *Frontiers in Psychology, 2*, 1–9.

Wagstaff, C. R. D., & Larner, R. J. (2015). A review of organizational psychology in elite performance domains: Recent developments and future directions. In S. D. Mellalieu and S. Hanton (Eds.), *Contemporary reviews in sport psychology* (pp. 91–110). London: Routledge.

Wagstaff, C. R. D., & Weston, N. J. V. (2015). Examining emotion regulation during an Antarctic expedition. *Sport, Exercise and Performance Psychology, 3*, 273–287.

Wagstaff, C. R. D., Fletcher, D., & Hanton, S. (2012a). Positive organizational psychology in sport: An ethnography of organizational functioning in a national sport organization. *Journal of Applied Sport Psychology, 24*(1), 26–47.

Wagstaff, C. R. D., Fletcher, D., & Hanton, S. (2012b). Positive organizational psychology in sport. *International Review of Sport and Exercise Psychology, 5*, 87–103.

Wagstaff, C. R. D., Fletcher, D., & Hanton, S. (2012c). Exploring emotion abilities and regulation strategies in sport organizations. *Sport, Exercise, and Performance Psychology, 1*, 268–282.

Wagstaff, C. R. D., Neil, R., Mellalieu, S. D., & Hanton, S. (2012d). Key movements in directional research in competitive anxiety. *Routledge Online Studies on the Olympic and Paralympic Games, 53*, 143–166. doi: 10.4324/9780203852293

Wagstaff, C. R. D., Hanton, S., & Fletcher, D. (2013). Developing emotion abilities and regulation strategies in a sport organization: An action research intervention. *Psychology of Sport and Exercise, 14*, 476–487.

Wagstaff, C. R. D., Gilmore, S., & Thelwell, R. C. (2015). Sport medicine and sport science practitioners' experiences of organizational change. *Scandinavian Journal of Medicine & Science in Sports, 25*(5), 685–698. doi: 10.1111/sms.12340

Wagstaff, C. R. D., Gilmore, S., & Thelwell, R. C. (2016). When the show must go on: Investigating repeated organizational change in elite sport. *Journal of Change Management. 16*(1), 38–54. doi:10.1080/14697017.2015.1062793

Watson, D., & Tellegen, A. (1985). Toward a consensual structure of mood. *Psychological Bulletin, 98*(2), 219–235.

Weiss, H. M., & Cropanzano, R. (1996). Affective events theory: A theoretical discussion of the structure, causes and consequences of affective experiences at work. *Research in Organizational Behavior, 18*, 1–74.

Weiss, M. R., Smith, A. L., & Theeboom, M. (1996). "That's what friends are for": Children's and teenagers' perceptions of peer relationships in the sport domain. *Journal of Sport & Exercise Psychology, 18*(4), 347–379.

Weiss, H. M., Nicholas, J. P., & Daus, C. S. (1999). An examination of the joint effects of affective experiences and job beliefs on job satisfaction and variations in affective experiences over time. *Organizational Behavior and Human Decision Processes, 78*, 1–24.

Williams, A. M., Vickers, J., & Rodrigues, S. (2002). The effects of anxiety on visual search, movement kinematics, and performance in table tennis: A test of Eysenck and Calvo's processing efficiency theory. *Journal of Sport and Exercise Psychology, 24*(4), 438–455.

Wilson, M. R., Wood, G., & Vine, S. J. (2009). Anxiety, attentional control, and performance impairment in penalty kicks. *Journal of Sport & Exercise Psychology, 31*(6), 761–775.

Woodman, T., Davis, P. A., Hardy, L., Callow, N., Glasscock, I., & Yuill-Proctor, J. (2009). Emotions and sport performance: An exploration of happiness, hope, and anger. *Journal of Sport & Exercise Psychology, 31*(2), 169–188.

Woodman, T., & Hardy, L. (2003). The relative impact of cognitive anxiety and self-confidence upon sport performance: A meta-analysis. *Journal of Sports Sciences, 21*(6), 443–457.

Wright, T. A., & Cropanzano, R. (1998). Emotional exhaustion as a predictor of job performance and voluntary turnover. *Journal of Applied Psychology, 83*(3), 486.

Wright, T. A., Bonnett, D. G., & Sweeney, D. A. (1993). Mental health and work performance: Results of a longitudinal field study. *Journal of Occupational and Organizational Psychology, 66*, 277–284.

Zeidner, M., Matthews, G., & Roberts, R. D. (2009). *What we know about emotional intelligence: How it acts learning, work, relationships, and mental health*. Cambridge, MA: MIT Press.

Zizzi, S., Deaner, H., & Hirschhorn, D. (2003). The relationship between emotional intelligence and performance among college basketball players. *Journal of Applied Sport Psychology, 15*(3), 262–269.

4

ATTITUDES TO EMPLOYMENT IN SPORT ORGANIZATIONS

Sarah Gilmore

Introduction

This chapter explores sport scientists' and sport medics' attitudes towards employment. Within the management and organization studies literatures, the study of worker attitudes to their employment has been a significant area of research for over sixty years. It is therefore curious to note the relative absence of this focus within the sport psychology field despite evidence – albeit from a different discipline – suggesting its centrality to experiences of work. Although it is not possible to give an accurate, contemporary account of the number of individuals employed within sport organizations, the number and the variety of roles offered have both risen steadily over the past few decades. For example, figures from the American Bureau of Labor Statistics estimate that approximately 138,700 people work in the spectator sport industry, an increase of nearly 10 percent since 2002 (Bureau of Labor Statistics, 2014) with the US sport industry predicted to grow by $145.3 billion between 2010 and 2015 (Belzer, 2014). In Australia, the 2011 census found that 95,590 people were employed in sport and recreation occupations, an increase of 17 percent compared to the 2006 findings (Australian Bureau of Statistics, 2011). Although comparable figures are not available for the UK context, the British Association of Sport and Exercise Sciences (BASES) – the professional body for sport and exercise science in the UK – has just over 2,000 members (BASES, 2015). A significant proportion of the BASES membership are students studying a range of sport science degrees with these programs having increased in the UK from around four in 1973 to over 100 in 2010 (Winter, 2010). Such figures highlight the growing and sustained attractiveness of careers within the sport context.

Historically, sport psychology has focused on athlete attitudes to their work rather than explore the attitudes of those who support their performance, such as coaches (see Scanlan, Chow, Sousa, Scanlan, & Knifsend, 2016; Chapter 2, this text) and it is only recently that research has emerged that highlights the salience of conducting studies with those in "other" roles such as performance directors (Fletcher & Arnold, 2011), executive boards and administrators (Wagstaff, Fletcher, & Hanton, 2012) and sport scientists and sport medics (Wagstaff, Gilmore, & Thelwell, 2015). Given the rising numbers of individuals employed in sport organizations and the research lacuna with reference to the orientation of much sport psychology study, focusing on employees' attitudes towards work in sport organization seems timely.

In this chapter, a brief overview of organizational behavior research concerning attitudes will be provided, demonstrating how attitudes are conceptualized and understood within this body of work. Following this, it will be argued that sport scientists' attitudes toward work need to be placed within the wider contours of change within the sector – whether the work is located within a (often privately owned) club setting or a publicly funded entity such as an Olympic or Paralympic organization (Bottenburg, 2010; Rowe, 2011) – and the increasing pressures on those working within sport organizations to attain and sustain competitive outcomes. Using contemporary research as a foundation for such arguments it will also be demonstrated that patterns of attitudinal change witnessed by sport scientists in professional sport are linked to a cycle whereby heightened staff turnover (particularly turnover generated by changes in management personnel), and concomitant precariousness of employment, is accompanied by attitudinal change. This is evidenced in weakened psychological contracts, declining employment engagement and commitment, potentially stalled professional identity and a high degree of cynicism. More positively, the cycle highlights sport workers engaging with changes to practices brought about by changes to the management team, assimilating them and reflecting on what had been learned through navigating this cycle. Much of the empirical evidence drawn on relates to the experiences of employees within UK sport organizations but, wherever possible, more international perspectives and accounts are included. Implications for research and practice are then outlined.

Attitudes at work

Within the organizational behavior domain, attitudes are understood as being evaluative statements or judgments concerning objects, people or events with people potentially holding multiple and even conflicting attitudes towards the same object – such as an employer or an occupation (Wood, 2000). Such ambivalence towards an object can be seen in ideas of cognitive dissonance, which argue that behavior within the workplace does not necessarily follow attitudes held towards a phenomenon. For example, where a planned organizational change is concerned, employees might hold the view generally that change is needed within the company, but emotionally recoil at demands for change within their own team (Festinger, 1957). Reducing the discomfort caused by cognitive dissonance will often see people changing attitudes, modifying behavior or engaging in processes of rationalization in order to reach a view that is stable and consistent. Ideas of cognitive dissonance show that attitudes are not monolithic and enduring, and such sentiments are an important consideration for this chapter given the rapidity and scope of change witnessed within contemporary sport organizations and the potential for concomitant changes in employee attitudes towards their work and their employer.

Research within the sphere of job attitudes, which is strongly influenced by organizational psychology, has focused on core themes with each theme creating huge bodies of research, as well as intersections between them. These include: job satisfaction, the degree to which we hold positive feelings about our job resulting from our evaluations of its characteristics (e.g., Bateman & Organ, 1983; Judge, Thoresen, Bono, & Patton, 2001; Mobley, 1977); job involvement, the extent of our psychological identification with our job where perceived performance is important to self-worth (e.g., Lodahl & Kejnar, 1965; Rabinowitz & Hall, 1977); and psychological empowerment, the belief in the degree of influence exerted over the job, its meaningfulness, and the degree of autonomy to enact it (e.g., Spreitzer, 1995; Zhang & Bartol, 2010). There has also been extensive research carried out in the area of organizational commitment, which explores the ways by which employees identify with an organization and its goals and wish to maintain membership of it (O'Reilly & Chatman, 1986; van Dierendonck & Jacobs, 2012). It has been argued that organizational commitment has declined in importance due to shifts in employment patterns with less experience of long-term employment in fewer companies, but ideas concerning *occupational* commitment are of interest and explore commitment shown towards a profession or occupation rather than an employer (Lee, Carswell, & Allen, 2000). Where sport scientists are concerned, this might raise the question as to whether greater commitment might be given to the professional role they undertake as opposed to the organization. Given the location of many professional sport employees (e.g., sport science and sport medicine practitioners) within a team setting, this could raise interesting tensions. Research in this area has also been accompanied by an increased focus on employee engagement (Saks, 2006), which refers to the degree of involvement employees might have, the levels of satisfaction with and enthusiasm for work, as well as ideas of perceived organizational support (POS). POS refers to the degree to which employees believe the organization values their contribution and cares about their well-being (CIPD, 2010). They are also important because they are linked to a higher incidence of organizational citizenship behaviors (OCBs) and enhanced performance outcomes. Given the performance requirements faced by sport scientists and sport medics to go beyond any existing job description in the furtherance of performance outcomes, such research has potentially profound implications.

Employee attitudes in context: professional sport and the nature of change

How we understand employee attitudes towards work within professional sport context requires an understanding of the general context the work is located within. There is a general consensus that the wider context of professional sport and the organization of professional sport have undergone a profound and radical change (Cunningham, 2006). From the early 1990s, the globalization of professional sports has been intertwined with its commercialization. This combination of forces has provided sport organizations with the opportunity for huge financial rewards through sponsorship, marketing, media, and broadcasting rights (Duke, 2002; Giulianotti, 1999; King, 1997; Garland, Malcolm & Rowe, 2000; Wagg, 2007) with access to these rewards being predicated on attaining and sustaining excellent team performance.

The need for sustained elite sport performance has increasingly been related to high degrees of organizational change (Wagstaff et al., 2015; Wagstaff, Gilmore, & Thelwell, 2016) – often associated with and instigated by the sacking of the manager when results are poorer than expected. As noted by Day, Gordon, and Fink (2012) the high rate of managerial turnover is one of the most enduring features of professional football with the League Managers Association (LMA) estimating a manager's average tenure as being 1.23 years with 64 manager movements and 47 dismissals across the English football league in the 2014/15 season alone (LMA, 2015). Mielke (2007) argues that this phenomenon of managerial team sackings is not solely a European matter or restricted to professional football, highlighting that top tier coaches across a range of sports in the USA are also regularly replaced for failing to meet team owners' expectations.

It is important to note that changes in manager or head coach (or equivalent) are often accompanied by the arrival of additional staff such as assistant managers, coaches, and other performance department employees such as sport scientists and medics who the new manager brings in. These people have usually worked with the manager before and are often trusted advisors in an environment more noted for the absence of trust. As a result, it is also common to see substantial changes to backroom and sport medicine and sport science (SM&SS) staff following managerial change in elite sport organizations as new philosophies, methodologies, and practices are ushered in (Gilmore & Sillince, 2014).

Even those SM&SS staff working within publicly funded contexts experience increasing volatility to their employment status linked to heightened competitiveness. The provision of monies to UK national governing bodies (NGBs) are awarded competitively on a payment-by-results basis demonstrating "value for money" (DCMS, 2012, p. 9). This means that failure to meet both performance and participation targets can result in a drop in income – as occurred in the British NGBs for basketball, weightlifting, and swimming after the London 2012 Olympiad (BBC, 2014). For those sport scientists and medics (SMSs) working with Olympic and Paralympic teams (predominantly under the aegis of country-specific divisions of UK Sport, such as the English Institute of Sport) such cuts in funding can mean that they face redeployment to other sports or even redundancy. In this way, it is possible to argue that the enhanced accountability seen across professional sports impact directly on employees such as SMSs as well as those who manage them (i.e., performance directors, heads of sport science and medicine).

In sum, the changes outlined above have resulted in an increasingly precarious work context and the decline of any "standard" form of employment. Such employment characteristics leave some employees in sport organizations (e.g., SMSs) increasingly susceptible to market imperatives and performance accountabilities as well as the need to develop "flexible subjectivities" (Pitts, 2013). That is, to combine and accept flexible working requirements (such as hours of work, frequent changes in work location and the demands of this changeable, performance-centric sport marketplace) with growing requirements to remake or shape their persona in ways that willingly embrace these demands, the aims and outcomes of this process being the alignment of SMSs attitudes towards work and work practices with the needs of the increasingly neo-liberal professional sport economy (Vallas & Cummins, 2015; Vallas, 1999).

The consequences of change for sport scientists

Despite the general acknowledgment of the ubiquity of change within the professional sport context, there remains a lack of empirical evidence as to how change is carried out at the macro, meso and micro levels within the industry (Cruickshank & Collins, 2012). Additionally, although the important contribution made by SMSs to the development of professional sport is slowly being acknowledged, it has been argued that little is known about these sport professionals (Dawson, Wehner, Gastin, Dwyer, Kremer, & Allan, 2013) or their attitudes towards work. Issues to do with nepotistic recruitment practices, and a lack of credentialism or a defined career pathway for sport scientists on leaving university plague the industry and have done for some considerable time (cf. Waddington, 2002; Waddington, Roderick, & Naik, 2001). Where empirical research exists, the findings indicate that SMSs are often required to work unsociable hours with additional service normally being unpaid. Much of the work often requires people management skills, which are often not included within the training undertaken at either undergraduate or postgraduate levels. Moreover, a recent Exercise and Sports Science Australia survey found that one third of the workforce included within the research were actively seeking other employment, with the most popular reasons for this being workload and perceptions of insufficient support – factors that are often linked to employee burnout (Dawson et al., 2013).

Attitudinal responses to change

At the organizational level, longitudinal research by Wagstaff et al. (2015) involving immersion within two Premier League football clubs and a County Championship cricket club found that rounds of managerial change resulted in SMSs navigating a change cycle. This cyclical process of change comprised four stages: anticipation and uncertainty, upheaval and realization, integration and experimentation, and normalization and learning. Characteristic responses at each stage began with uncertainty, often provoked by manager departure/sacking and the arrival of a new one. Emotional responses at this stage sometimes included disappointment, either at the loss of a manager or managerial team where working arrangements had been productive or at the prospect of having to acclimatize to a new senior management team. Nevertheless, for those who did not see eye to eye with the departing manager, this stage was often one of relief and positive anticipation. Alongside these responses, participants articulated a heightened climate of sensitivity, rumor, speculation, and gossip. Such environments were exacerbated when communication from the club's strategic leaders was poor and the workers concerned accessed their information from the sport media or the internet – as witnessed from one respondent after rumors began about the manager leaving, "everyone in the SM&SS department was talking and considering the consequences of a change of manager. There was a lot of uncertainty about how SM&SS practices would be impacted and who'd leave" (Wagstaff et al., 2015, p. 690).

As the managerial team "bedded into" their new context, respondents made comparisons with past practices and relationships. Where the comparisons were negative, this often led to resistance to new practices, opportunism, and protective behaviors with a focus on protecting the self or exploiting the situation to secure personal advantage. The final two stages in the cycle were reflected by a shift in focus to assimilating previous and new practices. This often led to challenging the initial attitudinal, emotional, and behavioral responses to change that might have resisted it. As a result, new norms could be developed and embedded, suggesting that not all experiences of managerial change were negative. Indeed, Wagstaff et al. (2015) noted that after the early resistance, turnover of staff, and people putting their head in the sand, employees reached a point where they began to build. New ways of working became the norm; people felt less threatened and were therefore more innovative and vocal about best practice with coaches.

The final stage reported by Wagstaff et al. – normalization and learning – related to a general focus on reflection and learning. This was often characterized by an individual's acknowledgement of change as a common facet of elite performance environments and the need for the sport scientists and medics to translate knowledge, skills, and abilities to relevant others, thus illustrating a shift from an earlier focus on the self to a broader regard for the collective. Wagstaff et al.'s findings support and extend non-sport organizational change research (e.g., Jaffe et al., 1994) in highlighting the importance of cognition and affect during the change process and how these influenced attitudinal responses to the organization.

More significantly for SMSs, Wagstaff et al.'s findings highlight the potentially negative impact of managerially oriented organizational change on sport science and medicine practices and roles, as previously embedded, even institutionalized, routines and ways of working are often "reset" with the arrival of a new manager. Given that it is not uncommon for SMSs in some sports to have experienced five changes in manager in as many years (Wagstaff et al., 2016), then there are questions as to how this cycle is persistently navigated over an extended time frame. Moreover, the findings from Wagstaff et al.'s (2015) study indicated that although repeated exposure to cycles of change may lead to an emotionally resilient SM&SS department, experimentation, and innovation over time, there was evidence of a more brittle and less trusting psychological contract between the sport scientists and their employer.

Implications for employee attitudes: the psychological contract

Rousseau (1995) defined the psychological contract as an individual's beliefs concerning the mutual obligations that exist between the employee and the employer. These obligations arise out of the belief that a promise has been made either explicitly or implicitly and the fulfillment of obligations by one party is contingent on the fulfillment of them by the other. In this way, the psychological contract comprises an individual's perception of the *mutual* obligations that exist in the exchange with the employer (often as represented by the line manager) and these are sustained through the norm of reciprocity. It is important to note that the psychological contract, unlike formal employment contracts, is not made once but is revised throughout an employee's tenure in the organization (Rousseau & McLean Parks, 1993). This means that the longer the relationship endures and the two parties interact with repeated cycles of contribution and reciprocity, the broader the array of contributions and inducements that might be included in the contract. In this way, the psychological contract may form a palimpsest over time where events in the form of new assignments, organizational restructuring, managerial change, and so on may overlay new terms upon old ones.

Should SMSs experience persistent change over time allied to the resetting of practices and routines, they will likely perceive this as a breach of the contract. Should this occur, responses are likely to be negative and result in reduced loyalty, commitment, and organizational citizenship behaviors (cf. Wagstaff et al., 2015; 2016). Given the long hours working culture of many high performance sport teams, a decline in OCBs could have a negative impact on the functioning of the specific sport science and medicine department. Finally, whilst the impact of the breach might be experienced by isolated individuals – as opposed to the whole group – should morale be more generally affected, the functioning of the performance department or team may decline with concomitant implications for performance. It is also pertinent to note that mismatches between the manager and employee may also cause a breach of the psychological contract. Given the nature of managerial turnover, it is highly likely that this in itself will be a major cause of tensions in the contract and in some cases lead to a cleavage. For others, repeated exposure to managerial turnover could potentially strain the psychological contract considerably and/or result in it breaking.

Exit, loyalty, voice, and cynicism

In the research by Wagstaff et al. (2015), although more experienced members of sport science and medicine staff were prepared to voice their opinions and to mobilize their networks to facilitate exit, less experienced workers deployed silence as a coping mechanism. Given that these roles are perceived – rightly or wrongly – as being "hot jobs in a cool industry" and prominently featured in popular discourse, especially in and associated with trendsetters, hipness, and cool (Neff et al., 2005), deploying silence when a neophyte is arguably a sensible strategy for maintaining employment given the uncertainty of continued employment in the sector – as one participant in Wagstaff et al.'s study reported:

> People who have been more vocal in terms of contributing to the new changes. Most of us who are going through this for the first time have stayed silent, and to be honest, I think that has been my best move during the whole process – just staying quiet. I can't say it's been easy, but at least I haven't lost my job by voicing my opinions too loudly.
>
> (Wagstaff et al., 2015, p. 689)

Nevertheless, remaining "silent" can have an emotional cost. Hirschman's (1970) seminal exit, loyalty, voice model was developed to explain employees' responses to "lapses from efficient, rational, law-abiding, virtuous, or otherwise functional organizational behavior" (1970, p. 1). His work captures and structures the ways by which employees might respond to sources of dissatisfaction and adverse workplace conditions. That is, within Hirschman's model, exit is generally (although not exclusively) viewed as a means of signaling discontent with the organization's products or behavior. Where the latter is concerned, Rusbult, Farrell, Rogers and Mainous (1988) conceived the exit option not only as actually quitting the job or voluntarily leaving the organization, but also as searching for a new job or thinking about leaving. Exit, therefore is as much about the *propensity* to leave as it is about actually departing. Indeed, Naus, van Iterson, and Roe (2007) noted, "whereas actually leaving the organization may not always be a viable option, due to real or perceived barriers to exit, leaving the organization in a psychological sense is something over which the employee has more control" (p. 688).

Voice was defined by Hirschman as, "any attempt at all to change an objectionable state of affairs, not only by petitioning to management or higher authorities, but also through protests including the mobilization of the public opinion" (1970, p. 30). When the model is used to describe the employment relationship, voice necessarily takes on a different meaning. Hence, Rusbult et al., (1988, p. 601) defined voice as "actively and constructively trying to improve conditions". This behavior was witnessed within Gilmore and Sillince's (2014) study where a senior member of performance staff attempted to negotiate between the manager and his increasingly alienated SM&SS workforce to no effect. Indeed, his "voice" was perceived as the offering of opinions that were counter to those of the manager and therefore as a form of opposition. It was not long before this sport scientist transitioned from "voice" to "exit".

Loyalty, the final element of the original model, refers to a special attachment to the organization with the loyalist being seen as a special attachment to an organization, someone who leaves no stone unturned before taking the decision to withdraw or exit. Loyalty has also been seen as a form of optimistically waiting for conditions to improve with this often being accompanied by offering support to the organization. For Hirschman, the importance of loyalty provides a psychological barrier to exit and in so doing strengthens the propensity to voice. Employees in Wagstaff et al.'s (2015) study articulated positive responses to change when they perceived greater autonomy or control over it. This suggests that loyalty to a club or team might be more likely when voice is possible:

> Right now, I feel immediately that I can leave behind what has mostly been a bad experience for me; I can take some control again; bring back old ways of doing things that we developed under [previous manager]. It's kind of a relief… and hopefully as players we can take a lead on cutting out all the crap things that [last manager] introduced… as long as our voices are heard.
> (Wagstaff et al., 2015, p. 692)

More recently, Naus et al. (2007) have proposed that the model be extended to include organizational cynicism, a response defined as "a negative attitude comprising three dimensions" (Naus et al., 2007, p. 689). The first dimension is a belief that the organization lacks integrity. The second, a negative affect toward the organization and, finally, the third dimension refers to tendencies to disparage and critical behavior toward the organization that is consistent with these beliefs. Cynicism is an important attitudinal response that may have profound implications for both the individual and the organization and can result in fractures to the psychological contract. It also serves as a form of self-defense, which allows the individual to cope with unpleasant thoughts and feelings of disappointment about the actions taken by the organization or its management. Confronted by persistent change, and insecurity, employees in sport organizations might find it difficult to discern coherence between organizational messages stressing unity, harmony and team spirit, and their role. Wagstaff et al. (2016) found that many participants reported becoming cynical about their club following repeated experiences of managerial change. In many instances, this led to further attitudinal, emotional and behavioral implications, including feelings of hopelessness:

> It seems to me that as time goes on the board has become less and less inclusive during the changeover of managers. I think they feel guilty and

embarrassed about the long contracts they have given new managers and
need to cover up the lies they have to tell us about stability.

(Wagstaff et al., 2015, p. 48)

Nevertheless, while researchers perceive cynicism as being associated with apathy, resignation, distrust, as well as poor performance, absenteeism, job-turnover, and burnout (Abraham, 2000), cynics can also act as the conscience for the organization. Moreover, cynics often care deeply about their organization and make careful and systematic recommendations of organizational problems (Bommer, Rich, & Rubin, 2005). This means that cynicism occupies an interesting and difficult position because it is neither wholly good nor wholly bad for the organization. Yet cynicism might be difficult to incorporate into a sport context that reifies teamwork as a core value. Nevertheless, as performance imperatives continue, it could be argued that there is a need for persistent questioning, thinking, and forms of cynicism that display care for the work, for the team, and for colleagues as well as a acknowledgement of the role cynicism plays as a mode of psychological self-defense.

Avoiding undesirable attitudes in sport organizations

It has been argued that individuals construct organizational norms, routines, and structures as a defense against anxiety in unconscious as well as conscious ways (Obholzer & Roberts, 1994). Should those structures be dismantled – as they often are during a period of change – then this is likely to cause feelings of uncertainty and anxiety. In doing so, employees in sport organizations might unwittingly unleash the very emotions they have worked hard to contain. Containing anxiety stemming from uncertainty allied with change will often require team members, managers, and leaders who can acknowledge and effectively manage such emotions. Gilmore and Sillince's (2014) study of the deinstitutionalization of sport science practices at a Premier League football club shows how the innovative use of sport science, developed over several years, was effectively disbanded within a short period of time. This was not solely due to staff departures to join the previous manager at a new club, but seemingly the failure of the senior management team to manage their own anxieties at a time of substantial change, which was accompanied by high staff turnover. An organizational climate marked by emotional warmth and a community of practice built up over time was replaced by a toxic one of suspicion, an "us and them" attitude between the managerial team and the "old" sport scientists and resulted in the decline of their innovative use of sport science as a strategic performance lever. What is required in such situations is not just tolerance of attitudinal responses and their unconscious and conscious evacuation but an ability to enable people to manage the nature of the experience, to digest it mentally, and give it meaning. If this occurs, employees are more likely to become able to internalize not only a "container" of feelings and attitudes (i.e., a manager who can manage their attitudes as well as those of their staff and their players) but also a mind that can hold thoughts (Bion, 1962).

The studies referred to within this chapter strongly highlight the importance of good and effective work relationships when sport organizations are undertaking change (e.g. Gilmore & Sillince, 2014). Vakola and Nikolaou (2005) argue that the ways by which conflict is handled, the building and maintenance of supportive work relationships, and effective communication all contributed to the formulation of positive attitudes to change and, therefore, to the success of a change program. Specifically, Vakola and Nikolaou found that employees experiencing strain demonstrated decreased levels of commitment and an increased reluctance to accept organizational change interventions. Should this be accompanied by poor work relationships, and work overload – often experienced when staff depart – then this would likely result in a significant, negative impact on attitudes to change. Finally, Vakola and Nikolaou's findings did not support the role of organizational commitment as a moderator in the relationship between occupational stress and attitudes to change. The authors suggest that organizations engaging in change should address the issue of employee well-being by actively ensuring that the increased demands being placed on them by virtue of the change process are counteracted with sufficient social support. In providing such support, the organization itself might become a healthier, and, in turn, more functional place for existing workers and a more attractive option for prospective employees.

Organizational responses

Responses to the rapidity of change are difficult to chart with any degree of certainty due to the lack of research across professional sport – mainly caused by problems academic researchers face with regards to access. This means that well-informed assessments are hard to make and even the claims made in this chapter are based on emerging evidence. Nevertheless, there are some observable response patterns appearing within elite sport organizations that will likely influence – and may have been implemented to address – the issues highlighted in this chapter regarding change and employee attitudes. From an organizational structure perspective, one response has been to install a "performance director" post at a very senior level within the organizational hierarchy, responsible to either the chief executive officer (CEO) or board of directors, and who is in charge of both the performance department (i.e., players, coaches) and, in some cases, the sport science and medicine department. Such posts are well established in, for example, Italian and Spanish football clubs, cricket, and rugby union. Interestingly, Premier League football clubs have experimented with this role and continue to do so as a means of instigating stability and continuity of practices, yet it is uncertain how well such roles will "gel" with the culture of either this or other sports. In some high-profile instances, these posts have been as volatile as those of the manager with no real security of tenure. For example, former director of football, Damien Comolli, has not been employed in such a post since his sacking by Liverpool and a turbulent relationship with manager Martin Jol at Tottenham Hotspur in 2012.

Other innovations in terms of attempting to ensure more beneficial approaches towards organizational change and, in turn, employee attitudes within sport organizations, include a focus on the culture of the performance department and an exploration and identification of high performance cultures elsewhere in sport or business (e.g. Cruickshank & Collins, 2012; Dawson & Dobson, 2002). For example, sport psychology research has highlighted the utility of 360-degree feedback (Cope, Eys, Schinke, & Bosselut, 2007) and organizational citizenship behavior (Aoyagi, Cox, & McGuire, 2008) for creating optimal team environments.

Other developments have seen some organizations offer managers extended employment contracts. The extent to which extended contracts have been successful in halting managerial turnover seems limited given the persistence of managerial departures; however, such outcomes are also difficult to gauge accurately given the private nature of contractual terms. Additionally, there has been a shift in terms of the number of staff managers are now permitted to bring with them when they join a new organization. Whereas the trend had been for new managers to bring a substantial team with them, the current expectation is for the manager to bring a smaller cluster of staff, including perhaps an assistant manager, a coach, and possibly a member of staff who, for example, might have a strength and conditioning remit or other specialist SM&SS expertise. Whilst the advent and integration of a new managerial team with the (often) closely knit SM&SS department will have ramifications for all parties as well as the outcomes of their work, this trend seems set to continue.

Agendas for practice and research

Having outlined the current research evidence regarding employee attitudes toward work in sport organizations, the chapter will conclude with agendas for practice and research. As noted by Wagstaff et al. (2015), CEOs and performance directors need to be aware that the changes they instigate and implement, often under the aegis of managerial change, have a direct impact on the productivity, creativity, engagement, and turnover in SM&SS staff (Wagstaff et al., 2016). One key recommendation for practice is for the education of those occupying strategically powerful rules (e.g., chairmen/women, CEOs, board members) as to the consequences of repeated cycles of change. This recommendation should also be accompanied by an agenda for research across the "public" and "private" sport sectors as the responses to change outlined in elite sport clubs are potentially experienced by those working in Olympic and Paralympic sports where fou- year funding cycles determine so much in the employment contracts of sport workers. Such research needs to establish whether a longer-term strategy is required for SM&SS; one that emphasizes the stability and endurance of philosophies and practices regardless of leader or managerial change. Such research should also investigate case studies of clubs who have adopted different structures and reporting arrangements. To what extent have performance directors engendered stability and endurance of sport science and medical practice and staff? To what extent do they foster cultures and climates of high performance practices over time as compared to more volatile entities? Should those postholders sit on the board of directors? Would it be preferable for SM&SS to report to a sporting director with organizational power than a head of sport science and medicine who is often located below the team manager or performance director and thus without any institutional clout? Finally, is there a need for greater institutionalization and even bureaucracy to sediment sport science and medicine work and, if so, what might be the implications for the contractual bases for sport scientists and medics? Would an expectation of greater stability be an outcome?

Any structural changes within sport organizations might have implications for the human resource management (HRM) function and sport psychologists, and their respective expertise. Professional organizations such as the Chartered Institution for Personnel and Development have argued for the function to take issues like challenges to the psychological contract seriously and, through their professional formation, HR specialists should be aware of the implications of open-ended change on a range of workplaces and workers. Additionally, as experts in areas such as recruitment, selection and staff development, the function should have much to offer strategic level staff in terms of securing better "fit" between organization and staff at the point of recruitment and to call an end to nepotistic hiring practices where preferred staff are imported and discarded as athletes are, but without the same rewards. Arguably a greater degree of professionalization of HR practices within sport psychology would result in a greater understanding of the range of SM&SS roles as well as the skills, knowledge, and education required for them to be carried out at the optimal level. Such a shift would also require taking HRM seriously within the playing and strategic levels of the organization and ensuring that the function was involved in *all* hires within the performance department. It would also require the HRM staff, or sport psychologists if they develop such skills, to be highly knowledgeable as to the nature of the jobs they are supporting. Given the trend for the HRM function to adopt a more "strategic" role within organizations (Boxall & Purcell, 2011), it is likely that resistance might be met as micro-level engagement in the details of key worker roles, careers, and so on could be perceived as a return to a former era of personnel management and as such it would denote a retrograde development and status for the function. It is also likely that "outsider" influence on key recruitment decisions within the playing side would be resisted. In sum, there is a need for more highly experienced SMSs in leadership positions and not just subordinate ones.

This is echoed by Wagstaff et al. (2012) and Wagstaff, Hanton, and Fletcher (2013) whose work on emotional intelligence within elite sport teams argues for an expansion of the sport psychologist role from a focus on psychological skills-centric work with individual athletes to a role inclusive of support at the team, senior management, and organizational levels. This role expansion would have implications for professional formation but, if successful, could bode well for the profession as well as the organizations they work within.

Allied to this argument for enhanced professionalization, there is an urgent need for a review of the professional formation of SMSs so that they are better prepared for the volatility of the professional sport environment and the emotional labor it entails (Wagstaff et al., 2015). To this end, it is pertinent to ask whether the working lives of sport employees would or could be improved by more powerful professional bodies who are able to set out requirements for accredited practitioners and to require sport organizations to adhere to them at the point of recruitment and to devote sufficient time/funds for continuous professional development. Research carried out in Australia to better understand the Australian high performance and sport science workforce found that the sport scientists surveyed, although inexperienced, were generally highly qualified yet did not necessarily belong to relevant professional bodies associated with their particular specialism. As the authors' noted, this provides a problem for the SM&SS industry as these concerns about either direct or indirect quality assurance or forms of professional accreditation still remain (Dawson et al., 2013).

Finally, focusing on issues of professionalization would require a fundamental shift in culture within many sport organizations, which remain dominated by competences largely achieved through a playing career – often referred to as "embodied competence" (Wacquant, 1995, p. 504) – and a rejection of the competences gained via the formal educational field (McGillivray, Fearn, & McIntosh, 2005; McGillivray & McIntosh, 2006). To take a professionalization strategy seriously requires taking education and training seriously across all levels of professional sport and ultimately refusing access to ineligibles (i.e., those who have not gained forms of accredited competence). Such forms of education and training exist in SM&SS professions, but are inconsistently integrated within employment processes (see Waddington, 2002; Waddington et al., 2001). Indeed, the lack of credence given to professions within sport organizations is somewhat contradictory to professions in other contemporary workplaces where arguments for "social closure" (Larson, 1977), the barring of ineligibles from practice, is expected. Thus, it is important that, in line with the HRM function, performance directors and heads of SM&SS departments ensure such restrictions to practice occur where unqualified applicants to jobs are concerned.

To conclude, there is a pressing need for research to fully ascertain employee attitudes towards work and the organizations that employ them in sport. While jobs in elite sport organizations are often perceived as being "cool jobs in hot industries" (Neff et al., 2005), research suggests that this is not necessarily the case and that they are prone to many of the ills that currently plague many other occupations (e.g., job insecurity). Nevertheless, employees in sport organizations are also heralded as being exemplars of a form of work akin to media and dot-com industries. As Neff et al. noted, while individuals are drawn to those kinds of jobs because of the excitement attached to them (as well as the autonomy and creativity), this work has a personal cost which involves the normalization of risks associated with this work, arguably exacerbated by the recency of many SM&SS professions. It is therefore imperative that a research agenda is constructed that explores these issues in-depth across a range of SM&SS functions and other key employees within sport organizations. Indeed, although the nascent body of research has largely sampled SMSs, there are a host of other relevant employee groups worthy of study and such diversification is an imperative of future research.

Applied implications

1 Evidence suggests that removing the manager to secure performance improvements rarely, if ever, yields the outcomes sought. It is about time HR practices, or sport psychologists with organizational psychology competencies, functioning together with the board and senior management of clubs, seriously reviewed their hiring (and firing) decisions and their processes – with a view to securing longer-term relationships with managers and managerial teams.
2 Improvements need to be made to the management of change by improving communication between the club's administrative arm and the performance departments, reviewing workload, managing undesirable attitude-inducing experiences, and looking at ways to improve the integration of a new manager and managerial team.
3 Professionalize, professionalize, professionalize. Embodied competence from a previous career as a professional athlete is insufficient qualification for the effective management of human assets.
4 Change the reporting lines for SMSs to a sporting director who has the equivalent status to the manager and can therefore ensure greater stability of practices, stability of staff, and institutionalize good practice in the SMS domain.
5 Owners, boards and CEOs need to understand how a performance department works. In turn, managers need to be productive colleagues, working with the club's administration, rather than seeing "their" department as a personal fiefdom to be kept from scrutiny by others.

Research directions

1 More research is needed with reference to SMSs' experiences of change in both private and publicly funded contexts. This is now urgent.
2 What factors might mediate change outcomes? What makes a change process better or worse within a professional sport context?
3 Research is required to further examine the patterns of employment for SMSs. How precarious is employment within professional sport?
4 The employment practices of professional sport urgently need to be reviewed. Research here is now old and we need to know what is occurring within publicly funded organizations and within professional clubs.

5 What forms of emotional labor do SMSs experience when change is occurring and they are expected to maintain stability of emotional and professional outcomes when interacting with others?

References

Abraham, R. (2000). Organizational cynicism: Bases and consequences. *Genetic, Social, and General Psychology Monographs,* 126(3), 269–292.

Aoyagi, M. W., Cox, R. H., & McGuire, R. T. (2008). Organizational citizenship behavior in sport: Relationships with leadership, team cohesion, and athlete satisfaction. *Journal of Applied Sport Psychology,* 20(1), 25–41.

Australian Bureau of Statistics (2011). Employment in sport and recreation. Retrieved from http://www.abs.gov.au/ausstats/abs@.nsf/mf/4148.0 (accessed December 1, 2015).

BASES (British Association of Sport and Exercise Sciences) (2015). Annual report and financial statements. http://www.bases.org.uk/Publications-Documents-and-Policies (accessed December 1, 2015).

Bateman, T. S. & Organ, D. W. (1983). Job satisfaction and the good soldier: The relationship between affect and employee "citizenship". *Academy of Management Journal,* 26(4), 587–595.

BBC (2014). Rio 2016: Four sports suffer Olympic funding cut. Retrieved from http://www.bbc.co.uk/sport/0/olympics/26036808 (accessed September 28, 2015).

Belzer, J. (2014, 5 February). Sports industry 101: Breaking into the business of sports. Retrieved from http://www.forbes.com/sites/jasonbelzer/2014/02/05/sports-industry-101-breaking-into-the-business-of-sports/#41d432c45491 (accessed 25 July 2016).

Bion, W. R. (1962). *Learning from experience.* London: Tavistock.

Bommer, W. H., Rich, G. A., & Rubin, R. S. (2005). Changing attitudes about change: Longitudinal effects of transformational leader behavior on employee cynicism about organizational change. *Journal of Organizational Behavior,* 26(7), 733–753.

Bottenburg, M. van (2010). Beyond diffusion: Sport and its remaking in and across cultural contexts. *Journal of Sport History,* 37(1), 41–53.

Boxall, N. & Purcell, J. (2011). *Strategy and human resource management.* London: Palgrave.

Bureau of Labor Statistics (2014, 31 January). Spectator sports employment. Retrieved from http://www.bls.gov/opub/ted/2014/ted_20140131.htm (accessed 25 July 2016).

CIPD (Chartered Institute of Personnel and Development) (2010). Creating an engaged workforce. https://www.cipd.co.uk/binaries/creating-an-engaged-workforce_2010.pdf (accessed December 9, 2015).

Cope, C. J., Eys, M. A., Schinke, R. J., & Bosselut, G. (2007). Coaches' perspectives of a negative informal role: The "cancer" within sport teams. *Journal of Applied Sport Psychology,* 22(3), 420–436.

Cruickshank, A. & Collins, D. (2012). Change management: The case of the elite sport performance team. *Journal of Change Management,* 12(2), 209–229.

Cunningham, G. B. (2006). The relationships among commitment to change, coping with change, and turnover intentions. *European Journal of Work and Organizational Psychology,* 15(1), 29–45.

Dawson, P. & Dobson, S. (2002). Managerial efficiency and human capital: An application to English association football. *Managerial and Decision Economics,* 23(8), 471–486.

Dawson, A., Wehner, K., Gastin, P., Dwyer, D., Kremer, P., & Allan, M. (2013). *Profiling the Australian high performance and sports science workforce.* Brisbane: Deakin & ESSA.

Day, D.V., Gordon, S., & Fink, C. (2012). The sporting life: Exploring organizations through the lens of sport. *Academy of Management Annals, 6*(1), 397–433.

DCMS (Department of Culture, Media and Spor) (2012). *Creating a sporting habit for life: A new youth sport strategy.* London: DCMS.

Duke, V. (2002). Local tradition versus globalization: Resistance to the McDonaldisation and Disneyisation of professional football in England. *Football Studies, 1*, 5–23.

Festinger, L. (1957). *A theory of cognitive dissonance.* Stanford, CA: Stanford University Press.

Fletcher, D. & Arnold, R. (2011). A qualitative study of performance leadership and management in elite sport. *Journal of Applied Sport Psychology, 23*(2), 223–242.

Garland, J., Malcolm, D., & Rowe, M. (2000). *The future of football: Challenges for the twenty-first century.* London: F. Cass.

Gilmore, S. E. & Sillince, J. A. A. (2014). Institutional theory and change: The deinstitutionalization of sports science at Club X. *Journal of Organizational Change Management, 27*(2), 313–330.

Giulianotti, R. (1999). *Football: A sociology of the global game.* Cambridge: Polity Press.

Hirschman, A. O. (1970). *Exit, voice and loyalty. Responses to decline in firms, organizations, and states.* Cambridge, MA: Harvard University Press.

Jaffe, D. T., Scott, C. D., & Tobe, G. R. (1994). *Rekindling commitment: How to revitalize yourself, your work, and your organization.* San Francisco, CA: Jossey-Bass.

Judge, T. A., Thoresen, C. J., Bono, J. E., & Patton, G. K. (2001). The job satisfaction–job performance relationship: A qualitative and quantitative review. *Psychological Bulletin, 127*(3), 376–407.

King, A. (1997). New directors, customers, and fans: The transformation of English football in the 1990s. *Sociology of Sport Journal, 14*, 224–242.

Larson, M. S. (1977). *The rise of professionalism.* Berkeley, CA: University of California Press.

Lee, K., Carswell, J. J., & Allen, N. J. (2000). A meta-analytic review of occupational commitment: Relations with person and work-related variables. *Journal of Applied Psychology, 85*(5), 799–811.

LMA (League Managers Association) (2015). LMA end of season review and manager statistics. Retrieved from http://www.leaguemanagers.com/news.html (accessed September 30, 2015).

Lodahl, T. M. & Kejnar, M. (1965). The definition and measurement of job involvement. *Journal of Applied Psychology, 49*(1), 24–33.

McGillivray, D. & McIntosh, A. (2006). "Football is my life": Theorizing social practice in the Scottish professional football field. *Sport in Society: Cultures, Commerce, Media, Politics, 9*(2), 371–387.

McGillivray, D., Fearn, R., & McIntosh, A. (2005). Caught up in and by the beautiful game. *Journal of Sport and Social Issues, 29*(1), 102–123.

Mielke, D. (2007). Coaching experience, playing experience and coaching tenure. *International Journal of Sports Science and Coaching, 2*(2): 105–108.

Mobley, W. H. (1977). Intermediate linkages in the relationship between job satisfaction and employee turnover. *Journal of Applied Psychology, 62*(2), 237–240.

Naus, F., van Iterson, A., & Roe, R. (2007). Organizational cynicism: Extending the exit, voice, loyalty, and neglect model of employees' responses to adverse conditions in the workplace. *Human Relations, 60*(5), 683–718.

Neff, G., Wissinger, E., & Zukin, S. (2005). Entrepreneurial labor among cutural producers: "Cool" jobs in "hot" industries. *Social Semiotics, 15*(3), 307–334.

Obholzer, A. & Roberts, V. Z. (1994). *The unconscious at work.* London: Routledge.

O'Reilly, C. A. & Chatman, J. (1986). Organizational commitment and psychological attachment: The effects of compliance, identification and internalization on prosocial behaviour. *Journal of Applied Psychology, 71*(3), 492–499.
Pitts, F. H. (2013). "A science to it": Flexible time and flexible subjectivity in the digital workplace. *Work, Organisation, Labour and Globalisation, 7*(1), 95–105.
Rabinowitz, S. & Hall, D. T. (1977). Organizational research on job involvement, *Psychological Bulletin, 84*(2), 265–288.
Rousseau, D. M. (1995). *Psychological contracts in organizations: Understanding written and unwritten agreements.* Thousand Oaks, CA: Sage.
Rousseau, D. M. & McLean Parks, J. M. (1993). The contracts of individuals and organizations. *Research in Organizational Behaviour, 15*, 1–43.
Rowe, D. (2011). *Global media sport: Flows, forms and futures.* London: Bloomsbury.
Rusbult, C. E., Farrell, D., Rogers, G., & Mainous, A. G. (1988). Impact of exchange variables on exit, voice, loyalty, and neglect: An integrative model of responses to declining job satisfaction. *Academy of Management Journal, 31*(3), 599–627.
Saks, A. M. (2006). Antecedents and consequences of employee engagement. *Journal of Managerial Psychology, 21*(7), 600–619.
Scanlan, T. K., Chow, G. M., Sousa, C., Scanlan, L. A., & Knifsend, C. A. (2016). The development of the Sport Commitment Questionnaire-2 (English version). *Psychology of Sport and Exercise, 22*, 233–246.
Spreitzer, G. M. (1995). Psychological empowerment in the workplace: Dimensions, measurement and validation. *Academy of Management Journal, 38*(5), 1442–1465.
Vakola, M. & Nikolaou, I. (2005). Attitudes towards organizational change: What is the role of employees' stress and commitment? *Employee Relations, 27*(2), 160–174.
Vallas, S. P. (1999). Re-thinking post-Fordism: The meaning of workplace flexibility. *Sociological Theory, 17*(1), 68–101.
Vallas, S. P. & Cummins, E. R. (2015). Personal branding and identity norms in the popular business press: Enterprise culture in an age of precarity. *Organization Studies, 36*(3), 293–319.
Van Dierendonck, D. & Jacobs, G. (2012). Survivors and victims, a meta-analytical review of fairness and organizational commitment after downsizing. *British Journal of Management, 23*(1), 96–109.
Wacquant, L. J. (1995). Pugs at work: Bodily capital and bodily labour among professional boxers. *Body & Society, 1*(1), 65–93.
Waddington, I. (2002). Jobs for the boys: A study of the employment of club doctors and physiotherapists in English professional football. *Soccer and Society, 3*(1), 51–64.
Waddington, I., Roderick, M., & Naik, R. (2001). Methods of appointment and qualifications of club doctors and physiotherapists in English professional football: Some problems and issues. *British Journal of Sports Medicine, 35*(1), 48–53.
Wagg, S. (2007). Angels of us all? Football management, globalization and the politics of celebrity. *Soccer & Society, 8*, 440–458.
Wagstaff, C. R. D., Fletcher, D., & Hanton, S. (2012). Positive organizational psychology in sport: An ethnography of organizational functioning in a national sport organization. *Journal of Applied Sport Psychology, 24*(1), 26–47.
Wagstaff, C. R. D., Gilmore, S. E., & Thelwell, R. C. (2015). Sport science and medicine practitioners' experiences of organizational change. *Scandinavian Journal of Medicine & Science in Sports, 25*(5), 685–698.
Wagstaff, C. R. D., Hanton, S., & Fletcher, D. (2013). Developing emotion abilities and regulation strategies in a sport organization: An action research intervention. *Psychology of Sport and Exercise, 14*(4), 476–487.

Wagstaff, C. R. D., Gilmore, S. E., & Thelwell, R. C. (2016). When the show must go on: Investigating repeated organizational change in elite sport. *Journal of Change Management. 16*(1), 38–54.

Winter, E. M. (2010). The history of sport and exercise science and BASES: Past. *The Sport and Exercise Scientist, 24,* 8–9.

Wood, W. (2000). Attitude change: Persuasion and social influence. *Annual Review of Psychology, 51,* 539–570.

Zhang, X., & Bartol, K. M. (2010). Linking empowering leadership and employee creativity: The influence of psychological empowerment, intrinsic motivation, and creative process engagement. *Academy of Management Journal, 53*(1), 107–128.

PART II
Stress and well-being in sport organizations

5

STRESS IN SPORT

The role of the organizational environment

David Fletcher and Rachel Arnold

Introduction

When one thinks of stress in sport one's mind is usually drawn to the worries or nerves that are typically experienced before performing in competition. Whether it's through personal sporting participation or via watching an Olympic or professional athlete prior to a race or a match, most people can relate in some way to competitive stress and anxiety experiences. There are probably two main reasons for this. The first is that such emotions are typically intense and therefore memorable. The second is that, given its intensity and closeness to competition, anxiety has the potential to affect the performance of athletes of all competitive standards. Notwithstanding these observations, there is another type of stress in sport that perhaps doesn't spring to mind as readily as competitive stress, but arguably has greater potential to impact on athletes' well-being and performance. Rather than stemming from athletes' competitive performance experiences, this type of stress originates from the complex social and organizational environment that athletes operate within. Indeed, for athletes who perform at the highest level, sport is "more than just a game" (cf. Jones, 1995) and functions as a profession that is inextricably linked to their stress experiences and personal well-being. In his reflections on performance excellence in sport and business, Jones (2002) went as far as to conclude "that organizational issues probably have the biggest impact [of any psychosocial factor] on performance" (p. 279).

Perhaps due to the prevailing scholarly focus on competitive stress and anxiety (cf. Woodman & Hardy, 2001b), scientific inquiry designed to further understanding of stress in sport organizations was slow to begin. However, since the publication of Fletcher, Hanton, and Mellalieu's (2006) review of organizational stress in competitive sport, research has gathered momentum over the past decade and it is timely to provide an updated review of the area. The purpose of this chapter is, therefore, to review the role of the organizational environment in sport performers' experiences of stress. To this end, the narrative addresses four important questions in this area. First, what is organizational stress? Second, how does organizational stress affect athlete performance and well-being? Third, how can athletes' experiences of organizational stress be optimized? Fourth, what does the future hold for organizational stress research in competitive sport?

What is organizational stress?

How stress is defined by sport psychologists should by now be recognized as important (Fletcher et al., 2006). As Cooper, Dewe, and O'Driscoll (2001) pointed out, definitions provide a context, a sense of coherence, and a framework for understanding research findings. What is generally agreed is that the term *stressor* refers to an environmental demand and the term *strain* to an individual's response (Beehr, 1998; Beehr & Franz, 1987). Strains can be psychological, physical, or behavioral reactions, but they are by definition indicators of an individual's negative evaluation of environmental events, which are more commonly known as stressors. The most recent definitional developments point to the notion of a transactional conceptualization of stress where the emphasis is on identifying the processes that link the individual with the environment (Lazarus, 1981; Lazarus & Folkman, 1984; Lazarus & Launier, 1978). Adopting a transactional perspective means that no one variable can be said to be stress because, as Lazarus (1990) has articulated, stress "has been defined as a continually changing relationship between the person and environment" (p. 4). Hence, stress is often defined "relationally" (Lazarus & Launier, 1978) involving ongoing transactions between an individual and the environment.

From an organizational stress in sport perspective, the transactional conceptualization implies a dynamic relationship between an individual and the sport organization within which he or she is operating (cf. Fletcher et al., 2006). In this transaction, the individual appraises an organizational-related event and his or her coping resources, while the organization's structure and climate influences these appraisals. Depending on the outcomes of these cognitive evaluations, an individual may engage thoughts and behaviors designed to deal with the situation, strategies which will likely change over time as efforts are reappraised and outcomes evaluated. This ongoing dynamic will affect subsequent appraisals of stressors and hence an individual's responses and possible choice of coping strategies. For example, a sport performer may evaluate (i.e., "appraise") an argument with a coach (i.e., the "stressor") as threatening to his or her aspirations, a reaction which is influenced by the coach's role in team selection (i.e., a "moderating variable"). Following an angry emotional response (i.e., "strain") the performer may watch television to calm down (i.e., "emotion-focused coping") and maybe later approach the coach about the issues underlying the altercation (i.e., "problem-focused coping"). Depending on how effective these strategies are in helping to achieve his or her desired outcome, the performer will likely respond to and cope with future disputes in different ways.

Within the sport psychology literature, early researchers investigating organizational stress made a notable attempt to define and delimit the scope of inquiry. Organizational stress in sport was originally conceived by Woodman and Hardy (2001a) as "an interaction between the individual and the sport organization within which that individual is operating" (p. 208). In quantitative research design, an interaction refers to the combined effect of two (or more) independent variables on a dependent variable. Hence, interaction implies a cause and effect, whereby, in this context, the individual and the sport organization give rise to cognitive-emotional reactions but nonetheless maintain their distinctiveness (cf. Appley & Trumbull, 1986; Lazarus, 1966; Lazarus & Folkman, 1984). However, although interaction is certainly relevant, it was pointed out by Fletcher et al. (2006) that it is also important to recognize that during stressful encounters the person and the organization can, and often do, mutually affect one another. Furthermore, the meaning the person construes from his or her relationship with the organization occurs at a higher level of abstraction than the distinct variables themselves (cf. Lazarus, 1981; Lazarus & Launier, 1978). Therefore, in addition to interaction, sport psychologists need to consider the dynamics of *transaction* and *relational meaning* (Fletcher et al., 2006). As noted above, transactional definitions of stress are less focused on the specific components of an interaction and more concerned with the psychological processes – such as the concepts of appraisal and coping – that underpin an encounter (cf. Dewey & Bentley, 1949; Lazarus & Launier, 1978). Rather than implying static correlations between variables, Lazarus (1998) argued that the term transaction adds meaning to a person's interaction with his or her environment: "*Transaction*... is much more than interaction... [it] brings the causal variables together at a higher level of abstraction; namely, the relational meaning constructed by the individual who is confronted by (or selects) a particular environment" (p. xix).

Despite the drawbacks associated with using the term "interaction", Woodman and Hardy (2001a) did go some way to recognizing the essence of the transactional conceptualization when they proposed that "organizational stress can be defined as the stress that is associated primarily and directly with an individual's appraisal of the structure and functioning of the organization within which he/she is operating" (p. 208). However, apart from the tautological imprecision of suggesting that "stress can be defined as the stress", there is another more subtle conceptual difficulty associated with this definition. Its emphasis on an individual's appraisal of the structure and functioning of the organization, combined with its neglect of the individual's appraisal of available coping resources, suggests that primary appraisal is in some way more relevant or important than secondary appraisal in the organizational stress process.

However, Lazarus (1999) specifically stated that his use of the term "secondary" was not intended to connote a process of less importance than primary appraisal, but rather an evaluative reaction to the identification of a significant encounter. Hence, rather than focusing on specific aspects or components of the transaction, definitions of organizational stress should attempt to encapsulate the essence of the overall process (cf. Lazarus, 1990, 1991). In view of these points, Woodman and Hardy's (2001a) work has been modified resulting in the following definition of organizational stress: "an ongoing transaction between an individual and the environmental demands associated primarily and directly with the organization within which he or she is operating" (Fletcher et al., 2006, p. 329; see also Arnold & Fletcher, 2012a; Arnold, Fletcher, & Daniels, 2013; Didymus & Fletcher, 2012; Fletcher, Hanton, Mellalieu, & Neil, 2012a; Hanton, Fletcher, & Coughlan, 2005; Hanton, Wagstaff, & Fletcher, 2012; Rumbold, Fletcher, & Daniels, 2012; Sohal, Gervis, & Rhind, 2013; Tabei, Fletcher, & Goodger, 2012).

Some sport psychology researchers have explicitly or implicitly suggested that the concept of organizational stress is too broad and that subdividing this type of stress has psychometric (Kristiansen, Halvari, & Roberts, 2012a) and practical (McKay, Niven, Lavallee, & White, 2008) value. Although organizational stress theorists (e.g., Arnold & Fletcher, 2012b; Fletcher et al., 2012a; Woodman & Hardy, 2001a) and psychometricians (e.g., Arnold & Fletcher, 2012a, Arnold et al., 2013) have recognized the need for conceptual (sub)classification in this area, the nomenclature, scope, and boundaries of subcategories has been a topic of discussion and debate (cf. Arnold & Fletcher, 2012b; Cruickshank & Collins, 2013; Fletcher et al., 2006).

How does organizational stress affect athlete performance and well-being?

Following an extensive review and synthesis of the stress literature, Fletcher and colleagues (Fletcher & Fletcher, 2005; Fletcher et al., 2006; Fletcher & Scott, 2010) developed a meta-model of stress, emotions, and performance that outlines the theoretical relationships among key processes, moderators, and consequences of the stress process. The model offers a supraordinate perspective of the stress–emotion–performance relationship by building on conceptual advances that emphasize the transactional nature of stress as a dynamic process (see Fletcher et al., 2006; Lazarus, 1998, 1999). Following the application of the meta-model to organizational stress in competitive sport, the model has provided the theoretical underpinning of several studies (see, for example Arnold & Fletcher, 2012b; Arnold et al., 2013, 2016; Knight, Reade, Selzler, & Rodgers, 2013). A detailed discussion of the meta-model is beyond the scope of this chapter (see, for reviews, Fletcher et al., 2006; Fletcher & Scott, 2010) but it is worth highlighting the main tenets and components of the model (see Figure 5.1). At its most fundamental level, the meta-model postulates that stressors arise from the environment an individual operates in, are mediated by the processes of appraisal and coping,

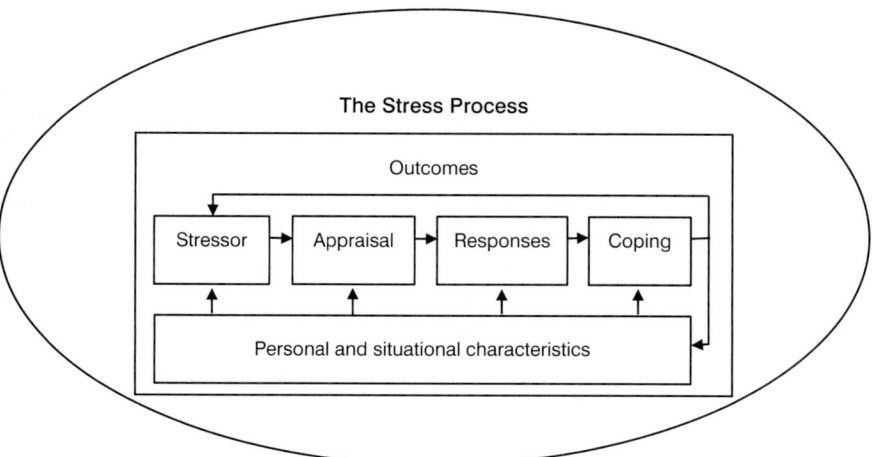

FIGURE 5.1 A simplified meta-model of stress, emotion, and performance

Source: Adapted with permission from Fletcher & Fletcher, 2005; Fletcher et al., 2006; Fletcher & Scott, 2010.

and, as a consequence, individuals respond in different ways. This ongoing process is moderated by personal and situational characteristics, and results in well-being- and performance-related outcomes. For the purpose of this chapter, we focus our attention on the organizational stress research conducted with sport performers pertaining to the stressors, appraisal, responses, coping, and outcomes components of the model.

Stressors

Organizational stressors are defined as "the environmental demands associated primarily and directly with the organization within which an individual is operating" (Fletcher et al., 2006, p. 359). In a number of early studies that identified different types of environmental demands, sport psychology researchers unearthed a variety of organizational-related stressors (see, for example Gould, Eklund, & Jackson, 1993; Scanlan, Stein, & Ravizza, 1991). At the turn of the century, Woodman and Hardy (2001a, 2001b) developed an exploratory framework that highlighted four main areas of organizational stress: environmental issues, personal issues, leadership issues, and team issues (cf. Carron, 1982). Empirical research that has adopted this framework has illustrated a wide range of organizational stressors that elite performers experience (see Fletcher & Hanton, 2003; Hanton et al., 2005; Woodman & Hardy, 2001a). However, due to its conceptual origins, the framework may reflect a bias toward group cohesion and interpersonal dynamics (Fletcher et al., 2006, 2012a). Fletcher and colleagues (2006, 2012a) proposed an alternative framework of organizational stressors that integrated recent developments in organizational psychology (see, for review, Cooper et al., 2001) and sport psychology (see, for a review, Fletcher et al., 2006). The model consists of a three-level hierarchical framework of organizational stressors with five general dimensions: factors intrinsic to the sport; roles in the sport organization; sport relationships and interpersonal demands; athletic career and performance development issues; and organizational structure and climate of the sport. Preliminary evidence for this framework was presented in a brief report (Hanton & Fletcher, 2005) and in studies of elite and non-elite performers (Fletcher et al., 2012a; Mellalieu, Neil, Hanton, & Fletcher, 2009; Tabei et al., 2012) and sport psychology academics and practitioners (Fletcher et al., 2011). Despite this support, Fletcher et al. (2012a) acknowledged that the framework was influenced by organizational stressors from a range of non-sport occupations; therefore, the extent to which it is free from bias or is entirely relevant to contemporary sport is questionable (Arnold & Fletcher, 2012b).

To advance the body of knowledge in this area, Arnold and Fletcher (2012b) synthesized the research that has identified the organizational stressors encountered by athletes and developed a taxonomic classification of these environmental demands. Using a meta-interpretative method, 34 studies (with a combined sample of 1809 participants) were analyzed and yielded 640 distinct organizational stressors. The demands were abstracted into 31 subcategories, which formed four categories: leadership and personnel issues; cultural and team issues; logistical and environmental issues; and performance and personal issues. Leadership and personnel issues consisted of the coach's behavior and interactions, the coach's personality and attitudes, external expectations, support staff, sport officials, spectators, media, performance feedback, and the governing body. Cultural and team issues consisted of teammates' behaviors and interactions, communication, team atmosphere and support, teammates' personalities and attitudes, cultural norms, and goals. Logistical and environmental issues consisted of facilities and equipment, selection, competition format, structure of training, weather conditions, travel, accommodation, rules and regulations, distractions, physical safety, and technology. Finally, performance and personal issues consisted of injuries, finances, diet and hydration, and career transitions. Several studies have provided support for this classification (Didymus & Fletcher, 2012, 2014; Sohal, Gervis, & Rhind, 2013) and identified some examples of culturally idiosyncratic stressors (Sohal et al., 2013; see also Tabei et al., 2012).

Beyond the identification of stressors encountered by athletes, researchers in this area have qualitatively explored the content and quantity of stressors in elite and non-elite sport performers. For example, Hanton et al. (2005) found that elite athletes experienced and recalled more demands associated primarily and directly with the sport organization than with competitive performance. Furthermore, this population appeared more likely to experience similar competitive stressors but varied organizational stressors, perhaps because the former are typically common to most athletes' experiences of performance, whereas the latter are generally disparate and subject to numerous sociocultural, political, economic, occupational, and technological influences. More recently,

Fletcher et al. (2012a) compared the frequency and content of organizational stressors between elite and non-elite sport performers. They found that the higher-skilled participants encountered more stressors than the lower-skilled participants. Their findings also suggest that across skill levels certain types of organizational stressors are experienced and recalled more frequently than others. More specifically, the elite performers mentioned travel and accommodation arrangements, income and funding, media attention, and a lack of participation in the decision-making process more often than their non-elite counterparts.

Rather than investigate organizational stressors per se, Didymus and Fletcher (2012) focused on the ubiquitous and cross-cutting characteristics – or situational properties – of stressors (Lazarus & Folkman, 1984). These were: 1) *novelty*, which refers to the effect of prior knowledge; 2) *predictability*, which implies that these are predicable environmental characteristics that can be discerned, discovered, or learned; 3) *event uncertainty*, which pertains to the probability of an event occurring; 4) *imminence*, which refers to the amount of time before an event occurs; 5) *duration*, which relates to how long stressful events persists; 6) *temporal uncertainty*, which pertains to situations when the necessary information required to make an appraisal is unavailable or insufficient; and 7) *timing* in relation to life cycle, which is concerned with the contextual properties that define the timing of an event. Didymus and Fletcher's (2012) findings suggest that it may be the situational property of the stressor, rather than the demand per se, that is fundamental to athletes' organizational stressor encounters.

Although much is known about the organizational stressors that sport performers encounter, until recently there was no method of assessing these phenomena. Following repeated calls for psychometric work in this area (see Arnold & Fletcher, 2012a, 2012b; Fletcher & Hanton, 2003; Fletcher et al., 2006; Hanton et al., 2005; Kristiansen et al., 2012a), Arnold et al. (2013) developed and validated the Organizational Stressor Indicator for Sport Performers (OSI-SP). The OSI-SP measures the frequency, intensity, and duration of demands across five main categories of organizational stressors: goals and development; logistics and operations; team and culture; coaching; and selection. Via a series of four related studies, the OSI-SP was shown to display adequate internal consistency and content, factorial, discriminant, and concurrent validity (Arnold et al., 2013). In addition, invariance testing supported the equality of factor loadings, variances, and covariances on the OSI-SP across gender, sport type, competitive level, and competitive experience, therefore making it possible for researchers to assess organizational stressors across different groups of sport performers and make more meaningful comparisons between them.

In the most recent study in this area, Arnold et al. (2016) used the OSI-SP and reported significant differences between male and female athletes, between team and individual-based athletes, and between varying competitive standard athletes in terms of their organizational stressor encounters. Specifically, it was found that males encounter significantly higher dimensions of logistics and operations organizational stressors than females, and that females encounter significantly higher dimensions of selection organizational stressors than males. For sport type, it was found that performers competing in team-based sports encounter higher dimensions of logistics and operations, team and culture, and selection organizational stressors than those competing in individual-based sports. Finally, when examining competitive level, it was evident that sport performers competing at higher performance levels (e.g., national or international) typically experience organizational stressors more frequently, at a higher intensity, and for a longer duration than those competing at lower levels (e.g., regional or university and county or club).

Appraisal

While stressors are clearly a salient feature of sport performers' lives, they only reflect one component of the stress process and say little about how performers evaluate or appraise organizational-related encounters. Neil, Hanton, Mellalieu, and Fletcher (2011) provided insights into athletes' transactions with their competition environment, including some organizational-related demands, and the relationships between appraisals, emotions, further appraisals, and subsequent behavior. In terms of the organizational stress experience, the findings indicated that athletes respond negatively to this type of stressor, although they have the potential to interpret their emotions in a positive way in relation to their performance. Hanton et al. (2012) supported and began to explain these findings by showing that sources of organizational strain are predominantly appraised as threatening or harmful (see also Didymus & Fletcher, 2012), with little perceived control, and few coping resources available. It also appears that the situational properties (e.g., imminence, novelty, duration) of the stressors encountered influence athletes' appraisal of organizational stressors (Didymus & Fletcher, 2012).

Responses

It is generally accepted that there are three major categories of possible stress responses or strain: physiological, psychological, and behavioral (Cooper et al., 2001; Kahn & Byosiere, 1992). Fletcher, Hanton, and Wagstaff (2012b) conducted a qualitative study to explore sport performers' responses to stressors encountered in sport organizations. The main emotional responses that were revealed were anger, anxiety, disappointment, distress, happiness, hope, relief, reproach, and resentment. The main attitudinal responses were beliefs, motivation, and satisfaction. The main behavioral responses were categorized as verbal and physical. Focusing on emotional responses, there is some quantitative evidence linking organizational stressor encounters with athletes' anxiety, dejection, anger, excitement, and happiness (Arnold et al., 2013) and a self-report measure to assess sport performers' emotional responses to organizational stressors was recently validated (Arnold & Fletcher, 2015).

Coping

Coping is closely linked to appraisal and is defined as "the cognitions and behaviors, adopted by the individual following the recognition of a stressful encounter, that are in some way designed to deal with that encounter or its consequences" (Dewe, Cox, & Ferguson, 1993, p. 7). Research investigating organizational stressor-coping relationships in sport performers has revealed that athletes employ some coping strategies in response to multiple stressors, whereas other strategies were unique to a particular stressor (Didymus & Fletcher, 2014; Kristiansen et al., 2012a, 2012b; Kristiansen & Roberts, 2010; Weston, Thelwell, Bond, & Hutchings, 2009). The strategies used by performers spanned a wide range of social support, cognitive strategies, avoidance, problem-focused, and emotion-focused coping. Further, Didymus and Fletcher (2014) found that appraisal mechanisms and coping effectiveness appear to be linked to the coping strategies employed.

Outcomes

Sport performers' experiences of organizational stress can result in number of well-being- and performance-related outcomes. In their study of organizational stress in Indian female international sport performers, Sohal et al. (2013) reported a perceived relationship between the stressors encountered and athletes' feelings of low environmental mastery and low personal growth. Comparable findings were reported in a study of English and Japanese soccer players who suggested that multiple organizational stressors were linked to their symptoms of burnout (Tabei et al., 2012). Although no research has investigated the effect of organizational stress on athletic performance, there is some qualitative (Fletcher et al., 2012a) and quantitative (Arnold et al., 2016) data that indicates athletes of different competitive standards have varying organizational stress experiences and that such encounters are related to their satisfaction with their performance (Arnold et al., 2013).

How can athletes' experiences of organizational stress be optimized?

When reflecting on the practical implications of the theory and research, perhaps the first observation that should be made is that it is neither possible nor desirable to eliminate all organizational stress from sport performers' lives. Some organizational stress is an inherent and inevitable aspect of the sport experience, particularly at higher levels of competitive performance. Although such demands and experiences can have a negative effect on performance and well-being, they can also have some stress inoculation, performance enhancing, and psychosocial benefits for athletes (Fletcher et al., 2006, 2012b). Indeed, Arnold et al. (2016) recognized the potential value of organizational stress inoculation training involving the exposure of performers to appropriate and progressively demanding stressors in a supportive and controllable environment so that performers can develop their resilience and stress management. Hence, rather than conceiving organizational stress management as predominately relating to the reduction of stressors, we prefer to focus on the holistic optimization of athletes' experiences (cf. Rumbold et al., 2012).

With the above observations in mind, we advocate a tripartite approach to organizational stress management in sport (see Fletcher et al., 2006; Fletcher & Scott, 2010). Primary interventions involve managing the organizational environment within which performers operate to optimize the demands placed on them (see Arnold & Fletcher, 2012b; Arnold et al., 2016; Didymus & Fletcher, 2012; Fletcher & Hanton, 2003; Fletcher et al., 2012a; Hanton & Fletcher, 2005; Hanton et al., 2005; Mellalieu et al., 2009; Sohal et al., 2013; Woodman & Hardy, 2001a). Secondary interventions focus on modifying performers' reaction and responses to stressors, rather than shaping the organizational conditions (see Didymus & Fletcher, 2012; Fletcher et al., 2012b; Hanton et al., 2012; Neil et al., 2011; Sarkar & Fletcher, 2014; Sohal et al., 2013; Tabei et al., 2012). Tertiary interventions are concerned with minimizing the damaging consequences of stress by helping performers cope more effectively with reduced well-being or performance as a result of strain (see Didymus & Fletcher, 2014; Sohal et al., 2013; Tabei et al., 2012). As Fletcher et al. (2006) noted, these interventions are not mutually exclusive and to some extent there is overlap between the different strategies (cf. Rumbold et al., 2012). Nevertheless, this framework presents a systematic approach to stress management that can aid consultants in optimizing athletes' well-being and performance.

To implement an organizational stress management intervention in sport, consultants will need to develop professional competence in optimizing team and organizational functioning. Such expertise will likely go well beyond their training in athlete psychological and performance enhancement, and span a range of leadership coaching and organizational consulting competencies (Fletcher & Hanton, 2003; Fletcher et al., 2006; Fletcher & Wagstaff, 2009; Hanton et al., 2005; Hanton & Fletcher, 2005; Jones, 2002; Rumbold et al., 2012; Tabei et al., 2012; Woodman & Hardy, 2001a, 2001b). To manage the organizational environment and demands encountered by those operating within it, sport psychologists will not only need to be aware of the potential threats to functioning (see Arnold & Fletcher, 2012b) but also the enablers of organizational effectiveness (see Arnold, Hewton, & Fletcher, 2015; Fletcher & Streeter, 2016; Fletcher & Wagstaff, 2009). A detailed discussion of organizational success in competitive sport is beyond the scope of this chapter, but Wagstaff and colleagues' work is informative in this regard (see, for review, Wagstaff, Fletcher, & Hanton, 2012a; Wagstaff, Fletcher, & Hanton, 2012b; Wagstaff & Larner, 2015).

In addition to broadening their competency, sport psychologists should be mindful of and sensitive to the realities of consulting in sport organizations (cf. Fletcher et al., 2006; Fletcher & Wagstaff, 2009). To elaborate, a climate and culture has prevailed in sport where organizations have tended to resist change when it has involved alterations to their practices and procedures. The reasons for this appear to relate predominately to a lack of knowledge on the part of senior management, keeping the size of support team staff to manageable levels (Gardner, 1995), the historical emphasis of placing the onus for psychological development on athletes, senior management's beliefs about the impact of the organizational environment on performers, and the financial, legal, and political repercussions of making organizational-level changes (Fletcher et al., 2006; Fletcher & Wagstaff, 2009). Further to these barriers, Ravizza (1988) recommended that consultants pay careful attention to the constantly unfolding "organizational politics" within elite sport. Of central importance is identifying the key decision-makers within an organization and the personnel (e.g., performance directors) whose input will likely influence any potential interventions (Gardner, 1995). Hardy et al. (1996) also noted that it is worth identifying who within the organization is receptive to psychological support. The extent of commitment from all layers of the organization – the executive board, managerial committees, technical and support staff, coaches, athletes – to implementing best practice is critical to the success of organizational-level interventions (Fletcher & Wagstaff, 2009). However, as Hardy et al. (1996) remarked, consultants should maneuver with caution in the milieu of organizational politics and not confuse political acuity with political activity.

What does the future hold for organizational stress research in competitive sport?

Although research investigating organizational stress in competitive sport has advanced considerably over the past decade, much work remains to be done. Most of the studies to date have focused on one component (e.g., stressors, appraisal, responses, coping, outcomes) of the organizational stress process in sport performers. Although such research provides fundamental knowledge about sport performers' stress experiences, the conceptualization of organizational stress as a complex, ongoing transaction between individuals and their organizational environment necessitates more diverse and rigorous research designs and methods. Although various qualitative (viz. interviews, diaries, content analysis, casual networks, grounded theory, meta-interpretation) and quantitative (viz. questionnaires, expert ratings, exploratory and confirmatory factor analysis, correlations, invariance testing, multivariate analyses of covariance) research methods have already been employed by researchers working in this area, the use of other qualitative (e.g., narrative inquiry, observational methods, the media, internet, and autobiographies) and quantitative (e.g., exploratory structural equation modeling and bifactor models, mediation and moderation analysis, multilevel modelling, Bayesian modelling, meta-analysis) research methods would help to further advance what is known about performers' subjective experiences and the complexity of organizational stress in sport. As in any area of psychosocial research, methodological partiality based on erroneous dogmatism should not, however, dictate the selection of methods in preference to their appropriateness for addressing original and significant research questions. Indeed, Hardy (2015; see also Hardy et al., 1996; Fletcher & Wagstaff, 2009) recently urged sport and exercise psychology researchers to

> use both qualitative and quantitative methods in their study of research questions. Although the philosophical underpinning of these two research methods are very different, there seems no reason why researchers should not be able to grasp both philosophies and behave in accordance with those different philosophies in different contexts.
>
> (Hardy, 2015, p. 266)

Regardless of the specific research method employed, it is important that researchers progress beyond investigating discrete aspects of the organizational stress process and, in accordance with the transactional perspective of stress, focus more on the features that link the components of the process and the reciprocal and adaptive nature of the process itself (Arnold et al., 2013; Didymus & Fletcher, 2012; Fletcher et al., 2006, 2012b; Tabei et al., 2012).

One of the most significant advances in this area of inquiry has been the development and validation of measures of organizational stressors (Arnold & Fletcher, 2012a; Arnold et al., 2013; Kristiansen et al., 2012a) and emotional responses (Arnold & Fletcher, 2015; Jones, Lane, Bray, Uphill, & Catlin, 2005). These measures require refinement within existing subscales and dimensions, expansion across a wider range of stressors and responses, and validation in different athletic populations and sport cultures. In addition, researchers could develop a scale that assesses the ubiquitous and cross-cutting characteristics of stressors (e.g., their situational properties; Didymus & Fletcher, 2012). An example of such an approach is the management standards which assess six salient risk factors (viz. demands, control, support, relationships, role, change) for organizational stress (Cousins, Mackay, Clarke, Kelly, Kelly, & McCaig, 2004; Mackay, Cousins, Kelly, Lee, & McCaig, 2004). Further, since extant measures rely solely on self-report data, future researchers should consider adopting a triangulation strategy, incorporating multiple methods (e.g., psychometric testing, observational techniques, physiological indices) within their studies so that the drawbacks of one method might be attenuated by the strengths of another (cf. Arnold & Fletcher, 2012a; Arnold et al., 2013; Fletcher et al., 2006).

Beyond methodological and psychometric issues, there are numerous research questions in this area that require attention, including: What is the interface between and interactive impact of organizational and other types of stressors on sport performers (Fletcher et al., 2006; Hanton et al., 2005)? How can researchers design studies to recognize the difference between objective and subjective organizational stressors (Fletcher et al., 2006, 2012a)? To what extent do performers actually express their felt responses (i.e., emotional labor; Fletcher et al., 2006, 2012b)? Do performers' responses to stressors spread throughout a sport team or organization (i.e., emotional contagion, group affective tone; Arnold et al., 2016; Fletcher et al., 2006, 2012b)? How do personal and situational characteristics influence the organizational stress process (Arnold et al., 2013, 2016; Didymus & Fletcher, 2012, 2014; Fletcher et al., 2006; Hanton et al., 2012; Sarkar & Fletcher, 2014; Tabei et al., 2012)? How much performance variance might be accounted for by organizational stress in elite sport (Arnold & Fletcher, 2012b; Fletcher et al., 2006, 2012a; Woodman & Hardy, 2001a)? What are the sources of organizational stress for "non-performing" members of the organization (cf. Fletcher & Scott, 2010; Fletcher et al., 2006, 2011; Harwood, Drew, & Knight, 2010; Harwood & Knight, 2009a, 2009b; Knight & Harwood, 2009; Knight et al., 2013; Levy, Nicholls, Marchant, & Polman, 2009; Rhind, Scott, & Fletcher, 2013; Thelwell, Weston, Greenlees, & Hutchings, 2008; Woodman & Hardy, 2001a)?

As discussed in the previous section, we are now able to theorize and make evidence-based recommendations regarding organizational stress management in competitive sport. However, what is lacking and is required are evaluations of such interventions (Didymus & Fletcher, 2014; Fletcher & Hanton, 2003; Fletcher et al., 2006; Rumbold et al., 2012; Tabei et al., 2012). In our opinion, the most rigorous way to design such evaluations is to attempt to establish the efficacy and effectiveness of a stress management intervention across a series of studies as part of a larger program of research (cf. American Psychological Association Presidential Task Force on Evidence-Based Practice, 2006). To elaborate, efficacious research using methods that substantiate evidence-based practice could be used to establish whether a particular stress management intervention has a specific, measurable effect at an organizational or group (i.e., randomized controlled trials) or an individual (i.e., single-case experimental designs) level. Effectiveness research that assesses stress management interventions as they are delivered in sport organizations could then be used to substantiate practice-based evidence and to identify whether a pre-established efficacious treatment has a discernible, beneficial effect across a range of populations and settings (cf. Barkham & Mellor-Clark, 2003). Some important considerations in such a program of intervention research are collecting follow-up assessments to evaluate the persistence of any treatment effects, using social validation and process evaluation to better understand the implementation of the intervention, and uploading online supplementary materials to provide adequate information about the research.

Concluding remarks

Research investigating organizational stress in competitive sport has gathered momentum since the publication of Fletcher et al.'s (2006) review of this area. We now have a good understanding of what causes organizational stress in sport and some knowledge of how athletes react and respond to such demands and cope with any issues that arise. Less is known, however, about how organizational stress affects athletes' performance and well-being. As the evidence and practice relating to organizational stress in competitive sport advances, so too will the support available to athletes and others operating in sport organizations. To conclude, we highlight five key messages of our review:

- Organizational stress is defined as "an ongoing transaction between an individual and the environmental demands associated primarily and directly with the organization within which he or she is operating" (Fletcher et al., 2006, p. 329)
- The meta-model of stress, emotions, and performance (Fletcher & Fletcher, 2005; Fletcher et al., 2006; Fletcher & Scott, 2010) and the associated research reviewed here provides a theoretical foundation and explanation for understanding individuals' stress experiences in sport organizations.
- Valid and reliable measures of the organizational stressors encountered by sport performers (Arnold et al., 2013) and of the emotions experienced by sport performers in organizational environments (Arnold & Fletcher, 2015; Jones et al., 2005) are available.
- Practitioners should adopt a tripartite approach to organizational stress management in sport whilst being mindful of and sensitive to the realities of consulting in sport organizations (cf. Fletcher et al., 2006; Fletcher & Wagstaff, 2009).
- Future researchers should employ more diverse and rigorous qualitative and quantitative research methods that are most appropriate for addressing the most original and significant research questions in this area (cf. Fletcher et al., 2006; Fletcher & Wagstaff, 2009).

References

American Psychological Association Presidential Task Force on Evidence-Based Practice. (2006). Evidence-based practice in psychology. *American Psychologist, 61,* 271–285.

Appley, M. H., & Trumbull, R. (1986). A conceptual model for the examination of stress dynamics. In M. H. Appley & R. Trumbull (Eds.), *Dynamics of stress: Physiological, psychological, and social perspectives* (pp. 21–45). New York: Plenum.

Arnold, R., & Fletcher, D. (2012a). Psychometric issues in organizational stressor research: A review and implications for sport psychology. *Measurement in Physical Education and Exercise Science, 16,* 81–100.

Arnold, R., & Fletcher, D. (2012b). A research synthesis and taxonomic classification of the organizational stressors encountered by sport performers. *Journal of Sport and Exercise Psychology, 34,* 397–429.

Arnold, R., & Fletcher, D. (2015). Confirmatory factor analysis of the Sport Emotion Questionnaire in organizational environments. *Journal of Sports Sciences, 33,* 169–179.

Arnold, R., Fletcher, D., & Daniels, K. (2013). Development and validation of the Organizational Stressor Indicator for Sport Performers (OSI-SP). *Journal of Sport and Exercise Psychology, 35,* 180–196.

Arnold, R., Fletcher, D., & Daniels, K. (2016). Demographic differences in sport performers' experiences of organizational stressors. *Scandinavian Journal of Medicine & Science in Sports, 26,* 348–358.

Arnold, R., Hewton, E., & Fletcher, D. (2015). Preparing our greatest team: The design and delivery of a preparation camp for the London 2012 Olympic Games. *Sport, Business and Management: An International Journal, 5*, 386–407.

Barkham, M., & Mellor-Clark, J. (2003). Bridging evidence-based practice and practice-based evidence: Developing a rigorous and relevant knowledge for the psychological therapies. *Clinical Psychology and Psychotherapy, 10*, 319–327.

Beehr, T. A. (1998). An organizational psychology meta-model of occupational stress. In C. L. Cooper (Ed.), *Theories of organizational stress* (pp. 6–27). Oxford: Oxford University Press.

Beehr, T. A., & Franz, T. M. (1987). The current debate about the meaning of job stress. In J. M. Ivancevich & D. C. Ganster (Eds.), *Job stress: From theory to suggestion* (pp. 5–18). New York: Haworth Press.

Carron, A. V. (1982). Cohesiveness in sport groups: Interpretations and considerations. *Journal of Sport Psychology, 4*, 123–138.

Cooper, C. L., Dewe, P. J., & O'Driscoll, M. P. (2001). *Organizational stress: A review and critique of theory, research, and applications*. Thousand Oaks, CA: Sage.

Cousins, R., Mackay, C. J., Clarke, S. D., Kelly, C., Kelly, P. J., & McCaig, R. H. (2004). "Management standards" and work-related stress in the UK: Practical implications. *Work and Stress, 18*, 113–136.

Cruickshank, C., & Collins, D. (2013). Culture change in elite sport performance teams: An important and unique construct. *Sport and Exercise Psychology Review, 9*, 6–21.

Dewe, P., Cox, T., & Ferguson, E. (1993). Individual strategies for coping with stress at work: A review. *Work and Stress, 7*, 5–15.

Dewey, J., & Bentley, A. F. (1949). *Knowing and the known*. Boston, MA: Beacon Press.

Didymus, F. F., & Fletcher, D. (2012). Getting to the heart of the matter: A diary study of swimmers' appraisals of organizational stressors. *Journal of Sports Sciences, 30*, 1375–1385.

Didymus, F. F., & Fletcher, D. (2014). Swimmers' experiences of organizational stress: Exploring the role of cognitive appraisal and coping behaviors. *Journal of Clinical Sport Psychology, 8*, 159–183.

Fletcher, D., & Fletcher, J. (2005). A meta-model of stress, emotions and performance: Conceptual foundations, theoretical framework, and research directions [Abstract]. *Journal of Sports Sciences, 23*, 157–158.

Fletcher, D., & Hanton, S. (2003). Sources of organizational stress in elite sports performers. *The Sport Psychologist, 17*, 175–195.

Fletcher, D., & Scott, M. (2010). Psychological stress in sports coaches: A review of concepts, research and practice. *Journal of Sports Sciences, 28*, 127–137.

Fletcher, D., & Streeter, A. P. (2016). A case study analysis of the high performance environment model in elite swimming. *Journal of Change Management, 16*, 123–141

Fletcher, D., & Wagstaff, C. R. D. (2009). Organizational psychology in elite sport: Its emergence, application and future. *Psychology of Sport and Exercise, 10*, 427–434.

Fletcher, D., Hanton, S., & Mellalieu, S. D. (2006). An organizational stress review: Conceptual and theoretical issues in competitive sport. In S. Hanton & S. D. Mellalieu (Eds.), *Literature reviews in sport psychology* (pp. 321–373). Hauppauge, NY: Nova Science.

Fletcher, D., Hanton, S., Mellalieu, S. D., & Neil, R. (2012a). A conceptual framework of organizational stressors in sport performers. *Scandinavian Journal of Medicine & Science in Sports, 22*, 545–557.

Fletcher, D., Rumbold, J. L., Tester, R., & Coombes, M. J. (2011). Sport psychologists' experiences of organizational stressors. *The Sport Psychologist, 25*, 363–381.

Fletcher, D., Hanton, S., & Wagstaff, C. R. D. (2012b). Performers' responses to stressors encountered in sport organizations. *Journal of Sports Sciences, 30*, 349–358.

Gardner, F. (1995). The coach and team psychologist: An integrated organizational model. In S. M. Murphy (Ed.), *Sport psychology interventions* (pp. 147–175). Champaign, IL: Human Kinetics.

Gould, D., Eklund, R. C., & Jackson, S. A. (1993). Coping strategies used by U.S. Olympic wrestlers. *Research Quarterly for Exercise and Sport, 64*, 83–93.

Hanton, S., & Fletcher, D. (2005). Organizational stress in competitive sport: More than we bargained for? *International Journal of Sport Psychology, 36*, 273–283.

Hanton, S., Fletcher, D., & Coughlan, G. (2005). Stress in elite sport performers: A comparative study of competitive and organizational stressors. *Journal of Sports Sciences, 23*, 1129–1141.

Hanton, S., Wagstaff, C. R. D., & Fletcher, D. (2012). Cognitive appraisals of stressors encountered in sport organizations. *International Journal of Sport and Exercise Psychology, 10*, 276–289.

Hardy, L. (2015). Epilogue. In S. D. Mellalieu and S. Hanton (Eds.), *Contemporary reviews in sport psychology* (pp. 258–269). London: Routledge.

Hardy, L., Jones, G., & Gould, D. (1996). *Understanding psychological preparation for sport: Theory and practice of elite performers*. Chichester: Wiley.

Harwood, C., & Knight, C. J. (2009a). Stress in youth sport: A developmental examination of tennis parents. *Psychology of Sport and Exercise, 10*, 447–456.

Harwood, C., & Knight, C. J. (2009b). Understanding parental stress: An investigation of British tennis parents. *Journal of Sports Sciences, 27*, 339–351.

Harwood, C., Drew, A., & Knight, C. J. (2010). Parental stressors in professional youth football academies: A qualitative investigation of specialising stage parents. *Qualitative Research in Sport and Exercise, 2*, 39–55.

Jones, G. (1995). More than just a game: Research developments and issues in competitive anxiety in sport. *British Journal of Psychology, 86*, 449–478.

Jones, G. (2002). Performance excellence: A personal perspective on the link between sport and business. *Journal of Applied Sport Psychology, 14*, 268–281.

Jones, M. V., Lane, A. M., Bray, S. R., Uphill, M., & Catlin, J. (2005). Development and validation of the Sport Emotion Questionnaire. *Journal of Sport and Exercise Psychology, 27*, 407–431.

Kahn, R. L., & Byosiere, P. (1992). Stress in organizations. In M. D. Dunnette (Ed.), *Handbook of industrial and organizational psychology* (pp. 571–648). Chicago, IL: Rand McNally.

Knight, C. J., & Harwood, C. (2009). Exploring parent-related coaching stressors in British tennis: A developmental investigation. *International Journal of Sports Science & Coaching, 4*, 545–565.

Knight, C. J., Reade, I. L., Selzler, A.-M., & Rodgers, W. M. (2013). Personal and situational factors influencing coaches' perceptions of stress. *Journal of Sports Sciences, 31*, 1054–1063.

Kristiansen, E., & Roberts, G. C. (2010). Young elite athletes and social support: Coping with competitive and organizational stress in "Olympic" competition. *Scandinavian Journal of Medicine & Science in Sport, 20*, 686–695.

Kristiansen, E., Halvari, H., & Roberts, G. C. (2012a). Organizational and media stress among professional football players: Testing and achievement goal theory model. *Scandinavian Journal of Medicine & Science in Sport, 22*, 569–579.

Kristiansen, E., Murphy, D., & Roberts, G. C. (2012b). Organizational stress and coping in U.S. professional soccer. *Journal of Applied Sport Psychology, 24*, 207–223.

Lazarus, R. S. (1966). *Psychological stress and the coping process*. New York: McGraw-Hill.

Lazarus, R. S. (1981). The stress and coping paradigm. In C. Eisdorfer, D. Cohen, A. Kleinman, & P. Maxim (Eds.), *Models for clinical psychopathology* (pp. 177–214). New York: Spectrum.

Lazarus, R. S. (1990). Theory-based stress measurement. *Psychological Inquiry, 1*, 3–13.

Lazarus, R. S. (1991). Psychological stress in the workplace. *Journal of Social Behavior and Personality*, 6, 1–13.
Lazarus, R. S. (1998). *Fifty years of the research and theory of R. S. Lazarus: An analysis of historical and perennial issues*. Mahwah, NJ: Erlbaum.
Lazarus, R. S. (1999). *Stress and emotion: A new synthesis*. London: Free Association.
Lazarus, R. S., & Folkman, S. (1984). *Stress, appraisal, and coping*. New York: Springer.
Lazarus, R. S., & Launier, R. (1978). Stress-related transactions between person and environment. In L. A. Pervin & M. Lewis (Eds.), *Perspectives in interactional psychology* (pp. 287–327). New York: Plenum.
Levy, A., Nicholls, A., Marchant, D., & Polman, R. (2009). Organizational stressors, coping, and coping effectiveness: A longitudinal study of an elite coach. *International Journal of Sports Science and Coaching*, 4, 31–45.
Mackay, C. J., Cousins, R., Kelly, P. J., Lee, S., & McCaig, R. H. (2004). "Management standards" and work-related stress in the UK: Policy background and science. *Work and Stress*, 18, 91–112.
McKay, J., Niven, A. G., Lavallee, D., & White, A. (2008). Sources of strain among elite UK track athletes. *Sport Psychologist*, 22, 143–163."
Mellalieu, S. D., Neil, R., Hanton, S., & Fletcher, D. (2009). Competition stress in sport performers: Stressors experienced in the competition environment. *Journal of Sports Sciences*, 27, 729–744.
Neil, R., Hanton, S., Mellalieu, S. D., & Fletcher, D. (2011). Competition stress and emotions in sport performers: The role of further appraisals. *Psychology of Sport and Exercise*, 12, 460–470.
Ravizza, K. (1988). Gaining entry with athletic personnel for season-long consulting. *The Sport Psychologist*, 2, 234–274.
Rhind, D. J. A., Scott, M., & Fletcher, D. (2013). Organizational stress in professional soccer coaches. *International Journal of Sport Psychology*, 44, 1–16.
Rumbold, J. L., Fletcher, D., & Daniels, K. (2012). A systematic review of stress management interventions with sport performers. *Sport, Exercise and Performance Psychology*, 1, 173–193.
Sarkar, M., & Fletcher, D. (2014). Psychological resilience in sport performers: A narrative review of stressors and protective factors. *Journal of Sports Sciences*, 32, 1419–1434.
Scanlan, T. K., Stein, G. L., & Ravizza, K. (1991). An in-depth study of former elite figure skaters: III. Sources of stress. *Journal of Sport and Exercise Psychology*, 1, 102–120.
Sohal, D., Gervis, M., & Rhind, D. (2013). Exploration of organizational stressors in Indian elite female athletes. *International Journal of Sport Psychology*, 44, 565–585.
Tabei, Y., Fletcher, D., & Goodger, K. (2012). The relationship between organizational stressors and athlete burnout in soccer players. *Journal of Clinical Sport Psychology*, 6, 146–165.
Thelwell, R. C., Weston, N. J. V., Greenlees, I. A., & Hutchings, N. V. (2008). Stressors in elite sport: A coach perspective. *Journal of Sports Sciences*, 26, 905–918.
Wagstaff, C. R. D., & Larner, R. J. (2015). A review of organizational psychology in elite performance domains: Recent developments and future directions. In S. D. Mellalieu & S. Hanton (Eds.), *Contemporary reviews in sport psychology* (pp. 91–110). London: Routledge.
Wagstaff, C. R. D., Fletcher, D., & Hanton, S. (2012a). Positive organizational psychology in sport. *International Review of Sport and Exercise Psychology*, 5(2), 87–103.
Wagstaff, C. R. D., Fletcher, D., & Hanton, S. (2012b). Positive organizational psychology in sport: An ethnography of organizational functioning in a national sport organization. *Journal of Applied Sport Psychology*, 24(1), 26–47.

Weston, N. J., Thelwell, R. C., Bond, S., & Hutchings, N. V. (2009). Stress and coping in single-handed round-the-world ocean sailing. *Journal of Applied Sport Psychology, 21*(4), 460–474

Woodman, T., & Hardy, L. (2001a). A case study of organizational stress in elite sport. *Journal of Applied Sport Psychology, 13*, 207–238.

Woodman, T., & Hardy, L. (2001b). Stress and anxiety. In R. N. Singer, H. A. Hausenblas, & C. M. Janelle (Eds.), *Handbook of sport psychology* (pp. 290–318). New York: Wiley.

6
WELL-BEING IN SPORT ORGANIZATIONS

Rich Neil, Helen M. McFarlane, and Andrew P. Smith

Introduction

The concept of *well-being* has generated considerable academic attention and debate over the past century, influenced by historical discussions about what feeling good or experiencing the 'good life' constitutes (Ryan & Deci, 2001). Indeed, entering the word 'well-being' into the Google Scholar search engine retrieves over 3.4 million associated articles. As will be identified in this chapter, a lot of the work that has examined well-being has been informed by models and theories relating to adversity, as opposed to optimal functioning or flourishing. Given Arnold and Fletcher's work on stress within their chapter in this volume, the purpose of this chapter will be to provide balance by focusing on well-being through the lens of *wellness*, utilizing concepts from positive psychology. First, we define well-being through the perspectives of hedonism and eudaimonism, illustrating how these approaches to understanding well-being differ and, potentially, complement each other both conceptually and empirically. Then, we will offer critical insight into well-being research within sport psychology that is relevant to the sport organization, discussing the predictors of athlete and coach well-being. The focus of the chapter then moves on to the strengths and limitations of the existing body of well-being research relevant to sport organizations, informing future research directions for the field. Potential intervention strategies that may promote well-being within sporting organizations are then suggested, including primary, secondary, and tertiary strategies.

What is well-being?

The growing interest in well-being within the academic community and further afield has been accompanied by a number of policy shifts. For example, in April 2011, the Office for National Statistics in the UK began measuring national well-being (Thomas & Evans, 2010), while in Scotland, national health and well-being indicators have been developed with a shift in emphasis from negative to more positive indicators of mental health (Parkinson, 2006). The academic literature has mirrored this increased interest in well-being within a number of diverse fields, such as psychology, economics, sociology, geography, and education (e.g., Dolan, Peasgood, & White, 2008; Fleuret & Atkinson, 2007). The renewed interest in well-being can partially be attributed to the burgeoning positive psychology field, the birth of which is usually dated to Martin Seligman's (1999) presidential address to the American Psychological Association. It should be noted, however, that research on well-being predated the birth of positive psychology by several decades (e.g., Bradburn, 1969). Nevertheless, despite decades of research and the recent resurgence of interest, there is still no accepted definition of well-being (Dodge, Daly, Huyton, & Sanders, 2012). Most researchers conceptualize well-being as a global, subjective, multi-dimensional construct but there is not yet consensus on its constituent factors (Jayawickreme, Forgeard, & Seligman, 2012), and a number of different approaches to understanding well-being can be identified within the research.

Historically, research on well-being has mainly been conducted within two traditions: hedonic well-being and eudaimonic well-being (Ryan & Deci, 2001). The hedonic approach to well-being measures subjective well-being which is comprised of life satisfaction, positive affect, and an absence of negative affect (Diener, Suh, Lucas, & Smith, 1999). Specifically, focusing on happiness from the perspective of pleasure versus pain including both cognitive evaluation (life satisfaction) and affect (with positive and negative affect comprising separate dimensions). In contrast, the eudaimonic approach to well-being is not simply interested in subjective happiness, but in the realization of human potential (Ryff & Keyes, 1995). Within this view, well-being is linked to a person living in a way which is congruent with their deeply held values: a meaningful life characterized by personal growth, as opposed to a pleasurable life characterized by hedonic enjoyment (Ryan & Deci, 2001).

Within the organizational psychology field, however, the study of well-being has not generally been undertaken within the hedonic and eudaimonic traditions. Research into well-being at work has been closely linked with the literature on stress at work and has developed differently to the general well-being literature (e.g., Häusser, Mojzisch, Niesel, & Schulz-Hardt, 2010). Within this literature, the term 'well-being' is used to refer to a wide range of outcomes, including physical health, depression, anxiety, burnout, job satisfaction, and engagement (e.g., de Jonge, Bosma, Peter, & Siegrist, 2000; Schaufeli, Taris, & Van Rhenen, 2008). This lack of consistency in the use of the term 'well-being' makes it difficult to compare studies or generalize findings and makes the concept less useful and meaningful. There is a need for researchers within organizational psychology to debate and come to a consensus about what the term well-being means within organizational contexts. A similar problem can be identified within the sport literature on well-being. Reviews of the literature on well-being in sport (e.g., Lundqvist, 2011; Ruoff, 1995) have identified that the term well-being is often poorly defined or not defined at all. Furthermore, Lundqvist found that researchers rarely attempted to locate the concept of well-being in sport within any wider theoretical or conceptual framework – an issue identified by Ruoff sixteen years earlier. There is, therefore, a need for researchers within both the sport and organizational fields to clarify the definition of well-being within these contexts and to make greater use of theory so that the study of well-being can be conducted in a more unified and consistent manner.

Theories and models of well-being

The hedonic approach to well-being has been predominant within the literature and the measurement of subjective well-being (sometimes simply referred to as 'happiness') has now been undertaken by a number of countries, including the UK (Thomas & Evans, 2010). The term 'subjective' is key, since the well-being of individuals in similar circumstances varies widely. Therefore, social indicators of well-being, such as income or funding, are not sufficient (Diener et al., 1999). Subjective well-being has both an affective and cognitive component – the affective aspect being comprised of both positive and negative affect (both are measured since they are to some extent independent, rather than opposite ends of a bipolar scale; Green & Salovey, 1999). The cognitive aspect of subjective well-being is measured by life satisfaction (within the organizational field, job satisfaction could be considered a subcategory of life satisfaction). Subjective well-being has been researched in a wide number of fields over several decades and is consistently correlated with good health, life expectancy, and positive relationships (see Diener, 2009 for a review). However, advocates of the eudaimonic approach to well-being have argued that subjective well-being is not adequate for understanding positive human functioning and that it is important for life to be meaningful and not merely pleasant (Ryan & Deci, 2001).

Eudaimonic well-being is an alternative approach to conceptualizing well-being which stresses the importance of individuals endeavoring to meet their true potential (Ryff & Singer, 2008). The term 'eudaimonia' is taken from the writings of Aristotle (translated by Ross, 1925), who stated that eudaimonia was the highest human good. Whilst eudaimonia has traditionally been translated as 'happiness', Aristotle argued that this was not about pleasure but about acting in accordance with virtue. Ryff and Singer argued that this implies that well-being depends upon goal-directed and purposeful action towards self-realization. Ryff (1989) posited that there are six aspects to eudaimonic well-being: self-acceptance; positive relations with others; autonomy; environmental mastery; purpose in life; and personal growth. Eudaimonic well-being has not been as widely studied as hedonic well-being but has been linked to improved health in a number of studies. For example, one study found that women with high eudaimonic well-being had lower salivary cortisol levels, lower pro-inflammatory cytokines, lower cardiovascular risk, and longer rapid eye movement (REM) sleep compared to those with low psychological well-being (Ryff, Singer, & Love, 2004). Another study found that individuals with high eudaimonic well-being were at lower risk of metabolic syndrome (Boylan & Ryff, 2015). Purpose in life is one aspect of well-being which has been studied separately and has been linked to a range of health outcomes such as lowered risk of Alzheimer's disease (Boyle, Buchman, Barnes, & Bennett, 2010), lower mortality (Boyle, Barnes, Buchman, & Bennett, 2009), reduced risk of stroke (Kim, Sun, Park, & Peterson, 2013), and reduced risk of myocardial infarction in coronary heart disease patients (Kim, Sun, Park, Kubzansky, & Peterson, 2013). Whilst both hedonic and eudaimonic well-being predict health, they appear to be somewhat distinct and predict different outcomes (Ryff, 2014). Including both hedonic and eudaimonic aspects of well-being in our definition and measurement may, therefore, give a fuller understanding of individuals' experiences of well-being (Ryan & Deci, 2001).

Despite our call for the inclusive approach alluded to above, and as previously noted, the literature on workplace well-being has rarely considered the concepts of hedonic and eudaimonic well-being. This area of study emerged from the literature on stress at work and as such has tended to have a less positive focus than the general well-being literature, often focusing on outcomes indicating 'ill-being' rather than well-being such as depression and burnout (e.g., de Jonge et al., 2000). This literature has also leaned heavily on traditional theories and models of stress such as the Demands-Control-Support Model (Karasek & Theorell, 1990) and Effort-Reward Imbalance Model (Siegrist, 1996). Recently, there has been increased interest in more positive concepts of well-being within organizational psychology, such as self-determination theory (SDT; e.g., Van den Broeck, Lens, De Witte, & Van Coillie, 2013). SDT is a theory of motivation, which has been used to predict well-being (Ryan & Deci, 2001). SDT proposes that there are three basic psychological human needs: autonomy; competence; and relatedness. It suggests that these three needs must be fulfilled in order for the individual to experience psychological growth, integrity, and well-being. There is an obvious overlap with the constructs which make up eudaimonic well-being; however, Ryan and Deci argued that autonomy, competence, and relatedness are the main contributors to well-being, rather than them defining well-being. In addition, they argued that SDT can predict hedonic well-being since the fulfilment of these needs would be likely to foster satisfaction with life and positive mood and to reduce negative mood. This theory has the potential to increase the understanding of well-being at work by examining how work environments can fulfil these three needs.

Recent years have seen the development of a validated scale to measure the fulfilment of these needs at work (Van den Broeck, Vansteenkiste, De Witte, Soenens, & Lens, 2010), as well as research supporting the hypothesis that the relationships between organizational factors and well-being is partially mediated by the fulfilment of the three basic needs (e.g., Gillet, Fouquereau, Forest, Brunault, & Colombat, 2012). SDT has also been used as a framework for researching well-being within the sport literature, proving a valuable concept in the pursuit of understanding what influences the well-being of athletes and, potentially, others employed within sport organizations. In considering how this literature might develop, we might note that the fulfilment of the basic needs in SDT is hypothesized to contribute to both optimal functioning and well-being, therefore this theory proposes that performance will increase alongside well-being. This has important implications for research on well-being in sport organizations, since it suggests that performance and well-being are not unrelated outcomes but rather that they stem from the fulfilment of the same needs. Consequently, fulfilment of these basic needs within a sporting performance and organizational setting will likely have a positive impact not only on well-being but also on performance. The integration of the concepts of well-being and performance has the potential, therefore, to contribute both to future research and to the provision of more effective support and management within sporting organizations.

Well-being in sport organizations

The importance of sport organizations appreciating the well-being of their employees has been recently voiced by Wagstaff and Larner (2015). Specifically, they emphasized the need for organizations to monitor the psychological states of employees at the workplace and at home (i.e., work–life balance) to promote effective functioning and engagement, with consideration for the factors that may influence well-being. Of the research that has considered well-being directly within the sporting literature, the majority has focused on the athlete or coach through the eudaimonic and/or hedonic lenses. As alluded to earlier, the focus on 'well-being' through such perspectives is important within sport – to counteract the plethora of work on such negative concepts as stress and anxiety and to guide practitioners on *developing* the 'functional' athlete. Indeed, in their interview study, Lundqvist and Sandin (2014) showed that athletes emphasized the importance of considering factors that characterize and signify their well-being both within and outside the sport – potentially due to the health related benefits, but also due to potential performance gains. Rathschlag and Memmett (2015) showed that athletes perform better in competitive sprinting when happy than when anxious or emotionally neutral.

Of the research that has considered hedonic and eudaimonic well-being within a sporting context, the majority have used well-being as an outcome variable and/or underpinned their work by self-determination theory due to the premise that having basic psychological needs met is beneficial for well-being. Within this section we will discuss those studies that are relevant to sport organizations and consider a number of predictors of well-being. Specifically, those at the organizational level including situational influences such as coach behavior and climate, and those at the personal level including individual influences such as personality, emotional intelligence, interpersonal skills, and goal motives.

Situational influences

Situational influences refer to the behaviors that coaches and teammates may exhibit within the workplace and the climate that coaches or leaders may create for their athletes to feel they can achieve their goals or feel connected to others within that particular organizational context. Generally, research has shown that supportive coaches who promote autonomy within the developmental environment are associated with athletes of higher well-being, possibly due to athletes perceiving their basic psychological needs are being met (Gunnell, Crocker, Mack, Wilson, & Zumbo, 2014; Mack, Wilson, Oster, Kowalski, Crocker, & Sylvester, 2011).

Balaguer, González, Fabra, Castillo, Mercé, and Duda (2012) examined coach interpersonal style, basic needs, and eudaimonic well-being (through vitality) and showed that coaches who supported autonomy improved the perceptions of basic needs being met, which, in turn, was positively associated with vitality. Adie, Duda, and Ntoumanis (2012) also showed increases in perceived autonomy support over time corresponded with increases in athlete vitality. Stenling, Lindwall, and Hassmen (2015) reported similar findings, but with subjective well-being as the outcome variable. Stenling et al. also showed that the more autonomously motivated athletes seek out environments that satisfy their needs to support their autonomous motivation and, in turn, improve well-being. In comparison to these findings, Reinboth, Duda, and Ntoumanis (2004) assessed eudaimonic well-being through vitality and intrinsic satisfaction, and found perceptions of autonomy support to be associated with autonomy, the latter being weakly associated with vitality and intrinsic satisfaction. Despite this finding, these collective results accentuate the importance of a coaching environment that aims to promote autonomy through continually fostering the athletes' perspective, conveying trust in their abilities, and initiating their choices and decision-making.

Kipp and Weiss (2013) examined the broader basic psychological needs of gymnastic performers, perceived coach behaviors, and well-being – focusing both on eudaimonic and hedonic variables. They also considered the motivational climate created by coach and teammate relatedness. The findings showed that a mastery climate did not directly relate to either indices of well-being. However, coach relatedness was associated with positive affect and team relatedness with increased self-esteem. Such findings support the examination of both eudaimonic and hedonic well-being, as different individuals within an organizational context can have an influence on different facets of athlete well-being. In this context, liking or feeling liked by the coach was associated with improved athlete happiness, while feelings of belonging within a team context was related to an improvement in how an athlete felt about him/herself. With regards to psychological needs, autonomy-supportive coach behaviors were associated to positive affect through coach relatedness, and quality of friendship to self-esteem through teammate relatedness. To elaborate, coaches who listened to and promoted more autonomy within their athletes improved the relationship with the athletes, which improved athlete affect. Similarly, athletes who reported high esteem support, loyalty, and companionship to be present within their teammates reported greater team association and, consequently, improved self-esteem.

Kipp and Weiss (2015) extended their work by investigating whether preseason social variables (i.e., motivational climate, coach behaviors, sport friendship quality) predicted well-being indicators in gymnasts during the competitive season, and if such a relationship was mediated by psychological needs. Interestingly, coach and team relatedness were not associated with well-being over time, whereas the performance climate and mastery/autonomy support at preseason both positively predicted self-esteem through perceived competence during the season. These findings emphasize the importance of monitoring well-being over time, given the changes due to fluctuating organizational influences (Wagstaff, Gilmore, & Thelwell, 2015). The findings also support the notion by Gagné, Ryan, and Bargmann (2003) that perceptions of coach autonomy support alongside connectedness with the team can help improve both eudaimonic and hedonic well-being in athletes.

Blanchard, Amiot, Perreault, Vallerand, and Provencher (2009) considered the impact of coach and team behavior on hedonic well-being through coach controlling style and team cohesion respectively. To elaborate, Blanchard et al. (2009) conducted a sequence analysis of the impact of both coach controlling style and team cohesion on perceptions of need satisfaction of athletes, which were hypothesized to impact self-determined motivation, which, in turn, was proposed to have an affect on positive emotions and life satisfaction. Blanchard et al. (2009) found partial support for this sequence, with controlling coach style negatively predicting autonomy and team cohesion and positively predicting all three basic needs. Perceptions of self-determined motivation were then found to mediate the relationship between basic needs and well-being outcomes. These findings may suggest that, irrespective of coach behavior, if other needs are met through being part of a cohesive team then hedonic well-being may be still be positive.

Smith, Ntoumanis, and Duda (2010) also focused on coach controlling behaviors and the impact on athlete hedonic well-being. They illustrated that coach controlling behaviors were positively associated with controlled goal motives, which, in turn, were negatively associated with hedonic well-being. Coach autonomy-supportive behaviors, on the other hand, were positively associated with autonomous goal motives within the athlete, which, in turn, were positively associated with hedonic well-being. Given that no indicators of team cohesion were considered, the findings indicate that in the absence of a cohesive environment, controlling coach behaviors can be to the detriment of hedonic well-being.

Felton and Jowett (2013) investigated the coach–athlete relationship with well-being (hedonic and eudaimonic) through a lens of athlete attachment style and basic psychological needs. That is, they examined whether the satisfaction of athletes' basic psychological needs transfers the effects of athletes' insecure attachment styles (anxious and avoidant) on their levels of hedonic and eudaimonic well-being.

Mediation effects for the satisfaction of basic needs through the coach–athlete relationship were only significant for avoidance attachment style and well-being. This would suggest that if the avoidant-attached athlete perceives low levels of need satisfaction from their coach, then this perception would have a negative effect on their well-being. Davies and Jowett (2014) focused on the linear associations between attachment style, the quality of the coach–athlete relationship, and hedonic well-being. They found that the higher the avoidance attachment style, the lower the perception of support received from the coach, the lower the sense of importance placed on the coach's role within the athlete's life, and the lower the perceived interpersonal conflict. Only interpersonal conflict was then found to be negatively associated with positive affect (hedonic well-being). Unfortunately, this particular study did not consider eudaimonic well-being, therefore not offering more of an insight into how such attachment styles and perceptions of coach behaviors impact the overall well-being of the athletes. Nevertheless, the findings from both these studies suggest that when considering the basic psychological needs of their athletes, coaches need to also be cognizant of whether the athletes need to feel connected to the coach, or are content with a distant relationship to begin with. With such information coaches could aim to create environments that support, nurture, and demonstrate caring for the athlete – this may enhance the athlete's feelings of belonging and benefit well-being.

The climate that the coach creates has been consistently linked to the well-being of the athlete, especially their eudaimonic well-being given the relevance to self-worth and growth. Reinboth and Duda (2004) investigated the influence of task- and ego-involvement climate on adolescent athlete eudaimonic well-being through self-esteem and self-worth. They found that a task-involving environment was positively associated with self-esteem, while ego-involving environments were associated with increases in self-worth. Despite this association, Reinboth and Duda suggested caution in using ego-involving climates, given the possibility that such motivational climates lead to less self-determined behavior and may thwart healthy adjustment. The benefit of a positive, task-involving coach or peer climate on both hedonic and eudaimonic well-being has also been supported, further accentuating the importance of promoting task-involving structures for athletes to feel self-worth, happy, and vigorous while participating in their sport (see Kipp and Weiss, 2015; Ntoumanis, Taylor, & Thøgersen-Ntoumani, 2012; Reinboth & Duda, 2006; Stark & Newton, 2014). Lundqvist and Raglin (2015) conducted a longitudinal investigation of social influence on both hedonic and eudaimonic well-being with elite athletes, and adopted a measure better aligned to the eudaimonic definition than that used in previous research; specifically, Ryff and Keyes's (1995) Psychological Well-being Scale. Findings from the study showed that within an elite sample, motivational climate, as defined by a mastery or performance-orientated climate, was not associated with athlete well-being. Lundqvist and Raglin suggested that these findings were potentially due to the simplicity of defining an elite sporting climate as one that is mastery and performance-orientated.

Other situational influences considered are the lack of selection for major games and the transition out of sport. Both are potentially significant life experiences for athletes and can have significant effects for well-being. For example, Martin, Malone, and Hilyer (2011) showed that those who made a Paralympian basketball team scored higher in vigor and lower in negative mood indices than those who did not get selected. Understanding the well-being profile of those not selected for such tournaments is vital for sport organizations to support these athletes to still feel self-worth and then challenged to grow towards future selection. Stephan, Bilard, Ninot, and Delignieres (2003) longitudinally assessed the transition process out of sport and found that former athletes shifted in psychological adaptation to changes in their lifestyle and socio-professional status over time. Well-being improved over time due to different strategies at different times through transition. That is, distraction-orientated activities early in the process, and the adoption of leisure activities and goals attached to a new professional identity during the later stages, helped the individuals gradually perceive a greater sense of personal control, job accomplishments, and competence.

Individual influences

In comparison to the research that has examined situational influences on, or correlates of, well-being, fewer studies have been conducted into the personal predictors of well-being. Those that have done so have considered such variables as personality, emotional intelligence, interpersonal skills, and goal motives. The personality predictors have included self-esteem, perfectionism, and self-compassion. Lundqvist and Raglin (2015) showed those athletes high in well-being and low in stress to have higher levels of trait self-esteem and lower levels of trait perfectionism than those low in well-being and high in stress – the latter finding having important implications for the athlete striving for excellence. That is, performers with high perfectionistic tendencies may experience regular stress and low well-being, outcomes that have been associated with burnout in sport (Martin, Kelley, & Eklund, 1999). Ferguson, Kowalski, Mack, and Sabiston (2014) examined the relationship between self-compassion on eudaimonic well-being and found a positive relationship. They suggested that self-compassionate athletes are actively engaged with the environment, take initiative, assume responsibility for their actions, emotions, and thoughts, and act of their own volition – the outcome of which is an increase in well-being. In a qualitative follow-up, participants suggested that self-compassion is valuable when failing to meet personal goals or expectations, making mistakes during competition, plateauing, and suffering from injuries. Taken together, this small body of research illuminates the potential influence of personality on the well-being of athletes within the sport organization.

The association between the emotional intelligence of student athletes and their well-being has also been considered (see Bai & Niazi, 2014). Bai and Niazi showed that those athletes with higher levels of emotional intelligence reported greater levels of happiness within their sporting environment, highlighting the importance of being aware of own and others' emotions. In relation to working effectively with 'others', Sharifi and Akbari (2014) compared the interpersonal skills and eudaimonic well-being in athletes and non-athletes. Athletes generally reported better interpersonal skills and well-being. Despite a greater level of well-being reported by the athletes, it is still important for coaches to attempt to develop the social life-skills of athletes further through their developmental sporting practices (Petitpas, Cornelius, & Van Raalte, 2008).

The influence of athletes' goal motives on their well-being was examined by Healey, Ntoumanis, Veldhuijzen van Zanten, and Paine (2014) in an attempt to support the premise that autonomous motives are associated with positive outcomes. They found that athletes who strive with more adaptive autonomous motives demonstrate higher levels of vitality. Smith, Ntoumanis, Duda, and Vansteenkiste (2011) showed that autonomous goals were linked to midseason effort, which positively predicted end of season goal attainment. Further, achieving goals satisfied the needs of these athletes, which, in turn, was positively associated with more positive affect. The promotion of autonomous goal motives, therefore, would seem to benefit the subjective and psychological well-being of athletes.

Only three studies that we identified considered the well-being of populations other than athletes. Specifically, Stebbings and associates have examined the factors that influence coach well-being, and the impact well-being has on their relationship with athletes. For example, Stebbings, Taylor, and Spray (2011) examined coach behaviors, psychological need satisfaction, and coach hedonic and eudaimonic well-being through affect and vitality respectively. They found that the competence and autonomy need satisfaction of the coaches positively predicted their levels of well-being, which, in turn, positively predicted the coaches' perceived autonomy support toward their athletes and negatively predicted their perceived controlling behavior. Stebbings, Taylor, Spray, and Ntoumanis (2012) extended this research and showed opportunities for development and job security predicted psychological need satisfaction, which, in turn, positively predicted affect and vitality. Better well-being was then associated with an adaptive interpersonal style (i.e., perceived autonomy supporting coaching behaviors). Finally, Stebbings, Taylor, and Spray (2015) examined whether changes in psychological well-being were related to perceived autonomy support and control behaviors when working with athletes. Findings showed positive affect and integration of self (eudaimonic well-being) to positively associate with perceived provision of autonomy support. Informed by these results, Stebbings et al. (2015) suggested that coaches high in well-being may be more likely to convey confidence in their athlete's abilities and encourage athletes to ask questions. The work by Stebbings and associates emphasizes the importance of understanding the factors that influence coach well-being for the benefit of both the coach and athlete.

Future research directions

Collectively, the body of research that has focused on the situational and individual influences on well-being with relevance to the sport organization has provided some insight into the ideal coach behaviors, the appropriate team and motivational climate, and the beneficial personal and interpersonal factors. The focus on the 'wellness' of athletes, as opposed to the negative outcomes of organizational and performance demands, has illustrated that athletes (and coaches) can feel happy, satisfied, and prosper within their organizational context – potentially influenced by the satisfaction of basic psychological needs. Despite this encouraging work, the majority of extant research has focused mostly on athletes, has been quantitative in nature, has not considered performance outcomes, and has adopted different conceptualizations of well-being.

Given that individuals at the elite sporting level now operate within an organizational structure that includes business managers, administrators, performance directors, development officers, coaches, medical doctors, psychologists, physiologists, physiotherapists, soft-tissue specialists, strength and conditioning coaches, performance analysts, and, more often than not, numerous interns, a narrow focus is adopted by solely looking at the coach as an influence on athlete well-being. Indeed, it would be beneficial to examine the detailed and complex elite sport environment to assess when and how a support structure works well and positively influences the well-being of athletes. In addition, when considering the potentially stressful support staff role, it is also imperative for researchers to focus on the well-being of these important performance department members. To elaborate, such demands as long, unsociable work hours, often poor remuneration, and excessive travel can have a gradual adverse effect on the well-being of support staff (McCrory, 2007), with the potential outcome being poorer performance, which may have negative implications for the athlete. Research could initially adopt a similar approach to that utilized by Stebbings et al. (2011, 2012, 2015) when they quantitatively examined the perceived influence of coach well-being on factors that could have an effect on the experiences of athletes within the sport organization. However, a more in-depth and longitudinal assessment of support staff well-being and implications for their performance and athlete well-being is warranted.

As noted earlier, the majority of sport research discussed within this chapter is quantitative in nature. This is by no means a criticism of the research, as a number of important predictors of well-being have been established. It is important, however, to extend this research by understanding the complex interplay between predictors and their effect on well-being. For example, future research could explore in-depth how certain coach behaviors help create environments that satisfy the athletes' basic psychological needs, and, in turn, affect self-determination and well-being. It is also important for sport psychology researchers to be more ambitious with their qualitative approaches, adopting more in-depth enquiries through ethnography or through multiple methods (e.g., diaries, questionnaires, observations, interviews), over a long period of time, and with a large proportion of personnel from the organization of interest. The data collected from such a venture would give a more detailed and holistic account of the workings of a sport organization and the impact on support staff and athlete well-being – potentially offering numerous benefits to the organization's structure, planning, communication, environment, and educational processes.

With regards to the well-being–performance relationship, it would not be unreasonable to suggest that an employee within the sport organization who is high in well-being (both hedonic and eudaimonic) would perform better than if he or she were experiencing low levels of well-being. Indeed, an employee who is happy, has high life/role satisfaction, and high perceptions of the factors associated with personal growth should be psychologically better prepared for a performance environment than an employee low in these constructs. Considering these tentative assumptions, it should be the purpose of researchers to examine the influence of well-being on performance – especially given the combined benefits to the individual and the organization. Indeed, it could be a cost-effective option to influence the organizational factors (such as motivational climate) that improve well-being in order to indirectly enhance performance (Reinboth & Duda, 2004).

For those researchers that decide to undertake any of the recommendations offered here to advance knowledge within the area of well-being within sport organizations, we would support Lundqvist's (2011) suggestions for the use of a more uniform definition that is founded in theory and measured by appropriate and reliable inventories. A more consistent approach to studying well-being will allow for comparisons across studies to be made more easily, leading to better conclusions about the climates, behaviors, and interventions that can positively influence well-being within sport organizations.

Interventions for positive well-being

Interventions focused on stress or well-being within organizations have traditionally been couched within primary, secondary, and tertiary categories (see Fletcher, Hanton, & Mellalieu, 2006). Specifically, these categories refer to interventions that: 1) aim to reduce or prevent stressors from occurring (primary); 2) help individuals manage situations as they happen (secondary); or, 3) promote reflection and learning about situations after they have happened (tertiary). Interventions which aim to make changes at an organizational level are often primary interventions aimed at reducing organizational stressors. Primary interventions with an organizational focus will be considered here as they are most relevant to the organizational focus of the chapter. Secondary interventions are also widely used in sport and usually target athletes. These interventions have been reviewed elsewhere (see Rumbold, Fletcher, & Daniels, 2012). Whilst this chapter mainly focuses on primary interventions, all three approaches can be employed by sport organizations for the benefit of employee well-being. At an organizational level, a primary intervention could focus on organizational change (Arnold & Fletcher, 2012). Sport organizations have specific pressures that can lead to a need for organizational change. Major demands have included a move from amateurism to professionalization (see O'Brien & Slack, 2003) and the need for commercialization (see Skinner, Stewart, & Edwards, 1999), as well as demands caused by the wider political and economic context (see Girginov & Sandanski, 2008). However, whilst organizational change has been an active area of study within management literature, few studies have focused on sport organizations (Cruickshank & Collins, 2012; Wagstaff et al., 2015; Wagstaff, Thelwell, & Gilmore, 2016). Moreover, while the studies that have been conducted within sport organizations have rarely considered well-being, those which have, have yielded some important findings. For example, Amis, Slack, and Hinings (2004) found that organizations whose members' values were congruent with change were more successful in transitioning quickly through change. Organizations where values were least congruent with change were unsuccessful in transitioning. Another study of the professionalization of a rugby club found that changes led to a loss of autonomy in volunteers, which resulted in resentment (O'Brien & Slack, 2003). The previous selection committee also had their role taken away, leading to questions about their value. This highlights the need for close collaboration and effective communication between various stakeholder groups during the process of change.

The management literature highlights a number of factors that facilitate positive organizational change, including organizational virtuousness (e.g., compassion and trustworthiness), effective leadership, positive relationships, and psychological capital (for a review of the evidence, see Cameron & McNaughton, 2014). There is a need for more research on organizational change and well-being in sport organizations, and particularly for organizational interventions to increase well-being during the process of organizational change (Wagstaff et al., 2015; Wagstaff et al., 2016). Organizational change management interventions can be difficult to evaluate due to the difficulty of having appropriate controls in place, and the current evidence base is in need of more high quality intervention studies (Barends, Janssen, ten Have, & ten Have, 2014). In general, however, organizational interventions that increase control, decrease demands, and increase support tend to increase employee well-being (Bambra, Egan, Thomas, Petticrew, & Whitehead, 2007; Egan, Bambra, Thomas, Petticrew, Whitehead, & Thomson, 2007), and change management interventions would benefit from considering these factors.

Given that most of the research on athlete well-being has focused on coach or climate influences, another recommended primary intervention is the education of coaches about potential implications of certain behaviors and climates on athlete well-being and performance (Wagstaff & Larner, 2015). In addition, guidance is needed on how to develop the appropriate coaching behaviors and climates that are proposed to facilitate the growth of the athlete through the satisfaction of their psychological basic needs. Coaches who can provide their athletes with choice in the developmental environment (Smith et al., 2010), a sense of mastery to improve competence through appropriate feedback (Kipp & Weiss, 2015), and a feeling of belonging through positive relations (Gagné et al., 2003), will likely nurture athletes with high levels of well-being.

The concept of eudaimonic well-being allows for interventions that promote psychological strength building. That is, strategies that acknowledge and facilitate such strengths as accepting one's self, positive relations with others, autonomy, environmental mastery, gaining and maintaining a purpose in life, and personal growth. One such tertiary strategy could be reflective practice (Knowles, Katz, & Gilbourne, 2012). Reflecting in a balanced manner (i.e., what went well and what could be better) after a situation has occurred might promote increased levels in eudaimonic well-being. At a basic level, guiding individuals to reflect on what they did well within a situation could help them to identify the strategies and behaviors that encouraged good relations and helped them master a task. By knowing what they did to make a situation go well could also improve their autonomy in similar future contexts. Focusing on what didn't go well, and what could be done to improve performance in future situations can promote acceptance of what occurred and instill purpose to do better next time. This balanced approach helps to identify personal growth and improves maintenance of appropriate strategies and behaviors (Neil, Cropley, Wilson, & Faull, 2013).

Conclusion

The concept of 'well-being' within a sporting organization has been narrow in focus and variably operationalized. The primary focus of researchers has been on a selection of situational and individual factors that may influence well-being, potentially mediated by the perceived satisfying of basic psychological needs, while the different definitions and methods adopted have limited between-study comparison. Despite these limitations, the findings of the current literature offer some insight into the appropriate intra- and interpersonal behaviors and environmental conditions to facilitate athlete well-being. The complexity of the organizational context was acknowledged within the discussion of future research directions, with emphasis placed on the need for an agreed conceptualization of well-being to guide examination into the impact of support staff on athlete well-being; the well-being of all employees within the sport organization and the conditions that facilitate well-being; and the association between well-being and performance. From an applied perspective, the current literature and theoretical lenses adopted within this chapter (i.e., hedonic and eudaimonic well-being) have steered interventions that target the organizational and individual levels. In summarizing this review, we would like to draw the reader to the following considerations:

- There needs to be a clearer definition of well-being within the sport literature and research needs to be more contextualized within a consistent and recognized theoretical framework (Lundqvist, 2011).

- Organizational factors including coach behaviors, motivational climate, and team relatedness can influence well-being.
- Individual factors which predict well-being include trait self-esteem, trait perfectionism, self-compassion, emotional intelligence, and autonomous goal motives.
- It is suggested that future research should focus on all staff working within sport organizations and not solely athletes; and should consider the effects of organizational environments on well-being and look at the relationship between well-being and performance. In addition, more qualitative research would complement and deepen our existing understanding of well-being in sport.
- Potential interventions to increase well-being in sport organizations include positive organizational change management and educating coaches on displaying behaviors and creating environments which facilitate well-being and reflective practice.

References

Adie, J. W., Duda, J. L., & Ntoumanis, N. (2012). Perceived coach-autonomy support, basic need satisfaction and the well- and ill-being of elite youth soccer players: A longitudinal investigation. *Psychology of Sport and Exercise, 13*, 51–59.

Amis, J., Slack, T., & Hinings, C. R. (2004). The pace, sequence and linearity of radical change. *The Academy of Management Journal, 47*(1), 15–39.

Aristotle. (1925). *The Nicomachean Ethics*. Ross, D., translator. New York: Oxford University Press.

Arnold, R., & Fletcher, D. (2012). A research synthesis and taxonomic classification of the organizational stressors encountered by sport performers. *Journal of Sport & Exercise Psychology, 34*, 397–429.

Bai, N., & Niazi, S. M. (2014). The relationship between emotional intelligence and happiness in collegiate champions (Case study: Jiroft University). *European Journal of Experimental Biology, 4*, 587–590.

Balaguer, I., González, L., Fabra, P., Castillo, I., Mercé, J., & Duda, J. L. (2012). Coaches' interpersonal style, basic psychological needs and the well- and ill-being of young soccer players: A longitudinal analysis. *Journal of Sports Sciences, 30*, 1619–1629.

Bambra, C., Egan, M., Thomas, S., Petticrew, M., & Whitehead, M. (2007). The psychosocial and health effects of workplace reorganisation. 2. A systematic review of task restructuring interventions. *Journal of Epidemiology & Community Health, 61*, 1028–1037.

Barends, E., Janssen, B., ten Have, W., & ten Have, S. (2014). Effects of change interventions: What kind of evidence do we really have? *The Journal of Applied Behavioral Science, 50*, 5–27.

Blanchard, C. M., Amiot, C. E., Perreault, S., Vallerand, R. J., & Provencher, P. (2009). Cohesiveness, coach's interpersonal style and psychological needs: Their effects on self-determination and athletes' subjective well-being. *Psychology of Sport and Exercise, 10*(5), 545-551.

Boylan, J. M., & Ryff, C. D. (2015). Psychological well-being and metabolic syndrome: findings from the midlife in the United States national sample. *Psychosomatic Medicine, 77*(5), 548–558.

Boyle, P. A., Barnes, L. L., Buchman, A. S., & Bennett, D. A. (2009). Purpose in life is associated with mortality among community-dwelling older persons. *Psychosomatic Medicine, 71*(5), 574–579.

Boyle, P. A., Buchman, A. S., Barnes, L. L., & Bennett, D. A. (2010). Effect of a purpose in life on risk of incident Alzheimer disease and mild cognitive impairment in community-dwelling older persons. *Archives of General Psychiatry, 67*, 304–310.

Bradburn, N. M. (1969). *The structure of psychological well-being.* Chicago, IL: Aldine.

Cameron, K., & McNaughton, J. (2014). Positive organizational change. *The Journal of Applied Behavioral Science, 50*(4), 445–462.

Cruickshank, A., & Collins, D. (2012). Change management: The case of the elite sport performance team. *Journal of Change Management, 12*, 209–229.

Davies, L., & Jowett, S. (2014). Coach-athlete attachment and the quality of the coach-athlete relationship: Implications for athlete's well-being. *Journal of Sports Sciences, 32*, 1454–1464.

de Jonge, J., Bosma, H., Peter, R., & Siegrist, J. (2000). Job strain, effort-reward imbalance and employee well-being: A large-scale cross-sectional study. *Social Science & Medicine, 50*, 1317–1327.

Diener, E. (2009). Subjective well-being. In E. Deiner (Ed.), *Social indicators of research series. The science of well-being* (Vol. 37, pp. 11–58). New York: Springer.

Diener, E., Suh, E. M., Lucas, R. E., & Smith, H. L. (1999). Subjective well-being: Three decades of progress. *Psychological Bulletin, 125*, 276–302.

Dodge, R., Daly, A. P., Huyton, J., & Sanders, L. D. (2012). The challenge of defining wellbeing. *International Journal of Well-being, 2*, 222–235.

Dolan, P., Peasgood, T., & White, M. (2008). Do we really know what makes us happy? A review of the economic literature on the factors associated with subjective well-being. *Journal of Economic Psychology, 29*, 94–122.

Egan, M., Bambra, C., Thomas, S., Petticrew, M., Whitehead, M., & Thomson, H. (2007). The psychosocial and health effects of workplace reorganisation 1: A systematic review of organisational-level interventions that aim to increase employee control. *Journal of Epidemiology & Community Health, 61*, 945–954.

Felton, L., & Jowett, S. (2013). Attachment and well-being: The mediating effects of psychological needs satisfaction within the coach-athlete and parent-athlete relational contexts. *Psychology of Sport and Exercise, 14*, 57–65.

Ferguson, L., Kowalski, K. C., Mack, D. E., & Sabiston, C. M. (2014). Exploring self-compassion and eudaimonic well-being in young women athletes. *Journal of Sport & Exercise Psychology, 36*, 203–216.

Fletcher, D., Hanton, S., & Mellalieu, S. D. (2006). An organizational stress review: Conceptual and theoretical issues in competitive sport. In S. Hanton & S. D. Mellalieu (Eds.), *Literature reviews in sport psychology* (pp. 321–374). Hauppauge, NY: Nova Science.

Fleuret, S., & Atkinson, S. (2007). Well-being, health and geography: A critical review and research agenda. *New Zealand Geographer, 63*, 106–118.

Gagné, M., Ryan, R. M., & Bargmann, K. (2003). Autonomy support and need satisfaction in the motivation and well-being of gymnasts. *Journal of Applied Sport Psychology, 15*, 372–390.

Gillet, N., Fouquereau, E., Forest, J., Brunault, P., & Colombat, P. (2012). The impact of organizational factors on psychological needs and their relations with well-being. *Journal of Business Psychology, 27*, 437–450.

Girginov, V., & Sandanski, I. (2008). Understanding the changing nature of sports organizations in transforming societies. *Sport Management Review, 11*, 21–50. doi:10.1016/S1441-3523(08)70102-5.

Green, D. P., & Salovey, P. (1999). In what sense are positive and negative affect independent?: A reply to Tellegen, Watson, and Clark. *Psychological Science, 10*, 304–306.

Gunnell, K. E., Crocker, P. R. E., Mack, D. E., Wilson, P. M., & Zumbo, B. D. (2014). Goal contents, motivation, psychological need satisfaction, well-being and physical activity: A test of self-determination theory over 6 months. *Psychology of Sport and Exercise, 15*, 19–29.

Häusser, J. A., Mojzisch, A., Niesel, M., & Schulz-Hardt, S. (2010). Ten years on: A review of recent research on the Job Demand-Control (-Support) model and psychological well-being. *Work & Stress, 24*, 1–35.

Healey, L. C., Ntoumanis, N., Veldhuijzen van Zanten, J. J. C. S., & Paine, N. (2014). Goal striving and well-being in sport: The role of contextual and personal motivation. *Journal of Sport & Exercise Psychology, 36*, 446–459.

Jayawickreme, E., Forgeard, M. J. C., & Seligman, M. E. P. (2012). The engine of well-being. *Review of General Psychology, 16*, 327–342.

Karasek, R. A, & Theorell, T. (1990). *Healthy work: Stress, productivity and the reconstruction of working life*. New York: Basic Books.

Kim, E. S., Sun, J. K., Park, N., Kubzansky, L., & Peterson, C. (2013). Purpose in life and reduced risk of myocardial infarction among older U.S. Adults with coronary heart disease: A two-year follow-up. *Journal of Behavioral Medicine, 13*, 124–133.

Kim, E. S., Sun, J. K., Park, N., & Peterson, C. (2013). Purpose in life and reduced stroke in older adults: The health and retirement study. *Journal of Psychosomatic Research, 74*, 427–432.

Kipp, L. E., & Weiss, M. R. (2013). Social influences, psychological need satisfaction, and well-being among female gymnasts. *Sport, Exercise, and Performance Psychology, 2*, 62–75.

Kipp, L. E., & Weiss, M. R. (2015). Social predictors of psychological need satisfaction and well-being among female adolescent gymnasts: A longitudinal analysis. *Sport, Exercise, and Performance Psychology, 4*(3), 153–169.

Knowles, Z., Katz, J., & Gilbourne D. (2012). Critical reflective practice within elite consultancy: A personal and elusive process. *The Sport Psychologist, 26*, 454–469.

Lundqvist, C. (2011). Well-being in competitive sports – The feel-good factor? A review of conceptual considerations of well-being. *International Review of Sport and Exercise Psychology, 4*, 109–127.

Lundqvist, C., & Raglin, J. (2015). The relationship of basic need satisfaction, motivational climate and personality to well-being and stress patterns among elite athletes: An exploratory study. *Motivation and Emotion, 39*, 237–246.

Lundqvist, C., & Sandin, F. (2014). Well-being in elite sport: Dimensions of hedonic and eudaimonic well-being among elite orienteers. *The Sport Psychologist, 28*, 245–254.

Mack, D. E., Wilson, P. M., Oster, K. G., Kowalski, K. C., Crocker, P. R. E., & Sylvester, B. D. (2011). Well-being in volleyball players: Examining the contributions of independent and balanced psychological need satisfaction. *Psychology of Sport and Exercise, 12*, 533–539.

Martin, J. J., Kelley, B., & Eklund, R. C. (1999) A model of stress and burnout in male high school athletic directors. *Journal of Sport & Exercise Psychology, 21*, 280–294.

Martin, J. J., Malone, L. A., & Hilyer, J. C. (2011). Personality and mood in women's Paralympic basketball champions. *Journal of Clinical Sport Psychology, 5*, 197–210.

McCrory, P. (2007). The long dark night of the sports medicine soul. *British Journal of Sports Medicine, 41*, 343–345

Neil, R., Cropley, B., Wilson, K., & Faull, A. (2013). Exploring the value of reflective practice interventions within applied sport psychology: Case studies with an individual athlete and a team. *Sport & Exercise Psychology Review, 9*(2), 42–56.

Ntoumanis, N., Taylor, I. M., & Thøgersen-Ntoumani, C. (2012). A longitudinal examination of coach and peer motivational climates in youth sport: Implications for moral attitudes, well-being, and behavioral investment. *Developmental Psychology, 48*, 213–233.

O'Brien, D., & Slack, T. (2003). An analysis of change in an organizational field: The professionalization of English Rugby Union. *Journal of Sport Management, 17*, 417–448.

Parkinson, J. (2006). Establishing national mental health and well-being indicators for Scotland. *Journal of Public Mental Health, 5*, 42–48.

Petitpas, A. J., Cornelius, A. E., & Van Raalte, J. (2008). Youth development through sport: It's all about relationships. In N. Holt (Ed.), *Positive youth development through sport* (pp. 61–70). New York: Routledge.

Rathschlag, M., & Memmett, D. (2015). Self-generated emotions and their influence on sprint performance: An investigation of happiness and anxiety. *Journal of Applied Sport Psychology, 27*, 186–199.

Reinboth, M., & Duda, J. L. (2004). The motivational climate, perceived ability, and athletes' psychological and physical well-being. *The Sport Psychologist, 18*, 237–251.

Reinboth, M., & Duda, J. L. (2006). Perceived motivational climate, need satisfaction and indices of well-being in team sports: A longitudinal perspective. *Psychology of Sport and Exercise, 7*(3), 269–286.

Reinboth, M., Duda, J. L., & Ntoumanis, N. (2004). Dimensions of coaching behavior, need satisfaction, and the psychological and physical welfare of young athletes. *Motivation and Emotion, 28*, 297–313.

Rumbold, J. L., Fletcher, D., & Daniels, K. (2012). A systematic review of stress management interventions with sport performers. *Sport, Exercise and Performance Psychology, 1*, 173–193.

Ruoff, M. K. (1995). *A literature review investigating the relationship between sports participation and psychological well-being.* Doctoral research paper. La Mirada, CA: Biola University.

Ryan, R. M., & Deci, E. L. (2001). On happiness and human potentials: A review of research on hedonic and eudaimonic well-being. *Annual Review of Psychology 2001, 52*, 141–166.

Ryff, C. D. (1989). Happiness is everything, or is it? Explorations on the meaning of psychological well-being. *Journal of Personality and Social Psychology, 57*, 1069–1081.

Ryff, C. D. (2014). Psychological well-being revisited: Advances in science and practice. *Psychotherapy and Psychosomatics, 83*, 10–28.

Ryff, C. D., & Keyes, C. L. M. (1995). The structure of psychological well-being revisited. *Journal of Personality and Social Psychology, 69*, 719–727.

Ryff, C. D., & Singer, B. H. (2008). Know thyself and become what you are: A eudaimonic approach to psychological well-being. *Journal of Happiness Studies, 9*, 13–39.

Ryff, C. D., Singer, B. H., & Love, G. (2004). Positive health: Connecting well-being with biology. *Philosophical Transaction of the Royal Society of London. Series, B, Biological Sciences, 359*, 1383–1394.

Schaufeli, W. B., Taris, T. W., & Van Rhenen, W. (2008). Workaholism, burnout and engagement: Three of a kind or three different kinds of employee well-being? *Applied Psychology: An International Review, 57*, 173–203.

Seligman, M. E. P. (1999). The president's address (annual report). *American Psychologist, 54*, 559–562.

Sharifi, T., & Akbari, R. (2014). Study and comparison of interpersonal skills and psychological well being of athletes and non-athletes female. *Journal of Applied Environmental and Biological Sciences, 5*, 40–45.

Siegrist, J. (1996). Adverse health effects of high-effort/ low-reward conditions. *Journal of Occupational Health Psychology, 1*(1), 27–41.

Skinner, J., Stewart, B., & Edwards, A. (1999). Amateurism to professionalism: Modeling organizational change in sporting organizations. *Sport Management Review, 2*, 173–192. doi:10.1016/S1441-3523(99)70095-1.

Smith, A., Ntoumanis, N., & Duda, J. L. (2010). An investigation of coach behaviors, goal motives, and implementation intentions as predictors of well-being in sport. *Journal of Applied Sport Psychology, 22*, 17–33.

Smith, A. L., Ntoumanis, N., Duda, J. L., & Vansteenkiste, M. (2011). Goal striving, coping, and well-being: A prospective investigation of the self-concordance model in sport. *Journal of Sport & Exercise Psychology, 33*(1), 124–145.

Stark, A., & Newton, M. (2014). A dancer's well-being: The influence of the social psychological climate during adolescence. *Psychology of Sport and Exercise, 15*, 356–363.

Stebbings, J., Taylor, I. M., & Spray, C. M. (2011). Antecedents of perceived coach autonomy supportive and controlling behaviors: Coach psychological need satisfaction and well-being. *Journal of Sport & Exercise Psychology, 33*, 255–272.

Stebbings, J., Taylor, I. M., & Spray, C. M. (2015). The relationship between well- and ill-being, and perceived autonomy supportive and controlling interpersonal styles: A longitudinal study of sport coaches. *Psychology of Sport and Exercise, 19*, 42–49.

Stebbings, J., Taylor, I. M., Spray, C. M., & Ntoumanis, N. (2012). Antecedents of perceived coach interpersonal behaviors: The coaching environment and coach psychological well- and ill-being. *Journal of Sport & Exercise Psychology, 34*, 481–502.

Stenling, A., Lindwall, M., & Hassmen, P. (2015). Changes in perceived autonomy support, need satisfaction, motivation, and well-being in young elite athletes. *Sport, Exercise, and Performance Psychology, 4*, 50–61.

Stephan, Y., Bilard, J., Ninot, G., & Delignieres, D. (2003). Repercussions of transition out of elite sport on subjective well-being: A one-year study. *Journal of Applied Sport Psychology, 15*, 354–371.

Thomas, J., & Evans, J. (2010). There's more to life than GDP but how can we measure it? *Economic & Labour Market Review, 4*, 29–36

Van den Broeck, A., Lens, W., De Witte, H., & Van Coillie, H. (2013). Unravelling the importance of the quantity and the quality of workers' motivation for well-being: A person-centered perspective. *Journal of Vocational Behavior, 82*, 69–78.

Van den Broeck, A., Vansteenkiste, M., De Witte, H., Soenens, B., & Lens, W. (2010). Capturing autonomy, competence, and relatedness at work: Construction and initial validation of the work-related basic need satisfaction scale. *Journal of Occupational and Organizational Psychology, 83*, 981–1002.

Wagstaff, C. R. D., & Larner, R. J. (2015). Organisational psychology in sport: Recent developments and a research agenda. In S. D. Mellalieu & S. Hanton (Eds.), *Contemporary advances in sport psychology: A review* (pp. 91–119). London: Routledge.

Wagstaff, C. R. D., Gilmore, S., & Thelwell, R. C. (2015). Sport medicine and sport science practitioners' experiences of organizational change. *Scandinavian Journal of Medicine & Science in Sports, 25*, 685–698.

Wagstaff, C. R. D., Gilmore, S., & Thelwell, R. C. (2016). When the show must go on: Investigating repeated organizational change in elite sport. *Journal of Change Management, 16*(1), 38–54. doi:10.1080/14697017.2015.1062793.

7

RESILIENCE IN SPORT

A critical review of psychological processes, sociocultural influences, and organizational dynamics

Christopher R. D. Wagstaff, Mustafa Sarkar, Claire L. Davidson, and David Fletcher

Introduction

The pressures faced by athletes who compete in sport around the world are extensive and can originate from a variety of sources (see, e.g., Arnold & Fletcher, 2012; Gould, Jackson, & Finch, 1993; Mellalieu, Neil, Hanton, & Fletcher, 2009; Scanlan, Stein, & Ravizza, 1991; Thelwell, Weston, & Greenlees, 2007). These stressors may be associated with an athlete's competitive performance, organizational environment, or personal "non-sporting" life events (Fletcher, Hanton, & Mellalieu, 2006; see also Sarkar & Fletcher, 2014). It is common for researchers as well as coaches, performance directors, and sport organizations to delineate between athletes and teams who thrive under pressure and achieve peak performances and those who yield to pressure and underperform. These differences are often attributed to the concept of resilience with some researchers indicating that resilience is a prerequisite for sporting success (Holt & Dunn, 2004; Mills, Butt, Maynard, & Harwood, 2012; Van Yperen, 2009).

Over the past couple of decades, our understanding of human behavior in demanding situations has developed rapidly, with resilience being examined across a range of contexts, including business organizations (see, e.g., Riolli & Savicki, 2003), education (see, e.g., Johnson et al., 2014), health care settings (see, e.g., Hart, Brannan, & De Chesnay, 2014), the military (see, e.g., Masten, 2013), and communities (see, e.g., Brennan, 2008). This research has been instrumental in developing our understanding of resilience and in creating successful intervention programs to develop resilience in some of these domains (see, e.g., Arnetz, Nevedal, Lumley, Backman, & Lublin, 2009; McDonald, Jackson, Wilkes, & Vickers, 2012,

2013; Reivich, Seligman, & McBride, 2011). Nevertheless, it is now widely agreed among researchers that resilience is best understood when it is considered in a context-specific domain (Luthar & Cicchetti, 2000), indicating that it is not wise to assume that models of resilience in other domains will necessarily be applicable to the context of competitive sport. Moreover, recent evidence suggests that problems may occur when applying key findings of resilience research to athletes. That is, the voluntary nature of sport sets it apart from many other domains because athletes often intentionally immerse themselves in challenging and stressful situations to develop and deliver their performance (Fletcher & Sarkar, 2012).

Recently, due to increasing popularity, a growing body of work has emerged exploring resilience specifically in athletes (Fletcher & Sarkar, 2012; Galli & Vealey, 2008; Machida, Irwin, & Feltz, 2013; Martin-Krumm, Sarrazin, Peterson, & Famose, 2003; Mummery, Schofield, & Perry, 2004; Schinke & Jerome, 2002; Seligman, Nolen-Hoeksema, Thornton, & Thornton, 1990) and teams (Morgan, Fletcher, & Sarkar, 2013, 2015). Further, a recent review of the literature has helped to clarify our understanding of resilience in these populations by evaluating current conceptualizations of resilience research in sport and offering areas of future research development (Galli & Gonzalez, 2015). Although Galli and Gonzalez (2015) provided a thorough overview of the literature in this domain, their review paid little attention to the practical applications of current knowledge or the influence of sociocultural factors and context, which have been identified as important for resilience in sport performers (Galli & Vealey, 2008; Machida et al., 2013) and an important area for future sport researchers to explore (Sarkar & Fletcher, 2014). The absence of the latter topic is somewhat surprising because, as highlighted by Ungar (2012), both "culture and context shape the environment in which processes associated with resilience occur, making some processes more crucial to adaptation and growth than others" (p. 387). We agree with this sentiment and argue here that sociocultural factors and organizational contexts hold significant implications for the definition and development of resilience.

In this chapter, we critically review the psychological processes underpinning the sociocultural influences on, and the organizational dynamics surrounding, resilience in athletes and teams. To this end, the narrative is divided into five main sections. The first section defines resilience. The second section reviews the psychological processes underpinning resilience in athletes and teams. The third section reviews the sociocultural influences on resilience in athletes and teams. The fourth section reviews the organizational dynamics surrounding resilience in athletes and teams. The fifth section proposes a research agenda for the future study of resilience in sport. The final section concludes the review with the main take-home messages for the reader.

Defining resilience

The term resilience in its most basic form refers to the ability of a substance to regain its shape following deformation (Geller et al., 2003). When used in relation to humans, resilience has been used to describe different types of people in a range of contexts. Literature across various domains of psychology has provided numerous definitions which vary significantly and are dependent on the context of activity investigated and conceptualization of resilience as a trait or process (see, for a review, Fletcher & Sarkar, 2013). Despite the construct being conceived in different ways, researchers generally agree that for resilience to be demonstrated both adversity and positive adaptation must be evident (Fletcher & Sarkar, 2013). Based on consistent themes in their review of the resilience literature, Fletcher and Sarkar recently defined psychological resilience as "the role of mental processes and behavior in promoting personal assets and protecting an individual from the potential negative effect of stressors" (2012, p. 675; 2013, p. 16). This definition extends previous conceptual work in this area in a number of ways. First, the focus on *psychological* resilience delimits the scope of the description, by definition, to "mental processes and behavior" and excludes other types of resilience such as physical, molecular, and structural resilience. Second, this definition encapsulates aspects of both trait and process conceptualizations of resilience (cf. Fletcher & Sarkar, 2012; 2013). Regarding the trait conceptualization, the "mental processes and behavior" enable individuals to adapt to the circumstances they encounter (cf. Connor & Davidson, 2003). The process conceptualization conceives resilience as a capacity that develops over time in the context of person–environment interactions (Egeland, Carlson, & Sroufe, 1993). Central to the process definition is the emphasis on the *role* that psychological-related phenomena play – rather than the mental processes and behavior per se – in avoiding negative consequences. Third, emphasis is placed on the neutral term "stressor" rather than the negative term "adversity" (cf. Fletcher & Sarkar, 2013). Fourth, the focus is on "promoting personal assets and protecting an individual from the potential negative effect of stressors" rather than positive adaptation per se, because resilience generally refers to the ability of individuals to maintain normal levels of functioning rather than the restoration or enhancement of functioning (cf. Bonanno, 2004).

In addition to the above definitional advances, several additional conceptual considerations are particularly worth highlighting in the context of this review. First, humanistic psychologists (see, e.g., Friedman & Robbins, 2012) have argued that the assumption that resilience is a virtue across all contexts leads well-intentioned theory, research, and praxis astray and is germane for resilience to become a vice instead of a virtue in some circumstances. That is, Friedman and Robbins proposed that positive psychology has tended to decontextualize resilience as a stand-alone virtue by locating it as an individual trait and leaving the concept open to misunderstanding and misapplication. It follows that researchers should provide a clear indication as to whether their work is focused on resilience as a process or a personality trait, or both. We concur with others' recommendations (e.g., Luthar et al., 2000; Masten, 1994) that competence despite adversity should be referred to by the term "resilience" but never "resiliency", which carries the misleading connotation of a discrete personal attribute. Thus, the term "resilience" should be used when referring to the process or phenomenon of competence despite adversity, with the term "resiliency" used only when referring to a specific personality trait (Luthar et al., 2000).

Second, and as alluded to earlier, additional conceptual considerations allied with the various definitions of resilience lie in their limited acknowledgment of sociological and cultural utility (Fletcher & Sarkar, 2013). For instance, following a review of resilience theory, disability researchers Hutcheon and Lashewicz (2014) argued that, to date, the concept of resilience is overly prescriptive and constrained by hegemony, positivism, and ability-centrism. The authors argued that, when unbounded, resilience might more robustly reflect the complexities of relationships and life processes of those deemed to be "impaired", and whom the authors concluded are marginalized by current definitions of resilience. In a data-driven follow-up, Hutcheon and Lashewicz (2015) argued that current definitions of family resilience are tied to notions of the traditional or normal family, which are often at odds with diverse forms taken by contemporary families. Moreover, the authors noted that, according to extant definitions, resilience is understood relative to normative definitions of health, wellness, and able-bodiedness and necessitates that resilience comprises demonstrations of competence, positive adaptation, or fulfillment of culturally appropriate milestones. In turn, these expectations are treated as universal, when in fact they are socially constructed and sanctioned (Walsh, 2002) and vary across cultures (Ungar, 2008). In sum, although psychological resilience is, by definition, centrally focused on intra-individual processes, greater consideration and sensitivity to sociocultural and organizational influences is required to gain a more complete understanding of the phenomenon (Fletcher & Sarkar, 2013; Sarkar & Fletcher, 2014).

Third, some researchers have problemized the use of the term "resilience" and put forward a case for understanding the resilience of soldiers with more complexity by linking the military imperative with the "inherent resilience" of the soldiers' body and mind within the military as a total institution (see McGarry, Walklate, & Mythen, 2015). Indeed, McGarry et al. hypothesized that the fostering of resilience within the moral careers of soldiers – perpetually working to a resilient military imperative – casts a dark shadow of hegemonic masculinity, gender-role conflicts, and stigma, resulting in demobilization and reintegration problems for some military veterans. Collectively, the concerns raised by scholars with current definitions of resilience have much to do with the absence of sociocultural and contextual sensitivity.

Psychological processes underpinning resilience in athletes and teams

Interest in resilience has a long history in general psychology (see, for a review, Fletcher & Sarkar, 2013; Windle, 2011), but until recently has only been sporadically studied by sport psychology researchers. We delineate these efforts between two chronologically-defined time periods: early studies (1990–2004) and recent studies (2008–present).

Psychological resilience in sport: early studies (1990–2004)

The earliest studies to explore resilience in sport performers largely centered on the role of resilience as a dependent variable in the stress–injury relationship or an individual's explanatory style. Specifically, Smith, Smoll, and Ptacek (1990) examined the ways in which moderator variables interact with one another to increase vulnerability or resilience in the life stress–athletic injury relationship. The authors' findings indicated that social support and psychological coping skills were statistically independent psychosocial resources and operated in a conjunctive manner to influence the relationship between life stress and subsequent athletic injury in adolescents. Adopting an explanatory style perspective, Seligman et al. (1990) examined failure in university swimmers by falsely notifying them that they had swam slower than their actual performance on a time trial. A comparison was then made between the first and second trial, which was completed later. The results indicated that swimmers in possession of an optimistic explanatory style swam a time on their second trial that was equal to, or faster, than their first trial. This work was later extended by Martin-Krumm et al. (2003) who manipulated the beliefs of high school students by telling them that they had not performed as well in a basketball task in comparison to others. In findings that were similar to those of Seligman et al. (1990), participants with an optimistic explanatory style performed better on the second trial than comparable participants with a pessimistic outlook. In Martin-Krumm et al.'s study, the relationship between explanatory style and participants' dribbling performance after perceived failure was also affected by their anxiety levels and success expectations. Here, an optimistic explanatory style was correlated with expectations of successful performance prior to the second trial and lower state anxiety which, in turn, were also linked to improved performance in the dribbling task.

More recently, Mummery et al. (2004) sought to improve the ecological validity of the then nascent findings by exploring resilience in swimmers who were competing in a real national competition. Swimmers were classified as resilient if they were able to improve their qualifying time after initially failing to do so during an earlier round. The results supported earlier findings (Martin-Krumm et al., 2003; Seligman et al., 1990), showing that athletes classified as resilient had higher perceptions of physical endurance, indicating a more optimistic outlook. Interestingly, the results also identified that these swimmers had lower levels of social support than those who did not perform well following initial failure. The authors explained these results by stating that the swimmers who displayed resilience may have been able to act in a more independent manner in unfamiliar surroundings than their non-resilient counterparts. In particular, placing less emphasis on requiring social support to achieve sporting success. However, it is important to note that the swimmers may not have perceived the inability to match their qualifying time as a stressor. This is because it is common practice for swimmers to limit their performance in earlier heats to preserve energy for later, more challenging, races where optimum performance is required.

The applied nature of these aforementioned studies and their examination of performance are important and the findings highlight that practitioners should consider explanatory styles when working with athletes to develop resilience. Indeed, based on these studies, Schinke and colleagues (e.g., Schinke & Jerome, 2002; Schinke, Peterson, & Couture, 2004) created the first sport resilience training program. Their interventions primarily focused on developing optimism skills and were deemed relatively successful by the authors in enhancing resilience in athletes and teams. Despite these positive outcomes, it is important to note that there are several limitations allied with the early interventions and the research on which it was based. For example, by focusing solely on optimism and its role in enabling athletes to overcome setbacks, these interventions elided other factors which play a role in athletes' resilience (see Galli & Gonzalez, 2015; Sarkar & Fletcher, 2014). In addition, the studies also exclusively explored the role of explanatory style in overcoming the stressor of failure. This approach restricts our practical understanding of how applicable an optimistic style is to athletes encountering other demands such as organizational stressors (Hanton, Wagstaff, & Fletcher, 2012). In addition, the research reviewed in this section generally establishes resilience based on the criteria of winning or increased performance such as swimming faster. From a sociocultural perspective, such criteria have limitations since they do not acknowledge the individual goals of the performer or characterize what success is for stakeholders, teams or organizations (cf. Ungar, 2008). Finally, by focusing on resilience from a trait perspective, the early studies reviewed in this section failed to capture the person–environment interactions characteristic of contemporary conceptualizations of resilience as a dynamic process (Fletcher & Sarkar, 2013; Windle, 2011).

Psychological resilience in sport: recent studies (2008–present)

More recently, researchers have adopted a more holistic approach to the conceptualization of resilience, incorporating the use of qualitative designs to unearth the processes that influence an athlete's ability to manage adversity and stressors. The first study to investigate resilience in this way was by Galli and Vealey (2008) who, through the use of interviews, explored athletes' perceptions of resilience in relation to the most difficult adversity they had encountered. The authors' used their findings to propose a framework highlighting that, following adversity, athletes experienced agitation (e.g., the use of a variety of coping strategies). In turn, this process resulted in positive outcomes including increased learning, motivation, and perspective. Further, the authors also remarked that these positive outcomes were in part a result of pre-existing sociocultural influences and personal resources.

Despite providing a valuable first insight into resilience as a process in sport, it could be argued that Galli and Vealey's (2008) study had some notable limitations. Specifically, during the interviews the athletes were asked to talk about only the most difficult adversity that they had overcome. Although pragmatic and amenable to a "tighter" research design, such foci might be considered an oversimplification of the participants' sporting experience and could limit the ecological validity of the study since athletes typically encounter various challenges concurrently rather than in isolation (cf. Galli & Reel, 2012). Furthermore, Galli and Vealey's study has received criticism for being overly reliant on Richardson (2002) and colleagues' (Richardson, Neiger, Jensen, & Kumpfer, 1990) resiliency model (Fletcher & Sarkar, 2012; Sarkar & Fletcher, 2014). Indeed, although there has been some support for Richardson's model in relation to health promotion (e.g., Walker, 1996), the linear stage framework evident within its structure, absence of meta-cognitive and meta-emotive processes, and its bias toward coping-oriented processes might be considered limitations (cf. Fletcher & Sarkar, 2013). These drawbacks are of particular concern since "the resiliency model (Richardson et al., 1990) served to drive and direct . . . [our] study" (Galli & Vealey, 2008, p. 321).

In an attempt to address the limitations of Galli and Vealey's (2008) work, several groups of researchers (e.g., Fletcher & Sarkar, 2012; White & Bennie, 2015) have employed inductive qualitative designs to explore resilience free from the constraints of a preconceived model. To illustrate, Fletcher and Sarkar (2012) developed a grounded theory of psychological resilience in Olympic champions. They interviewed 12 Olympic gold medalists to explore and explain the relationship between psychological resilience and optimal sport performance. The findings revealed that numerous psychological factors (relating to a positive personality, motivation, confidence, focus, and perceived social support) protected Olymic champions from the potential negative effect of stressors by influencing their challenge appraisal and meta-cognitions. These constructive cognitive reactions promoted facilitative responses that led to the realization of optimal sport performance.

In another qualitative study, to clarify how sport might cultivate resilience, White and Bennie (2015) recently investigated gymnast and coach perceptions about the development of resilience through gymnastics participation. Underpinned by a qualitative design, 22 female gymnasts and seven gymnastics coaches participated in semi-structured interviews. Data analysis revealed that aspects of the gymnastics environment created stress and exposed gymnasts to many challenges in training and competition. Features of the sport environment, such as interpersonal relationships and positive coach behaviors, supported gymnasts through these challenges and encouraged them to overcome failure. Gymnastics participation was perceived to develop resilience, as well as life skills, self-efficacy, and self-esteem. These findings support the notion that youth sport may be an appropriate avenue for the development of resilience and have implications for future coaching practice.

In addition to the holistic exploratory studies reviewed above, researchers have recently turned their attention to psychometric issues and the use of questionnaires to examine variables that correlate with resilience or moderate its relationship with dependent variables. In one of the initial studies in this area,

Gucciardi, Jackson, Coulter, and Mallett (2011) examined the dimensionality and measurement invariance of the 25-item Connor-Davidson Resilience Scale (CD-RISC; Connor & Davidson, 2003) across samples of adult and adolescent Australian cricketers. Confirmatory factor and item level analyses supported the psychometric superiority of a revised 10-item, unidimensional model of resilience over the original 25-item, five-factor measurement model. Despite this, the authors concluded that there was a need to develop a sport-specific measure of resilience to advance psychologists' understanding of this area. To enhance researchers' knowledge of measuring psychological resilience in athletes, and in line with a recommendation by Gucciardi et al. (2011), Sarkar and Fletcher (2013) reviewed psychometric issues in resilience research and discussed the implications for sport psychology. One of the key recommendations to emerge from their discussion, for sport psychology researchers seeking to develop a measure of psychological resilience in athletes, is that measures of resilience need to consider three pivotal components – adversity, positive adaptation, and protective factors – in a tripartite fashion to realize a complete and accurate representation of resilience in sport. Nevertheless, in the absence of a sport-specific measure of resilience, researchers using questionnaire designs to examine resilience in sport have typically employed the CD-RISC.

Over a dozen measures of resilience have been developed and validated by various researchers during the past three decades (see, for a review, Windle, Bennett, & Noyes, 2011). Although Windle et al. (2011) "found no 'gold standard' amongst 15 measures of resilience" (p. 8), one measure that has received considerable research attention – more so than other scales – is the CD-RISC. Several studies using the CD-RISC have revealed: resilience to be positively associated with sport achievement and psychological well-being, and negatively associated with psychological distress (Nezhad & Besharat, 2010); coping strategies to be predictive of self-reported resilience (Belem, Caruzzo, Nascimento Jr, Vieira, & Vieira, 2014); and adolescent athletes to report higher levels of resilience than their peers, with differences observed between male and female athletes in undertaking risky behavior (Lipowski, Lipowski, Jochimek, & Krokosz, 2015). Despite some initial evidence for the use of the CD-RISC in sport performers, it is worth noting some of the limitations of the scale. These include its focus on individual resilience qualities, the limited evidence base for the selection of items, its development and use in non-sport (clinical) contexts, and its conceptual overlap with coping (cf. Sarkar & Fletcher, 2013; Windle et al., 2011).

Elsewhere, researchers have considered the predictive role of resilience on well-being, drawing on Smith's (1986) cognitive-affective model of athletic burnout (see, e.g., Lu et al., 2016; Vitali, Bortoli, Bertinato, Robazza, & Schena, 2015). To illustrate, Vitali et al. (2015) examined the role of personal factors (perceived competence and resilience) and situational variables (motivational climate) on burnout in young athletes participating in team sports. The findings showed a mastery (i.e., task-involving) climate to correlate positively with resilience and perceived competence, and negatively with the three dimensions of burnout (viz. emotional/physical exhaustion, reduced sense of accomplishment, and sport devaluation). In contrast, a performance (i.e., ego-involving) climate related positively with the three dimensions of burnout. Regression analysis results showed a perceived mastery climate to significantly contribute to the amount of the variability in two burnout dimensions (viz. reduced sense of accomplishment and sport devaluation). In addition, resilience and perceived competence were shown to moderate the effects of the motivational context towards burnout. Lu et al. (2016) examined the conjunctive effect of athletes' resilience and coaches' social support on the relationship between life stress and burnout in a sample of student-athletes. The findings showed resilience and coaches' social support conjunctively moderated the stress–burnout relationship. Specifically, the interaction of athletes' resilience with coaches' informational and tangible social support moderated athletes' stress–burnout relationship in high and low life stress conditions.

The recent work reviewed above arguably advances early resilience research by providing psychologists, coaches, and national sport organizations with context-relevant frameworks to understand resilience (e.g., Fletcher & Sarkar, 2012; Galli & Vealey, 2008). Nevertheless, much of the exploratory qualitative research has been based on singular retrospective accounts of athletes' past experiences of successfully managing adversity, which may raise issues of retrospective recall bias (Schiller & Phelps, 2011). In addition, the nascent sport models do not appear to fully recognize the impact of sociocultural factors on athletes' capacity to withstand stressors, despite such factors being previously identified as pivotal in some qualitative studies of resilience in sport (e.g., Galli & Vealey, 2008; Machida et al., 2013). Finally, an ongoing limitation of the extant resilience research is the notably few studies exploring how athletes develop resilience. Hence, in summarizing, more work is needed to develop theoretically coherent interventions which are evaluated using conceptually grounded measures (cf. Robertson, Cooper, Sarkar, & Curran, 2015). Moreover, little is known about the generalizability of emerging models to other populations of sport performers such as non-Olympic athletes or regarding how resilience is developed in athletes. One way of addressing these questions would be to conduct longitudinal studies across different sports with multiple interaction points to explore how the resilience process changes over time and elucidate how it may differ depending on the stage of the athlete's career (Fletcher & Sarkar, 2012; Galli & Vealey, 2008).

Team resilience in sport studies

Resilience researchers, in various domains of psychology, have recently devoted attention to the group level (e.g., Carmeli, Friedman, & Tishler, 2013; Stephens, Heaphy, Carmeli, Spreitzer, & Dutton, 2013). Within the sport psychology literature, Morgan, Fletcher, and Sarkar (2013) conducted the first study of team resilience in sport. Employing focus groups with members of five elite sport teams, a definition of team resilience was developed and the resilient characteristics of elite sport teams were identified. Specifically, team resilience was defined as a "dynamic, psychosocial process which protects a group of individuals from the potential negative effect of the stressors they collectively encounter. It comprises processes whereby team members use their individual and collective resources to positively adapt when experiencing adversity" (p. 552). Team resilience was described as a dynamic phenomenon with participants stating that it was "dependent upon what time of the season it is" or "whether there is an injury in the team". In terms of its protective function, the participants described team resilience as akin to "having a barrier around you" and "having a thick skin". Furthermore, the participants emphasized that team resilience involved a shared experience of stressors (e.g., team disruptions, low team morale) and this was revealed through comments such as "we have been through so many setbacks together". Four resilient characteristics of elite sport teams emerged from this study: group structure (i.e., conventions that shape group norms and values), mastery approaches (i.e., shared attitudes and behaviors that promote an emphasis on team improvement), social capital (i.e., the existence of high quality interactions and caring relationships within the team), and collective efficacy (i.e., the team's shared beliefs in its ability to perform a task).

The recent developments in resilience research have advanced psychologists' knowledge of the nature, meaning, and scope of team resilience. In the sport psychology literature, Morgan et al.'s (2013) study provided greater definitional clarity on resilience at the team level (i.e., what team resilience is) and a framework to profile the resilient characteristics of elite sport teams (i.e., what resilient teams "look" like). Although such knowledge provided descriptive information about the factors that enable teams to withstand stressors, these characteristics do not explain how resilient teams function. Morgan et al. described team resilience as a "dynamic, psychosocial process" (p. 552) which points to operational aspects of this construct and how it changes over time. The authors concluded their manuscript by calling for future research that seeks to identify the processes that underpin the resilience characteristics in light of the contextual and temporal nature of team resilience. In an attempt to address this gap in our knowledge, Morgan, Fletcher, and Sarkar (2015) subsequently explored the psychosocial processes underpinning team resilience in elite sport. Using narrative inquiry, Morgan et al. (2015) analyzed the autobiographies of eight members of the 2003 England rugby union World Cup winning team. Findings revealed five main psychosocial processes underpinning team resilience: transformational leadership; shared team leadership; team learning, social identity; and positive emotions. The results indicated that these processes enabled the England rugby team to effectively utilize their cognitive, affective, and relational resources to act as leverage points for team resilience when facing stressors. Furthermore, the findings of this study revealed that team resilience was illuminated through a progressive narrative form. This was portrayed by team members evaluating stressors in a positive fashion and focusing on moving forward as a team despite setbacks.

Collectively, the emerging research exploring team resilience in sport has contributed to our understanding of what team resilience is, providing a framework of resilient characteristics, and has also highlighted some of the processes by which resilient teams function. Nevertheless, there remains much to be explored regarding the interplay of sociocultural and organizational dynamics and both individual and team resilience. Indeed, some of the themes to emerge from Morgan et al.'s (2013) study of team resilience (e.g., psychosocial conventions shaping group norms and roles, managing change, and social capital) intersect with those highlighted in research on organizational functioning in sport (cf. Wagstaff, Fletcher, & Hanton, 2012a).

Sociocultural influences on resilience in athletes and teams

As alluded to earlier in this chapter, research examining resilience has been critiqued for being too focused on individual capacities (see Ungar et al., 2008). Although some scholars have pointed to the potential salience of sociocultural factors (e.g., Galli & Vealey, 2008), most of the resilience research conducted in sport has focused on athletes' *psychological* processes hitherto eliding the sociocultural context within which this process occurs (Sarkar & Fletcher, 2014). It follows that research which aims to address this omission is essential to the development of effective resilience interventions. The argument for such research endeavors is further supported by the identification of social and cultural factors that influence resilience in non-sport domains (see, e.g., Clauss-Ehlers, 2008) and an emerging recognition of social and cultural variations that exist within sport (see, e.g., Blodgett, Schinke, McGannon, & Fisher, 2014; Schinke & Hanrahan, 2009). Indeed, Blodgett et al. recently took stock of the growing body of conceptual research aligned with the cultural sport psychology (CSP) agenda. In doing so, the authors highlighted the centrality of cultural praxis to CSP as a means of overcoming the "taken for granted" way of "doing" sport psychology steeped in a post-positivist, white, Euro-American, male, performance-based discourse.

Cultural praxis in sport psychology grew out of early writings that drew on cultural studies that highlighted how issues of power and privilege were being perpetuated in and through the practices of the domain. Through cultural praxis, researchers and practitioners strive to consider their own, as well as others', cultural identities. The intent is to draw attention to issues of sociocultural difference, power, ethics, and politics, which are often concealed, and facilitate a more contextualized understanding of marginalized identities and a plurality of differences (e.g., race, ethnicity, class, gender, sexuality, dis/ability, physicality, nationality). For example, athletes originate from a diverse range of family backgrounds with varying cultural and religious beliefs, factors which have been found to influence the resilience process (cf. Clauss-Ehlers, 2008). Athletes also operate within organizational environments that have similar, yet idiosyncratic, economic, political, and sociocultural characteristics (Fletcher & Wagstaff, 2009). In light of these influences, it would appear that "off-the-shelf" resilience interventions are unlikely to be effective across all athletes, teams, and sport organizations, and there is a need to better incorporate lessons from sociocultural and organizational dynamics research.

Within the general psychology literature, Ungar and colleagues (Theron et al., 2011; Ungar, 2008; Ungar et al., 2008; Ungar, 2010) have written widely about the need for a more culturally and contextually embedded understanding of resilience. In doing so, these authors have used the tenets of ecological theory to draw from research and clinical experience with children, youth, and families to argue that resilience is not a phenomenon solely related to the individual, but also exists as a facet of one's social and political setting, thus being *negotiated* by individuals and their community. For other scholars (e.g., Gilligan, 2004; Seccombe, 2002), an approach to resilience development wherein "changing the odds" is preferable to resourcing individuals to "beating the odds". To illustrate, in his manual for child and youth care workers, Gilligan (2004) argued that "resilience… is now more usefully considered as a variable quality that derives from a process of repeated interactions between a person and favorable features of the surrounding context in a person's life" (p. 94). Hence, and in line with a more culturally and contextually embedded view of resilience, "the degree of resilience displayed by a person in a certain context may be said to be related to the extent to which that context has elements that nurture this resilience" (p. 94).

Recently, Ungar (2012) highlighted three main sociocultural influences relevant for resilience. The first centers on the observation that facilitative environments can be more powerful than individual-level variables in the resilience process (see Ungar, 2012). To illustrate, Chauhan and colleagues (2010) found that, when matching for individual factors such as delinquency and psychological risk factors, the recidivism rates amongst girls were shown to be correlated with sociocultural factors and racial background. In the context of sport, Galli and Vealey (2008) noted that the majority of African American athletes in their study believed that the notion of success and overcoming challenges was a central part of their culture and a key influence on their ability to deal with the adverse events they encountered. In practical terms, these studies underline the need for researchers to not only focus interventions on athletes' personal qualities, but also to utilize aspects of their sociocultural environment to facilitate the development of resilience.

Ungar's (2012) second observation concerns the access to, and the meaningfulness of, the findings from non-diverse samples. Policymakers in sport need to develop organizations and services that facilitate the development of resilience whilst being considerate of different contexts and cultures. Beyond sport, resilience researchers in general psychology have acknowledged that minority groups (Ungar, 2008) and disadvantaged individuals (Hutcheon & Lashewicz, 2014) are frequently not included in discussions when designing services to aid their resilience. Accordingly, the aforementioned researchers recognized that interventions that target these populations are often not specific to their backgrounds or properly suited to their specific needs. This omission can have dramatic (negative) effects, as highlighted by Hansson and colleagues (Hansson, Tuck, Lurie, & McKenzie, 2012), who found that adult immigrants who assimilate into a culture and lack specific cultural support report more mental health issues than those who do not. Hence, and given the global nature of contemporary sport, it is vital that practitioners work with athletes to ensure that resources are tailored to the specific sociocultural context in which they originate or identify with. Only then are resilience interventions likely to be both effective and efficacious.

The last observation made by Ungar (2012) was that individuals benefit more from protective factors developed to alleviate risks when the level of exposure to the risk is at its greatest. Indeed, it is generally accepted that individuals with the greatest perceived needs benefit from unique individual provision rather than general resilience programs designed for wider populations and situations (cf. Robertson et al., 2015). In addition, the support required can be disproportionately larger for an athlete facing substantial demands. Away from sport, education studies have shown smaller class sizes and a caring teacher are more advantageous to pupils with the most complex educational needs and disrupted home lives (Shernoff & Schmidt, 2008). Despite the different domains, the overall picture is that a homogenous approach to developing resilience is not appropriate and it is possible that athletes who are most at risk will benefit the most from resilience intervention resources.

Organizational dynamics surrounding resilience in athletes and teams

Since the turn of the century it has become increasingly apparent that a need exists to better understand the pivotal role that organizations play in preparing athletes and teams for competition (Fletcher & Wagstaff, 2009; Wagstaff, Fletcher, & Hanton, 2012b; Wagstaff & Larner, 2015). In line with the growing acknowledgement of the importance of organizational issues in elite sport, three recent reviews have summarized the emergence, application, and potential futures for this domain. Specifically, in a 2009 article published in a *Psychology of Sport and Exercise* special issue concerning topical themes in contemporary psychology, Fletcher and Wagstaff reviewed six lines of inquiry pointing to the salience of organizational issues in elite sport. These were: factors affecting Olympic performance (see, for a review, Gould & Maynard, 2009); organizational stress (see, for a review, Arnold & Fletcher, 2012); perceptions of roles (see, e.g., Reid, Stewart, & Thorne, 2004); organizational success factors (see, e.g., Weinberg & McDermott, 2002); performance environments in elite sport (see, e.g., Jones, Gittins, & Hardy, 2009); and organizational citizenship behavior (see, e.g., Aoyagi, Cox, & McGuire, 2008). The convergence of evidence indicates that such influences have the potential to have a significant positive impact on organizational functioning and resilience. Interestingly, in their 2009 article, Fletcher and Wagstaff recognized that an area of inquiry that merits further research in contemporary elite sport is that of organizational resilience:

> Since international level sport has never been so competitive, National Sport Organizations (NSOs) will likely need to meet the challenges, adversities and changes associated with the developments in elite sport governance. Despite these observations, there is currently no rigorous research that specifically addresses... organizational resilience in elite sport.
> (Fleatcher and Wagstafll, 2009, p. 433)

Wagstaff et al. (2012b) reviewed the literature relating to positive organizational psychology in sport (POPS), defined as "the study of positive attributes, processes and outcomes associated with sport organizations and their members" (p. 88). In their review, Wagstaff et al. defined and delimited relevant concepts (viz. organizational psychology, positive psychology, positive organizing), provided an overview of extant research relating to positive environments, behaviors, and outcomes in sport, and speculated about the future of this area of inquiry, suggesting that attention needs to be paid to topics such as culture, climate and change, in addition to those aligned with positive organizational behavior and scholarship, in order to advance our understanding and practice. Wagstaff et al.'s review stimulated an ongoing program of research examining organizational functioning in sport (see Wagstaff, Fletcher, & Hanton, 2012a; Wagstaff, Hanton, & Fletcher, 2013). Most recently, Wagstaff and Larner (2015) summarized the recent developments in organizational psychology research and outlined a research agenda to structure current and future lines of inquiry into four core dimensions of research and application: emotions and attitudes; stress and well-being; behaviors, and environments. This research agenda later provided the foundation for this text.

Organizational change

In their call for a research agenda on POPS, Wagstaff et al. (2012b) highlighted a construct that characterizes organizational dynamics and is a particularly pertinent issue surrounding resilience in athletes and teams, namely organizational change. Organizational change occurs both naturally and intentionally, requiring those operating within an organization to forge new paths and learn new strategies to attain redefined goals, often with unstable resources. Subsequently, Wagstaff et al. (2012b) noted that individuals, teams, and organizations "… must have the efficacy to adapt to organizational change as well as the resilience to bounce back from setbacks that occur during the change process" (pp. 95–96). This assertion has been supported by recent research on organizational change in elite sport (Wagstaff, Gilmore, & Thelwell, 2015; 2016). To illustrate, Wagstaff et al. (2015) explored sport medicine and science practitioners' experiences of organizational change using a longitudinal design over a two-year period. Specifically, data were collected in three temporally defined phases via 49 semi-structured interviews with 20 sport medics and scientists (SMSs) employed by three organizations competing in the top tiers of English football and cricket. The findings indicated that change occurred over four distinct stages: anticipation and uncertainty; upheaval and realization; integration and experimentation; normalization and learning. Moreover, the data highlighted salient emotional, behavioral, and attitudinal experiences of medics and scientists following organizational change. With regards to job attitudes, Wagstaff et al. (2015) asserted that the transition from one stage to another appeared to be dependent on appraisals and that SMSs who had experienced repeated cycles of change had become more resilient in their response to change. Moreover, the authors noted that the learning opportunities in the fourth and final stage of change were essential for promoting resilience among employees.

Responding to calls for the investigation of individuals' responses to recurrent change events, Wagstaff et al. (2016) recently studied employees' experiences of repeated organizational change. Data were gathered via 20 semi-structured interviews with 10 individuals fulfilling a range of roles within two organizations competing in English football's Barclays Premier League. The results indicated that employees in sport organizations responded to recurring organizational change in positive and negative emotional, behavioral, and attitudinal ways. Moreover, one of the main positive response themes related to resilience. That is, although participants generally reported a largely negative experience of change, many of the participants who had experienced repeated change recognized resilience as an inherent characteristic of working in high-performance domains. That is, although participants commonly reported a largely negative perception of change events, they stated that they were developing more positive responses to subsequent change events than their first experience of such change. Thus, organizational scholars in sport might look to further examine how resilience influences individuals' response to change. Indeed, in a similar fashion to Fletcher and Wagstaff (2009), Wagstaff et al. (2012b) recognized the merits of further investigating organizational resilience to advance knowledge:

> A POPS research agenda which complements negative-oriented research may… help researchers better understand positive states and traits such as organizational resilience… to buffer against the demands that are placed on individuals within organizations.
>
> (Wagstaff et al. 2012, p. 99)

Organizational resilience

As mentioned earlier in this chapter, recent resilience research has shifted away from individuals toward the study of groups and teams (see, e.g., Alliger et al., 2015; Bennett, Aden, Broome, Mitchell, & Rigdon, 2010; Meneghel, Salanova, & Martinez, 2014; Morgan et al., 2013; 2015; Stephens et al., 2013). Over the past decade or so, the concept of resilience has also been applied to organizations (e.g., Coutu, 2002; Gittell, Cameron, Lim, & Rivas, 2006; Lengnick-Hall, Beck, & Lengnick-Hall, 2011; McManus, Seville, Vargo, & Brunsdon, 2008; Somers, 2009; Stephenson, Vargo, & Seville, 2010). Organizational resilience has been defined as "the maintenance of positive adjustment under challenging circumstances such that the organization emerges from those conditions strengthened and more resourceful" (Vogus & Sutcliffe, 2007, p. 3418) and as "an organization's propensity to absorb, deflect or exploit the demands on, and threats to, its efficient and effective operation" (Fletcher & Wagstaff, 2009, p. 433). Scholars have advanced arguments for a wide array of critical dimensions. As a result, different models have been conceptually developed to describe which factors enhance organizational resilience.

An early conceptualization proposed by Weick (1993) suggested that organizational resilience is comprised of *bricolage* (viz. an ability to remain creative under pressure), *attitude of wisdom* (viz. an ability to combine previous experience with a set of heuristics to evaluate a situation both knowledgeably and flexibly), and *virtual role system* (viz. an advanced form of work team relationships). This conceptualization was built upon by Mallak (1998) who developed a scale designed to measure organizational resilience in the health care provider industry. The analyses resulted in six factors labelled *goal-directed solution-seeking* (viz. the need for goals and a vision to guide creative processes in seeking solutions to problems), *avoidance* (e.g., escaping chaotic situations, approaching new situations with skepticism), *critical understanding* (e.g., making sense of a situation when chaos ensues, knowing what resources to access), *role dependence* (viz. the ability to take on and perform team members' roles), *source reliance* (viz. relying on multiple sources of information), and *resource access* (e.g., the knowledge needed to do the job and access to resources).

Another stream of research suggests that organizational resilience consists of three main dimensions (see, for a review, McManus et al., 2008). These are *situation awareness* (viz. an organization's understanding and perception of its entire operating environment), *management of keystone vulnerabilities* (viz. those aspects of an organization, operational and managerial, that have the potential to have significant negative impacts in a crisis situation), and *adaptive capacity* (viz. the culture and dynamics of an organization that allow it to make decisions in a timely and appropriate manner, both in day-to-day business and also in crises). McManus et al. (2008) introduced a facilitated process that assists organizations to enhance their performance in relation to these attributes. This process is called resilience management and was developed and tested with 10 case study organizations in New Zealand (see also Stephenson et al., 2010). Preliminary findings from the use of this process revealed that some of the key indicators of resilience include awareness of stakeholder roles and responsibilities, hazard events and their consequences, together with recovery priorities. The use of specific planning, such as risk management and business continuity planning, together with the ability to link and test these plans using exercises, were also significant indicators of resilience. Moreover, silo mentality, poor communications and relationships with stakeholders, and inflexible and uncreative decision-making appeared to have considerable impacts on overall organizational resilience.

Most recently, Lengnick-Hall et al. (2011) proposed that an organization's capacity for resilience is developed through strategically managing human resources to create competencies among core employees that, when aggregated at the organizational level, make it possible for organizations to achieve the ability to respond in a resilient manner when they experience severe shocks. Specifically, their proposition is based on three elements central to developing an organization's capacity for resilience: *cognitive factors* (e.g., strong core values, sense of purpose, constructive sense-making), *behavioral characteristics* (e.g., learned resourcefulness, bricolage, behavioral preparedness), and *contextual conditions* (e.g., psychological safety, deep social capital, diffused power and accountability). Lengnick-Hall et al. then explained how these three elements might operate at three different levels: individual employee contributions; human resource (HR) principles; and HR policies. To illustrate, under the behavioral characteristics element, a desired employee contribution of "collaborative behavior" would be related to the HR principle of "share information as broadly as possible within the organization" and the HR policy of "open book management". Indeed, Lengnick-Hall et al. (2011) argued that, "it is the particular configuration of employee contributions, HR practices, and HR policies... that work together to create a capacity for resilience and that transforms individual actions into this collective organizational capability" (p. 252).

Organizational resilience has been investigated in a number of sectors such as business and industry (e.g., Coutu, 2002; Gittell et al., 2006), health (e.g., Mallak, 1998), and public administration (e.g., Somers, 2009). Somewhat surprisingly, the sport sector has been neglected within this research. To the best of our knowledge, the only study on organizational resilience in sport was conducted by Wicker, Filo, and Cuskelly (2013). Specifically, this study explored the organizational resilience of community sport clubs in the aftermath of natural disasters, particularly major cyclone and flood events. Within the study, organizational resilience was conceptualized as a function of *robustness* (viz. the ability to withstand stress), *redundancy* (viz. the capability to substitute different resources to ensure the ongoing functioning of the organization), *resourcefulness* (viz. the capacity to identify problems, establish priorities, and mobilize resources when conditions exist that threaten to disrupt the organization), and *rapidity* (viz. the capacity to meet priorities and achieve goals in a timely manner in order to contain losses and avoid future disruption). Using data from a survey of sport clubs ($n = 200$) in Queensland, Australia, the findings showed that clubs predominantly used human and financial resources in their recovery efforts. Organizational resilience, number of members, and the use of government grants had a significant positive effect on the extent of the club's perceived overall recovery. To elaborate, smaller clubs and those that typically use outdoor sport facilities exclusively (viz. equestrian, golf, and motor sports) recovered to a significantly lesser extent than larger clubs providing other sports. Further, proactively pursuing government grants, suitable insurance coverage, and inter-organizational relationships were identified as factors that assisted clubs in becoming more resilient. Thus, sport organizations and senior managers should be aware of the importance of organizational resilience and specific resources that are critical to facilitate recovery. For example, larger sport clubs, who do not have the sole financial responsibility for their facilities, might be at some advantage in recovery from natural disasters, likely due to having access to more human (e.g., volunteers) and financial resources (e.g., total revenues), yet such organizations are likely to also suffer from heterogeneous interests among members and be at the mercy of government support in recovery situations. Moreover, future similar research in sport should explore demands beyond natural disasters.

Overall, a convergence of evidence points to organizational dynamics as having the potential to significantly influence resilience in athletes and teams. Nevertheless, the body of knowledge in this area remains at a nascent stage and empirical examination of organizational resilience is rather scant both in general and sport psychology contexts. Researchers investigating organizational resilience face challenges concerning conceptualization and more research is needed to understand the complex relationships between individual, team, and organizational resilience. The landscape that has revealed itself to sport psychologists to explore is vast, the opportunities to elucidate the complex relationship between individuals and organizations are inviting, and the research agenda that beckons is exciting. Indeed, Vogus and Sutcliffe (2007) highlighted that "given the dearth of empirical work exploring resilience in organization theory, many (if not all) avenues are open for future research in resilience" (p. 3420).

A research agenda for the future study of resilience in sport

In this section, we outline a number of directions that future researchers can explore to advance knowledge of resilience in sport. This agenda organizes many extant (see, for reviews, Galli & Gonzalez, 2015; Sarkar & Fletcher, 2014) and possible future lines of inquiry into two broad areas: the nature of resilience and methodological advancements in resilience research.

Regarding the nature of resilience, we will discuss three main avenues that we believe will advance sport psychologists' knowledge and understanding of this area. First, as discussed earlier in this chapter, an important consideration when investigating resilience is the sociocultural context in which an individual or group operates. Research to date has predominantly focused on *psychological* processes underpinning resilience in athletes and teams and, thus, resilience researchers need to explore the sociocultural and organizational context within which this occurs. Ungar et al. (2008) noted that resilience definitions are often equivocal when observed through different cultures. Thus, the meaning of resilience may be culturally and contextually dependent. It is important to identify what the benchmark for "success" might be for different cultures or organizations, who might place different values on such criteria (Fletcher & Sarkar, 2013; Windle, 2011). To illustrate, Ungar and colleagues (Ungar, 2008; Ungar & Liebenberg, 2011; Ungar et al., 2008) argued that resilience research has predominantly defined positive adaptation from a Western psychological discourse with an emphasis on individual and relational capacities, such as academic success and healthy relationships. According to Ungar and colleagues, these outcomes lack sensitivity to cultural factors that contextualize how resilience is defined by different populations and manifested in different practices. Rather than assuming neutrality or objectivity in the use of competence indicators across settings (i.e., an etic perspective), they propose that understanding positive adaptation from within the cultural frame from which competence emerges (i.e., an emic perspective) is a more ecologically sensitive approach. This perspective is supported by Mahoney and Bergman (2002) who stated that the specific sociocultural conditions in which an individual functions must be considered when examining competence, and that "failing to do so may lead to a view of positive adaptation as a static phenomenon with relevance to only a minority of persons in select circumstances" (p. 212). Thus, due to resilience being manifested across a variety of contexts, scholars need to be sensitive to the sociocultural factors that contextualize how it is defined by different populations.

Second, although extant research has provided insight into individuals' and teams' perceptions of resilience, future researchers should incorporate physiological indices into study designs to attenuate the drawbacks of the self-report nature of resilience inquiry to date. For decades, resilience research has focused on psychological variables but "we are now into a new era with concerted attention to biology" (Luthar, Sawyer, & Brown, 2006, p. 109). In a seminal review paper, Curtis and Cicchetti (2003) explained the role of diverse biological processes ranging from neuroendocrinology to capacities for emotion regulation. Indeed, due to the importance of the person–environment interaction in resilience inquiry (cf. Egeland, Carlson, & Sroufe, 1993), "it will be necessary to combine psychosocial and biological research approaches" (Rutter, 2006, p. 10). In the athletic context, Fletcher and Sarkar (2012) noted that it may be beneficial for sport psychologists interested in examining the stress–resilience–performance relationship to consider recent evidence from cognitive neuroscience. Specifically, researchers interested in further investigating resilience in sport should consider the neurochemical factors that characterize psychobiological resilience and that has predictive value regarding successful adaptation to stress (see, for a review, Charney, 2004; Haglund, Nestadt, Cooper, Southwick, & Charney, 2007). For example, neuropeptide Y (NPY) is a 36-amino acid neuropeptide that acts as a neurotransmitter in the brain and in the autonomic nervous system of humans. Preliminary work with combat veterans and special operations soldiers has indicated that higher levels of NPY may be associated with resilience against posttraumatic stress disorder (Yehuda, Brand, & Yang, 2006), and, by dampening the fear response, allows individuals to perform better under stress (Morgan et al., 2000). NPY's protective effects against post-traumatic psychopathology, in addition to its beneficial effects on performance under stress, suggest that the peptide could be an effective pharmacotherapy for enhancing resilience to stress (Haglund et al., 2007). Furthermore, cortisol is a hormone that is released in response to stress, sparing available glucose for the brain, and generating new energy from stored reserves. Nevertheless, excessive and sustained cortisol secretion can have serious adverse physiological (Whitworth, Williamson, Mangos, & Kelly, 2005) and psychological (Carroll et al., 2007) effects. Preliminary work has indicated that resilience training can lead to large reductions in cortisol response during a critical incident (police work) simulation (Arnetz et al., 2009), and that trait reappraisal is associated with resilience to acute psychological stress as measured by cortisol, heart rate, and self-report measures (Carlson, Dikecligil, Greenberg, & Mujica-Parodi, 2012). Thus, future sport psychology researchers should collect well-established physiological indicators of resilience to further corroborate the self-report accounts of resilience to date.

Third, to elucidate the unique nature of resilience, future research in sport needs to examine the relationships between resilience and other pertinent concepts. For example, although resilience and coping are often used interchangeably, there is a growing body of evidence to suggest that these are conceptually distinct constructs (Campbell-Sills et al., 2006; Compas, Connor-Smith, Saltzman, Thomsen, & Wadsworth, 2001; Karoly & Ruehlman, 2006; Major, Richards, Cozzarelli, Cooper, & Zubek, 1998). Based on the collective body of work supporting the distinction between resilience and coping, Fletcher and Sarkar (2013) proposed that resilience "is characterized by its influence on one's appraisal prior to emotional and coping responses and by its positive, protective impact, whereas coping is characterized by its response to a stressful encounter and by its varying effectiveness in resolving outstanding issues" (p. 16). Future research in sport needs to empirically test this postulation. That is, sport psychology researchers should test whether resilience can be considered a distinct construct from that of coping. To provide another example, resilience and growth are often confused in the psychology literature (Westphal & Bonanno, 2007). For instance, it is debated as to whether or not growth is a form of resilience, and argued whether or not growth confers certain advantages over resilience. The two studies that have examined the relationship between resilience and growth are somewhat inconclusive (Bensimon, 2012; Levine, Laufer, Stein, Hamama-Raz, & Solomon, 2009). Levine et al. (2009) found that high levels of resilience were associated with the lowest growth scores and Bensimon (2012) found that resilience was positively associated with growth. Thus, future research in sport is needed to elucidate the relationship between resilience and growth.

Regarding methodological advancements in resilience research, we will discuss four main avenues that we believe will advance sport psychologists' knowledge in this area. First, there exists an urgent need to develop sport-specific measures of psychological, team, and organizational resilience. At the individual level (see, for a review, Sarkar & Fletcher, 2013), Fletcher and Sarkar (2012) stated, "it will be difficult to advance our understanding of this area without a valid and reliable assessment instrument" (p. 676). Most recently, Galli and Gonzalez (2015) noted, "knowledge will be enhanced by the development of a sport-specific resilience measure" (p. 243). For team resilience research and measurement in sport, Morgan, Fletcher, and Sarkar

(2015) indicated that "team resilience should be operationalized and assessed differently at different levels of analysis" (p. 99). Specifically, researchers should disaggregate individuals' perceptions of the team's resilience from team-level resilience. At the organizational level, Wicker et al.'s (2013) study represented initial quantitative assessment of organizational resilience in a sport context. Nevertheless, the (exploratory factor) analysis demonstrated that further testing and item development is necessary and the authors concluded that "the measurement of [organizational] resilience [in sport] should be refined and expanded in future research" (p. 510).

Second, although cross-sectional designs have been appropriate for initially exploring concepts and relationships in this area, future research should adopt longitudinal designs to better capture the complex and dynamic nature of resilience. In terms of the quantitative assessment and examination of psychological resilience, Gucciardi et al. (2011) argued that it is crucial that researchers explore the factor structure stability and item consistency – within and across individuals – in a longitudinal fashion. In terms of the qualitative exploration of resilience at the individual level, Galli and Vealey (2008) noted that future research should employ longitudinal qualitative designs (e.g., multiple interviews with athletes over time) to explore the dynamic nature and temporal course of psychological resilience. Moreover, Fletcher and Sarkar (2012) stated that lifespan-based studies, examining relationships between resilience, stress, and performance from a longitudinal perspective, is warranted. At the team level, due to the contextual and temporal nature of team resilience, Morgan et al. (2015) emphasized that "longitudinal research is required to further explore the resilience processes identified in this study [elite sport]" (p. 98). At the organizational level, Wicker et al. (2013) acknowledged as a limitation their use of cross-sectional data and called on future researchers to "collect longitudinal data to evaluate resilience among community sport clubs over time and to investigate how the concept and its dimensions evolve as time from the natural disaster passes and changes in personnel and resources may occur" (p. 523). As an example from non-sport organizational psychology research, Kimberlin, Schwartz, and Austin (2011) analyzed organizational histories spanning several decades to portray organizational resilience processes.

Third, to address potential interpretive ambiguities in sport-related resilience studies that may initially arise due to a lack of a quantitative benchmark, sport psychology researchers should provide qualitative characterizations of a subset of individuals within the group being examined (Sarkar & Fletcher, 2013). That is, resilience researchers in sport should consider adopting mixed-method research designs (cf. Alex, 2010; West, Buettner, Stewart, Foster, & Usher, 2012). To illustrate, West et al. (2012) conducted an explanatory sequential mixed-methods study to measure and explore family resilience. In this type of design, the researcher first gathers and analyses the quantitative data, which is followed by a qualitative phase undertaken to help explain the quantitative results (Creswell & Clark, 2011). According to West et al. (2012), the combination of both quantitative and qualitative data in the final phase enhanced the overall outcome of the study by providing a more comprehensive explanation of the results. Similarly, Alex (2010) noted that integrating both sets of data (i.e., quantitative and qualitative) can offer a new perspective on our understanding of resilience. Specifically, Alex (2010) used the Resilience Scale (RS; Wagnild & Young, 1993) to identify elderly individuals with estimated high resilience before using thematic narrative interviews to investigate their resilience in more depth. This mixed-method approach may be useful for researchers interested in further investigating resilience in sport.

Fourth, resilience intervention studies are required in sport. As a caveat to this recommendation, Fletcher and Sarkar (2012) argued that:

> From a research perspective… it is important that such work is grounded in systematic resilience research programs rather than piecemeal and incomplete strategies based on, for example, the mental toughness, hardiness or coping literatures. Such research programs, which should be underpinned by the conceptual and theoretical advances already made in this area in general psychology (cf. Fletcher & Sarkar, 2013), will provide the most rigorous and robust platform from which to develop resilience training in sport.
>
> (p. 676)

To provide an illustration, albeit in another performance context, the Comprehensive Soldier Fitness (CSF) program designed to develop resilience in soldiers was adapted primarily from the Penn Resiliency Program (PRP; see, for a review, Brunwasser, Gillham, & Kim, 2009). Notwithstanding the program's foundation, Eidelson, Pilisuk, and Soldz (2011) voiced a number of conceptual and ethical concerns with the CSF intervention. To illustrate, Eidelson et al. contended that the resilience program's outcomes should have been convincingly demonstrated first in carefully conducted randomized controlled trials before being rolled out under less-controlled conditions, that the model on which the CSF program is based was developed on dramatically different (non-military) populations and therefore cannot be generalized to the challenges that soldiers face in combat, and that the PRP's effects seemed to be unrelated to the "resilience" theory underpinning the program. Ethically, Eidelson et al. argued that "resilience training could… harm… soldiers by making them more likely to engage in combat actions that adversely affect their psychological health" (Eidelson et al., 2011, p. 643). Moreover, they provided a general critique of positive psychology that was the foundation of CSF. This included the failure of positive psychology to appreciate the valuable functions played by "negative" emotions such as anger, guilt, and fear; its disregard for harsh societal realities such as poverty and oppression; and its promotion of claims without sufficient scientific support (cf. Coyne & Tennen, 2010). In light of the criticisms of the CSF resilience program, sport psychologists attempting to develop similar interventions should ensure that a rigorous methodological design is employed (ideally a randomized controlled trial), that the intervention is underpinned by conceptual and theoretical context-specific knowledge of resilience, that the "dark side" of resilience is considered, and that the program draws on humanistic and other perspectives that may not be covered in the field of positive psychology (cf. Robertson et al., 2015).

Concluding remarks and take-home messages

Resilience is viewed here as a prerequisite for sustained sporting success and a key area of development for athletes, teams, and organizations. In an attempt to help researchers and practitioners gain a better practical understanding of resilience at multiple levels of analysis and intervention, this review has examined the literature with the intention to highlight the praxis of the current research. Specifically, it is hoped that this synthesis of literature will help researchers and practitioners to gain a better practical understanding of resilience in athletes, teams, and organizations, while providing a rigorous and robust platform for the development of sport-specific interventions to facilitate resilience. In drawing together our observations, the emerging research examining resilience in sport has provided practitioners with nascent sport-specific frameworks for understanding what resilience at different levels of analysis is, how it develops, and what functions it serves. In addition, this review has also raised a number of research and practice implications regarding resilience. Indeed, we finish the chapter by reiterating five key messages for future research on resilience in sport organizations:

- Research to date has predominantly focused on *psychological* processes underpinning resilience in athletes and teams and, thus, resilience researchers need to explore the sociocultural and organizational context within which this occurs.
- To elucidate the unique nature of resilience, future research in sport needs to examine the relationships between resilience and other pertinent concepts such as coping and growth.
- Researchers should incorporate physiological indices into study designs to attenuate the drawbacks of the self-report nature of resilience inquiry to date and consider the neurochemical factors that characterize psychobiological resilience and that have predictive value regarding successful adaptation to stress.
- There exists an urgent need to develop sport-specific measures of and interventions to develop psychological, team, and organizational resilience.
- Although cross-sectional designs have been appropriate for initially exploring concepts and relationships in this area, future research should adopt longitudinal designs to better capture the complex and dynamic nature of resilience.

References

Alex, L. (2010). Resilience among very old men and women. *Journal of Research in Nursing, 15*, 419–431.
Alliger, G. M., Cerasoli, C. P., Tannenbaum, S. I., & Vessey, W. B. (2015). Team resilience: How teams flourish under pressure. *Organizational Dynamics, 44*, 176–184.
Aoyagi, M. W., Cox, R. H., & McGuire, R. T. (2008). Organizational citizenship behavior in sport: Relationships with leadership, team cohesion, and athlete satisfaction. *Journal of Applied Sport Psychology, 20*(1), 25–41
Arnetz, B. B., Nevedal, D. C., Lumley, M. A., Backman, L., & Lublin, A. (2009). Trauma and resilience training for police: Psychophysiological and performance effects. *Journal of Police Criminal Psychology, 24*(1), 1–9. doi: 10.1007/s11896-008-9030-y.
Arnold, R., & Fletcher, D. (2012). A research synthesis and taxonomic classification of the organizational stressors encountered by sport performers. *Journal of Sport and Exercise Psychology, 34*, 397–429.
Belem, I. C., Caruzzo, N. M., Nascimento Junior, J. R. A. D., Vieira, J. L. L., & Vieira, L. F. (2014). Impact of coping strategies on resilience of elite beach volleyball athletes. *Revista Brasileira de Cineantropometria & Desempenho Humano, 16*(4), 447–455.
Bennett, J. B., Aden, C. A., Broome, K., Mitchell, K., & Rigdon, W. D. (2010). Team resilience for young restaurant workers: Research-to-practice adaptation and assessment. *Journal of Occupational Health Psychology, 15*, 223–236.
Bensimon, M. (2012). Elaboration on the association between trauma, PTSD and posttraumatic growth: The role of trait resilience. *Personality and Individual Differences, 52*, 782–787.
Blodgett, A. T., Schinke, R. J., McGannon, K. R., & Fisher, L. A. (2014). Cultural sport psychology research: Conceptions, evolutions, and forecasts. *International Review of Sport and Exercise Psychology, 8*, 24–43.
Bonanno, G. A. (2004). Loss, trauma and human resilience: Have we underestimated the human capacity to thrive after extremely aversive events? *American Psychologist, 59*, 20–28.
Brennan, M. A. (2008). Conceptualizing resiliency: An interactional perspective for community and youth development. *Child Care in Practice, 14*(3), 55–64.
Brunwasser, S. M., Gillham, J. E., & Kim, E. S. (2009). A meta-analytic review of the Penn Resiliency Program's effect on depressive symptoms. *Journal of Consulting and Clinical Psychology, 77*, 1042–1054.
Campbell-Sills, L., Cohan, S. L., & Stein, M. B. (2006). Relationship of resilience to personality, coping, and psychiatric symptoms in young adults. *Behavior Research and Therapy, 44*, 585–599.
Carlson, J. M., Dikecligil, G. N., Greenberg, T., & Mujica-Parodi, L. R. (2012). Trait reappraisal is associated with resilience to acute psychological stress. *Journal of Research in Personality, 46*, 609–613.
Carmeli, A., Friedman, Y., & Tishler, A. (2013). Cultivating a resilient top management team: The importance of relational connections and strategic decision comprehensiveness. *Safety Science, 51*(1), 148–159.
Carroll, B. J., Cassidy, F., Naftolowitz, D., Tatham, N. E., Wilson, W. H., Iranmanesh, A., et al. (2007). Pathophysiology of hypercortisolism in depression. *Acta Psychiatrica Scandinavica Supplementum, 433*, 90–103.
Charney, D. S. (2004). Psychobiological mechanisms of resilience and vulnerability: Implications for successful adaptation to extreme stress. *American Journal of Psychiatry, 161*, 195–216.

Chauhan, P., Reppucci, N. D., Burnette, M., & Reiner, S. (2010). Race, neighborhood disadvantage, and antisocial behavior among female juvenile offenders. *American Journal of Community Psychology, 38*(4), 532–540. doi: 10.1002/jcop.20377.

Clauss-Ehlers, C. S. (2008). Sociocultural factors, resilience, and coping: Support for a culturally sensitive measure of resilience. *Journal of Applied Developmental Psychology, 29*(3), 197–212. doi: 10.1016/j.appdev.2008.02.004.

Compas, B. E., Connor-Smith, J. K., Saltzman, H., Thomsen, A. H., & Wadsworth, M. E. (2001). Coping with stress during childhood and adolescence: Problems, progress, and potential in theory and research. *Psychological Bulletin, 127*, 87–127.

Connor, K. M., & Davidson, J. R. T. (2003). Development of a new resilience scale: The Connor-Davidson resilience scale (CD-RISC). *Depression and Anxiety, 18*(2), 76–82.

Coutu, D. L. (2002). How resilience works. *Harvard Business Review, 80*, 46–55.

Coyne, J. C., & Tennen, H. (2010). Positive psychology in cancer care: Bad science, exaggerated claims, and unproven medicine. *Annals of Behavioral Medicine, 39*, 16–26.

Creswell, J., & Clark, V. L. P. (2011). *Designing and conducting mixed methods research*. Thousand Oaks, CA: Sage.

Curtis, W. J., & Cicchetti, D. (2003). Moving research on resilience into the 21st century: Theoretical and methodological considerations in examining the biological contributors to resilience. *Development and Psychopathology, 15*, 773–810.

Egeland, B., Carlson, E., & Sroufe, L. A. (1993). Resilience as process. *Development and Psychopathology, 5*(4), 517–528. doi: 10.1017/S0954579400006131

Eidelson, R., Pilisuk, M., & Soldz, S. (2011). The dark side of Comprehensive Soldier Fitness. *American Psychologist, 66*, 643–644.

Fletcher, D., & Sarkar, M. (2012). A grounded theory of psychological resilience in Olympic champions. *Psychology of Sport and Exercise, 13*(5), 669–678.

Fletcher, D., & Sarkar, M. (2013). Psychological resilience: A review and critique of definitions, concepts, and theory. *European Psychologist, 18*(1), 12–23.

Fletcher, D., & Wagstaff, C. R. D. (2009). Organizational psychology in elite sport: Its emergence, application and future. *Psychology of Sport and Exercise, 10*, 427–434.

Fletcher, D., Hanton, S., & Mellalieu, S. D. (2006). An organizational stress review: Conceptual and theoretical issues in competitive sport. In S. Hanton, & S. D. Mellalieu (Eds.), *Literature reviews in sport psychology* (pp. 321–374). Hauppauge, NY: Nova Science.

Friedman, H. L., & Robbins, B. D. (2012). The negative shadow cast by positive psychology: Contrasting views and implications of humanistic and positive psychology on resiliency. *The Humanistic Psychologist, 40*(1), 87–102.

Galli, N., & Gonzalez, S. P. (2015). Psychological resilience in sport: A review of the literature and implications for research and practice. *International Journal of Sport and Exercise Psychology, 3*, 243–257. doi: 10.1080/1612197X.2014.946947.

Galli, N., & Reel, J. J. (2012). "It was hard, but it was good": Exploring stress-related growth in Division I athletes. *Qualitative Research in Sport, Exercise, and Health, 4*(3), 297–319. doi: 10.1080/2159676X.2012.693524.

Galli, N., & Vealey, R. S. (2008). "Bouncing back" from adversity: Athletes' experiences of resilience. *Sport Psychologist, 22*(3), 316–335.

Geller, E., Weil, J., Blumel, D., Rappaport, A., Wagner, C., & Taylor, R. (2003). *McGraw-Hill dictionary of engineering (2nd edn.)*. London: McGraw-Hill.

Gilligan, R. (2004). Promoting resilience in child and family social work: Issues for social work practice, education and policy. *Social Work Education, 23*(1), 93–104.

Gittell, J. H., Cameron, K., Lim, S., & Rivas, V. (2006). Relationships, layoffs, and organizational resilience. *The Journal of Applied Behavioral Science, 42*, 300–329.

Gould, D., & Maynard, I. (2009). Psychological preparation for the Olympic Games. *Journal of Sports Sciences, 27*(13), 1393–1408.

Gould, D., Jackson, S. A., & Finch, L. M. (1993). Sources of stress in national champion figure skaters. *Journal of Sport and Exercise Psychology, 15*(2), 134–159.

Gucciardi, D. F., Jackson, B., Coulter, T. J., & Mallett, C. J. (2011). The Connor-Davidson Resilience Scale (CD-RISC): Dimensionality and age-related measurement invariance with Australian cricketers. *Psychology of Sport and Exercise, 12*, 423–433.

Haglund, M. E. M., Nestadt, P. S., Cooper, N. S., Southwick, S. M., & Charney, D. S. (2007). Psychobiological mechanisms of resilience: Relevance to prevention and treatment of stress-related psychopathology. *Development and Psychopathology, 19*, 889–920.

Hansson, E. K., Tuck, A., Lurie, S., & McKenzie, K. (2012). Rates of mental illness and suicidality in immigrant, refugee, ethnocultural, and racialized groups in Canada: A review of the literature. *Canadian Journal of Psychiatry, 57*(2), 111–121.

Hanton, S., Wagstaff, C., & Fletcher, D. (2012). Cognitive appraisals of stressors encountered in sport organizations. *International Journal of Sport and Exercise Psychology, 10*(4), 276–289. doi: 10.1080/1612197X.2012.682376.

Hart, P. L., Brannan, J. D., & De Chesnay, M. (2014). Resilience in nurses: An integrative review. *Journal of Nursing Management, 22*(6), 720–734.

Holt, N. L., & Dunn, J. G. (2004). Toward a grounded theory of the psychosocial competencies and environmental conditions associated with soccer success. *Journal of Applied Sport Psychology, 16*(3), 199–219. doi: 10.1080/10413200490437949.

Hutcheon, E., & Lashewicz, B. (2014). Theorizing resilience: Critiquing and unbounding a marginalizing concept. *Disability and Society, 29*(9), 1383–1397.

Hutcheon, E. J., & Lashewicz, B. (2015). Are individuals with disabilities and their families "resilient"? Deconstructing and recasting a well-intended concept. *Journal of Social Work in Disability & Rehabilitation, 14*(1), 41–60.

Johnson, B., Down, B., Le Cornu, R., Peters, J., Sullivan, A., Pearce, J., & Hunter, J. (2014). Promoting early career teacher resilience: A framework for understanding and acting. *Teachers and Teaching, 20*(5), 530–546. doi: 10.1080/13540602.2014.937957.

Jones, G., Gittins, M., & Hardy, L. (2009). Creating an environment where high performance is inevitable and sustainable: The high performance environment model. *Annual Review of High Performance Coaching and Consulting, 1*, 139–150.

Karoly, P., & Ruehlman, L. S. (2006). Psychological "resilience" and its correlates in chronic pain: Findings from a national community sample. *Pain, 123*, 90–97.

Kimberlin, S. E., Schwartz, S. L., & Austin, M. J. (2011). Growth and resilience of pioneering nonprofit human service organizations: A cross-case analysis of organizational histories. *Journal of Evidence-Based Social Work, 8*, 4–28.

Lengnick-Hall, C. A., Beck, T. E., & Lengnick-Hall, M. L. (2011). Developing a capacity for organizational resilience through strategic human resource management. *Human Resource Management Review, 21*, 243–255.

Levine, S. Z., Laufer, A., Stein, E., Hamama-Raz, Y., & Solomon, Z. (2009). Examining the relationship between resilience and posttraumatic growth. *Journal of Traumatic Stress, 22*, 282–286.

Lipowski, M., Lipowska, M., Jochimek, M., & Krokosz, D. (2015). Resiliency as a factor protecting youths from risky behaviour: moderating effects of gender and sport. *European Journal of Sport Science, 16*(2), 246–255.

Lu, F. J., Lee, W. P., Chang, Y. K., Chou, C. C., Hsu, Y. W., Lin, J. H., & Gill, D. L. (2016). Interaction of athletes' resilience and coaches' social support on the stress-burnout relationship: A conjunctive moderation perspective. *Psychology of Sport and Exercise, 22*, 202–209.

Luthar, S. S., & Cicchetti, D. (2000). The construct of resilience: Implications for interventions and social policies. *Development and Psychopathology, 12*(2), 857–885.

Luthar, S. S., Cicchetti, D., & Becker, B. (2000). The construct of resilience: A critical evaluation and guidelines for future work. *Child Development, 71*(3), 543–562.

Luthar, S. S., Sawyer, J. A., & Brown, P. J. (2006). Conceptual issues in studies of resilience: Past, present, and future research. *Annals of the New York Academy of Sciences, 1094*, 105–115.

Machida, M., Irwin, B., & Feltz, D. (2013). Resilience in competitive athletes with spinal cord injury: The role of sport participation. *Qualitative Health Research, 23*(1), 1054–1065.

Mahoney, J. L., & Bergman, L. R. (2002). Conceptual and methodological considerations in a developmental approach to the study of positive adaptation. *Applied Developmental Psychology, 23*, 195–217.

Major, B., Richards, C., Cozzarelli, C., Cooper, M. L., & Zubek, J. (1998). Personal resilience, cognitive appraisals and coping: An integrative model of adjustment to abortion. *Journal of Personality and Social Psychology, 74*, 735–752.

Mallak, L. A. (1998). Measuring resilience in health care provider organizations. *Health Manpower Management, 24*, 148–152.

Martin-Krumm, C. P., Sarrazin, P. G., Peterson, C., & Famose, J. (2003). Explanatory style and resilience after sports failure. *Personality and Individual Differences, 35*(7), 1685–1695.

Masten, A. S. (1994). Resilience in individual development: Successful adaptation despite risk and adversity. In M. C. Wang and E. W. Gordon (Eds.), Educational resilience in inner-city America: Challenges and prospects (pp. 3–25). Hillsdale, NJ: Erlbaum.

Masten, A. S. (2013). Competence, risk, and resilience in military families: Conceptual commentary. *Clinical Child and Family Psychology Review, 16*(3), 278–281.

McDonald, G., Jackson, D., Wilkes, L., & Vickers, M. H. (2012). A work-based educational intervention to support the development of personal resilience in nurses and midwives. *Nurse Education Today, 32*(4), 378–384. doi: 10.1016/j.nedt.2011.04.012.

McDonald, G., Jackson, D., Wilkes, L., & Vickers, M. H. (2013). Personal resilience in nurses and midwives: Effects of a work-based educational intervention. *Contemporary Nurse, 45*(1), 134–143. doi: 10.5172/conu.2013.45.1.134.

McGarry, R., Walklate, S., & Mythen, G. (2015). A sociological analysis of military resilience: Opening up the debate. *Armed Forces and Society, 41*(2), 352–378.

McManus, S., Seville, E., Vargo, J., & Brunsdon, D. (2008). Facilitated process for improving organizational resilience. *Natural Hazards Review, 9*, 81–90.

Mellalieu, S. D., Neil, R., Hanton, S., & Fletcher, D. (2009). Competition stress in sport performers: Stressors experienced in the competition environment. *Journal of Sports Sciences, 27*(7), 729–744. doi: 10.1080/02640410902889834.

Meneghel, I., Salanova, M., & Martinez, I. M. (2014). Feeling good makes us stronger: How team resilience mediates the effect of positive emotions on team performance. *Journal of Happiness Studies, 17*(1), 239–255.

Mills, A., Butt, J., Maynard, I., & Harwood, C. (2012). Identifying factors perceived to influence the development of elite youth football academy players. *Journal of Sports Sciences, 30*(15), 1593–1604. doi: 10.1080/02640414.2012.710753.

Morgan, P. B. C., Fletcher, D., & Sarkar, M. (2013). Defining and characterizing team resilience in elite sport. *Psychology of Sport and Exercise, 14*(4), 549–559.

Morgan, P. B. C., Fletcher, D., & Sarkar, M. (2015). Understanding team resilience in the world's best athletes: A case study of a rugby union World Cup winning team. *Psychology of Sport and Exercise, 16*(1), 91–100.

Morgan, C. A., Wang, S., Mason, J., Southwick, S. M., Fox, P., Hazlett, G., et al. (2000). Hormone profiles in humans experiencing military survival training. *Biological Psychiatry, 47*, 891–901.

Mummery, W. K., Schofield, G., & Perry, C. (2004). Bouncing back: The role of coping style, social support and self-concept in resilience of sport performance. *Athletic Insight: The Online Journal of Sport Psychology of Sport and Exercise, 6*(3), 1–18.

Nezhad, M. A. S., & Besharat, M. A. (2010). Relations of resilience and hardiness with sport achievement and mental health in a sample of athletes. *Procedia-Social and Behavioral Sciences, 5*, 757–763.

Reid, C., Stewart, E., & Thorne, G. (2004). Multidisciplinary sport science team in elite sport: Comprehensive servicing or conflict and confusion. *The Sport Psychologist, 18*, 204–217.

Reivich, K. J., Seligman, M. E. P., & McBride, S. (2011). Master resilience training in the US Army. *American Psychologist, 66*(1), 25–34. doi: 10.1037/a0021897

Richardson, G. E. (2002). The metatheory of resilience and resiliency. *Journal of Clinical Psychology, 58*(3), 307–321.

Richardson, G. E., Neiger, B. L., Jensen, S., & Kumpfer, K. L. (1990). The resiliency model. *Health Education, 21*(6), 33–39. doi: 10.1080/00970050.1990.10614589

Riolli, L., & Savicki, V. (2003). Information system organizational resilience. *Omega: The International Journal of Management Science, 31*(3), 227–233.

Robertson, I., Cooper, C. L., Sarkar, M., & Curran, T. (2015). Resilience training in the workplace from 2003–2014: A systematic review. *Journal of Occupational and Organizational Psychology, 88*, 533–562.

Rutter, M. (2006). Implications of resilience concepts for scientific understanding. *Annals of the New York Academy of Sciences, 1094*, 1–12.

Sarkar, M., & Fletcher, D. (2013). How should we measure psychological resilience in sport performers? *Measurement in Physical Education and Exercise Science, 17*, 264–280.

Sarkar, M., & Fletcher, D. (2014). Psychological resilience in sport performers: A review of stressors and protective factors. *Journal of Sports Sciences, 32*, 1419–1434.

Scanlan, T. K., Stein, G. L., & Ravizza, K. (1991). An in-depth study of former elite figure skaters: III. Sources of stress. *Journal of Sport & Exercise Psychology, 13*(2), 103–120.

Schiller, D., & Phelps, E. A. (2011). Does reconsolidation occur in humans? *Frontiers in Behavioral Neuroscience, 5*, 24.

Schinke, R. J., & Hanrahan, S. J. (Eds.) (2009). *Cultural sport psychology*. Champaign, IL: Human Kinetics.

Schinke, R. J., & Jerome, W. C. (2002). Understanding and refining the resilience of elite athletes: An intervention strategy. *Athletic Insight, 4*(9), 1–13. Retrieved from http://www.athleticinsight.com.

Schinke, R. J., Peterson, C., & Couture, R. (2004). A protocol for teaching resilience to high performance athletes. *Journal of Excellence, 9*, 9–18.

Seccombe, K. (2002). "Beating the odds" versus "changing the odds": Poverty, resilience, and family policy. *Journal of Marriage and Family, 64*(2), 384–394.

Seligman, M. E., Nolen-Hoeksema, S., Thornton, N., & Thornton, K. M. (1990). Explanatory style as a mechanism of disappointing athletic performance. *Psychological Science, 1*(2), 143–146. doi: 10.1111/j.1467-9280.1990.tb00084.x.

Shernoff, D. J., & Schmidt, J. A. (2008). Further evidence of an engagement-achievement paradox among U.S. high school students. *Journal of Youth and Adolescence, 37*(5), 564–580. doi: 10.1007/s10964-007-9241-z.

Smith, R. E. (1986). Toward a cognitive-affective model of athletic burnout. *Journal of Sport Psychology, 8*(1), 36–50.

Smith, R. E., Smoll, F. L., & Ptacek, J. T. (1990). Conjunctive moderator variables in vulnerability and resiliency research: Life stress, social support and coping skills, and adolescent sport injuries. *Journal of Personality and Social Psychology, 58*(2), 360–370.

Somers, S. (2009). Measuring resilience potential: An adaptive strategy for organizational crisis planning. *Journal of Contingencies and Crisis Management, 17*, 12–23.

Stephens, J. P., Heaphy, E. D., Carmeli, A., Spreitzer, G. M., & Dutton, J. E. (2013). Relationship quality and virtuousness: Emotional carrying capacity as a source of individual and team resilience. *Journal of Applied Behavioral Science, 49*, 13–41.

Stephenson, A., Vargo, J., & Seville, E. (2010). Measuring and comparing organizational resilience in Auckland. *Australian Journal of Emergency Management, 25*, 27–32.

Thelwell, R. C., Weston, N. J. V., & Greenlees, I. A. (2007). Batting on a sticky wicket: Identifying sources of stress and associated coping strategies for professional cricket batsmen. *Psychology of Sport and Exercise, 8*(2), 219–232.

Theron, L., Cameron, C. A., Didkowsky, N., Lau, C., Liebenberg, L., & Ungar, M. (2011). A "day in the lives" of four resilient youths: Cultural roots of resilience. *Youth & Society, 43*(3), 799–818.

Ungar, M. (2008). Resilience across cultures. *British Journal of Social Work, 38*, 218–235.

Ungar, M. (2010). What is resilience across cultures and contexts? Advances to the theory of positive development among individuals and families under stress. *Journal of Family Psychotherapy, 21*(1), 1–16.

Ungar, M. (2012). Researching and theorizing resilience across cultures and contexts. *Preventive Medicine, 55*(5), 387–389. doi: 10.1016/j.ypmed.2012.07.021.

Ungar, M., & Liebenberg, L. (2011). Assessing resilience across cultures using mixed methods: Construction of the Child and Youth Resilience Measure. *Journal of Mixed Methods Research, 5*, 126–149.

Ungar, M., Liebenberg, L., Boothroyd, R., Kwong, W. M., Lee, T. Y., Leblanc, J., Duque, L., & Makhnach, A. (2008). The study of youth resilience across cultures: Lessons from a pilot study of measurement development. *Research in Human Development, 5*, 166–180.

Van Yperen, N. W. (2009). Why some make it and others do not: Identifying psychological factors that predict career success in professional adult soccer. *The Sport Psychologist, 23*(3), 317–329.

Vitali, F., Bortoli, L., Bertinato, L., Robazza, C., & Schena, F. (2015). Motivational climate, resilience, and burnout in youth sport. *Sport Sciences for Health, 11*(1), 103–108

Vogus, T. J., & Sutcliffe, K. M. (2007). Organizational resilience: Towards a theory and research agenda, *IEEE Systems, Man, and Cybernetics 2007 Conference Proceedings*, 3418–3422.

Wagnild, G., & Young, H. (1993). Development and psychometric evaluation of the Resilience Scale. *Journal of Nursing Management, 1*, 165–178.

Wagstaff, C. R. D., & Larner, R. J. (2015). A review of organizational psychology in elite performance domains: Recent developments and future directions. In S. D. Mellalieu and S. Hanton (Eds.), *Contemporary reviews in sport psychology* (pp. 91–110). London: Routledge.

Wagstaff, C. R. D., Fletcher, D., & Hanton, S. (2012a). Positive organizational psychology in sport: An ethnography of organizational functioning in a national sport organization. *Journal of Applied Sport Psychology, 24*(1), 26–47.

Wagstaff, C. R. D., Fletcher, D., & Hanton, S. (2012b). Positive organizational psychology in sport. *International Review of Sport and Exercise Psychology, 5*, 87–103.

Wagstaff, C. R. D., Gilmore, S., & Thelwell, R. C. (2015). Sport medicine and sport science practitioners' experiences of organizational change. *Scandinavian Journal of Medicine & Science in Sport, 25*, 685–698.

Wagstaff, C. R. D., Gilmore, S., & Thelwell, R. C. (2016). When the show must go on: Investigating repeated organizational change in elite sport. *Journal of Change Management, 16*(1), 38–54. doi:10.1080/14697017.2015.1062793.

Wagstaff, C. R. D., Hanton, S., & Fletcher, D. (2013). Developing emotion abilities and regulation strategies in a sport organization: An action research intervention. *Psychology of Sport and Exercise, 14*(4), 476–487.

Walker, R. J. (1996). Resilient reintegration of adult children of perceived alcoholic parents. Unpublished doctoral dissertation, University of Utah.

Walsh, F. (2002). A family resilience framework: Innovative practice applications. *Family Relations, 51*, 130–137.

Weick, K. E. (1993). The collapse of sensemaking in organizations: The Mann Gulch disaster. *Administrative Science Quarterly, 38*, 628–652.

Weinberg, R., & McDermott, M. (2002). A comparative analysis of sport and business organizations: Factors perceived critical for organizational success. *Journal of Applied Sport Psychology, 14*, 282–298.

West, C., Buettner, P., Stewart, L., Foster, K., & Usher, K. (2012). Resilience in families with a member with chronic pain: A mixed methods study. *Journal of Clinical Nursing, 21*, 3532–3545.

Westphal, M., & Bonanno, G. A. (2007). Posttraumatic growth and resilience to trauma: Different sides of the same coin or different coins? *Applied Psychology: An International Review, 56*, 417–427.

Whitworth, J. A., Williamson, P. M., Mangos, G., & Kelly, J. J. (2005). Cardiovascular consequences of cortisol excess. *Vascular Health and Risk Management, 1*, 291–299.

Wicker, P., Filo, K., & Cuskelly, G. (2013). Organizational resilience of community sport clubs impacted by natural disasters. *Journal of Sport Management, 27*, 510–525.

Windle, G. (2011). What is resilience? A review and concept analysis. *Reviews in Clinical Gerontology, 21*(2), 152–169.

Windle, G., Bennett, K. M., & Noyes, J. (2011). A methodological review of resilience measurement scales. *Health and Quality of Life Outcomes, 9*, 1–18.

Yehuda, R., Brand, S., & Yang, R. K. (2006). Plasma neuropeptide Y concentrations in combat exposed veterans: Relationship to trauma exposure, recovery from PTSD, and coping. *Biological Psychiatry, 59*, 660–663.

PART III
Behaviors in sport organizations

8
LEADERSHIP IN SPORT ORGANIZATIONS

Calum A. Arthur, Christopher R. D. Wagstaff, and Lew Hardy

Introduction

The ability to lead, inspire, and motivate people is an important human characteristic. Indeed, it has been suggested that leadership is vital for effective organizational and societal functioning (Antonakis, Cianciolo, & Sternberg, 2004), with great or poor organizational, military, or sport performances frequently credited to great leadership or lack thereof. Therefore, it is not surprising that leadership has become one of the most studied topics within the social sciences (Antonakis et al., 2004). Leadership has been analyzed from a number of different perspectives (e.g., trait, behavioral, contingency, relational, skeptic, information-processing based approaches) which has resulted in a large number of different theories and models of leadership. Indeed, as long ago as 1971, Fiedler (1971) stated that, "there are almost as many definitions of leadership as there are theories of leadership – and there almost as many theories of leadership as there are psychologists working in the field" (p. 1).

Since the pioneering work of the influential Ohio State and Michigan research programs in the 1950s, the behavioral approach has dominated the leadership research. These programs of research categorized leader behaviors into the broad categories of *consideration* and *initiating* structure (e.g., Stogdill & Coons, 1957), or *task-orientated*, *relations-orientated*, and *participative leadership* (e.g., Katz, Maccoby, Gurin, & Floor, 1951). Following the Ohio State and Michigan research programs, the interest in identifying and categorizing effective leader behaviors burgeoned, with many different theories and behaviors being identified. In line with the extant literature, the current chapter adopts primarily a behavioral approach to leadership. Whilst there have been many theories of leadership within organizational psychology, relatively little theoretical work has been directed specifically at sport organization leadership. The nature of elite sport organizations tend to differ from the typical non-sport organizations in several ways (for an elaboration of this please see Chapter 1 of this book). Therefore, it is important to consider the unique facets of sport organizations when developing theories and models of leadership for use in such domains. It follows that the identification of leader behaviors that facilitate effective functioning across the sport organization is important. Indeed, Fletcher and Arnold (2011) in their research on performance directors stated:

> Future researchers should go beyond global models of leadership and the identification of perceived roles of leaders, and examine (a) differentiated models of leadership in elite sport, and (b) what leaders do in terms of their behaviors and communication in specific contexts and situations.
>
> (p. 237)

Hence, there is a need to focus on what leaders *do* at different levels of sport organizations.

The leadership research that has been conducted from a sport psychology perspective has tended to focus on the dyadic process between the coach and the athlete, or the coach and their teams. This line of research typically tries to identify coach behaviors or styles that impact athlete outcomes and has been underpinned by a number of different perspectives, for example autonomy supportive or controlling coach behaviors (e.g., Pelletier, Fortier, Vallerand, & Briere, 2001), coach-created motivational climate (e.g., Newton, Duda, & Yin, 2000), transformational leadership perspectives (e.g., Arthur, Woodman, Ong, Hardy, & Ntoumanis, 2011), multidimensional leadership perspective (e.g., Riemer & Chelladurai, 1995), the mediational model perspective (e.g., Smoll & Smith, 1984), and the relationship between the coach and the athlete (e.g., Jowett, 2009). This research has demonstrated that different coach behaviors impact a wide range of athlete variables, including organizational citizenship behaviors (Aoyagi, Cox, & McGguire, 2008), group cohesion (Callow, Smith, Hardy, Arthur, & Hardy, 2009; Cronin, Arthur, Hardy, & Callow, 2015; Smith, Arthur, Hardy, Callow, & Williams, 2012), intrinsic motivation (Hollembeak & Amorose, 2005), fun and self-esteem (Smoll, Smith, Barnett, & Everett, 1993), motivational climate (Smith et al., 2005), extra effort, satisfaction with coach, and attendance (Rowold, 2006), athlete self-talk (Zourbanos et al., 2011), satisfaction (Baker, Yardley, & Côté, 2003), anxiety (Williams et al., 2003), win–loss record (Weiss & Friedrichs, 1986), self-ratings of performance (Horne & Carron, 1985), coping (Nicolas, Gaudreau, & Franche, 2011), goal attainment (Nicolas et al., 2011), communication (Smith et al., 2012), and athlete sacrifice (Cronin et al., 2015). However, this research has typically been conducted as if coach–athlete interactions occur in a vacuum with little consideration given to the antecedent factors or the climate in which these effects occur. Indeed Stebbings, Taylor, Spray, and Ntoumanis (2012) recently stated, "…scant research addresses potential reasons why coaches employ these contrasting interpersonal styles" (p. 482). In their study, Stebbings and colleagues found coaches' perceptions of their environment influenced their psychological health and their interpersonal behavior toward athletes. Thus, there would appear to be a need to consider the wider environment in which the coach operates. Within the sport context the wider environment might manifest to effect coaches in two broad ways: by influencing the behaviors that the coach displays with their athletes; and by moderating the effectiveness of coach behaviors on athlete outcomes.

The majority of leadership and coaching theories and models that have been developed within sport have been underpinned by social cognitive approaches (cf. Arthur, 2014), yet very little research has actually been conducted within a social cognitive paradigm. That is, the environmental factors that influence coach behaviors or moderate coach behaviors have received scarce research attention. This is surprising given that one of the key underpinning factors of social cognitive approaches is that interactions and relationships do not occur in isolation; rather they are part of a reciprocal causal network whereby environmental, personal, and behavioral factors interact to determine a range of attitudinal and behavioral consequences. Thus, coach–athlete interaction occurs within a broader environment. This notion is similar to the sentiment of Hardy, Jones, and Gould (1996) who stated that athletes do not perform in a vacuum; rather they are part of a complex social and organizational structure. Interestingly, this sentiment is not unique to the sport leadership literature and has been acknowledged in organizational psychology; for example, House and Aditya (1997) stated, "it is almost as though leadership scholars… have believed that leader-follower relationships exist in a vacuum" (p. 445).

While research (see Weinberg & McDermott, 2002) indicates that leaders in both sport (i.e., coaches) and business (i.e., executives) agree on the factors relating to organizational success (viz. leadership characteristics, interpersonal skills, leadership style), it is important to recognize that the nature of a sport organization is somewhat different to many non-sport organizations. For example, sport organizations are typically evaluated by the performance of athletes and teams, whereas for-profit business organizations are evaluated by outcomes such as market share, operations, customer service, financial profit, or product quality. Within this domain, the coach–athlete interaction can be considered a special case of leadership as it occurs at the bottom of a hierarchical schematic, yet it is arguably the most important in determining organizational outcomes. Moreover, while the coach plays a pivotal role in developing and shaping the environment for their athletes, the coach also has to perform within the broader organizational environment. The aim of the current chapter is to extend Hardy et al.'s (1996) notion in calling for leadership researchers to move beyond the coach–athlete interaction. Although very important, sport leadership research is limited by its narrow focus on the coach–athlete dyad and like non-sport organizations, we should turn our attention to leadership throughout the organizational structure. In this way the leadership that the coach receives from their line manager will impact on their interactions with their athlete. Likewise the leadership that the coach's line manager (e.g., head coach or performance director) receives from their line manager (e.g., executive board or chief executive officer; CEO) will impact their behaviors with the coach's line manager, and so on. In essence it is argued that there is a cascading of leadership effects at play within sport organizations that have implications for leadership throughout the organization, not least for coach–athlete interactions. This has been described in the literature as "in the shadow of the Boss's Boss" (Tangirala, Green, & Ramanujam, 2007). Tangirala et al. (2007) demonstrated that nurse outcomes (i.e., organizational identification, perceived organizational support, and depersonalization toward customers) were, in part, determined by the quality of the relationship that the nurse's supervisor had with their supervisor.

An important consideration when discussing organizational leadership is the distinction between *leadership in* and *leadership of* organizations (see Dubin, 1977). Leadership *in* organizations refers to lower level leadership that involves direct leader–follower interactions. Whereas leadership *of* refers to leadership near the top of the organizational hierarchy where interactions are typically more distant and strategically orientated. Leaders at the top of the hierarchy will also engage in direct interactions with their immediate subordinates that are typical of the *in* approach (Hunt, 2004). The current chapter briefly discusses hierarchical structures and will then integrate leader distance theories into the sport organizational context. Last, a behavioral taxonomy that is cognizant of leader distance and leadership *of* and *in* will be developed. An aim of the behavioral taxonomy is to help better understand and integrate leadership practices throughout the different hierarchical structures within sport organizations (leadership *of* and *in*). The resultant intention is that the behavioral taxonomy will help to create integrated and coherent leadership practices within sport organizations.

Hierarchical structures in sport organizations

Hierarchical structures and role differentiation are omnipresent in organizations and are used to coordinate the actions of individuals within organizations (Gruenfeld & Tiedens, 2010; Halevy, Chou, Galinsky, & Murnighan, 2012). Indeed, Halevy, Chou, and Galinsky (2011) stated that hierarchies allow the social organization of groups that enables them to achieve high levels of coordination and cooperation that ensure survival and success. Organizations have different hierarchical structures, for example, mechanistic organizations that are governed by an authority-centered philosophy will have greater hierarchical distance than organic organizations where decision-making is distributed throughout the organization (Courtright, Fairhurst, & Rogers, 1989). "Sport governance" includes many of the usual features of governance, such as: vision; strategy; effective running of an organization; accountability; and supervision. Nevertheless, there are aspects of "sport governance" such as anti-doping, betting and gambling policies inter alia on the safeguarding children and vulnerable adults, diversity, and equality which feed into, and contribute to, the effective running of the organization and the sport at large. They make "sport governance" unique. "Sport governance" includes not only regulatory but also ethical procedures and processes which aim to ensure the effective and fair administration and development of the sport beyond the organization itself. Good governance in sport and recreation goes beyond the oversight of an organization (structure), and extends to the context and environment that the organization operates within. In this sense, good governance in the sport sector must be lived throughout not just the organization but through the membership and experience of the participants of the activity.

In an attempt to optimize sport governance, sport management scholars have dedicated substantial effort to examining organizational design to better understand the optimal structure of sport organizations. Importantly for sport psychologists, management scholars have observed increasing alignment of structures with few clear differences in configuration (see Theodoraki & Henry, 1994), a process referred to as institutional isomorphism. Where differences in organizational structure exist, it is mainly because they operate with different contextual situations. For example, differences in organizational design in elite sport might be due to the not-for-profit (e.g., governing bodies) or for-profit (e.g., professional sport organizations) goals of the organization. Nevertheless, a common governance structure exists and is encouraged. In the United Kingdom, in an effort to ensure that public funds are invested in well-governed and managed national governing bodies (NGBs), UK Sport and Sport England have developed a "Governance Framework" consisting of required standards, funding triggers, and conditions of grants for NGBs, all of which are based on good practice principles. Specifically, organizations must adhere to proscribed organizational structures, policies, and board composition guidance to uphold the highest standards of leadership and governance in order to be recognized as eligible to receive government funding.

Leadership style varies as a function of the hierarchical level of the leader with more senior leaders typically engaging in policy making, articulation of visions, and having limited contact with their subordinates (*leadership of*), whereas lower level leaders typically engage in daily interactions with their subordinates and engage in behaviors such as goal setting and mentoring (*leadership in*) (Avolio & Bass, 1995; Waldman & Yammarino, 1999). Senior leaders will typically communicate with their subordinates using speeches addressing larger groups with little opportunity to interact on an individual basis. Individual interactions with senior leaders will typically be few and far between and will likely be associated with greater importance or having greater consequence (the importance will likely increase with greater hierarchical differentiation). The specific interactions that more distal and proximal leaders tend to engage in can be categorized along a continuum from more abstract (distal leaders) to more concrete (proximal leaders) (Berson et al., 2015). For example, more distal leaders are likely to engage in more abstract type behaviors such as articulating a strategic vision (typically long term), hypothetical aspirations, shared values, and collective identity, whereas more proximal leaders are more likely to engage in more concrete day-to-day behaviors such as goal setting and individualized feedback (cf. Kluger & DeNisi, 1996; Locke & Latham, 2002). Importantly, there is evidence that hierarchal leader distance moderates the effectiveness of leader behaviors based on the level of abstractness (e.g., Berson & Halevy, 2014). Consequently, when attempting to determine what effective leadership is from an organizational perspective it is important to consider the level at which the leader operates in the organization and with whom they are interacting.

Leader distance

The concept of how "close" or "distant" followers are from their leaders can change the influence process of leader behaviors. Antonakis and Atwater (2002) define leader distance as "the configual effect (i.e., the coexistence of a cluster of independent factors) of leader-follower physical distance, perceived social distance, and perceived interaction frequency" (p. 674). To elaborate, social distance can be elevated or reduced by leader behaviors; for example, leader behaviors that maximize their status and displays of power differentials will enhance leader distance. That is, leaders who interact with their followers less frequently might contribute toward creating greater distance between the leader and their follower. The hierarchical structure of the organization will likely also contribute to leader distance. In extending Napier and Ferris's (1994) work on leader distance, Antonakis and Atwater (2002) conceptualized leader distance as having three distinct dimensions. The first dimension, *perceived social or psychological distance*, was based on Napier and Ferris's psychological distance and Bass and Stogdill's (1990) psychosocial distance concepts. Antonakis and Atwater (2002) defined perceived social or psychological distance as, "…perceived differences in status, rank, authority, social standing, and power, which affect the degree of intimacy and social contact that develop between followers and their leader" (p. 682). The second dimension, *physical distance*, refers to how close followers are located to their leader. Antonakis and Atwater drew a distinction between social and physical distance in that proximally located leaders are likely to be socially distant and distally located leaders are likely to be socially close. The third dimension, *perceived frequency of leader-follower interaction*, was defined as "the perceived degree to which leaders interact with their follower" (p. 686). Importantly, Antonakis and Atwater suggest that these three dimensions are distinct and can occur concurrently in various levels. Furthermore, according to Antonakis and Atwater, no particular combination of the three factors necessarily determine leader effectiveness; rather effectiveness will be determined by a combination of the dimensions of leaders' distance and other (moderating) factors that will include leader behaviors, situation, and context.

Berson, Halevy, Shamir, and Erez (2015) offered an explanation of the effects of leader distance that is based on Construal-Level Theory (CLT) of psychological distance (Trope & Liberman, 2010). At the heart of CLT is the notion of psychological distance, which refers to an abstract mental construal of objects measured as a metaphorical or actual distance from the self (Trope & Liberman, 2010). These distances can be construed in terms of spatial distance, temporal distance, social distance, and hypothetically, and are all, to some extent, interchangeable. CLT predicts that when different objects are construed as similar in terms of relative distance from the self then response patterns are quicker and will lead to more positive outcomes (cf. Berson & Halevy, 2014). The extent to which different objects are construed as similar in terms of psychological distance is referred to as "construal fit" (Berson & Halevy, 2014). That is, if two different objects that are congruent in terms of perceived psychological distance from the self, this would be labelled as having construal fit. An important premise of CLT is that distant situations such as future events, physically or socially remote individuals, and hypothetical events are construed as abstract representations, whereas more proximal near future events, closeness to others, and probable events use concrete representations (Berson et al., 2015). From a leadership perspective the construal fit relates to the fit between the situation (i.e., psychological distance between leader and follower) and the behaviors of the leader (i.e., abstract or concrete). Therefore, following this logic, a large social distance between leader and follower would require more abstract communication from the leader and a small social distance between leader and follower would require more concrete communication styles from the leader.

In a series of studies, Berson and Halevy (2014) tested the construal fit hypothesis in a leadership context where the hierarchical distance between leaders and followers were hypothesized to moderate the effectiveness of leader behaviors. Specifically, abstract leader behaviors (e.g., articulation of a vision) when enacted across a large hierarchical distance produced more positive effects than when enacted across smaller hierarchical distances. The results supported their hypothesis in that the relationship between job satisfaction and articulation of a vision (abstract leader behavior) was stronger when a large hierarchical distance was present. That is, articulation of a vision only impacted employee's job satisfaction when it originated from distant leaders and there was no relationship between the articulation of a vision and job satisfaction when it originated from proximal leaders. Conversely, the effects of feedback and mentoring (concrete leader behaviors) on job satisfaction was only significant at a small hierarchical distance. Hence, feedback and mentoring positively impacted job satisfaction only when it was provided by hierarchically proximal leaders. The results were replicated and extended in two further studies that tested and supported the construal fit hypothesis in a hypothetical situation (Study 2) and in a crisis situation (Study 3). The theoretical predictions of CLT and leader distance and the empirical research testing them strongly suggest that it is vital to consider the psychological distance between the leader and the follower when examining leader effectiveness in an organizational setting.

Given the salience of leader–follower psychological distance in organizations, it is worth highlighting two factors that will influence the usefulness of such findings in the context of sport. Namely, perceived leader distance is caused by at least two factors, one of these being the structure of the organization and is thus less amenable to change. The other factor that can influence leader distance are the behaviors and communication style that leaders use with their followers. For example, leaders can distance themselves from their followers or get closer to them (Berson et al., 2015) depending on the way they choose to interact. Specifically, greater one-to-one interaction with followers will likely lead to a minimized perceived distance. Nevertheless, it is important to note that the results from the Berson et al. (2015) studies suggest that leaders from different hierarchical levels would need to be careful in how they try to reduce the distance between them and their follower. This is because feedback and mentoring, which might be used to increase interaction and thus reduce distance, did not impact job satisfaction when feedback was provided from a leader who was one step hierarchically above their direct leader (i.e., the boss's boss).

In this brief review of leader distance and CLT a number of factors become apparent when discussing leadership within sport organizations. First, a very complex picture of leadership emerges highlighting a need to simplify the leadership process. Second, the effectiveness of leader behaviors are likely impacted by perceived leader distance. Third, perceived leader distance is likely impacted by hierarchical level and leader behaviors. Fourth, models of organizational leadership would be incomplete if they solely focus on the dyadic coach–athlete relationship without considering the broader context in which leaders operate. One way to simplify a phenomenon is to organize it into meaningful and understandable sub-units. To this end, the next section of the chapter outlines a model that provides a taxonomy of leader behaviors categorized according to their typical content and primary outcomes.

The Tripartite Model of Leadership

A review of the leadership literature in sport reveals that the vast majority of this research has focused on the coach–athlete dyad (see Fletcher & Arnold, 2011; Stebbings et al., 2012). Another observation from the literature is that a large number of different leadership behaviors have been identified. Indeed in our review of the sport literature which included models such as the ones developed by Smith and Smoll (1989), Cushion, Harvey, Muir, and Nelson (2012), Gallimore and Tharpe (2004), Chelladurai (1993), Mageau and Vallerand (2003), Balaguer, Duda and Crespo (1999), Côté, Yardley, Sedgwick, and Baker (1999), and Callow et al. (2009) we identified over 30 different behaviors that have been articulated in the literature. As described earlier, these models typically focus on the coach–athlete dyad. In order to best utilize this rich research, we have developed a model of organizational leadership that makes use of the sport coaching literature and applies it to the sport organizational context. Although it is unlikely that any one theory or model would be able to incorporate all the different approaches to leadership that currently exist in the literature, we believe that it is possible to synthesize the current literature into a number of higher order leadership factors and apply the principles to sport organization leadership. This section presents a possible categorization of the different leader behaviors that have been identified in the literature. It is important to note that we have primarily focused on developing a taxonomy of typical leader behaviors but we will also delineate the primary mechanisms by which the different behavioral categories will operate. That is, the behavioral typologies can be differentiated based on the content of the actual behavior and the primary outcomes the behaviors are theorized to influence. Furthermore, it is clear from the review of leader distance literature that leader–follower interactions do not occur in a vacuum and that a theory or model of sport organizational leadership will need to include concepts of distance in its formation, or at least in its application. The current behavioral taxonomy presents a generic model of leader behaviors that can be applied across the hierarchical levels of an organization (leadership that relates to both *of* and *in*) and across different situations.

In the current model we outline leader behaviors that are directed at followers and organize these into behavioral categories that are likely common to all leaders in any (sport) organization. A leader in the current model is defined as an individual who is hierarchically more senior than another individual within a formalized organizational structure. Being hierarchically more senior than another individual in the organization usually means that the person who is in a more senior position typically possesses certain responsibilities, skills, knowledge, and experience that are different to individuals that are below them. The person on the next hierarchical level of an organization is likely more experienced, has more knowledge, has a greater sphere of influence, will need to take a broader perspective, has more job complexity, and will typically have more diverse areas of responsibility when compared to their subordinates. For example, athletes are led by coaches, who typically use their advanced knowledge of skill development to advance skill execution. Coaches are led by a performance director or head coach, who must assimilate multiple aspects of team selection, preparation, and performance, while integrating sport science and medicine support. Further up the hierarchy, performance directors and head coaches are typically led by senior management (CEOs, chairs, boards), whose remit focuses on both strategic and operational factors. However, a role that all leaders have, regardless of their hierarchical level within an organization, is the need to influence the motivation of those under their charge, and the better they are at doing this the more effective a leader they are likely to be (cf. Berson et al., 2015). Of course, this is predicated on the caveat that the leader is motivating their followers in the right direction. Thus, the leader is required to both generate motivation (energy) and direct this toward optimal targets. An exceptionally motivated team, that is, a team willing to put extra effort into achieving their goals, will not be successful if they are not directed toward appropriate goals. Additionally, an exceptionally motivated team will likely not be successful if the team members are pulling in different directions toward contradictory goals. Conversely, a demotivated team that is going in the right direction are also unlikely to perform optimally. Another key leader role is to ensure that their subordinates have sufficient skills and knowledge to carry out their jobs. Hence, there are three basic fundamental roles fulfilled by a leader to promote the likelihood of success: to generate motivation; point this motivation in the right direction; and ensure subordinates have sufficient knowledge and skills. In turn, we propose that there are three higher order behavioral typologies that can be used to achieve these (either in combination or on their own): *leadership/ inspirational type behaviors*; *coaching type behaviors*; and *instructing type behaviors* (see Figure 8.1). These constructs are defined and described in the following sections.

It is intended that the current classification provides a reasonable basis from which leadership, coaching, and instruction can be meaningfully differentiated, both with regard to the content of the behavior and the primary mechanisms by which they operate. Indeed, we believe the application of the Tripartite Model of Leadership (TML) within sport organizations will assist with the provision of a consistent message about the leadership *of* and *in* the organization along with the behaviors that are consistent with this message. That is, the TML is a single overarching model of leadership that can be used and adapted to the different levels within a sport organization that will generate a consistent leadership strategy and, in turn, consistent behaviors.

Inspirational leadership behaviors

The inspirational leadership category in the TML draws from the "new paradigm" of leadership theories (Bryman, 1992) such as transformational leadership (Bass, 1985; Burns, 1978), charismatic leadership (Conger & Kanungo, 1987), and visionary leadership (Sashkin, 1984). At the heart of the new paradigm of leadership is the separation of transactional exchanges from transformational leadership. Transactional exchanges are in essence about rewards and punishments, whereas transformational leadership centers on affective components as the key influence process. That is, transformational leadership is often described as a process of engagement whereby the leader develops each follower to achieve their full potential by engaging the emotions and values of their followers. In his seminal work Bernard Bass (1985) stated, "to sum up, we see the transformational leader as one who motivates us to do more than we originally expected to do" (p. 20). Bass went on to delineate the processes by which this expectancy-surpassing takes place, namely that it includes raising awareness and level of consciousness about the value of designated outcomes along with ways of reaching these outcomes, and transcending self-interest for the greater good.

The inspirational leadership component of the TML focuses on behaviors that motivate and inspire athletes to achieve beyond expectations. The articulation of a compelling and inspirational vision forms a central component of the leader typology. Visions typically focus on future-orientated idealizations of shared organizational goals that refer to purpose, beliefs, and values (Bass,

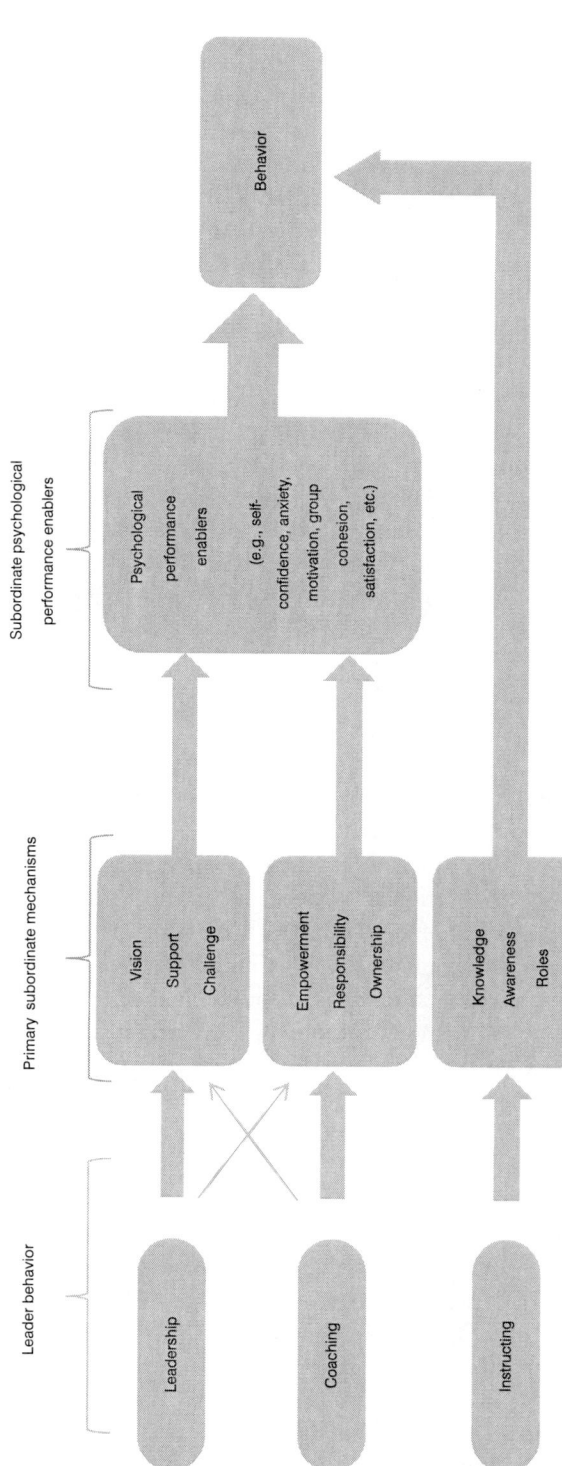

FIGURE 8.1 The Tripartite Model of Leadership (TML)

Note: The TML is a behavioral taxonomy that separates leader behaviors (interactions with subordinates) into three higher order categories and it is intended to be applied throughout all hierarchical levels of the sport organization. While it is likely that there are many moderators of the relationships proposed in the TML, we have not included them in the model for aid of understanding.

1985; Conger & Kanungo, 1998; Nanus, 1992; Sashkin, 1984). They generally relate to a desirable end state ("What") and the reasons underpinning this end state ("Why") but rarely focus on the mechanisms by which visions are achieved ("How") (Conger & Kanungo, 1998). Further, visions tend to emphasize team or individual aspirations that can span many years or will draw attention to superordinate goals of a greater purpose and meaning. Along with the visionary component, other leader behaviors such as role modeling, individual consideration, fostering acceptance of group goals, and high performance expectations are also included in the leadership typology. This typology is underpinned by the conceptualization of transformational leadership developed by Arthur and colleagues (Arthur et al., 2011; Callow et al., 2009; Hardy et al., 2010). However, the Arthur and colleagues' conceptualization is not exhaustive and most behaviors aligned with the "new paradigm" will likely occupy this category. The transactional type behaviors (e.g., reward, praise, punishment, scolding, and discipline type behaviors) are also included in the leadership typology as this component is often described as forming the foundations upon which transformational leadership operates (e.g., Bass, 1985).

The leadership category can also be differentiated from coaching and instructing type behaviors based on the primary mechanisms by which the leadership behaviors are theorized to operate. That is, leadership type behaviors are theorized to provide individuals with a positive vision of the future, perceptions of support, and challenge. The notion of vision, support, and challenge in relation to transformational leadership has been discussed elsewhere (Arthur, Hardy, & Woodman, 2012; Arthur & Lynn, 2017; Hardy et al., 2010) and as such only a brief synopsis is provided below. Leader behaviors which articulate a positive vision of the future will be related to followers' perceptions of vision. Leader behaviors instill belief in their followers that they can achieve the vision; for example, expressions of confidence and the provision of support will be related to the support component. Praise and rewarding type behaviors are also proposed to be related to the support component. Finally, leader behaviors that emphasize high performance expectations, challenge followers to solve problems, and punishment or discipline orientated behaviors will predict perceptions of challenge.

We believe that any leader in a sport organization can use the leader typology behaviors regardless of their hierarchical level, but the effectiveness and the behavioral manifestation of them (i.e., what they look like) will likely differ across hierarchical level. For example, the use of vision will likely be more effective when articulated by more senior members of an organization. This is because visions tend to be about the organization or larger polities and are more abstract in nature. Berson and Halevy (2014) recently demonstrated that visionary leadership (measured by the inspirational motivation scale from the Multifactor Leadership Questionnaire-5X) was more effective when used by more senior leaders than when it was used by less senior leaders. Contrastingly, leader behaviors that were described as being more concrete, such as individual level goal setting (contained in both the instructional and coaching categories, the main difference being the method by which goals are set), were found to be more effective for lower level leaders. Expanding these results to other leader behaviors, it is plausible that leader behaviors that are focused on individual level interactions, such as individual consideration and contingent reward, would be more effective for lower level leaders, or those with small leader distance.

Coaching behaviors

Similar to the leadership literature, the definition of coaching remains somewhat elusive and can range from more instructional and directive type approaches to more self-directed type approaches. For example, Parsloe (1995) defined coaching as, "directly concerned with the immediate improvement of performance and the development of skills by a form of tutoring and instruction" (p. 18). Elsewhere, Druckman and Bjork (1991) stated that coaching "consists of observing students and offering hints, feedback, reminders, [or] new tasks, or redirecting a student's attention to a salient feature – all with the goal of making the student's performance approximate the expert's performance as closely as possible" (p. 61). Other scholars have proposed more self-directed definitions of coaching, such as Whitmore (2009), who argued that, "coaching is unlocking a person's potential to maximize their own performance. It is helping them learn rather than teaching them" (p. 8). The definitions of coaching are diverse and appear to, in places, overlap with the definition of leadership or have an instructional component. Nevertheless, a central theme of the definitions of coaching is that they all, to some extent, either explicitly refer to, or implicitly imply, the facilitation of self-awareness and self-directed learning. Furthermore, the role of asking questions is almost always central to the coaching process (e.g., Grant & Stober, 2006; Whitmore, 2009). In summing up the various coaching definitions, Grant and Stober (2006) stated, "it is clear that coaching is more about asking the right questions than telling people what to do" (p. 3). In the current model, we define coaching as a process that uses a questioning technique to enhance self-awareness, ownership, responsibility, and goal commitment that ultimately seeks to facilitate more internalized regulation of motivation for goal attainment and performance.

The coaching process is essentially about the extent which leaders encourage their followers to engage in their own self-development by promoting self-reflective practices. In turn, the primary behaviors the coach will engage in will be effective questioning techniques and the facilitation of goal setting. The main difference between the coaching and instructing type category is that, in the latter, the leader will act as an educator and will typically tell or show their followers what to do, whereas in the coaching type category the leader will typically avoid telling their followers what to do but will encourage them to reflect and identify their own strengths and weaknesses and set their own goals (in the instructional category the leader will set goals for their subordinates).

Another crucial difference is that to be effective in the coaching mode, the leader does not necessarily need to have an in-depth knowledge of the content they are coaching, but the leader will need to possess an in-depth knowledge of the coaching process. This is consistent with Whitmore (2009) who stated, "coaching requires expertise in coaching but not in the subject at hand. That is one of its great strengths" (p. 14). Nevertheless, it is also important to note that not all types of questions will be considered coaching questioning, for example, rhetorical, closed, and cynical questioning styles that are intended to scold, clearly do not belong in the coaching category.

The primary mechanisms by which the coaching behaviors are theorized to facilitate are self-awareness, ownership, and empowerment. That is, we propose that the process of asking effective questions is theorized to stimulate active engagement and problem solving that will elicit greater cognitive load. This proposition is consistent with the notions that have been articulated in the sport coaching literature with regards to the use of questioning techniques to promote reflective thinking and active learning (see, for example, Anderson, Magill, Sekiya, & Ryan, 2005; Chambers & Vickers, 2006). The concepts of ownership and empowerment are not dissimilar to key aspects of self-determination theory (Deci & Ryan, 1985). We suggest that the use of coaching type behaviors will promote the likelihood that athletes will have greater levels of internalized motivation. Indeed, in a coaching context Mageau and Vallerand (2003) proposed a model of the coach–athlete relationship which was underpinned by the principles of self-determination theory. They proposed that the positive impact of the coach (i.e., coach's autonomy supportive behaviors) would impact athlete motivation via the satisfaction of autonomy, relatedness, and competence. Similar to Mageau and Vallerand, the current model adopts key aspects of self-determination theory that propose that leaders who satisfy athletes' needs of autonomy, relatedness, and competence will engender more internalized regulation of behavior. However, the current model differs in that we specifically propose that leaders will satisfy such needs primarily via the use of coaching type behaviors.

Beyond the potential gains to motivation in terms of self-determined motivation, the principles of the coaching behaviors category are also consistent with contextual interference (Battig, 1979), where optimum learning (skill transfer and retention) is proposed to occur as a result of internal feedback mechanisms and more effortful processing (e.g., Brady, 2008). One of the ways contextual interference is proposed to enhance learning is, in conditions of increasing task difficulty, more effortful processes are engaged and, thus, enhanced learning occurs (cf. Shea & Zimny, 1988). It is posited here that questioning techniques will increase task focus, thereby encouraging more effortful processing. Another key research finding from the skill acquisition research is that augmented feedback can be detrimental to skill acquisition (for a review, see Magill, 1994). One of the explanations for why augmented feedback can be detrimental to skill learning is that subordinates can become overly reliant on the external feedback and when such feedback is no longer present they can struggle to execute the skill. Furthermore, augmented feedback is also proposed to interfere with the internal feedback mechanisms thus making them less effective. It follows that withholding immediate feedback and using questioning prompts might stimulate the development of more independent processing mechanisms and facilitate enhanced understanding of skill mechanisms.

The implementation and effectiveness of the questioning process will be affected by many factors including the leader–follower relationship and the situation. For example, in order for the questioning to be effective it must be done in a suitable environment where there are no direct time pressures and affectivity of the follower is neutral. Also, it might also be unadvisable to engage in coaching type behaviors early in the stages of learning given the research evidence that demonstrates that early learners benefit from block practice (a conceptually simple learning environment) rather than random practice (a conceptually more challenging environment) (e.g., Landin & Hebert, 1997). We also propose leader distance to play a role in determining the optimal times or situations to use the coaching behaviors. For example, the use of the coaching type behaviors will likely lead to reduced leader–follower distance because the leader essentially asks their subordinate(s) to work with them to solve problems. Such acts often require relatively close and frequent contact with their follower. It is important to note that the coaching behavior category is not about the leader simply delegating and taking a laissez-faire approach to leadership; rather a questioning technique and working through the problems will be required. Another proposition that we make is that the coaching type behaviors will typically take longer to achieve the desired outcomes compared to instructing type behaviors (see next section) but the follower will likely remain engaged for longer because they have ownership of the solution and will thus likely be more intrinsically motivated. Evidence to support the coaching dimension of the TML model comes from the self-determination theory research where autonomy supportive behaviors (an example of which is adopting a questioning technique) is related to enhanced intrinsic motivation which, in turn, is related to enhanced persistence (e.g., Hardre & Reeve, 2003; Robbins et al., 2004; Vallerand, Fortier, & Guay, 1997). The observable outcome of coaching behaviors may be fairly similar to the one obtained via instructing, yet the long term motivational effects of the coaching mode will be far stronger and will promote greater levels of perseverance. Of course, the downside is that remaining in the coaching mode will take more time and the leader has less control over the final solution. And, finally, it is suggested that a fairly strong leader–follower relationship is required for the coaching behaviors to have optimal effects.

Instructing behaviors

Instructing type behaviors include all those behaviors that are focused on the transference of knowledge from the leader to their followers in the form of detailed instructions. The essence of this behavior is that the leader will communicate to their followers exactly what and how things should be done or, in other words, the leader will adopt a "telling" approach. The underlying assumption of the instructional typology is that the leader has useful or important knowledge, at that moment in time, beyond that of his or her followers that is transferred via demonstrations and/or verbal descriptions. Consequently, leaders will have detailed knowledge of what needs to be achieved and how to achieve it. This implies that to be effective in this domain the leader has to possess superior knowledge and or insight which are not necessarily fundamental to the coaching domain. Instructions can be the provision of informational feedback in response to a specific event, where the feedback provides insight into what went wrong, perhaps why, and offer alternatives for future events. Of course, were the leader to adopt a coaching approach then no instructions would be provided; rather a questioning technique would be employed to try and elicit the solutions from their subordinate.

It is hypothesized that the instruction type behaviors will primarily operate via mechanisms such as explicit knowledge of what is expected of followers and role clarity. It is important to note that the instructing behavioral typology will not necessarily be beneficial for follower motivation in terms of the internalization of motivation. Indeed, it may even contribute to more external regulation types. However, the potential benefits of the instructional type behaviors are that subordinates will have a clear idea of what is to be achieved from their leader's or the organization's perspective (which is important for promotion and retaining contracts etc.), and how to achieve it in a relatively short period of time, provided they have the necessary skills and that the leader can communicate in such a way that the follower understands. Additionally, an instructional reminder of a process goal prior to an Olympic final, or an important board meeting, could have beneficial effects on motivation (reducing doubts) and technique/performance. Too much use of instructional type behaviors outside a pressured environment and the leader will likely be perceived as controlling and micromanaging their followers, yet there will be times when telling or instructing is the optimal behavior. In time-pressured and other stressful (high performance) environments the instructing type behaviors will likely be optimal because the performer is not required or are perhaps not able to problem solve or make complex decisions themselves, thereby reducing the pressure on them.

With regards to hierarchical level within a sport organization, we again believe that leaders at all levels of the hierarchy can use the instructional type behaviors to good effect. However, in line with leader distance and construal fit hypothesis, the instructional type behaviors are by their nature concrete, and are thus likely to be more effective when the leader distance is small (Berson & Halevy, 2014), or when leading *in* rather than *of*. That is, instructing will likely be more effective when used by leaders with their direct followers under time constraints and will become increasingly less effective with greater leader distance or where there are few additional demands. Within a sport organization, the coach will likely make most use of this behavioral typology. Indeed, the coach observational literature consistently reports that coaches use the instructional behavioral typology more than any other (e.g., Cushion, Harvey, Muir, & Nelson, 2012; Partington & Cushion, 2013).

Conclusion

The TML is a behavioral taxonomy that categorizes leader behaviors into three higher order factors, namely inspirational leadership, coaching, and instructing. While these categories can be differentiated at a behavioral and outcome level, there are grey areas between them and they will likely be used in combination and, to some extent, have interactive effects. It is also important to note that no one behavioral category is better or more desirable than any other, and we perceive each behavior type to have value depending on contextual demands. The model provides a behavioral framework which can help to raise awareness of and reflection on the behavior of leaders in sport organizations. Such use of the framework might support assessment and development of effective leader behaviors and guide reflection. Thus, it is hoped that the model will help to disentangle the complex nature of leading people within sport originations by providing a clear behavioral framework to help evaluate and guide behavior. Moreover, in developing the model, we were cognizant that leaders do not operate in a vacuum; rather they have to perform within an organizational structure which will be characterized by climatic and cultural factors. Indeed, a primary determinant of the organizational climate is the leadership that is displayed throughout (i.e., leadership *in*) the organization, with a key mechanism of this being the hierarchical nature of the organization and leader distance. Furthermore, the construal level (Trope & Liberman, 2010) and leader distance perspectives offer indications of which behaviors will be more effective at different levels of leader distance. Namely, that the greater the leader distance, the more abstract the leader behaviors should be. Likewise, the closer the leader distance, the more concrete the behavior should be. While research is required to test the theoretical propositions of incorporating CLT into leadership theory in sport organizations, the TML appears to provide a solid foundation from which to test these propositions.

The TML has many potential applied uses. For example, it might be used as a framework for leader education, intervention, and assessment. The model might allow for bespoke interventions to be developed, whereby leaders can be evaluated against the criteria with the information generated being used to tailor interventions. For example, if the leader is very good at inspirational leadership type behaviors but not questioning techniques, then the intervention could focus on the latter behavioral aspects. The typology could also be used as a broader educational framework that might help the leader to understand their behaviors and the impact that different behaviors are likely to have on their subordinates in different situations. In reality, it is likely that the different behavior types will be used in combination and interchangeably, with the effectiveness of each behavioral typology being determined by a variety of situational and contextual variables. Hence, a leader may switch between them concurrently and adapt their style to the situation and context. Similarly, they may plan to use one type of style but recognize that it is not working and switch to another. For example, if the leader adopts a coaching style but recognizes that this is not having the desired effect, then switching to the instructional style might seem prudent. The different behavioral categories might also be used in conjunction with each other or have interactional type effects. In a situation when the coaching style is not applicable but the leader is concerned about the potential negative motivational effects of the instructional style, the leader may pair an instructional type behavior with leadership (e.g., explanation of why it is important, how it relates to the values of the sport etc.) to mitigate against negative motivational effects. Thus the behavioral typologies may have an interactional effect that is different to their main effects. In this case, it might be that the leadership style raises the importance and value of the task and thus motivation will at least be maintained. Furthermore, the personality of the follower will likely also play a role in determining the effectiveness of the behavioral typology.

The TML taxonomy categorizes leader behaviors into three distinct factors, inspirational leadership, coaching, and instructing, that are theorized to contain leader behaviors that will be a key determinant of the organizational climate and ultimately the behaviors of individuals within the organization. As with any behavior taxonomy there are likely behaviors that are not included or do not fall neatly within our categories and there is likely to be some conceptual overlap between the categories. For example, intellectually stimulating type behaviors (included in most conceptualizations of transformational leadership) that we have placed in the leadership category of the TML is fairly close in nature to the coaching dimension. That is, intellectually stimulating behaviors will likely involve using questioning techniques. Hence, it may be that when the model is empirically tested, this behavior will gravitate towards the coaching dimension. Such "grey areass around the edges of our dimensions are due to the categories that we have imposed on what is a vast and complex system of interacting behaviors. Nevertheless, one of the aims of science is to try and categorize and arrange complex phenomenon into understandable, useful, and theoretically distinct meaning units that facilitate better understanding of the phenomenon. In this case we have categorized sport organizational leadership, which is a highly complex and somewhat elusive construct, into discrete meaning units.

To summarize, in proposing the TML we hoped to stimulate both theoretically guided research and conceptual advancement to help leaders better understand their own behavior and the possible associated consequences. With future research, further guidance on when to use each style might be forthcoming. While the model will not be able to classify every subordinate focused behavior, we believe it provides a useful framework by which to theoretically advance the sport organizational leadership literature and to provide a useful applied framework for coaches and leaders to use within organizations. In the words of George Box (Box & Draper, 1987) we hope that the TML will be useful to leaders and organizations in helping to shape leadership practice: "essentially, all models are wrong, but some are useful". We finish with five key messages from this chapter:

- In sport organizations the environment might manifest to affect coaches in two broad ways: by influencing the behaviors that the coach displays with their athletes and by moderating the effectiveness of coach behaviors on athlete outcomes.
- The majority of leadership and coaching theories and models that have been developed within sport have been underpinned by social cognitive approaches, yet the environmental factors that influence or moderate leader and coach behaviors have received scarce research attention.
- Hierarchical structures and role differentiation are omnipresent in organizations and are therefore an important consideration when discussing the behavioral taxonomies aligned with *leadership in* and *leadership of* sport organizations.
- How "close" or "distant" followers are from their leaders in terms of perceived social or psychological distance, physical distance, and the perceived frequency of leader–follower interaction can change the influence process of leader behaviors.
- We propose a tripartite model of leadership that encapsulates three higher order behavioral typologies identified in the literature: leadership/inspirational type behaviors; coaching type behaviors; and instructing type behaviors.

References

Anderson, D. I., Magill, R. A., Sekiya, H., & Ryan, G. (2005). Support for an explanation of the guidance effect in motor skill learning. *Journal of Motor Behavior, 37*(3), 231–238.

Antonakis, J., & Atwater, L. (2002). Leader distance: A review and a proposed theory. *The Leadership Quarterly, 13*(6), 673–704.

Antonakis, J., Cianciolo, A. T., & Sternberg, R. J. (2004). Leadership: Past, present, and future. In J. Antonakis, A. T. Cianciolo, & R. J. Sternberg (Eds.), *The nature of leadership* (pp. 3–15). Thousand Oaks, CA: Sage Publications, Inc.

Aoyagi, M. W., Cox, R. H., & McGguire, R. T. (2008). Organizational citizenship behavior in sport: Relationships with leadership, team cohesion, and athlete satisfaction. *Journal of Applied Sport Psychology, 20*(1), 25–41. doi:10.1080/10413200701784858.

Arthur, C. A. (2014). Leadership in sport: Social cognitive approaches. In R. C. Eklund & G. Tenenbaum (Eds.), *Encyclopedia of sport and exercise psychology* (Vpl 1 ed., pp. 410–416). Thousand Oaks, CA: Sage.

Arthur, C. A., Woodman, T., Ong, C. W., Hardy, L., & Ntoumanis, N. (2011). The role of athlete narcissism in moderating the relationship between coaches' transformational leader behaviors and athlete motivation. *Journal of Sport & Exercise Psychology, 33*(1), 3–19.

Arthur, C. A., Hardy, L., & Woodman, T. (2012). Realising the Olympic dream: Vision, support, and challenge. *Reflective Practice International and Multidisciplinary Perspectives, 13*(3), 399–406. doi:10.1080/14623943.2012.670112.

Arthur, C. A., & Lynn, A. (2017). Transformational leadership and the role of the coach. In R. C. Thelwell, C. Harwood and I. Greenlees (Eds.), *The psychology of sports coaching: Research and practice* (pp. 187–202). Abingdon; Routledge.

Avolio, B. J., & Bass, B. M. (1995). Individual consideration viewed at multiple levels of analysis: A multi-level framework for examining the diffusion of transformational leadership. *The Leadership Quarterly, 6*(2), 199–218.

Baker, J., Yardley, J., & Cote, J. (2003). Coach behaviors and athlete satisfaction in team and individual sports. *International Journal of Sport Psychology, 34*(3), 226–239.

Balaguer, I., Duda, J. L., & Crespo, M. (1999). Motivational climate and goal orientations as predictors of perceptions of improvement, satisfaction and coach ratings among tennis players. *Scandinavian Journal of Medicine & Science in Sports, 9*(6), 381–388.

Bass, B. M. (1985). *Leadership and performance beyond expectations* (4th ed.). New York: Free Press.

Bass, B. M., & Stogdill, R. M. (1990). *Bass & Stogdill's handbook of leadership: Theory, research, and managerial applications.* New York: Simon and Schuster.

Battig, W. F. (1979). The flexibility of human memory. *Levels of processing and human memory.* Hillsdale, NJ: Lawrence Erlbaum Associates.

Berson, Y., & Halevy, N. (2014). Hierarchy, leadership, and construal fit. *Journal of Experimental Psychology: Applied, 20*(3), 232–246.

Berson, Y., Halevy, N., Shamir, B., & Erez, M. (2015). Leading from different psychological distances: A construal-level perspective on vision communication, goal setting, and follower motivation. *The Leadership Quarterly, 26*(2), 143–155.

Box, G. E. P., and Draper, N. R., (1987), *Empirical Model Building and Response Surfaces.* New York; John Wiley & Sons.

Brady, F. (2008). The contextual interference effect in sport skills. *Perceptual and Motor Skills, 106*, 461–472.

Bryman, A. (1992). *Charisma and leadership in organizations.* London: Sage.

Burns, J. M. (1978). *Leadership.* New York: Harper and Row.

Butler, R. J., & Hardy, L. (1992). The performance profile: Theory and application. *Sports Psychologist, 6*(3), 253–264.

Callow, N., Smith, M. J., Hardy, L., Arthur, C. A., & Hardy, J. (2009). Measurement of transformational leadership and its relationship with team cohesion and performance level. *Journal of Applied Sport Psychology, 21*(4), 395–412.

Chambers, K. L., & Vickers, J. N. (2006). Effects of bandwidth feedback and questioning on the performance of competitive swimmers. *The Sports Psychologist, 20*, 184–197.

Chelladurai, P. (1993). Leadership. In R. N. Singer, M. Murphey, & L. K. Tennant (Eds.), *Handbook of research on sport psychology* (pp. 647–671). New York: Macmillan.

Conger, J. A., & Kanungo, R. N. (1987). Toward a behavioral-theory of charismatic leadership in organizational settings. *Academy of Management Review, 12*(4), 637–647. doi:10.2307/258069.

Conger, J. A., & Kanungo, R. N. (1998). *Charismatic leadership in organizations.* Thousand Oaks, CA: Sage Publications.

Côté, J., Yardley, J., Hay, J., Sedgwick, W., & Baker, J. R. (1999). An exploratory examination of the coaching behaviour scale for sport. *Avante, 5*(3), 82–92.

Courtright, J. A., Fairhurst, G. T., & Rogers, L. E. (1989). Interaction patterns in organic and mechanistic system. *Academy of Management Journal, 32*(4), 773–802.

Cronin, L. D., Arthur, C. A., Hardy, J., & Callow, N. (2015). Transformational leadership and task cohesion in sport: The mediating role of inside sacrifice. *Journal of Sport & Exercise Psychology, 37*(1), 23–36. doi:10.1123/jsep.2014-0116.

Cushion, C., Harvey, S., Muir, B., & Nelson, L. (2012). Developing the coach analysis and intervention system (CAIS): Establishing validity and reliability of a computerised systematic observation instrument. *Journal of Sports Sciences, 30*(2), 203–218. doi:10.1080/02640414.2011.635310.

Deci, E. L., & Ryan, R. M. (1985). *Intrinsic motivation and self-determination in human behavior.* New York: Springer Science & Business Media.

Deci, E. L., & Ryan, R. (1989). Parent styles associated with Druckman, D., & Bjork, R. A. (Eds). (1991). *In the mind's eye: Enhancing human performance.* Washington, DC: National Academy Press.

Dubin, R. (1977). Metaphors of leadership: An overview. In J. G. Hunt & L. L. Larson (Eds), *Cross current in leadership* (pp. 225–238). Carbondale, IL: Southern Illinois University Press.

Fiedler, F. E. (1971). *Leadership.* Morristown, NJ: General Learning Press.

Fletcher, D., & Arnold, R. (2011). A qualitative study of performance leadership and management in elite sport. *Journal of Applied Sport Psychology, 23*(2), 223–242. doi:10.1080/10413200.2011.559184.

Gallimore, R., & Tharp, R. (2004). What a coach can teach a teacher, 1975–2004: reflections and reanalysis of John Wooden's teaching practices. *Sport Psychologist, 18,* 119–137.

Grant, A. M., & Stober, D. R. (2006). Introduction. In D. R. Stober & A. M. Grant (Eds.), *Evidence based coaching handbook: Putting best practices to work for your clients.* (pp. 1–14). Hoboken, NJ: John Wiley & Sons.

Gruenfeld, D. H., & Tiedens, L. (2010). Organizational preferences and their consequences. In S. T. Fiske, D. T. Gilbert, & G. Lindzey (Eds.), *Handbook of social psychology* (5th ed., Vol. 2, pp. 1252–1287). Hoboken, NJ: John Wiley & Sons.

Halevy, N., Chou, E. Y., & Galinsky, A. D. (2011). A functional model of hierarchy why, how, and when vertical differentiation enhances group performance. *Organizational Psychology Review, 1*(1), 32–52.

Halevy, N., Chou, E. Y., Galinsky, A. D., & Murnighan, J. K. (2012). When hierarchy wins evidence from the national basketball association. *Social Psychological and Personality Science, 3*(4), 398–406.

Hardre, P. L., & Reeve, J. (2003). A motivational model of rural students' intentions to persist in, versus drop out of, high school. *Journal of Educational Psychology, 95,* 347–356. doi:10.1037/0022-0663.95.2.347.

Hardy, L., Arthur, C. A., Jones, G., Shariff, A., Munnoch, K., Isaacs, I., & Allsopp, A. J. (2010). The relationship between transformational leadership behaviors, psychological, and training outcomes in elite military recruits. *Leadership Quarterly, 21*(1), 21–32. doi:10.1016/j.leaqua.2009.10.002.

Hardy, L., Jones, J. G., & Gould, D. (1996). *Understanding psychological preparation for sport: Theory and practice of elite performers.* Hoboken, NJ: John Wiley & Sons.

Hollembeak, J., & Amorose, A. J. (2005). Perceived coaching behaviors and college athletes' intrinsic motivation: A test of self-determination theory. *Journal of Applied Sport Psychology, 17*(1), 20–36. doi:10.1080/10413200590907540.

House, R. J., & Aditya, R. N. (1997). The social scientific study of leadership: Quo vadis?. *Journal of Management, 23*(3), 409–473.

Horne, T., & Carron, A. V. (1985). Compatibility in coach-athlete relationships. *Journal of Sport Psychology, 7*(2), 137–149.

Hunt, J. G. J. (2004). *What is leadership?* Thousand Oaks, CA: Sage Publications, Inc.

Jowett, S. (2009). Factor structure and criterion-related validity of the metaperspective version of the coach-athlete relationship questionnaire (CART-Q). *Group Dynamics: Theory Research and Practice, 13*(3), 163–177. doi:10.1037/a0014998

Katz, D., Maccoby, N., Gurin, G., & Floor, L. G. (1951). *Productivity, supervision and morale among railroad workers.* Ann Arbor, MI; Institute for Social Research, University of Michigan.

Kluger, A. N., & DeNisi, A. (1996). The effects of feedback interventions on performance: A historical review, a meta-analysis, and a preliminary feedback intervention theory. *Psychological Bulletin, 119*(2), 254–284.

Landin, D., & Hebert, E. P. (1997). A comparison of three practice schedules along the contextual interference continuum. *Research Quarterly for Exercise and Sport, 68*, 357–361.

Locke, E. A., & Latham, G. P. (2002). Building a practically useful theory of goal setting and task motivation: A 35-year odyssey. *American Psychologist, 57*(9), 705–717.

Mageau, G., & Vallerand, R. (2003). The coach-athlete relationship: A motivational model. *Journal of Sports Sciences, 21*(11), 883–904. doi:10.1080/0264041031000140374.

Magill, R. A. (1994). The influence of augmented feedback on skill learning depends on characteristics of the skill and the learner. *Quest, 46*(3), 314–327.

Nanus, B. (1992). *Visionary leadership: Creating a compelling sense of direction for your organization.* San Francisco, CA: Jossey-Bass.

Napier, B. J., & Ferris, G. R. (1994). Distance in organizations. *Human Resource Management Review, 3*(4), 321–357.

Newton, M., Duda, J. L., & Yin, Z. (2000). Examination of the psychometric properties of the perceived motivational climate in sport questionnaire-2 in a sample of female athletes. *Journal of Sports Sciences, 18*(4), 275–290.

Nicolas, M., Gaudreau, P., & Franche, V. (2011). Perception of coaching behaviors, coping, and achievement in a sport competition. *Journal of Sport & Exercise Psychology, 33*(3), 460–468.

Parsloe, E. (Ed.) (1995). *Coaching, mentoring, and assessing: A practical guide to developing competence.* New York: Kogan Page.

Partington, M., & Cushion, C. (2013). An investigation of the practice activities and coaching behaviors of professional top-level youth soccer coaches. *Scandinavian Journal of Medicine & Science in Sports, 23*(3), 374–382. doi:10.1111/j.1600-0838.2011.01383.x.

Pelletier, L. G., Fortier, M. S., Vallerand, R. J., & Briere, N. M. (2001). Associations among perceived autonomy support, forms of self-regulation, and persistence: A prospective study. *Motivation and Emotion, 25*(4), 279–306.

Riemer, H. A., & Chelladurai, P. (1995). Leadership and satisfaction in athletics. *Journal of Sport & Exercise Psychology, 17*(3), 276–293.

Robbins, S. B., Lauver, K., Huy, L., Davis, D., Langley, R., & Carlstrom, A. (2004). Do psychosocial and study skill factors predict college outcomes? A meta-analysis. *Psychological Bulletin, 130*, 261–288. doi: 10.1037/0033-2909.130.2.261.

Rowold, J. (2006). Transformational and transactional leadership in martial arts. *Journal of Applied Sport Psychology, 18*(4), 312–325. doi:10.1080/10413200600944082.

Sashkin, M. (1984). *The visionary leader: The leader behavior questionnaire.* Bryn Mawr, PA: Organization Design and Development.

Shea, J. B., & Zimny, S. T. (1988). Knowledge incorporation in motor representation. In O. G. Meijer & K. Roth (Eds.), *Complex movement behavior: "The" motor action controversy* (pp. 289–314). Amsterdam: Elsevier.

Smith, S. L., Fry, M. D., Ethington, C. A., & Li, Y. H. (2005). The effect of female athletes' perceptions of their coaches' behaviors on their perceptions of the motivational climate. *Journal of Applied Sport Psychology, 17*(2), 170–177. doi:10.1080/10413200590932470.

Smoll, F. L., & Smith, R. E. (1984). Leadership research in youth sports. In M. J. Silva & R. S. Weinberg (Eds.), *Psychological foundations of sport* (pp. 371–386). Champaign, IL: Human Kinetics.

Smoll, F. L., & Smith, R. E. (1989). Leadership Behaviors in Sport: A Theoretical Model and Research Paradigm. *Journal of Applied Social Psychology, 19*(18), 1522–1551.

Smoll, F. L., Smith, R. E., Barnett, N. P., & Everett, J. J. (1993). Enhancement of children's self-esteem through social support training for youth sport coaches. *Journal of Applied Psychology, 78*(4), 602–610.

Stebbings, J., Taylor, I. M., Spray, C. M., & Ntoumanis, N. (2012). Antecedents of perceived coach interpersonal behaviors: The coaching environment and coach psychological well-and ill-being. *Journal of Sport & Exercise Psychology, 34*(4), 481–502.

Stogdill, R., & Coons, A. (Eds.) (1957). *Leader behavior: Its description and measurement.* Columbus, OH: Ohio State University, Bureau of Business Research.

Tangirala, S., Green, S. G., & Ramanujam, R. (2007). In the shadow of the boss's boss: Effects of supervisors' upward exchange relationships on employees. *Journal of Applied Psychology, 92*(2), 309–320.

Theodoraki, E. I., & Henry, I. P. (1994). Organisational structures and contexts in British national governing bodies of sport. *International Review for the Sociology of Sport, 29*(3), 243–265.

Trope, Y., & Liberman, N. (2010). Construal-level theory of psychological distance. *Psychological Review, 117*(2), 440–463.

Vallerand, R. J., Fortier, M. S., & Guay, F. (1997). Self-determination and persistence in a real-life setting: Toward a motivational model of high school dropout. *Journal of Personality and Social Psychology, 72*, 1161–1176.

Waldman, D. A., & Yammarino, F. J. (1999). CEO charismatic leadership: Levels-of-management and levels-of-analysis effects. *Academy of Management Review, 24*(2), 266–285.

Weinberg, R., & McDermott, M. (2002). A comparative analysis of sport and business organizations: Factors perceived critical for organizational success. *Journal of Applied Sport Psychology, 14*(4), 282–298.

Weiss, M. R., & Friedrichs, W. D. (1986). The influence of leader behaviors, coach attributes, and institutional variables on performance and satisfaction of collegiate basketball teams. *Journal of Sport Psychology, 8*(4), 332–346.

Whitmore, J. (2009). *Coaching for performance: Growing human potential and purpose.* London: Nicholas Brealey International.

Williams, J. M., Jerome, G. J., Kenow, L. J., Rogers, T., Sartain, T. A., & Darland, G. (2003). Factor structure of the coaching behavior questionnaire and its relationship to athlete variables. *Sport Psychologist, 17*(1), 16–34.

Zourbanos, N., Hatzigeorgiadis, A., Goudas, M., Papaioannou, A., Chroni, S., & Theodorakis, Y. (2011). The social side of self-talk: Relationships between perceptions of support received from the coach and athletes' self-talk. *Psychology of Sport and Exercise, 12*(4), 407–414. doi:10.1016/j.psychsport.2011.03.001.

9

PROSOCIAL AND ANTISOCIAL BEHAVIORS IN SPORT ORGANIZATIONS

Maria Kavussanu and Nicholas Stanger

Introduction

Sport by nature is a social context that provides opportunities to engage in behaviors that can have positive consequences for others. For example, athletes may congratulate teammates for good play, help them to learn a new skill, or console them following failure. At the same time, sport has the potential for behaviors that can have negative consequences for others, for instance cheating, insults, and physically injurious acts, such as elbowing and kicking. These behaviors occur in sport, particularly at the elite level. An example is the biting incident of Louis Suarez in the last FIFA World Cup that resulted in his elimination from further play. Behaviors with more severe consequences are not uncommon. A recent example is the punch by Ben Flower to his opponent Lance Hohaia in the 2014 Rugby League Grand Final resulting in Hohaia being knocked unconscious. Such behaviors can have serious negative consequences for their recipients, but also question the integrity of sport as an institution.

Intentional behaviors that have consequences for others' welfare are the subject of the moral domain (see Turiel, 1983). Although moral behavior in sport has been studied using a variety of theoretical frameworks, the theory that has guided many recent studies is the social cognitive theory of moral thought and action (Bandura, 1991), which focuses on behavior and its consequences for others' rights and well-being. Bandura (1999) has also distinguished between proactive morality, which is the power to behave humanely, and inhibitive morality, which is the power to refrain from behaving inhumanely. In the context of sport, the terms prosocial and antisocial behavior have been used to refer to the two dimensions of morality (see Kavussanu, 2012). Prosocial behavior is behavior intended to help or benefit another (Eisenberg & Fabes, 1998), for example, helping an opponent off the floor, congratulating a teammate, and lending equipment to an opponent. In contrast, antisocial behavior is behavior intended to harm or disadvantage another (Sage, Kavussanu, & Duda, 2006), for instance, trying to injure an opponent and verbally abusing a teammate.

In this chapter, the term moral behavior is used to refer to a broad range of intentional acts that could result in positive or negative consequences for others' psychological and physical welfare. We review the literature pertaining to prosocial and antisocial behaviors in sport. These behaviors can have important implications for the effective functioning of sport organizations. First, we discuss empirical research that has examined consequences of prosocial and antisocial behaviors. Second, we elaborate on antecedents of these behaviors distinguishing between moral and motivational variables. Third, we discuss organizational citizenship behavior. Finally, we conclude with practical implications and directions for future research.

Consequences of prosocial and antisocial behaviors in sport

It has been suggested that prosocial and antisocial behaviors can have important positive and negative consequences, respectively, for the recipient (Kavussanu, 2012). Specifically, prosocial behaviors toward teammates can facilitate achievement, because they have the potential to enhance motivation and subsequent performance (Kavussanu & Boardley, 2009). For example, giving constructive feedback, congratulating a teammate after good play, and encouraging a teammate should lead the recipient to try harder and perform better during a match. In contrast, antisocial behaviors such as verbally abusing a teammate, swearing, arguing, criticizing, and expressing frustration at a teammate's poor play may lead the recipient of this behavior to lower their effort with subsequent negative consequences for their performance.

These proposals were examined in two independent samples of football and basketball players, who were asked, shortly after a match, to respond to a questionnaire about their experiences during the match they had just played (Al-Yaaribi, Kavussanu, & Ring, 2016). Both football and basketball players, who perceived that their teammates engaged in prosocial behaviors toward them during the match, reported that they had tried harder and performed better. Mediation analysis indicated that the effects of prosocial teammate behavior on effort and performance were partially mediated by enjoyment. In the basketball players, perceived prosocial teammate behavior was also positively associated with commitment to continue playing for their team, both directly and indirectly through enjoyment, effort, and perceived performance. Finally, in both samples, players who perceived that their teammates acted antisocially toward them during the match, reported lower effort and more anger.

Although this study was cross-sectional, thus precluding firm conclusions about the direction of causality, it provides important preliminary information for the potential consequences of prosocial teammate behavior on the recipient. The results highlight the significance of positive social behaviors within the team, during a match, for several important variables. Based on these findings, we could speculate that prosocial and antisocial behaviors of other members of the sport organization, such as coaches, managers, and support staff, would also have positive consequences for the recipient. For example, when coaches and managers act toward players in a prosocial manner by offering encouragement, support, and positive feedback, athletes may be more motivated to train harder and subsequently perform better.

In sport, antisocial behavior is most often directed at one's opponents during a match. One specific form of antisocial behavior is sledging, which – according to the Oxford and Cambridge dictionaries – is the act of one sports player making taunting or teasing remarks, or insulting an opposing player during a game, in order to make them angry and disturb their concentration. The ultimate aim of sledging is to impair an opposing player's performance, and anecdotal examples of this occurring are plentiful. One famous sledging incident took place during the 2006 FIFA World Cup final between France and Italy. Mattarazi, an Italian player, verbally provoked the French footballer Zidane, by allegedly insulting a member of his family. This infuriated Zidane, who head-butted Mattarazi in the chest. Zidane was sent off and France lost the final, thus the ultimate aim of sledging of impairing performance of the opposing team was achieved on this occasion.

The effects of sledging on anger, attention, and performance were examined in one experiment (Ring et al., in revision), where participants performed a competitive basketball free-throw task under three conditions: insult (i.e., sledging designed to offend and upset the performer), distraction (i.e., sledging designed to draw attention away from the task), or control (i.e., no sledging). The sledges in the insult condition led to more anger compared to the control and distraction conditions; also, both the insult and distraction sledges increased distraction and reduced self-focus compared to the control group. However, sledging had no effect on performance, perhaps due to the sledges not being perceived as sufficiently strong to lead to a decline in performance.

Despite the promising findings outlined above, in general, research examining consequences of prosocial and antisocial behaviors in sport is in its infancy. However, preliminary evidence suggests that these behaviors can have important consequences for both one's teammates and opponents. Prosocial and antisocial behaviors can also be directed toward other members within sport organizations, such as coaches and support staff. For example, athletes could act in an antisocial manner toward these agents and this could in turn influence the relationships within the organization. Similarly, coaches can be prosocial toward players by encouraging and supporting them, and this can increase the cohesion of the organization. It would be interesting for future research to investigate these possibilities.

Antecedents of prosocial and antisocial behaviors

If prosocial and antisocial behaviors have consequences for the recipient, it is important to understand what leads sport participants to engage in these behaviors.

Several factors have been identified as potential antecedents of moral behavior in sport and will be discussed in this section. Some of them (e.g., moral identity, moral disengagement) can be classified as "moral" variables, while others (e.g., achievement goals and motivation types) are "motivational" variables. As moral variables appear to have been more consistently and more strongly associated with moral behavior, we turn our attention to these first. Some of the variables reviewed in this section are also individual difference variables (e.g., moral disengagement, motivation types), while others refer to the social environment (e.g., moral atmosphere, motivational climate). Social environmental variables have been measured via athlete perceptions in the studies described in this section. It is through the individuals' perceptions that social environmental factors such as motivational climate exert their influence on outcomes (see Ames, 1992).

Moral variables

The moral variables discussed in this section are moral emotion, moral disengagement, moral identity, empathy, and moral atmosphere. We begin by discussing the moral emotion of guilt. Not only is this emotion a key predictor of moral behavior in sport, it is also an important mediator of the effects of other moral variables on moral behavior. We continue by discussing research pertaining to moral disengagement, empathy, and moral identity and conclude with work relevant to moral atmosphere.

Moral emotion

Moral emotion is a strong motivator of moral action. A few studies have investigated the emotion of guilt in relation to antisocial behavior in sport. Guilt is a "moral" emotion because it results from behavior that is considered unethical. It is also an adaptive emotion characterized by reparative action tendencies (i.e., making amends) following a transgression (Tangney, Stuewig, & Mashek, 2007). Guilt involves unpleasant feelings accompanied by tension and regret and plays a central role in regulating transgressive behavior: people refrain from such behavior due to anticipated affective sanctions (Bandura, 1991). They tend to behave in ways that match their moral standards to avoid experiencing negative emotions such as guilt and shame, which result from behavior that violates their moral standards (Bandura, 1991).

Anticipated guilt has been investigated both as a predictor and as a mediator in two of our studies (e.g., Kavussanu, Stanger, & Ring, 2015; Stanger, Kavussanu, Boardley, & Ring, 2013). In this line of research, we have asked participants to imagine themselves in a hypothetical situation, where they decide to foul their opponent, resulting in the opponent being seriously injured. Thus, the hypothetical act is intentional and has negative consequences for the recipient, thereby representing antisocial behavior (see Kavussanu & Boardley, 2009, 2012). Participants are then asked to indicate the extent to which they would anticipate feeling guilt after engaging in the antisocial act. Anticipated guilt was inversely and modestly associated with antisocial behavior in both studies (Kavussanu et al., 2015; Stanger et al., 2013).

Moral disengagement

Moral disengagement is a central construct in Bandura's (1991) social cognitive theory of moral thought and action. Bandura proposed that in the course of socialization, individuals develop moral standards from a variety of influences, such as observation of others and approving and disapproving reactions of their behavior by others. These moral standards regulate behavior through evaluative self reactions: people feel good when behaving in ways that match their moral standards; and experience self reproof when their actions violate their moral standards. Thus, anticipated self sanctions in reaction to one's behavior, keep behavior in line with moral standards. However, people are able to disengage moral self sanctions from reprehensible behavior, through the use of one or more of eight psychosocial mechanisms, collectively known as moral disengagement. This allows different types of behavior from individuals with the same moral standards (Bandura, 2002).

Psychosocial mechanisms operate by cognitively restructuring transgressive behavior and its consequences, minimizing or obscuring one's role in the harm one causes, disregarding or distorting the detrimental consequences of one's behavior, and dehumanizing or blaming one's victim. For example, cheating could be justified as a way of helping one's team or organization (moral justification); athletes may talk about "bending the rules" rather than breaking them (euphemistic labelling); they could compare transgressive behavior with more harmful acts, making the behavior in question appear relatively benign (advantageous comparison); they could displace responsibility for action on the coach, manager, or support staff (displacement of responsibility); they could downplay the harm they cause (distortion of consequences); and attribute blame for their behavior onto their victim (attribution of blame).

Qualitative investigations have shown that although all mechanisms are used to some extent in sport, displacement of responsibility, attribution of blame, moral justification and distortion of consequences are particularly common (Corrion, Long, Smith, & d'Arripe-Longueville, 2009; Traclet, Romand, Moret, & Kavussanu, 2011). Athletes often report diffusing responsibility on to teammates for cheating and deliberately fouling opponents because their teammates also commit such acts. Additionally, displacement of responsibility on to the coach is common, such as when athletes report that their coaches encouraged antisocial behavior and sometimes showed athletes how to cheat while competing in sport (Traclet et al., 2011). The numerous quantitative studies, which have investigated moral disengagement in sport, have consistently revealed strong positive relationships with antisocial behavior, particularly toward opponents (Boardley & Kavussanu, 2009, 2010; Hodge & Gucciardi, 2015;

Hodge & Lonsdale, 2011; Stanger et al., 2013). Moreover, moral disengagement has been associated with reduced negative emotional reactions to antisocial acts, as reflected in self-reports and physiological measures (Stanger, Kavussanu, Willoughby, & Ring, 2012).

Finally, in an experiment with university athletes from a variety of sports, Stanger et al. (2013) manipulated attribution of blame, one of the moral disengagement mechanisms, via a scenario describing a hypothetical situation that involved the potential to deliberately foul and hurt an opponent. Participants were allocated to either an experimental group or a control group; both groups read a scenario referring to the same act. However, in the experimental group scenario, participants were asked to imagine that they had been provoked by their opponent; this was designed to elicit attribution of blame. Participants in the experimental group were more likely to report that they would deliberately foul and hurt their opponent in this hypothetical situation, and they anticipated feeling less guilt for doing so, compared to the control group participants; guilt partially mediated the effect of attribution of blame on antisocial behavior (Stanger et al., 2013).

These findings suggest that provocation could lead one to experience less guilt for deliberately fouling and hurting the opponent. This may be because the individual feels that justice is achieved, if he or she retaliates when provoked. Although this study manipulated attribution of blame by describing a situation that involved provocation so that the participant had the opportunity to blame the victim for his or her own actions, it may also be that provocation simply makes one feel justified for acting aggressively.

Empathy

Empathy has been defined as an affective response that stems from the comprehension of someone else's emotional state or condition and is similar to what the other person is feeling or expected to feel in a certain situation (Eisenberg & Strayer, 1987). It is an other-oriented response, which is more congruent with another person's situation or perceived welfare than to one's own (Batson, Early, & Salvarani, 1997). Empathy includes a cognitive component, known as perspective taking, and an affective component, known as empathic concern. Perspective taking refers to the ability to understand the psychological point of view of others, while empathic concern is the ability to feel sympathy and compassion for unfortunate others (Davis, 1983). When individuals adopt the perspective of others and attend to their feelings and needs, they are more likely to behave prosocially and refrain from acting antisocially.

Dispositional empathy has been positively associated with prosocial behaviors such as helping an opponent off the floor, and negatively linked to antisocial behavior in several studies (Kavussanu & Boardley, 2009; Kavussanu et al., 2009; Kavussanu, Stanger, & Boardley, 2013). In one experiment, Stanger, Kavussanu, and Ring (2012) presented participants with a scenario describing a hypothetical situation occurring during a regular game, where they had the opportunity to foul and risk injuring their opponent, when the referee was not looking. Then, the high empathy group was asked to take their opponent's perspective and imagine how he or she would feel in this situation, while the low empathy group was instructed to take an objective perspective toward the opponent and remain detached. Participants were also asked how likely they would be to engage in this behavior and to indicate the feelings of guilt they anticipated experiencing. Men in the high empathy group reported lower likelihood to aggress and greater anticipated guilt than men in the low empathy group. Importantly, the effects of empathy on aggression were mediated by anticipated guilt, such that the high empathy group experienced more guilt, which led to a lower reported likelihood to aggress.

In a second experiment, Stanger and colleagues (Stanger, Kavussanu, McIntyre, & Ring, 2016) examined whether empathy inhibits *actual* aggression in a competitive reaction time task against a fictitious opponent over a number of trials. The researchers measured aggression as the intensity of the electrical stimulation participants chose to administer to the (fictitious) opponent, when they won a trial. Provocation was also manipulated by administering to participants, on losing trials, low or high painful electrical stimulations to their non-dominant arm. Guilt was measured by asking participants how guilty they felt about shocking their opponent in winning trials. An interesting interaction was revealed, whereby at low provocation, empathy suppressed aggression in both men and women, but at high provocation the effect was evident only in women. In addition, at low – but not high – provocation, guilt mediated the suppressing effects of empathy on aggression in men, but not in women.

These findings highlight the important moderating role of gender and provocation on the empathy–aggression relationship. Men appear to react to provocation differently to women, such that the reaction may be so strong that the typical effect of empathy on aggression is overridden. Therefore, strategies aimed to enhance empathy to reduce aggression need to be tailored specifically for men and women. Guilt appears to play an important role in mediating the effect of empathy on aggression, but only in men at low provocation. One can clearly justify aggression under high provocation. Perhaps participants view this as restoring fairness; when provoked, individuals may feel justified to act aggressively against others.

Moral identity

Moral identity refers to the cognitive schema that people hold about their moral character (Aquino et al., 2009); it is the degree to which being moral is a defining or central characteristic of one's sense of self. Moral identity is organized around a set of moral traits, such as being honest, fair, caring, kind, and generous (Aquino & Reed, 2002). Although we have a number of identities, only some of them can be salient at a given point in time in our working self-concept. When moral identity is cognitively salient, it is more likely to influence our thoughts, emotions, and behavior. Moral identity is typically measured by listing the nine traits around which it is organized and asking participants to indicate how important it would be for them to be someone with those traits (Aquino & Reed, 2002). Using this approach, studies have shown a positive link between moral identity and prosocial behavior toward teammates and opponents (Kavussanu et al., 2013) and a negative relationship with antisocial behavior toward opponents (Kavussanu et al., 2013, 2015; Sage et al., 2006).

In one experiment, the effect of moral identity on athletes' emotional reactions to unpleasant sport pictures was investigated (Kavussanu, Willoughby, & Ring, 2012). Researchers asked participants to copy nine words referring to moral traits (e.g., fair, honest, caring, hardworking, kind) and write a story about themselves using these words; a control group did the same using nine neutral words (e.g., chair, table). The moral identity group had stronger negative emotional reactions – as indicated by accentuated startle blinks – to pictures of players badly injured or deliberately hurt. In a second experiment, using the same manipulation for moral identity, participants were presented with a scenario describing a hypothetical situation, in which they had the opportunity to hurt an opponent during a match. Then they indicated the likelihood they would aggress if they were in that hypothetical situation and their concomitant anticipated guilt, if they had committed the act (Kavussanu et al., 2015). The moral identity group were less likely to aggress compared to the control group and the suppressing effect of moral identity on likelihood to aggress was mediated by anticipated guilt. These findings clearly point to the important role guilt plays in aggression in sport and indicate that a strong sense of moral identity is a source of moral motivation.

Moral atmosphere

The constructs discussed so far refer to individual difference variables. One feature of the social environment of sport is the moral atmosphere of the team or organization, a construct based on the work of Kohlberg and colleagues (e.g., Power, Higgins, & Kohlberg, 1989). In the sport psychology literature, moral atmosphere has been operationally defined as a set of collective norms regarding moral action on the part of group members (Shields & Bredemeier, 1995). In a sport team, certain philosophies are developed over time regarding what is appropriate behavior; these are the outcome of the characteristics of the coach and team members. Teammates' perceptions of their peers' choices in situations that give rise to moral conflict are also part of the moral atmosphere (Shields & Bredemeier, 1995).

In the first study that examined moral atmosphere in sport, Stephens and Bredemeier (1996) measured footballers' perceptions of the number of teammates willing to tackle an opponent from behind as a dimension of moral atmosphere. Players who perceived that a large number of their teammates would behave aggressively in a hypothetical situation also indicated greater likelihood to behave aggressively. Athletes' perceptions of their team's pro-aggressive norms were also the main predictor of reported likelihood to aggress in basketball and football players (e.g., Chow, Murray, & Feltz, 2009; Stephens, 2001). Similar findings have been reported in other studies, which have examined not only perceived teammate but also perceived coach behavior. Basketball and football players who thought that their coach encouraged antisocial conduct and that their teammates would engage in the described behaviors if it was necessary for the team to win also reported lower levels of moral functioning (Kavussanu, Roberts, & Ntoumanis, 2002; Kavussanu & Spray, 2006). Thus, the moral atmosphere of sport teams appears important in determining the moral functioning of its members.

Motivational variables

Sport is an achievement context and, as such, achievement motivation is important. Two major theories of motivation have contributed to our understanding of behavior in the context of sport: achievement goal theory (Nicholls, 1989) and self-determination theory (Deci & Ryan, 2000). In this section, we outline the main tenets of these two theories that are relevant to moral behavior and discuss relevant empirical research conducted in the sport context.

Achievement goal theory

Achievement goal theory was developed by Nicholls (1989), who argued that individuals engage in achievement contexts such as sport in order to demonstrate competence. However, the way people define success and evaluate competence varies, and conceptions of competence or ability are embedded within two achievement goals: task and ego orientation. The task-oriented individual tends to define competence and evaluate success using self-referenced criteria, such as skill mastery and improvement, whereas the ego-oriented athlete tends to define success and evaluate competence using other-referenced criteria, for example doing better than others. Due to their focus on normative superiority, ego-oriented individuals may show a lack of concern about justice and fairness (Nicholls, 1989). In contrast, task-oriented people are expected to play by the rules, as breaking the rules cannot provide a true test of their competence (Duda, Olson, & Templin, 1991).

Research has supported the above assertions. In several studies, ego orientation has been positively associated with antisocial behavior (Boardley & Kavussanu 2010; Kavussanu, 2006; Sage et al., 2006); typically, the link has been stronger for opponent than teammate behavior (e.g., Boardley & Kavussanu, 2010; Kavussanu et al., 2013). Ego orientation has also been inversely related to prosocial behavior (Kavussanu, 2006). The opposite pattern of relationships is evident for task orientation, which has been positively associated with prosocial behavior and inversely linked to antisocial behavior in sport (Kavussanu, 2006; Kavussanu et al., 2013). In the only experiment to date that has manipulated the two achievement goals to observe their effects on moral behavior, Sage and Kavussanu (2007) found that participants in the ego-involving group engaged in more antisocial acts than those in the task-involving and control groups during two table-football games.

The criteria of success are evident not only in the achievement goals one pursues while taking part in sport, but also in the situational goal structure, known as motivational climate (Ames, 1992). Thus, similar to individuals, contexts also have their own achievement goals: significant others such as coaches, teachers, and parents convey to the participants what is important in the achievement context. These significant others determine the evaluation procedures and distribution of rewards, and, via their behavior, they communicate to the athletes what is valued in that context. Coaches can create a performance motivational climate by rewarding only the top athletes and valuing normative ability, or a mastery climate by focusing on skill development and rewarding participants for effort and improvement. Several studies have shown that when players perceive a performance motivational climate in their team they tend to report more frequent antisocial behavior (e.g., Boardley & Kavussanu, 2009; Kavussanu & Spray, 2006; Ommundsen et al., 2003) and more instrumental aggression (Rascle, Coulomb-Cabagno, & Delsarte, 2005). In contrast, a mastery climate has been positively associated with prosocial behavior (Boardley & Kavussanu, 2009; Kavussanu, 2006).

Self-determination theory

Self-determination theory (SDT; Deci & Ryan, 1985; Ryan & Deci, 2000) is the second motivational theory that has been used to investigate moral behavior in sport. The theory distinguishes between autonomous motivation, which is evident when actions emanate from one's sense of self, for example, when individuals volitionally engage in an activity for its own sake or for the benefits it can provide; and controlled motivation, which is evident when individuals engage in the activity purely for extrinsic reasons, such as prestige and financial rewards, because they are pressured, or to avoid feelings of guilt and shame (Ryan & Deci, 2000). It has been suggested that athletes who take part in sport for extrinsic reasons may use any means necessary to achieve their goals, including committing antisocial behaviors (Donahue et al., 2006; Gagné, 2003). In empirical research, autonomous motivation has been positively associated with prosocial behavior toward teammates (Hodge & Lonsdale, 2011), whereas controlled motivation has been positively linked to antisocial behavior toward both teammates and opponents (Hodge & Lonsdale, 2011).

Autonomy support and control can also be features of the social environment. In an autonomy supportive environment, athletes are provided with a sense of control and choice over tasks, their feelings are acknowledged, and opportunities to demonstrate initiative and independent problem solving are provided (Mageau & Vallarand, 2003). Controlling behaviors place value on control and using techniques that assert one's power and pressure others to comply (Grolnick &

Ryan, 1989). For example, the team manager can support athletes' autonomy by giving them choice, or control them using extrinsic rewards linked to their performance and controlling language. Performance directors may support coaches' autonomy by allowing them to implement their own coaching plans, or they can control them by demanding that they adopt a certain approach to their coaching.

The relationship between athletes' perceptions of the autonomy supportive or controlling features of their team environment and prosocial and antisocial behavior has been examined in two studies. Hodge and Lonsdale (2011) found that perceptions of an autonomy supportive coaching style positively predicted autonomous motivation, which in turn predicted prosocial behavior toward teammates. This climate was also a negative predictor of controlled motivation, which had an indirect positive effect, via moral disengagement, on antisocial behavior toward both teammates and opponents (Hodge & Lonsdale, 2011). In the second study, Hodge and Gucciardi (2015) extended this research to include psychological need satisfaction and controlling behaviors by the coach and one's teammates, in university athletes. Some of the behaviors examined were controlling use of rewards, negative conditional regard, intimidation, and excessive personal control (Bartholomew, Ntoumanis, & Thøgersen-Ntoumani, 2010). Perceived controlling coach and teammate behavior predicted moral disengagement, which in turn positively predicted antisocial behavior toward opponents and teammates. Perceived coach autonomy support had a positive indirect effect on prosocial behavior toward teammates via the satisfaction of relatedness and competence needs.

Integration of motivational theories

An interesting integration of constructs of a revised version of achievement goal theory (Elliot & McGregor, 2001) and self-determination theory was conducted by Vansteenkiste and his colleagues in two studies (2010, 2014). In the first study, Vansteenkiste, Mouratidis, and Lens (2010) investigated whether pursuing performance approach goals (i.e., the aim to do better than others; Elliot & McGregor, 2001) for autonomous or controlling reasons influenced moral functioning. Participants completed measures of whether athletes pursued performance approach goals for autonomous (e.g., because the goals were challenging to them) or controlling (e.g., because others expect them to do so) reasons. Immoral functioning was assessed by measures of how frequently athletes engaged in antisocial behaviors. Pursuing approach goals for controlling reasons positively predicted objectifying attitudes (i.e., the tendency to downgrade opponents and perceive them as barriers to overcome at all costs to achieve their aim), which in turn positively predicted immoral functioning.

In the second study, Vansteenkiste, Mouratidis, Van Riet, & Lens (2014) examined whether game-to-game variations in situational achievement goal pursuit was related to game-to-game variation in prosocial behavior. Volleyball players completed a questionnaire right after the end of six volleyball matches. After controlling for the outcome of the game, participants with a dominant mastery approach situational goal (i.e., aim to master the requirements of the task and doing as well as they possibly can) reported, on average, more prosocial behavior toward their teammates, compared to participants with a dominant performance approach (i.e., aim to outperform others), performance avoidance (i.e., aim to avoid performing worse than others), or mastery avoidance (i.e., aim to avoid not meeting task requirements or one's potential) goals. After controlling for the outcome of the game, autonomous reasons (e.g., "because I liked to pursue this goal"; "because I found this a personally important goal") underlying dominant mastery approach goal pursuit were also related positively to prosocial behavior toward teammates. Interestingly, victory was also a positive predictor of prosocial behavior toward one's teammates.

Organizational citizenship behaviors

One important form of morally relevant behavior that could facilitate organizational functioning is organizational citizenship behavior (OCB), defined as behavior that is "discretionary, not directly or explicitly recognized by the formal rewards system, and that in the aggregate promotes the effective functioning of the organization" (Organ, 1988, p. 4). In this definition, two key distinctions are implicit: first, the emphasis is on volitional behaviors because the behaviors are not requirements that can be enforced by the job description, and second, individual OCBs may not be significant in terms of organizational functioning, but the accumulation of these behaviors will enhance performance. Although Organ (1988) described five categories of OCB, only three of them have been examined in sport research: helping, which refers to aiding others with preventing the occurrence of work-related problems; sportspersonship, which pertains to tolerating problems and daily hassles without complaining; and civic virtue, which is behaving responsibly and showing concern about the life of the organization. OCB can be viewed as a form of prosocial behavior as it involves behaviors intended to help, for the benefit of others.

To date, only one study has examined OCB in sport. Specifically, Aoyagi, Cox, and McGuire (2008) investigated the relationship between the three types of OCB described above and team cohesion, athlete satisfaction, and congruence between preferred and perceived leadership behavior in student athletes from a variety of sports. Results revealed that both team cohesion and leadership congruence positively predicted OCB. Thus, when student-athletes perceived that their team had high task and social cohesion, and that their leader displayed training and instruction, democratic behavior, social support, and positive feedback when these behaviors were also preferred by the athletes, they were more likely to also report engaging in the OCBs described above (Aoyagi et al., 2008).

Applied implications and future research directions

The literature discussed in this chapter has some important applied implications for sport organizations. In this section, we indicate some of these implications and provide directions for future research. The first three bullet points below refer to applied implications, and the last four refer to future research directions.

- Prosocial teammate behaviors could have a positive influence on the recipients' effort, enjoyment, and commitment to continue playing for the team (Al-Yaaribi et al., 2016). Thus, this type of behavior should be encouraged among teammates, but also at all levels of the sport organization. For example, chief executive officers (CEOs) and performance directors could act in a prosocial manner toward coaches and support staff, when the opportunity arises.
- The negative link between antisocial teammate behavior and effort (Al-Yaaribi et al., 2016) suggests that this kind of behavior could have a negative influence on its recipient. Coaches, managers, and support staff need to be aware that acting toward others in an antisocial manner could demotivate them; thus, this type of behavior should be kept to a minimum.
- Certain features of the social environment, such as the moral atmosphere of the team, the motivational climate, and the coaches' interpersonal style can influence prosocial and antisocial behaviors. In order to promote prosocial behavior, coaches can reward effort and treat athletes fairly, but also support their autonomy by giving them choices (see Mageau & Vallerand, 2003). Coaches should also avoid rewarding only the best athletes, creating intrateam rivalry, and using controlling behaviors, to minimize antisocial behavior in sport.
- Most studies to date have focused on the moral conduct of athletes toward teammates and opponents. Research is needed to investigate the prosocial and antisocial behaviors of other members of the sport organization such as coaches, support staff, and performance directors.
- We know little about the role of various members of the sport organization on athletes' decisions to use banned performance-enhancing drugs, or about the organizational dynamics that may be involved in other morally questionable behaviors, such as match-fixing and bribery. Research is needed to examine these issues.
- Research is needed to understand the consequences of moral behavior in sport. For example, researchers could examine the potential influence of prosocial and antisocial behaviors on relationships, conflict resolution, and burnout.
- Finally, researchers could examine the experiences and behavior of elite athletes, a population that has not been sampled extensively.

Conclusion

In conclusion, our understanding of the moral and motivational antecedents of prosocial and antisocial behaviors in sport has been enhanced in the last decade. A number of personal and social variables have been linked to these behaviors, while teammate behavior appears to play a role in the effectiveness of sport organizations. When athletes behave more prosocially and refrain from acting antisocially toward their teammates, effort, performance, enjoyment, and commitment are likely to occur. Sport organizations would benefit from focusing on dedicating effort on strategies that promote prosocial and deter antisocial behaviors within the organization.

References

Al-Yaaribi, A., Kavussanu, M., & Ring, C. (2016). Consequences of perceived prosocial and antisocial behaviors in sport for the recipient. *Psychology of Sport and Exercise, 26*, 102–112.

Ames, C. (1992). Achievement goals, motivational climate, and motivational processes. In G. C. Roberts (Ed.), *Motivation in sport and exercise* (pp. 161–176). Champaign, IL: Human Kinetics.

Aoyagi, M. W., Cox, R. H., & McGuire, R. T. (2008). Organizational citizenship behavior in sport: Relationships with leadership, team cohesion, and athlete satisfaction. *Journal of Applied Sport Psychology, 20*, 25–41.

Aquino, K., & Reed, A. (2002). The self-importance of moral identity. *Journal of Personality and Social Psychology, 83*, 1423–1440.

Aquino, K., Freeman, D., Reed, A., Lim, V. K. G., & Felps, W. (2009). Testing a social cognitive model of moral behavior: The interactive influence of situations and moral identity centrality. *Journal of Personality and Social Psychology, 97*, 123–141.

Bandura, A. (1991). Social cognitive theory of moral thought and action. In W. M. Kurtines & J. L. Gewirtz (Eds.), *Handbook of moral behavior and development: Theory, research, and applications* (Vol. 1, pp. 71–129). Hillsdale, NJ: Lawrence Erlbaum Associates.

Bandura, A. (1999). Moral disengagement in the perpetration of inhumanities. *Personality and Social Psychology Review, 3*, 193–209.

Bandura, A. (2002). Social cognitive theory in cultural context. *Applied Psychology, 51*(2), 269–290.

Bartholomew, K. J., Ntoumanis, N., & Thøgersen-Ntoumani, C. (2010). The controlling interpersonal style in a coaching context: Development and initial validation of a psychometric scale. *Journal of Sport & Exercise Psychology, 32*, 193–216.

Batson, C. D., Early, S., & Salvarani, G. (1997). Perspective taking: Imagining how another feels versus imagining how you would feel. *Personality and Social Psychology Bulletin, 23*, 751–758. doi: 10.1177/0146167297237008.

Boardley, I. D., & Kavussanu, M. (2009). The influence of social variables and moral disengagement on prosocial and antisocial behaviors in field hockey and netball. *Journal of Sports Sciences, 27*, 843–854.

Boardley, I. D., & Kavussanu, M. (2010). Effects of goal orientation and perceived value of toughness on antisocial behavior: The mediating role of moral disengagement. *Journal of Sport & Exercise Psychology, 33*, 176–192.

Chow, G. M., Murray, K. E., & Feltz, D. L. (2009). Individual, team, and coach predictors of players' likelihood to aggress in youth soccer. *Journal of Sport & Exercise Psychology, 31*, 425–443.

Corrion, K., Long, T., Smith, A. L., & d'Arripe-Longueville, F. (2009). "It's not my fault; it's not serious": Athlete accounts of moral disengagement in competitive sport. *The Sport Psychologist, 23*, 388–404.

Davis, M. H. (1983). Measuring individual differences in empathy: Evidence for a multidimensional approach. *Journal of Personality and Social Psychology, 44*, 11–26.

Deci, E. L., & Ryan, R. M. (1975). *Intrinsic motivation*. Chichester: John Wiley & Sons.

Deci, E. L., & Ryan, R. (1985). *Intrinsic motivation and self-determination in human behavior*. New York: Springer.

Donahue, E. G., Miquelon, P., Valois, P., Goulet, C., Buist, A., & Vallerand, R. J. (2006). A motivational model of performance-enhancing substance use in elite athletes. *Journal of Sport & Exercise Psychology, 28*, 511–520.

Duda, J. L., Olson, L. K., & Templin, T. J. (1991). The relationship of task and ego orientation to sportsmanship attitudes and the perceived legitimacy of injurious acts. *Research Quarterly for Exercise and Sport, 62*, 297–334.

Eisenberg, N., & Fabes, R. A. (1998). Prosocial development. In N. Eisenberg (Ed.), *Handbook of child psychology, Vol. 3: Social, emotional, and personality development* (pp. 701–778). New York: Wiley.

Eisenberg, N., & Strayer, J. (1987). Critical issues in the study of empathy. In N. Eisenberg and J. Strayer (Eds.), *Empathy and its development* (pp. 3–16). Cambridge: Cambridge University Press.

Elliot, A. J., & McGregor, H. A. (2001). A 2 × 2 achievement goal framework. *Journal of Personality and Social Psychology, 80*, 501–519.

Gagné, M. (2003). The role of autonomy support and autonomy orientation in prosocial behavior engagement. *Motivation and Emotion, 27*, 199–223.

Grolnick, W., & Ryan, R. (1989). Parent styles associated with children's self-regulation and competence in school. *Journal of Educational Psychology, 81*(2), 143–154.

Hodge, K., & Gucciardi, D. F. (2015). Antisocial and prosocial behavior in sport: The role of motivational climate, basic psychological needs, and moral disengagement. *Journal of Sport & Exercise Psychology, 37*, 257–273.

Hodge, K., & Lonsdale, C. (2011). Prosocial and antisocial behavior in sport: The role of coaching style, autonomous vs. controlled motivation, and moral disengagement. *Journal of Sport & Exercise Psychology, 33*, 527–547.

Kavussanu, M. (2006). Motivational predictors of prosocial and antisocial behavior in soccer. *Journal of Sports Sciences, 24*(6), 575–588.

Kavussanu, M. (2012). Moral behavior in sport. In S. Murphy (Ed.), *The Oxford handbook of sport and performance psychology* (pp. 364–383). Oxford: Oxford University Press. .

Kavussanu, M., & Boardley, I. D. (2009). The Prosocial and Antisocial Behavior in Sport Scale. *Journal of Sport & Exercise Psychology, 31*, 1–23.

Kavussanu, M., & Boardley, I. D. (2012). Moral behavior in sport. In G. Tenenbaum, R. J. Eklund, & A. Kamata (Eds.), *Handbook of measurement in sport and exercise psychology*. Champaign, IL: Human Kinetics.

Kavussanu, M., & Spray, C. M. (2006). Contextual influences on moral functioning of male youth footballers. *The Sport Psychologist, 20*, 1–23.

Kavussanu, M., Roberts, G. C., & Ntoumanis, N. (2002). Contextual influences on moral functioning of college basketball players. *The Sport Psychologist, 16*(4), 347–367.

Kavussanu, M., Stamp, R., Slade, G., & Ring, C. (2009). Observed prosocial and antisocial behaviors in male and female football players. *Journal of Applied Sport Psychology, 21(Supp. 1)*, S62–S76.

Kavussanu, M., Stanger, N., & Boardley, I. D. (2013). The Prosocial and Antisocial Behaviour in Sport Scale: Further evidence for construct validity and reliability. *Journal of Sports Sciences, 31*, 1208–1221.

Kavussanu, M., Willoughby, A., & Ring, C. (2012). Moral identity and emotion in athletes. *Journal of Sport & Exercise Psychology, 34*, 695–714.

Kavussanu, M., Stanger, N., & Ring, C. (2015). The effects of moral identity on moral emotion and antisocial behavior in sport. *Sport, Exercise and Performance Psychology, 4*, 268–279.

Mageau, G. A., & Vallerand, R. J. (2003). The coach-athlete relationship: A motivational model. *Journal of Sports Sciences, 21*, 883–904.

Nicholls, J. G. (1989). *The competitive ethos and democratic education*. Cambridge, MA: Harvard University Press.

Ommundsen, Y., Roberts, G. C., Lemyre, P. N., & Treasure, D. (2003). Perceived motivational climate in male youth soccer: Relations to social-moral functioning, sportspersonship and team norm perceptions. *Psychology of Sport and Exercise, 4*, 397–413.

Organ, D. W. (1988). *Organisational citizenship behavior: The good soldier syndrome*. Lexington, MA: Lexington Books.

Power, C., Higgins, A., & Kohlberg, L. A. (1989). *Lawrence Kohlberg's approach to moral education*. New York: Columbia University Press.

Rascle, O., Coulomb-Cabagno, G., & Delsarte, A. (2005). Perceived motivational climate and observed aggression as a function of competitive level in youth male French handball. *Journal of Sport Behavior, 28*(1), 51–67.

Ring, C., Kavussanu, M., Stanger, N., McVittie, H., Condie, R., & Tenenbaum, G. (in revision). The ethics of competition: An experimental study of sledging. *International Journal of Sport and Exercise Psychology*.

Ryan, R. M., & Deci, J. L. (2000). Self-determination theory and the facilitation of intrinsic motivation, social development, and well-being. *The American Psychologist, 55*, 68–78.

Sage, L. D., & Kavussanu, M. (2007). The effects of goal involvement on moral behavior in an experimentally manipulated competitive setting. *Journal of Sport & Exercise Psychology, 29*, 190–207.

Sage, L. D., Kavussanu, M., & Duda, J. L. (2006). Goal orientations and moral identity as predictors of prosocial and antisocial functioning in male association football players. *Journal of Sports Sciences, 24*(5), 455–466.

Shields, D. L., & Bredemeier, B. J. L. (1995). *Character development and physical activity*. Champaign, IL: Human Kinetics.

Stanger, N., Kavussanu, M., & Ring, C. (2012). Put yourself in their boots: Effects of empathy on emotion and aggression. *Journal of Sport & Exercise Psychology, 34*, 208–222.

Stanger, N., Kavussanu, M., Willoughby, A., & Ring, C. (2012). Psychophysiological responses to sport-specific affective pictures: A study of morality and emotion in athletes. *Psychology of Sport and Exercise, 13*, 840–848.

Stanger, N., Kavussanu, M., Boardley, I. D., & Ring, C. (2013). The influence of moral disengagement and negative emotion on antisocial sport behavior. *Sport, Exercise and Performance Psychology, 2*, 117–129.

Stanger, N., Kavussanu, M., McIntyre, D., & Ring, C. (2016). Empathy inhibits aggression in competition: The role of provocation, emotion, and gender. *Journal of Sport & Exercise Psychology, 38*(1), 4–14.

Stephens, D. E. (2001). Predictors of aggressive tendencies in girls' basketball: An examination of beginning and advanced participants in a summer skills camp. *Research Quarterly for Exercise and Sport, 72*(3), 257–266.

Stephens, D. E., & Bredemeier, B. J. L. (1996). Moral atmosphere and judgments about aggression in girls' soccer: Relationships among moral and motivational variables. *Journal of Sport & Exercise Psychology, 18*, 158–173.

Tangney, J. P., Stuewig, J., & Mashek, D. J. (2007). Moral emotions and moral behavior. *Annual Review of Psychology, 58*, 345–372.

Traclet, A., Romand, P., Moret, O., & Kavussanu, M. (2011). Antisocial behavior in soccer: A qualitative study of moral disengagement. *International Journal of Sport and Exercise Psychology, 9*(2), 143–155.

Turiel, E. (1983). *The development of social knowledge: Morality and convention*. Cambridge, UK: Cambridge University Press.

Vansteenkiste, M., Mouratidis, A., & Lens, W. (2010). Detaching reasons from aims: Fair play and well-being in soccer as a function of pursuing performance-approach goals for autonomous or controlling reasons. *Journal of Sport & Exercise Psychology, 32*, 217–242.

Vansteenkiste, M., Mouratidis, A., Van Riet, T., & Lens, W. (2014). Examining correlates of game-to-game variation in volleyball players' achievement goals pursuit and underlying autonomous and controlling reasons. *Journal of Sport & Exercise Psychology, 36*, 131–145.

10
MEDIA BEHAVIOR IN SPORT

Elsa Kristiansen, Frank E. Abrahamsen, and Paul M. Pedersen

Introduction

The growth and influence of the mass media have expanded to the point where the affiliated professionals, whose work in the past mainly involved a narrow focus on the reporting of sport results, are now part of an institutional complex of enormous economic (e.g., television rights fees), social, organizational, cultural, and political importance (Pedersen, 2013; Rowe, 2004). While over the years the symbiotic and influential relationship between sport and the mass media has been strengthened at all levels, this relationship is particularly noteworthy in major sport because, as noted by Wenner (2015), "there could be no big-time sport without big-time media" (p. 629). With the integration of the two institutions of sport and the mass media, terms such as *mediasport* (Wenner, 1998), *mediated sport* (Maguire, Jarvie, Mansfield, & Bradley, 2002), and *mediatization* (Frandsen, 2014) have been adopted to describe the sport–media nexus within various academic fields (e.g., sport sociology, sport communication). Given the mass medias often serve as the voice for telling sport stories, "mediasport strategically reaches out to us to narrate understandings of sport in the context of broader social relations" (Wenner, 2013, pp. 83–84). The influence of the mass media – as well as social media – on the growth (e.g., economical) and significance (e.g., societal) of sport has resulted in a proliferation of research into how sport behavior is framed and understood.

For the most popular mediated sports such as soccer in Europe and American football in the United States, the daily media "news" is disseminated instantly by trained media professionals as well as amateur citizen journalists via various social media platforms and multimedia devices. Such dissemination keeps the players (e.g., athletes at all levels, but especially professional athletes and high-profile amateurs such as intercollegiate student-athletes) in the public eye (Pedersen, 2014). Even in the offseason the many communication platforms (e.g., newspaper sports pages, sports websites, smartphone apps, and social media services) will often include updates on player transactions, contract negotiations, training regimens, and even unauthorized private videos and candid photographs of prominent sport stars during their vacations and other non-sport engagements. While many athletes may appreciate and even embrace the seemingly incessant media coverage because of what may be perceived as certain intrinsic and extrinsic benefits (e.g., exposure, recognition, popularity, personal branding, endorsement opportunities, fame), because contemporary media coverage – whether wanted or unwanted – is hard to control, there is the possibility that media attention will be intrusive, embarrassing, exhausting, and even debilitating. Thus, both professional and private life press coverage may catch even the most seasoned sport professionals by surprise and the media attention and interaction demands might pose unpredictable environmental demands (Kristiansen, Hanstad, & Roberts, 2011) and impose behavioral requirements.

While the sport industry has benefited in numerous ways from the growth and influence of the media (e.g., mass media, social media, emerging media), a wide variety of sport industry stakeholders ranging from managers (e.g., Carter, 2007), coaches (e.g., Nesti, 2010), athletes and journalists (Kristiansen & Hanstad, 2012), referees (e.g., Anshel & Weiberg, 1995), sport psychologists (e.g., Lindsay & Thomas, 2014), and even medical personnel (e.g., Gibson, 2015) need to manage behaviors *with* and *of* the media. Indeed, the outcome of *not* managing the behavior of sport individuals and the media may result in stress due to the heightened and, at times, seemingly incessant media coverage and attention.

The sport-focused research on media behavior has mainly examined the subject from the athletes' perspective, with the focus being on the negative aspect of media stressors as a result of the athletes' interactions with journalists or athletes' exposure to published media reports (Kristiansen & Lines, 2014). Sport organizations need to offer their stakeholders (e.g., athletes, staff members, coaches) education and media training (e.g., practice sessions) in dealing with the media. Such opportunities can be used to help athletes to cope both with the media coverage they receive and with their interactions (i.e., interviews) with journalists. Indeed, researchers have recently highlighted that the impact of media coverage on athletes and their affiliated entourage remains an understudied topic in sport psychology (Kristiansen & Lines, 2014). Although media stressors are often evident in the competitive, organizational, and personal segments of athletic involvement, the limited scholarly work regarding these demands may be a result of scholars' placing media-induced stress under the general research umbrella of organizational stress (e.g., McKay et al., 2008). Based on recent scholarly work (e.g., Kristiansen & Hanstad, 2012) it might be postulated that the media have the power to initiate, affect, and at times aggravate the entire interplay between competitive, organizational, and personal stressors for athletes and support staff. One reason for this broad potential influence is that the mass (and social) media are pervasive throughout the sport industry, and especially in elite sport. For instance, new technologies have made it harder for sport stars to hide, escape, or live a life unnoticed. The ubiquitous presence and extensive use of social media have made it possible for previously private statements (e.g., a racist comment by an athlete during a concert) and personal incidents (e.g., an act of domestic violence by an athlete in a hotel elevator) public – and often career ending – in a matter of seconds. Professional sports stars (e.g., Ray Rice), coaches (e.g., former Rutgers University basketball coach Mike Rice), intercollegiate athletes (e.g., former Florida State University quarterback De'Andre Johnson), and even interscholastic players (e.g., high school football players attacking a game official) have seen their lives and careers altered by video footage that has gone viral. One need only log onto a website such as Deadspin.com or TMZ.com and scroll through the web pages to find numerous images of athletes videoed or photographed saying or doing things that just a decade ago the public never would have seen because such media outlets did not exist. Nevertheless, while there is no public video of the incident that changed Tiger Woods's image (and career), back in 2009, the once dominating golfer quickly realized how media coverage created intense personal stress (on his family relations, social life, etc.) as well as organizational stress (on his sponsors, agency, handlers, foundation, etc.). One can only speculate how much the controversies contributed to Woods going from being Number One in the world ranking (2010) to dropping out of the tTop 200 in 2015. Of course, media attention may also have positive outcomes. For example, Holt and Hogg (2002) did not find media attention as a distraction for female football players preparing for the World Cup. Instead, the footballers in their study welcomed some media attention during their preparation because their performances were not normally mentioned in the press. For the athletes, the media coverage of their participation was an excellent opportunity to present their sport and thus they enjoyed their media interactions and whatever media coverage they could get.

In this chapter, we will look more closely at media behavior for athletes and organizations and give practical advice for sport psychologists and organizations to better help their employees (e.g., athletes, coaches, managers) cope with media coverage and increase the effectiveness of their interactions with the media.

Media as a stressor

In order to examine how the media might be perceived as a stressor by individuals in the sport industry, it is best to first look at how the media cover and influence sport. Social science researchers have explored the messages contained within media platforms for some time (Yoo, Smith, & Kim, 2013). According to Hargreaves (1986), mass media's coverage of sport has to do with "skilled, exciting and above all entertaining leisure activity" (p. 138). In his opinion, through their use of often-stereotypical depictions of athletes, the media have built up and even prepared their audiences for how to react to the coverage. This is apparent in the language used in some media outlets (e.g., wording and phrasing regarding heroes and villains) along with the "notoriously stereotyped" (Hargreaves, 1986, p. 151) use of language among journalists. One example is the sport coverage of football in Britain, which has been extensive since the 1980s. While effective teamwork in football is essential for success, Hargreaves noted that the media attention has "focused on the individual through the routine practice in British TV coverage of making frequent close-ups of players, showing their problems, achievements and failures" (p. 150). Beyond the televised coverage, Hargreaves noted that the print media provided coverage that was "substantially the same, except that personalization and dramatization are carried further in competition with TV and rival newspapers" (p. 150). Since Hargreaves' observation three decades ago, the proliferation of media channels and technologies as well as the phenomenal rise of social media platforms and usage have dramatically changed the media landscape and the sport media scene in particular.

Living in the eyes of the media

Journalists often use dramaturgical techniques to enhance the entertainment factor of the athletes or sporting events they cover, and for decades the sport media have used protagonists and antagonists to captivate their media audiences (Langer, 1981). More time and resources have typically been devoted to male sports (Cooky, Messner, & Hextrum, 2013), and members of the media have a history of trying to compare the participation and accomplishments of girls and women in sport to that of their male counterparts (Pirinen, 2002). Such comparisons to male athletes can have a negative impact on female athletes. For example, Kristiansen, Broch, and Pedersen (2014) observed female soccer players to express perceptions of an internal hierarchy between male and female players and a sense that they (the female athletes) would never be equal to male athletes. Some players found it annoying that outsiders would even take the time and effort to make the female–male comparisons because the players themselves see women's and men's soccer as two different sports and are therefore incomparable. The study also found that some players indicated that the media sometimes fuel this comparison and make it harder for athletes to cope with such demands.

Sometimes the media coverage is so complex that it makes it hard to figure out who – if anyone – is wrong or right in a framed or actual conflict. For instance, endurance cycling is a sport when the team leader needs team members willing to sacrifice themselves for him or her in order to win. Few cyclists will be in opposition with this system, though the athletes' significant others (e.g., spouses, partners) are obviously not constrained by this loyalty. Take, for example, the 2012 Tour de France, in which Team Sky's Sir Bradley Wiggins was poised to win. Chris Froome's loyalty was questioned twice when he left his team leader (Wiggins) and twice attempted to go for a stage win for himself (Beattie, 2013); leaving your leader is usually regarded as unacceptable in cycling. While Froome returned to Wiggins in compliance with team orders, Beattie noted that the two incidents caused a significant media storm. During the competition itself Wiggins and Froome remained quiet concerning their views about each other, but their significant others made heated statements on social media, including a complaint by Froome's girlfriend about how his loyalty was being abused (*Daily Mail*, 2012). While the cyclists did not participate in the media (and social media) controversy, it could be argued that the swirling conflict may have affected both riders to some degree (e.g., energy draining, future competitions). Regardless, in order to be prepared for such media scenarios, it is advisable that athletes' entourages – whether they be significant others or sponsors – are media-trained, media-savvy, and fully aware of the direct and indirect consequences their actions could have on the performers. The rise in social media engagement, interaction, and influence requires athletes, their stakeholders, and sport organizations overall – as well as the members of the sport media – be appropriately educated and trained regarding the opportunities and pitfalls related to this medium (Clavio, Bowles, Vooris, & Pedersen, 2013; Pedersen, 2014). For example, the Olympic champion Norwegian handball team recently outlined new organization-wide guidelines due to the challenges presented by the changing media landscape (Kristiansen, 2014). After a few incidents where spontaneous tweets took several days – and an abundance of energy and human resources – to resolve, the new guidelines allow players the freedom to use the social media as they please with regard to their own feelings. However, any issues regarding the team may not be shared with the public. In the United States, numerous incidents on social media have prompted the implementation of social media policies for both the athletes and employees of the sport organizations (e.g., owners, managers, support staff). Clavio et al. (2013) noted that with the increasing oversight of social media activities, professional leagues are making it clear that they "believe athletes should take personal responsibility for their comments and strive to portray themselves and their leagues in a positive light" (p. 69). Further, Clavio et al. added that the leagues believe "this can be accomplished by players' taking caution before posting to their social media accounts. The leagues stress that players should be respectful to their fans, their teammates, other teams, officials and the game itself" (p. 69).

Interactions with journalists

Athletes (and also their support staff) sometimes have an ambivalent relationship with the journalists who cover them (Kristiansen & Hanstad, 2012). While the athletes often may not care for the media members and their activities (e.g., questions, coverage), Kristiansen and Hanstad noted that athletes are more capable of coping with demands if they acknowledge that the athletes and the media representatives have distinct roles as actors and distributors, respectively, in major events. Nevertheless, the rise in source publicity has allowed athletes more opportunities to take on dual roles as both actors on the field of play and as media distributors when they post social media messages or distribute their own articles and press releases on their own websites and outlets. The former general manager of Boston Bruins (National Hockey League), Mike O'Connell, revealed an understanding of these distinct roles when he noted that, "there are three components to the sport industry: the entertainment component, the talent and competitive component, and the business component" (O'Connell, 2004, p. 30). We would argue that an awareness of the role of media is beneficial to help manage media interactions, and this awareness can start with athletes' undertaking appropriate preparation (e.g., media training, mock Q&A sessions) before interviews. "The journalists don't ask about our goals or what you hope to achieve," noted one Olympic athlete – a participant in a study (Kristiansen & Hanstad, 2012) that investigated the relationship (e.g., contact, communication) between athletes and journalists – "all they want is to find out the other stuff, things that I am not prepared for, and their questions may sweep my focus on task away" (p. 237). In the study, which focused on the 2010 Olympic Winter Games in Vancouver, Canada, the participating journalists were presented with the athletes' perceptions of them shortly after they interviewed the athletes. Interestingly, the journalists emphasized that at the Olympic level sports journalism is both circus and entertainment and as such coaches and athletes need to be aware of this unique situation. The journalists, who highlighted the importance of making entertaining and engaging stories instead of more mundane articles about athletic performances, regarded coping with media and their questions as an ingredient of being an elite performer. The members of the media involved in the study also emphasized that they should not be perceived as the enemy, even though the athletes who find themselves portrayed in a negative light (e.g., criticized for a performance below expectations) might have a tendency to feel as if they are. The journalists argued that they shouldn't be considered the enemy for simply fulfilling their role, as they have a different job or agenda (e.g., create quality, engaging, interesting stories that, in turn, help to sell newspapers, promote the media entity, get website clicks, and so forth) than athletes. In an attempt to work around these issues, some athlete participants reported maintaining a closer relationship with a few journalists that they trusted. As one noted, "I can tell him (reporter) things without it being broadcasted, and in return he gets exclusives and the opportunity to call me privately" (p. 239). Hence, it is important for the sport performers to behave in ways that regulate the information flow while at the same time being accessible; an active use of social media is another way of controlling the information flow.

Media coverage and mediated interaction

A good working relationship between athletes and the sport media is viewed here as a two-way street – a symbiotic relationship – for both parties; elite athletes depend on the media for publicity, which, in turn, often assists the athlete in intangible (e.g., fame) and tangible (e.g., sponsors) ways. Journalists need to create articles that will be of interest to the public and thus they need to sell stories (i.e., the media outlet needs to make money through subscriptions, purchases, website clicks and affiliated advertising, and so forth), but at the same time they need to maintain access to and sustain relationships with the athletes and organizations they cover (Pedersen, Miloch, & Laucella, 2007). Tension may easily arise during major events when all journalists want a story and the athletes or coaches do not want to offer controversial sound bites or responses that might create headlines. Thus, as one athlete noted in a study by Kristiansen and Roberts (2011), "you do not say something controversial and create a media storm two days before a major competition like the Olympics!" (p. 241). Media behavior can even lead to physical altercations. Take, for instance, the former coach of the Mexican national soccer team, Miguel Herrera, who was accused of hitting and threatening a journalist who had been one of his harshest media critics. Shortly after the incident Herrera was fired by the Mexican Soccer Federation (*Daily Telegraph*, 2015).

While there are controversial moments, challenging interactions, and often competing goals and roles, for the most part athletes and media personnel are in it together (Kristiansen & Hanstad, 2012). Depending on the specific role of the credentialed media member (e.g., columnist, reporter, broadcaster, blogger, and social media editor), the goals for the media may range from informational to entertainment. Thus, injuries and failures are often issues about which the athletes are interviewed (Kristiansen & Roberts, 2011). Because of the mass media's gatekeeping role and agenda-setting function (the influence of both may be said to be decreasing with the ability of athletes and organizations to tell their own stories through their own mass media and social media outlets), the mass media continue to hold a certain amount of power regarding what gets reported, highlighted, minimalized, marginalized, or ignored. As a consequence, some athletes realize the power of the media to frame a story and thus they try to be prepared for everything, and are also helped in their preparation by advice and guidance from media relations professionals and sports information directors (Kristiansen, 2014). As alluded to above, both national and professional teams tend to rely more on these professional staff members to coordinate and organize press meetings, to give advice and protect athletes, to deal with unforeseen press incidents, and to act as an overall liaison between athletes and the media. High-profile intercollegiate athletics in the United States often involve pre-season press conferences. For American college football teams, the head coaches often select the attendees at these media days. The individuals selected are often experienced student-athletes. "Cautious coaches tend to lean toward rewarding upperclassmen with a trip to media day" noted one report, adding, "part of the reason is that experienced seniors can be relied upon to stay on message" (*Bloomington Herald-Times*, 2015).

There are many key points that athletes, coaches, and other sport personnel should consider when interacting with the media in order both to better cope with the inherent media stress that comes with such interactions, and to better navigate some of the issues and pitfalls that have been reported by athletes in extant research. Table 10.1 provides advice for how stakeholders in sports organizations (e.g., athletes, coaches, managers) might optimize media behavior.

TABLE 10.1 Advice and examples for media interactions

Advice	Examples
Have respect and understanding for each other's nuanced roles	• In some countries, the National Olympic Committee (NOC) officials create various rules regarding how the athletes should be contacted by the media during the games. In order to obtain press credentials, the rules – presented as an agreement – are signed by the sport media as well as the NOC • All staff are trained by media personnel in the different roles that media have • The evaluations after the games are given to both parties in order to improve the collaboration
Be well-mannered and on time for interviews	• Respect that journalists are on a deadline. Typically, a suggestion for interactions involve the adage that one must show respect in order to receive respect. Nevertheless, some media members may take advantage of the respect shown and thus the athlete should stay on guard even in a perceived respectful dialogue or arrangement • Respect the other person even if you disagree with her/his perspective and arguments • If in a disagreement, remember that you are disagreeing about the subject and not about the person
If provided the option, ask for questions in advance and agree on topics in advance as well. Then on commencing of media interactions, stick to the questions and topics agreed upon	• Ask for the topics of the interview in advance and, if possible, request a list of the questions that might be asked • While it doesn't hurt to ask to read the proof before printing if possible, keep in mind that most professional – objective/independent – sports journalists would not provide such a copy • Plan for what to say before meeting the media. Do not "wing it" during the interview
Comment only on your own performance or responsibilities	• Speak on behalf of yourself, or for the subject you have been assigned responsibility • Tell what you know and do not guess. Refer to other experts if outside your area of expertise

Advice	Examples
	• If needed, ask for more time to investigate the issue rather than making inferences from journalists' remarks or questions
	• If there is any confusion or if you need additional time to think, ask for a clarification of the question, ask for a rewording of the question, or ask that the interviewer come back to the question later on during the interview
If a (media) break is needed during the interview process, ask for it in advance rather than simply stepping away	• Instead of avoiding the media (right after a performance) or if asked for an interview at an inconvenient time, simply ask the journalist to call back later in the day (or whenever you are free and prepared to finish the interview). While the journalist may give the impression that they are upset/disappointed with your decision to postpone the interview, letting sports journalists know your status or need for privacy can help them prepare (e.g., go to another source, write a different story)

Coping with the media

Media attention can be a lot of fun, especially for those athletes just commencing their careers. For example, elite soccer players in Kristiansen and Roberts's (2011) media behavior study reported running out early in the morning for newspapers the day after they played. Athletes from minor sports or those that often do not receive much coverage, as well as young athletes in major sports, are sometimes enamored by and even desire media attention. While media may be enjoyable and embraced by athletes early in their media interactions, after a certain point, the attention can become a stressor for athletes and, as such, the media coverage and interactions can serve as a distraction that must be dealt with (Kristiansen & Roberts, 2011). Stress theory suggests that being able to cope is related to the development and execution of learned responses that successfully lower arousal by neutralizing or minimizing the importance of a threatening condition (Lazarus & Folkman, 1984). In other words, coping with the media is a learned response that may take time and training to develop. Consequently, what the athletes experience and understand may change over time. For example, Kristiansen (2011) illustrated this change by an experienced soccer goalkeeper who had received media coverage throughout his athletic career:

> Now that I am older and have had the media say both good and bad things about me, what I have realized is that you really have to take it all with a

pinch of salt... There have been games where I had a very normal game, and the media praised me, saying I had an amazing game, and for me reading article it is like: *REALLY?* I had a very basic and simple game. And then there have been times where... I maybe have let in a bad goal, but had a really solid game, and I took a lot of media scrutiny, and so ... you know, when they say good things you need to brush it off, and when they say bad things, you have to brush it off, too. That is easier said than done ... but, that is what you have to accept, and in the end of the day ... if you are overly concerned about what other people think about you, you are going to have a tough time and you will not last.

(pp. 57–58)

As revealed in the quotation above, the media can be a source of substantial strain for elite athletes given the demands they must learn to deal with (Kristiansen & Roberts, 2011). Both young and old athletes might mobilize social support when attempting to cope with media demands. Social support is a multidimensional construct and according to Schaefer, Coyne, and Lazarus (1982) it can be divided into function types: emotional support (e.g., love and care); tangible support (e.g., direct aid, practical help); and informational support (e.g., feedback). Social support is considered to be an important a priori buffer against stress, as well as being an ad hoc coping resource (Lazarus & Folkman, 1984) which is an effective strategy when coping with acute stressors (Cohen & Wills, 1985). However, media stress may represent a chronic stressor and, thus, might require more than social support. Hence, in order to cope more effectively with the media as a chronic stressor, alternative long-term coping strategies should also be developed. Some athletes choose coping strategies that may be placed under the heading of avoidance coping, such as listening to music or by not reading newspapers, social media postings, or sport blogs. In doing so, athletes try to shut out the media and reduce the likelihood that media coverage could influence their thinking (e.g., Kristiansen, Hanstad, et al., 2011). However, avoidance coping strategies are often ineffective given the prevalence of media coverage and for compliance one would likely need help from one's family or media relations officers to avoid media reports (Kristiansen, Roberts, et al., 2011). Nevertheless, even though friends and family may wish to support athletes, they often want to discuss performance, and the information and knowledge that they wish to discuss is often drawn from media reports (Kristiansen & Roberts, 2011). Thus, it is not easy or effective for athletes to use avoidance coping behaviors in dealing with media demands.

Avoiding contact with journalists is even harder, as there are certain expectations and regulations from sponsors and sport organizations. Of course, an athlete can remain reticent so not even the most eager journalist finds them interesting to talk to (Kristiansen, Roberts, et al., 2011). Indeed, even when sport organizations have media interaction requirements, some athletes refuse to be highly engaging and only do the bare minimum. For instance, recently retired National Football League (NFL) star Marshawn Lynch was fined for his failure to engage with the media in accordance with league (NFL) rules (Buchanan, 2015). With ongoing media interest, taking a media break, that is, getting time off from the media attention, in order to focus on an upcoming event, might be a behavioral solution (Kristiansen, Hanstad, et al., 2011). However, such behavioral approaches require media personnel agreement and if an athlete walks away from the press conference to avoid being questioned, the media will likely be even more critical of them. Therefore, avoidance strategies will be unlikely to help athletes to effectively cope with media; indeed, such behavior might only serve to exacerbate the strain experienced. The media does not easily accept violation of the media rules previously agreed upon with governing bodies and sport organizations. Specifically, our research findings indicate that professional sport performers must accomplish the art of coping with the media, as it is part of the job (Kristiansen, Hanstad, et al., 2011). Of course, age, some sort of automatization, and experience teach athletes how to rationalize these demands and understand the importance of being appropriately prepared (Kristiansen & Roberts, 2011).

Despite the points above, it has been suggested that the use of avoidance–coping behaviors might actually protect individuals' self-confidence as they might avoid conflicting narratives about themselves (e.g., Giddens, 2006). For example, during major competitions and tournaments, athletes may be in agreement with team leaders to avoid reading newspapers and checking what is written about them online. However, only the coverage might be possible to avoid, not the actual interaction with media representatives. While the effectiveness of this in the short term may be debated, in the long term some sort of acceptance of the situation and adopting other strategies to fight disruptive thoughts may be needed. Sport performers have limited influence on what the media cover, though the social media have given them an opportunity to present their side of the story. Hence, to fight back might be considered one problem-focused approach. Problem-focused coping strategies are usually perceived to facilitate performance (e.g., Ntoumanis & Biddle, 1998), and are commonly employed concurrently with avoidance coping strategies (Reeves et al., 2009). From the extant literature, it has been argued that avoidance–coping strategies are beneficial in the initial stages of coping, with problem-focused strategies being beneficial at the latter stages of coping (e.g., Roth & Cohen, 1986). Further, use of avoidance strategies might also facilitate problem-focused strategies when they serve as a "time-out" to refocus (Aldwin, 2007). During long tournaments such as the FIFA World Cup, the Olympic Games, and the Tour de France, such behaviors might be necessary in order to effectively cope during the competition.

In team sports, individual coping strategies might not be sufficient when an entire team has to cope with negative media exposure. Park (2000) argued that athletes in team sports require more coping strategies than individual sports, and that team players face different stressors (e.g., roster competition and inter-team rivalry). Hence, team senior management and administrators within sport organizations must understand that publicly calling for a "change of results" increases the pressure on the coach who, in turn, may increase the pressure on the players – a scenario often found in performance slumps when athletes or teams fail to live up to certain expectations based on previously successful outings (Kristiansen & Roberts, 2011). Hence, facilitating a mastery climate as a team coping strategy, might be advisable (see Table 10.2). The terms mastery and performance climate are used in the achievement goal theory of motivation (for a review, see for instance Roberts, 2012), with motivational climate regarded as a team atmosphere emphasizing personal development and improvement, as opposed to a performance climate that emphasizes inter-team rivalry and normative evaluation. Indeed, our findings indicate that when a coach or team emphasizes the mastery aspect of the perceived climate, this was associated with the perception that a mastery climate seems to reduce the impact of negative media coverage (Kristiansen, Halvari, & Roberts, 2012).

In the next section, we consider specific components of media behavior and how sport organizations can prepare their employees to meet challenges that might occur and in order to help their athletes to better manage media behavior.

TABLE 10.2 Overview of behavior strategies to use with media

	Social support (coach, family, friends)	*Avoidance strategies*	*Problem-focused strategies*
Individual coping with the media	Coach support (informational and emotional)	Avoid buying newspapers or reading articles about yourself on the internet	Rationalize what they (the journalists) write about you
	Tangible support from team leaders and family	Give "boring" answers and not draw attention to your person	Focus on the next task and plan ahead (also during game)
	Emotional support from family (and help with avoidance)	Avoid giving interviews that will appear on game day	Team debriefing and analysis of the game
		Avoid journalists via a media break	See things in perspective
Team coping with the media	Mastery climate as team support and encourage collective effort	Mastery climate as team support to help with avoidance coping and distractions	Mastery climate as team support with coach debriefing to keep players focused on task

Note: This table is based on data published by Kristiansen and Roberts (2011) and Kristiansen, Roberts, and Sisjord (2011).

Media behavior and sport organizations

Professional sport organizations and high-profile amateur sport organizations, such as intercollegiate athletic departments within universities across the United States, have for some time acknowledged the need for media training and guidance of their players by having media relations or sports information departments. Within these organizational units are professional staff members who not only manage media interactions and disseminate information about their teams and players, but increasingly the staff train other employees (e.g., players, coaches, managers) in areas such as how to interact with the media; how to respond to controversial news coverage; and how to use the media for personal or organizational gain. Even when training is not involved, sometimes the more experienced individuals (e.g., seasoned coaches, veteran players) can take on some of the media pressure (thus reducing the media demands for the inexperienced individuals) or can serve as role models for how others might interact with the media. For example, in the United States even at the high school football level (interscholastic athletics) it is not uncommon for the head coach to make assistant coaches "off limits" to the media, ensuring all media interactions at the coaching level can only go through the (typically) veteran head coach. At the intercollegiate level, media and public relations officers often assist in managing the media interactions and help coaches to deflect media criticism, prevent media intrusion (e.g., allowing the media to interact with athletes at certain times), and help athletes deal with challenging media environments. An example of this is the well-publicized dispute that former collegiate athlete turned successful American football head coach, Mike Gundy, had with the media several years ago. Frustrated with the perceived negative media coverage a sports columnist had given regarding one of his players, Gundy went on a tirade during a press conference, shouting "come after me. I'm a man, I'm 40! I'm not a kid" (Friend, 2008). Regardless of whether his behavior was appropriate or not in "calling out" the journalist for what Gundy perceived to be inappropriate criticism of his young athlete, it has been debated as to whether Gundy may have used this interaction with the media in order to advance his own agenda, as the athlete was embarrassed by the situation and eventually transferred. Whether or not the coach's motives were pure, the incident – which has been rated as the number one most heated exchange between a sports personality and the media (Kian, Ketterer, Nichols, & Poling, 2014) – demonstrates that sport industry stakeholders (e.g., coaches, athletes, agents) might use the media to serve their own interests.

Another example of this optimizing behavior includes when an athlete or their agent might talk to the media during contract negotiations. The most media-savvy athletes who have substantial star power (e.g., highly recognized and celebrated athletes such as Cristiano Ronaldo, LeBron James) sometimes simply bypass the media altogether and post comments, photos, and articles on their own websites (e.g., Derek Jeter as the publisher of *The Players' Tribune*). Such publicity, when generated and managed by the athlete, is often done through social media platforms such as Facebook, Instagram, and Twitter, and is increasingly used by athletes at all levels to break news personally, interact with their fans, avoid interactions with the media, and control information flow.

Some sport organizations offer their best-known athlete(s) to the media because of the exposure that this brings to the organizations. However, this purposeful promotion has been reported to add to feelings of pressure on the part of the athlete being presented (Kristiansen, Roberts, et al., 2011). Given that this perception of pressure might manifest in stress response, such strategies could backfire on organizations by inhibiting performance, which, in turn, could lead to negative media exposure. Thus, sport organizations should carefully supervise the media workload placed on their athletes in order to avoid potential negative spirals, where negative results lead to negative media coverage and more pressure and possibly even worse results. As an example, we would like to share a story from our applied work as an illustration of how media attention can impede an athlete's development and long-term results. When working with a talented young athlete, the athlete surprised both the sport community, as well as herself, when she won the X-games for the first time. From being an unknown talent to becoming a worldwide star overnight changed a lot for her. In particular, the athlete went from training in solitude to having the media showing up at every training session. The athlete wanted to protect the media's image of her "talent" by only working on existing skills and became afraid of working on new skills, because she feared failing in the eyes of the media. This shift would be analogous to a shift from being mastery-involved to ego-involved, in accordance with achievement goal theory (Roberts, 2012). Hence, in order to help the athlete, it was initially decided that more closed training sessions would be arranged where the media were not allowed to observe or participate. However, the athlete's marketing team did not like this, and it led to a lot of conflict and resulted in compromises that were presented as having the athlete's best interests in mind. The athlete also undertook training in psychological skills and media management.

As mentioned previously, neophyte athletes sometimes desire and enjoy media attention, but this might come with a cost. Additionally, marketing is a large part of professional sport (as well as many amateur sport organizations), where the results of the teams and athletes are just part of a bigger picture (e.g., revenue streams/sharing). Hence, the dualism between getting publicity and being distracted by the media is only one of the issues to which organizations should be attentive.

The differences between minor and major media sports also present different challenges for athletes, coaches, and media attachés (e.g., media relations officers). With minor sports it is reasonable to assume that when many people think of these sports they think of sports that have more limited historical roots in a particular nation (e.g., cross-country skiing in the United States), Paralympic sports with lesser media attention, many of the amateur sports engaged in by young people and high school athletes, or sports that have few international competitors (e.g., race walking). Alternatively, major sports (hallmark sporting events such as the Olympic Games, the Super Bowl, and the World Cup) might have restrictive media credential requirements because of space and quality concerns, and will by necessity develop a systematic and restrictive handling process to deal with the significant media interest. Minor sports might try to do the exact opposite (e.g., a less restrictive media credentialing process) in order to gain as much media attention, secure as much sponsorship as possible – even if the brand is diluted as a result – and get as many people as possible participating and attending competitions. Our experience is that individuals and organizations operating in sports that receive little media attention in between the major games (e.g., Olympic Games) face more media difficulties in the weeks and days leading up to the major games due to the unfamiliarity of the spotlight they come under. Several difficulties typically surface. Those athletes who receive such sporadic media attention have less training to handle media interactions than athletes from more mediated sports, and often say or do things that cause trouble. The inexperience with media can generate additional stress (for instance, in the mixed zone – where the media interview athletes – for extended periods and often for the first time) and some encounter problems when experienced journalists lure them into making headline-grabbing comments. A typical example of being lured is by accepting the premise of the journalists› questions. For instance, in soccer a common question might start with the journalist saying, "today you lost because of the goalkeeper's error – what do you think should have been done differently?" While an inexperienced player might assign blame, an experienced player might avoid making scapegoats by saying something like

> well, we did not lose today because of one error, we had a lot of shots on the goal that we did not convert and we made some mistakes in our defense – so we have to fix those issues before the upcoming game.

New challenges with the shifting media landscape

Mo'ne Davis has quickly risen to fame within the United States and the baseball-interested world. Born in 2001, the Little League Baseball player has broken many barriers by being the first African-American girl to play in the Little League World Series; the first girl to throw a shutout; and also the first Little League Baseball player to appear on the cover of *Sports Illustrated*. Due to these feats she has received star treatment (e.g., appearing on *The Tonight Show with Jimmy Fallon* and having her story made into a Disney movie). Amid substantial media attention she has acted with grace, calmness, and maturity in the different settings in which she has appeared. However, as with many young sport stars, heightened media (and social media) attention can sometimes have unknown and unintended consequences. For instance, in 2015, a university baseball player was kicked off his collegiate team after he tweeted a vulgar statement regarding Davis (Lepard, 2015). While the vulgar tweet resulted in personal consequences for the university player, on hearing about the repercussions Davis publicly forgave the player and asked that the university reinstate him (Young, 2015). There are many discussion points to this story: first, as public figures, those involved in sport must realize that tweeting might have consequences. Indeed, Sanderson (2013) noted, "sports teams must be interested in the social media activity of their prospective employees" (p. 62) and apparently also the current ones. Second, Davis's response was very untypical for a 14 year old, and this has made others state "we need to be saving and protecting her" (Young, 2015). Thus, sport organizations should also be cognizant of when an athlete should be exposed to this level of media attention in order to protect both personal and athletic development processes.

More research about engagement in social media is needed; however, at the moment it is recommended that practitioners help athletes become aware of the consequences (and opportunities) that come with participation in new media platforms. Some of the emerging advice from our research has been summarized in Table 10.1, but below are some further recommendations. For instance, the media attaché of the Olympic training center in Norway, Halvor Lea, stated, "a tweet may be more spontaneous than some well-chosen words in a formal interview. We have had instances where athletes uttered observations and remarks which we have had to take several days to 'clean up after'" (Kristiansen, 2014, p. 444). For a sport organization it is a good idea to have a written strategy for how its employees (coaches, athletes, support staff, etc.) should behave when they use any media platform. As noted above, many sport entities in the United States have specific rules regarding when athletes and management cannot engage in social media (e.g., shortly before, during, and shortly after the game). Clavio et al. (2013) stated that, "there are no circumstances under which a player in the National Football League, National Basketball Association, National Hockey League, or Major League Baseball is allowed to communicate on social media during games. This rule also extends to halftimes and breaks between game periods" (p. 69). Furthermore, the four leagues noted above prevent "players from communicating with fans before they are interviewed by the media while in the locker room or at a press conference" (p. 69).

Even an innocent action such as clicking on a "like" button can cause problems. For instance, in June 2015, Boston Red Sox (Major League Baseball) player Pablo Sandoval was benched after it was discovered that he simply "liked" an Instagram photo while he was in the bathroom during a game (Bonesteel, 2015). Thus, in addition to providing specific rules regarding social media usage, many sport organizations monitor, manage, and assess penalties and fines for the social media postings of their employees. The monitoring, which at times involves training employees on how to engage in social media, can result in sport employees being reprimanded, fined, and even having their employment terminated for inappropriate postings or social media activities. For instance, in 2015 an employee of the National Basketball Association's Houston Rockets was fired for tweeting a message that the organization deemed inappropriate. Further, it is not uncommon for athletes and those in management to be reprimanded or fined for what a league or sports organization views as social media violations. During the Olympic Games, these rules have sometimes spurred debate among athletes, and some athletes feel that their freedom of expression is compromised when they cannot talk freely about some subjects. Thus, there is a need to establish a balance between rules and regulations and employees' freedom of speech. Nevertheless, media training is advisable for athletes who will deal with traditional media (e.g., print, television, and radio) as well as for their usage of social media platforms (e.g., Snapchat, Twitter, Instagram, Facebook) and other emerging (new) media.

Conclusion

The way sport media professionals do their jobs (see Pedersen, 2014) and the way athletes interact with the media (e.g., bypassing the media, posting comments on social media) and fans will continue to change (see Billings & Brown, 2013). Thus, media relations professionals and sport organization leaders need to be cognizant of both the challenges and opportunities that frequently arise as a consequence of the dynamic and evolving nature of the sport and media interaction. For instance, having athletes interact with personal and team stakeholders (e.g., fans) on social media will become more important and will most likely become a significant revenue stream for sport enterprises when they figure out a way to monetize such activities. However, because of the direct communication (e.g., retweets, comments, postings) the general population can have with athletes who are on social media, those athletes who choose to be active will need advice and assistance in ways to increase their self-confidence and buffer against social media trolls and antagonists, as well as their effectiveness in engaging with the media and public. Athletes, coaches, and sport industry professionals have, at times, deleted their social media accounts for a variety of reasons, thus reflecting the salience of further empirical attention examining social media behavior in sport. Regardless, in sum, there is a need for athletes, coaches, and managers to engage in behavioral training to both optimally interact with the media (and social media) and cope with the media (and social media) interactions and coverage. We finish by reiterating the key messages emerging from this chapter for future research and applied practice.

Key messages for future research

- There is a difference between athletes that undergo media attention for an extended period of time, and those that "meet" the media for the first time in major competitions. New research should examine how different organizations train their athletes to cope with media.
- Research is required to study athletes that have been under immense media pressure, and examine how they coped with it. In cases where athletes have coped with the stress that extreme media attention causes, researchers should examine what the organizations did to support their athletes.

- Researchers should sample public relations personnel (e.g., press attachés) in order to examine what their advice is, and to establish whether this is in line with the best interests of athletes.
- While difficult to access, international sport stars should be interviewed in order to examine their best media behavior advice regarding coping with and exploiting media attention.

Key messages for applied practice:

- Protect adolescent athletes when dealing with the media, and educate the young athletes regarding the media and how to best handle media interactions.
- Control the amount of media access provided to the athletes and monitor their overall media exposure.
- Explain the value of mutually beneficial interactions with the media and encourage sport organization stakeholders (e.g., administrators, coaches, athletes) to build good relationships with the press.
- Be proactive in both source publicity (e.g., athletes and organizations publishing stories and information on their own without going through the media), as well as embracing opportunities for media engagement (e.g., media releases, updates), and interactions (e.g., press access, media days).
- Encourage athletes (and organizational stakeholders overall) to be active in promoting their team and sport through social media, but be aware that anything posted could be seen by the public and possibly exploited (e.g., a tweet that goes viral).

References

Aldwin, C. M. (2007). *Stress, coping, and development: An integrative perspective*. New York; Guilford Press.s

Anshel, M., & Weiberg, R. (1995). Sources of acute stress in American and Australian basketball referees. *Journal of Applied Sport Psychology*, 7(1), 11–22.

Beattie, M. (2013, November 28). Bradley Wiggins held back Tour de France bonus payments from Chris Froome for 14 months. *Telegraph Sport*. Retrieved from http://www.telegraph.co.uk/sport/othersports/cycling/tour-de-france/10480146/Bradley-Wiggins-held-back-Tour-de-France-bonus-payments-from-Chris-Froome-for-14-months.html

Billings, A. C., & Brown, N. (2013). Understanding the biggest show in media: What the Olympic Games communicates to the world. In P. M. Pedersen (Ed.), *Routledge handbook of sport communication* (pp. 155–164). Abingdon, Oxon: Routledge.

Bloomington Herald-Times (2015, July 28). At college media days, star QBs can be fleeting. Retrieved from http://www.heraldtimesonline.com/sports/at-college-media-days-star-qbs-can-be-fleeting/article_2e868c38-febb-5a88-9a10-50c8610d7f53.html

Bonesteel, M. (2015, June 18). Pablo Sandoval benched for liking photos on Instagram during Red Sox game. *The Washington Post*. Retrieved from http://www.washingtonpost.com/blogs/early-lead/wp/2015/06/18/some-are-wondering-if-pablo-sandoval-was-on-instagram-during-a-red-sox-game/

Buchanan, Z. (2015, January 28). Why Marshawn Lynch hates talking, and why that bugs the NFL. azcentral.com (*The Arizona Republic*). Retrieved from http://www.azcentral.com/story/sports/nfl/super-bowl/2015/01/26/seattle-seahawks-super-bowl-marshawn-lynch-media-day-nfl/22380229/

Carter, N. (2007). Managing the media: The changing relationship between football managers and the media. *Sport in History*, 27(2), 217–241.

Clavio, G., Bowles, J., Vooris, R., & Pedersen, P. M. (2013). The integration of social media and sport: Perspectives and examples from the United States. In A. Hebbel-Seeger & T. Horky (Eds.), *International symposium on sport & economics: Sports, journalism, & social media* (pp. 59–72). Aachen: Meyer & Meyer-Verlag.

Cohen, S., & Wills, T. A. (1985). Stress, social support, and the buffering hypothesis. *Psychological Bulletin*, 98, 310–357.

Cooky, C., Messner, M. A., & Hextrum, R. H. (2013). Women play sport, but not on TV: A longitudinal study of televised news media. *Communication & Sport*, 1, 203–230.

Daily Mail (2012, July 22). Battle of the Tour de France WAGs: Bradley Wiggins' wife in Twitter spat with cycling teammate's girlfriend who took umbrage at her man being forced to play second fiddle. Retrieved from http://www.dailymail.co.uk/femail/article-2177461/Bradley-Wiggins-wife-Catherine-Twitter-spat-Chris-Froomes-girlfriend.html

Daily Telegraph (2015, 29 July). Miguel Herrera fired as Mexico coach after allegedly punching TV reporter. Retrieved from http://www.telegraph.co.uk/sport/football/teams/mexico/11769992/Miguel-Herrera-fired-as-Mexico-coach-after-allegedly-punching-TV-reporter.html

Frandsen, K. (2014). Mediatization of sports. In K. Lundby (Ed.), *The handbook of mediatization of communication* (pp. 525–543). Berlin: Mouton de Gruyter.

Friend, T. (2008, April 15). Reid: Gundy's rant "basically ended my life." *ESPN*. Retrieved from http://sports.espn.go.com/ncf/news/story?id=3341578

Gibson, O. (2015, March 5). Sexist chanting at Chelsea's Eva Carneiro cannot be swept under the carpet. *The Guardian*. Retrieved from http://www.theguardian.com/football/blog/2015/mar/05/sexist-chanting-chelsea-eva-carneiro

Giddens, A. (2006). *Sociology* (5th edn). Cambridge: Polity Press.

Hargreaves, J. (1986). *Sport, power and culture. A sociological and historical analysis of popular sports in Britain*. New York: St. Martin's Press.

Holt, N. L., & Hogg, J. M. (2002). Perceptions of stress and coping during preparations for the 1999 women's soccer World Cup finals. *The Sport Psychologist*, 16(3), 251–271.

Kian, E. M., Ketterer, S., Nichols, C., & Poling, J. (2014, March 10). Watchdogs of the fourth estate or homer journalists? Newspaper coverage of local BCS college football programs. *The Sport Journal*. Retrieved from http://thesportjournal.org/article/watchdogs-of-the-fourth-estate-or-homer-journalists-newspaper-coverage-of-local-bcs-college-football-programs/

Kristiansen, E. (2011). Perception of and coping with organizational and media stress in elite sport: Does the coach matter? (Unpublished doctoral thesis). Norwegian School of Sport Sciences, Oslo, Norway.

Kristiansen, E. (2014). Interview with Halvor Lea, Head of Communications at the Norwegian Olympic Sports Centre (Olympiatoppen). *International Journal of Sport Communication*, 7, 441–444.

Kristiansen, E., & Hanstad, D. V. (2012). Journalists and Olympic athletes: A Norwegian case study of an ambivalent relationship. *International Journal of Sport Communication*, 5, 231–245.

Kristiansen, E., & Lines, G. (2014). Media. In A. Papaioannou & D. Hackfort (Eds.), *Companion to sport and exercise psychology: Global perspectives and fundamental concepts* (pp. 236–259). New York: Taylor & Francis.

Kristiansen, E., & Roberts, G. C. (2011). Media exposure and adaptive coping in elite football. *International Journal of Sport Psychology, 42*, 339–367.

Kristiansen, E., Hanstad, D. V., & Roberts, G. C. (2011). Coping with the media at the Vancouver Winter Olympics: "We all make a living out of this." *Journal of Applied Sport Psychology, 23*(4), 443–458.

Kristiansen, E., Roberts, G. C., & Sisjord, M. K. (2011). Coping with negative media coverage: The experiences of professional football goalkeepers. *International Journal of Sport and Exercise Psychology, 9*(4), 295–307.

Kristiansen, E., Halvari, H., & Roberts, G. C. (2012). Organizational and media stress among professional football players: Testing an Achievement Goal Theory model. *Scandinavian Journal of Medicine & Science in Sports, 22*, 569–579.

Kristiansen, E., Broch, T. B., & Pedersen, P. M. (2014). Negotiating gender in professional soccer: An analysis of female footballers in the United States. *Choriga: Sport Management International Journal, 10*(1), 5–27.

Langer, J. (1981). Television's personality system. *Media, Culture, and Society, 3*(4), 351–365.

Lazarus, R. S., & Folkman, S. (1984). *Stress, appraisal, and coping*. New York: Springer.

Lepard, C. (2015, March 22). Bloomsburg University athlete kicked off team after offensive Mo'ne Davis tweet. Retrieved from http://wnep.com/2015/03/22/bloomsburg-university-athlete-kicked-off-team-after-offensive-mone-davis-tweet/

Lindsay, P., & Thomas, O. (2014). Reflections on being a neophyte sport psychologist in the media: Conversations with my younger self. *The Sport Psychologist, 28*, 290–301.

Maguire, J., Jarvie, G., Mansfield, L., & Bradley, J. (2002). *Sports worlds. A sociological perspective*. Champaign, IL: Human Kinetics.

McKay, J., Niven, A. G., Lavallee, D., & White, A. (2008). Sources of strain among elite UK track athletes. *The Sport Psychologist, 22*(2), 143–163.

Nesti, M. (2010). *Psychology in football. Working with elite and professional players*. New York: Routledge.

Ntoumanis, N., & Biddle, S. (1998). The relationship between competitive anxiety, achievement goals, and motivational climates. *Research Quarterly for Exercise and Sport, 69*(2), 176–187.

O'Connell, M. (2004). The three components of the sport industry. In K. Nguyen (Ed.), *Career insight: Landing a job with a sports team* (pp. 30–41). Boston, MA: Aspatore.

Park, J. K. (2000). Coping strategies used by Korean national athletes. *Sport Psychologist, 14*(1), 63–80.

Pedersen, P. M. (2013). Introduction. In P. M. Pedersen (Ed.), *Routledge handbook of sport communication* (pp. 1–6). Abingdon, Oxon: Routledge.

Pedersen, P. M. (2014). The changing role of sports media producers. In A. C. Billings & M. Hardin (Eds.), *Routledge handbook of sport and new media* (pp. 101–109). Abingdon, Oxon: Routledge.

Pedersen, P. M., Miloch, K. S., & Laucella, P. (2007). *Strategic sport communication*. Champaign, IL: Human Kinetics.

Pirinen, R. (2002). Catching up with men? Finnish newspaper coverage of women's entry into traditionally male sports. In S. Scraton & A. Flintoff (Eds.), *Gender and sport: A reader* (pp. 94–105). London: Routledge.

Reeves, C. W., Nicholls, A. R., & McKenna, J. (2009). Stressors and coping strategies among early and middle adolescent premier league academy soccer players: Differences according to age. *Journal of Applied Sport Psychology, 21*(1), 31–48.

Roberts, G. C. (2012). Motivation in sport and exercise for an achievement goal theory perspective: After 30 years, where are we? In G. C. Roberts & D. C. Treasure (Eds.), *Advances in motivation in sport and exercise* (Vol. 3, pp. 5–58). Champaign, IL: Human Kinetics.

Roth, S., & Cohen, L. J. (1986). Approach, avoidance, and coping with stress. *American Psychologist, 41*(7), 813–819.

Rowe, D. (2004). *Sport, culture and media* (2nd ed.). London: Open University Press.

Sanderson, J. (2013). Social media and sport communication. In P. M. Pedersen (Ed.), *Routledge handbook of sport communication* (pp. 56–65). Abingdon, Oxon: Routledge.

Schaefer, C., Coyne, J. C., & Lazarus, R. S. (1982). The health related functions of social support. *Journal of Behavioural Medicine, 4*, 381–406.

Wenner, L. A. (1998). Playing mediasport. In L. A. Wenner (Ed.), *Mediasport* (pp. 3–13). London: Routledge.

Wenner, L. A. (2013). The mediasport interpellation: Gender, fanship, and consumer culture. *Sociology of Sport Journal, 30*, 83–103.

Wenner, L. A. (2015). Assessing the sociology of sport: On the mediasport interpellation and commodity narratives. *International Review for the Sociology of Sport, 50*, 628–633.

Yoo, S. K., Smith, L. R., & Kim, D. (2013). Communication theories and sport studies. In P. M. Pedersen (Ed.), *Routledge handbook of sport communication* (pp. 8–19) Abingdon, Oxon: Routledge.

Young, D. (2015, March 26). It's great Mo'ne Davis had it in her to forgive that guy. But still, f**k that guy. *The Huffington Post*. Retrieved from http://www.huffingtonpost.com/damon-young/its-great-mone-davis-had-it-in-her-to-forgive-that-guy-but-still-fk-that-guy-_b_6946230.html

PART IV

Environments in sport organizations

11
THE SOCIAL ENVIRONMENT IN SPORT ORGANIZATIONS

Luc Martin, Mark Eys, and Kevin Spink

Introduction

There are several certainties in life, and while death and taxes likely come to mind, another that should ring true is that people are social beings. Admittedly, we share this characteristic with many other living organisms, be they on land (e.g., gorillas, wolves) or in the sea (e.g., dolphins, orcas). However, it has been suggested that the single most important characteristic of human beings is the need for group membership (Forsyth & Burnett, 2010).

As noted by researchers, people have a strong need to belong to groups (cf. Baumeister & Leary, 1995). Evidence abounds about this need, whether it is to be part of a family, club, or work group collection; and it is perhaps not surprising that sport is no exception with respect to the proclivity to be in groups. As such, the social environment is a key component of sport, and one worthy of examination by sport psychologists. To be clear, when we use the phrase "social environment" in this chapter, we are referring to the group environment. Further, we acknowledge that our call for the examination of groups in the sport setting is not a new suggestion. Over three decades ago, Albert Carron (1980)—a pioneer in group-related research in sport, and at one time a mentor to all of us involved in writing this chapter—noted that:

> From a social psychological perspective, both generally and in the specific context of sport and physical activity, a considerable proportion of individual behaviour occurs within groups. Thus, in order to gain an understanding of the antecedents and consequences of behaviour it is imperative to focus on the group.
>
> (p. 193)

In attempting to understand the group, we are not alone in the sport area, as we can draw on the field of study that focuses on the behavior of groups—group dynamics. According to Cartwright and Zander (1968), this field focuses on gaining knowledge about the nature of groups and their development, and on understanding the interrelationships between groups and individuals, between groups, and between groups and organizations. While most of the sport research has focused on the interrelationships between the team and the individual, the focus in this chapter will be on a specific aspect of the "between-groups" interrelationship that, to date, has received little attention in the literature.

What likely comes to mind when thinking about interrelationships between groups in the sport setting is the comparison of one team to another, and for good reason. Competition between teams is meaningful to members, and shapes interactions in predictable ways even when groups are established at random. For example, flipping a coin to create a "blue" versus "red" team (Locksley, Ortiz, & Hepburn, 1980) or creating short-lived teams that compete for meaningful rewards (Sherif & Sherif, 1953) result in in-group favoritism almost immediately, where preferential treatment and more favorable attitudes are shown to members of one's own group versus other groups (Tajfel, 1981). Extending this idea further, the presence of out-groups in the form of a sport opponent also may contribute to the level of cohesiveness developed within a team (Baumeister & Bushman, 2011). A team working together to achieve a successful outcome against a common opponent is likely to feel more united than a team that simply practices without ever encountering an opponent.

While this between-group interrelationship is undeniably important in helping one understand the social environment in sport, the fact is that there are different groups within the sport organization itself that are likely to be just as important in facilitating this understanding. While we readily recognize the athletes as one of these groups, coaches and management also form other potential groups within a sport organization. Understanding how these subgroups might influence each other and the overall group environment is important given the possibility that each of these subgroups might be pursuing different outcomes, and research in other areas has shown that these different outcomes can be related to one another in complex ways (Argote & McGrath, 1993). Further, effectiveness at one group level could interfere with effectiveness at another. Consider the following sport examples.

At the level of professional sport, what happens to the cohesiveness and subsequent effectiveness of one subgroup (athletes) when the goal of another subgroup (management) is to obtain a higher selection in the next draft (a procedure where new athletes are made available for selection by teams in a league, with earlier choices allocated to the weaker teams; *Oxford Dictionaries*, 2015)? This may involve shedding current athletes, which invariably contributes to subpar team performance, but results in a more favorable drafting position (i.e., lower final league standing = better draft position; McGran, 2015). Or, at the grassroots level in sport, what happens to the experience of child and youth athletes when another level (league management) decides to "improve" the game by eliminating the need to keep score, without a clear understanding of the athletes' desires (Carlson, 2012)?

The purpose of this chapter is to provide a case for examining an aspect of the social environment within sport organizations that typically receives little attention—the group(s) within the group. Again, this is not a new idea as McGrath, Arrow, and Berdahl (2000) defined groups as "open and complex systems that interact with the smaller systems (i.e., the members) embedded within them and the larger systems (e.g., organizations, communities) within which they are embedded" (p. 98). When this is coupled with the definition of group dynamics presented earlier by Cartwright and Zander (1968), the message is clear that we need to acknowledge and discuss the presence and interrelatedness of various subgroups in order to fully understand the social environment in sport. In line with this proposition, four main sections will provide the structure for the remainder of the chapter. The first outlines the importance of accounting for different subgroups, and the identification of key groups. The second outlines and discusses the interrelatedness of the various subgroups. The third provides suggestions for future research, whereas the fourth advances practical implications based on the information introduced in the preceding sections.

Group boundaries in sport organizations

A prerequisite to discussing the social environment in a sport organization is defining the boundaries of the various groups that exist within it, as well as recognizing that these boundaries are permeable and likely to vary across sport organizations. For example, a professional sport organization has several reasonably defined subgroups (e.g., athletes, coaching staff, management) that communicate with each other at regular intervals and are each represented by a number of members. In contrast, a youth sport organization may include dozens of teams, small numbers of coaching staff (perhaps one coach per team at times), and a management group that may be largely unfamiliar with the majority of athletes and coaches. In the former case, the various subgroups may identify strongly with one another, blurring the lines of how they think about their "group." In the latter, youth athletes likely give little thought to the administration of their sport organization. Thus, in trying to understand the social environment and, more specifically, the group dynamics present within these organizations, critical preliminary questions involve who constitutes "we" and who constitutes "they"?

Clearly, the degree to which individuals view others as part of a collective can vary, and understanding what constitutes a group has occupied social psychology researchers for some time. Campbell (1958) noted that certain collections of individuals could have more "entitativity" than others; in other words, they hold certain social and physical properties that may classify them as groups (or not). In a similar vein, Spink, Wilson, and Priebe (2010) advocated for the need to consider the degree of groupness perceived within physical activity contexts. Groupness, in this case, refers to the relative presence of five characteristics of the collective including (a) common fate (e.g., a group outcome), (b) mutual benefit (i.e., participation with others is necessary and rewarding), (c) social structure (e.g., presence of group norms, individual roles), (d) group processes (e.g., meaningful and sustained communication), and (e) self-categorization (i.e., members view themselves as a group). As such, the perceived degree of the presence or absence of these characteristics helps us to determine the boundaries of a true group (i.e., "we"), and aids in the ability to differentiate between other associations that might be present within an organization as well as external to it (i.e., "they").

In the industrial/organizational (I/O) setting, Lawrence (2011) noted several layers of social contextual boundaries within organizations that include dyadic relationships, task groups, potentially overlapping social networks, and a larger organizational reference group; the latter defined as "the set of people an individual perceives as belonging to his or her work environment … including people with whom the individual does and does not communicate and those with whom awareness is the only connection" (Lawrence, 2006, p. 80).

From a sport perspective, popular media and researchers alike have traditionally created social contextual divides between the athletes, coaching staff, and management, although the boundaries among these groups can dissipate or further fragment depending on other environmental variables. For example, locker room celebrations after winning major sport championships (e.g., the Stanley Cup, Champions Cup) evoke perceptions of togetherness and a sense of groupness among all participants (athletes, coaches, managers). In contrast, failure to win or develop cohesion within one of the groups can result in clique formations and a greater focus on smaller subgroups (e.g., offense vs. defense). Zucchermaglio (2005) demonstrated this potential "divide" while working with professional football (soccer) players. After a victory, athletes attributed their success to the entire group, whereas after defeat they distanced themselves from the group and attributed the loss to various subgroups (e.g., defenders).

In the remaining sections of this chapter, we suggest that understanding the social environment in sport organizations requires consideration of both the group dynamics that occur within these entities but also make a case for developing an understanding of the dynamics that span the organization as a whole.

The group of athletes

Without question, the vast majority of research pertaining to group dynamics within sport has focused on athletes. The literature that continues to be developed within the field of sport psychology has been summarized in texts and chapters devoted to this area (e.g., Beauchamp & Eys, 2014; Carron & Eys, 2012; Jowett & Lavallee, 2007). Suffice to say, this body of research has provided ample evidence to suggest that the dynamics of the group are incredibly important for an array of individual and team outcomes. The cohesion of the group, for example, is one of the most widely investigated topics in sport group dynamics and is positively linked with performance (both in individual and team sports; Carron, Colman, Wheeler, & Stevens, 2002) as well as adherence (Spink, Wilson, & Odnokon, 2010). Furthermore, the perceptions that athletes hold about their interdependent role functions have been shown to be associated with precompetitive anxiety (Beauchamp, Bray, Eys, & Carron, 2003), task self-efficacy (Bray, Balaguer, & Duda, 2004; Eys & Carron, 2001), satisfaction (Eys, Carron, Bray, & Beauchamp, 2003), and intentions to return to the team (Eys, Carron, Bray, & Beauchamp, 2005). As a final example, Loughead, Munroe-Chandler, Hoffmann, and Duquay (2014) highlighted support for the development and consequences of athlete-to-athlete leadership behaviors, noting that peers offer a unique source of leadership in contrast to the coaching staff.

While the above topics reflect only a small subset of intra-team variables that have been examined within sport, the accumulated evidence has sparked a need to consider how to facilitate effective group dynamics. Efforts directed toward team building (TB) in sport, defined as "a method of helping the group to (a) increase its effectiveness, (b) satisfy the needs of its members, or (c) improve work conditions" (Brawley & Paskevitch, 1997, p. 13), have used different conceptual frameworks. In terms of the relationship between the overall TB interventions and specific outcomes, positive relationships have been reported for performance effectiveness and adaptive cognitions like self-efficacy or satisfaction, for athletes exposed to TB protocols in comparison to those not exposed (Martin, Carron, & Burke, 2009). Although these efforts have been shown to be effective, further examination with a broad spectrum of age and skill levels is still needed (Martin et al., 2009).

The group of coaches

Coach-oriented research predominantly tackles issues related to tactics, strategies, and the skill development of athletes, in addition to understanding how coaches influence athletes through the process of leadership. With respect to the latter, transformational leadership (Hoption, Phelan, & Barling, 2014), motivational climate (Duda, 2001), and the coach–athlete relationship (Jowett & Poczwardowski, 2007) are some of the many topics that explore the interactions between the decision-makers and the performers. Less frequent are studies that explore the dynamics that occur *within* the coaching staff, although available research provides insight and areas for future work. For example, Cunningham (2009) explored the effect of heterogeneity of group member attributes within 71 National Collegiate Athletic Association (NCAA) coaching staffs. His findings suggest that greater actual and perceived diversity within the coaching staff (based on age, tenure, and race) are associated with decreased congruence of values and subsequent perceptions of life satisfaction. In discussing his results, Cunningham was clear that further research is necessary to understand the advantages (e.g., greater inclusion; Doherty & Chelladurai, 1999) and disadvantages (e.g., conflict; van Knippenberg & Schippers, 2007) of coaching staff heterogeneity.

From a group structure and process standpoint, the clear transmission of role responsibilities to members of a coaching staff is also an important consideration. For example, applied researchers have suggested that delegating specific roles to staff members with respect to communicating with athletes, both generally (Gilbert, Gilbert, & Trudel, 2001) and in specific instances (e.g., timeouts; Andrews, 2015), should facilitate collaboration and cohesion. This latter outcome, coaching staff cohesion, which refers to "the degree of teamwork among head and assistant coaches that is derived from personal and professional factors and assists in developing a pleasing work environment and fulfillment of the individual" (Martin, 2002, p. 25) has also received attention. Coaches who took part in the Atlanta (1996) and Nagano (1998) Olympics perceived that their coaching effectiveness was, in part, determined by the chemistry displayed by the coaching staff as a whole (Gould, Guinan, Greenleaf, & Chung, 2002). In summarizing their work demonstrating a positive association between coaching staff cohesion and the athletes' perceptions of team cohesion, Zakrajsek, Abildso, Hurst, and Watson (2007) concluded that, "the coaching staff can be viewed as a team within the team, which must function together with a shared purpose" (p. 12).

The management group

The field of I/O psychology provides a wealth of knowledge pertaining to management issues, and researchers have encouraged greater integration of such themes within sport (e.g., Fletcher & Wagstaff, 2009). At the more elite levels of sport, there are indications that group dynamics across the management group are important. For example, qualitative research conducted by Fletcher and Arnold (2011) examining national performance directors' (Olympic sports) perceptions of best practices for elite sport leadership and management revealed several themes related to group processes. These included the need for a positive team atmosphere, effective communication, and the transmission of role knowledge. In a similar manner, Doherty and colleagues demonstrated the importance of group norms (Doherty, Patterson, & Van Bussel, 2004) and cohesion (Doherty & Carron, 2003) among volunteer executives within non-profit sport organizations.

Although the above sections highlight that it is necessary to consider the "within-group" dynamics of athletes, coaches, and management, it is also clear that these groups are interwoven in pursuit of larger sport objectives. The following sections discuss how these groups intersect to create another layer to the social environment of sport organizations.

Group interrelatedness in sport organizations

We now take our discussion pertaining to the social environment in sport organizations one step further, and highlight the embeddedness of the various levels. We acknowledge that while it is necessary to continue our efforts at better understanding the dynamics present within the various levels, it is a certainty that athletes, coaches, and managers do not function in isolation, and that the behaviors demonstrated by each level influence, and are influenced by, other organizational groups.

Sport organizations are "composed of individuals or groups who transact with each other to perform functions essential to the organization" (Wagstaff, Fletcher, & Hanton, 2012a, p. 87). With respect to athletes, recent research supports the influence of the organization on both their cognitions and behaviors. Through qualitative interviews, Fletcher, Hanton, and Wagstaff (2012) found that athletes experienced stressors induced from various levels within the organization (e.g., issues with teammates, coaches and training/medical staff, management and administration), and that these led to a wide range of emotions, attitudes, and behaviors. Similarly, this same research group had four elite athletes complete stress-appraisal logs throughout the duration of a competitive season (Hanton, Wagstaff, & Fletcher, 2012). It became apparent that athletes cognitively appraised organizational stressors, largely felt a lack of control pertaining to the environment, and because of a lack of coping resources, often were unable to adequately respond to the stressors. These studies demonstrate the various stressors present within the organization as a whole, and how athletes concede to spending time appraising the environment, which, inter alia, detracts attention from sport performance.

The influence of the organization on athletes is not limited to elite sport. In the youth setting, recent work conducted by Williams, Whipp, Jackson, and Dimmock (2013) found the social structure within a golf club offered important sources of relatedness support for female golfers. In addition to the more "expected" social influencers such as peers, parents, and coaches, the authors described how these adolescents felt connected to the golf club (through the policies of management, among other things), and how this resulted in perceptions of affiliation, feelings of security, and resultant retention.

In understanding the relative salience of the sport organization for athlete development, Henriksen, Stambulova, and Roessler (2010a, 2010b) conducted a series of projects involving a holistic ecological approach. The objective was to focus on the athletic talent development environment (ATDE) within successful sailing and track and field milieus by conducting in-depth interviews with athletes, coaches, and administrators. The takeaway was that these organizations were perceived as having a high degree of cohesiveness within and between the various levels, and the authors outlined factors inherent in both settings that contributed to their success, that ranged from athletes and coaches openly sharing their knowledge to strong organizational cultures pervading daily aspects of the environments.

In terms of coaches, we discussed previously the relationships between coaches, as well as those with their athletes. Undoubtedly, these relationships are influenced by organizational practices. Researchers have made the argument that such practices can influence coach experiences and performance, and that coaches should be perceived as performers within the organization (e.g., Gould et al., 2002). Coincidently, a lack of investigation pertaining to the influence of the organization on coaches has been deemed unfortunate (e.g., Giges, Petitpas, & Vernacchia, 2004). Allen and Shaw (2009) identified this lack of research attention, and subsequently interviewed eight elite female coaches to better understand the extent to which their psychological needs were being met. Those involved in organizations providing an autonomy-supportive environment felt a greater sense of relatedness and belonging. This is an important consideration as coaches are often evaluated based on the performances of their athletes and teams; however, their abilities to coach are largely facilitated or restricted by the organization (Jones & Wallace, 2005).

It is apparent that both athletes and coaches are influenced by the culture established within the organization, and this is typically initiated at the management level. Sport researchers suggest that individuals at the management level are aware of the impact of their decisions. From the example provided earlier, the national performance directors interviewed by Fletcher and Arnold (2011) reported taking care in sharing their vision for the organizations, because they understood the importance of dealing with all organizational members to develop a positive culture. As an extension to this work, these same authors synthesized the literature pertaining to organizational stressors from 34 studies, and four main themes emerged—leadership and personnel, culture and the team, logistics and environment, and personal issues (Arnold & Fletcher, 2012). Across these themes, we see elements emanating from within and between the various levels that we discuss in this chapter.

Considering that athletes, coaches, and managers must interact with those within their subgroups, and also with those from other levels within the organization, a concept that has emerged in the sport literature is emotional intelligence (EI). Several studies have demonstrated the benefits of being able to manage self and others' emotions in order to maintain stronger interpersonal relationships at the individual level, but also within the organizational environment as a whole (e.g., Wagstaff, Fletcher, & Hanton, 2012b, 2012c). When demonstrated by leaders, EI is related to increased leader (i.e., coach) efficacy (Thelwell, Lane, Weston, & Greenlees, 2008) and team cohesion (e.g., Wang & Huang, 2009), and when present at the team level, predicts cohesion and performance (e.g., Crombie, Lombard, & Noakes, 2009; Rapisarda, 2002). Importantly, recent research has shown that adaptive emotional regulation behaviors and the development of EI can be taught (e.g., Wagstaff, Hanton, & Fletcher, 2013). Presumably, seeing the organization from the perspective of other members (e.g., the chief executive officer (CEO) or performance director from the perspective of the athletes, and vice versa) should enable better member-wide understanding of organizational objectives, cultures, and values. An extension from the promising work conducted by Wagstaff et al. (2013) in relation to EI intervention protocols could be to specifically increase member awareness of the interconnectedness of the various organizational levels.

Future directions

We have discussed how group dynamics research explores not only the group influences on individuals, and the individual influences on the group, but also the various environments that are present within a larger group (i.e., the organization). Although researchers are venturing into many exciting new areas, we take this opportunity to discuss five concepts that, with a specific focus on the various groups within an organization, could prove fruitful for furthering our understanding of the social environment in sport.

Shared knowledge

The notion of shared knowledge refers to a common understanding of the taskwork and teamwork that is required by members of a group (e.g., Eccles & Tenenbaum, 2004). In the I/O literature, this concept is termed "shared mental models" (SMMs), and is defined as "an organized understanding or mental representation of knowledge that is shared by team members" (Mathieu, Heffner, Goodwin, Cannon-Bowers, & Salas, 2005, p. 38). Originally, SMMs were believed to portray the common beliefs within a team pertaining to technology, the task, team interaction, and the team as a whole (Cannon-Bowers, Salas, & Converse, 1993). More recently, however, task (when members share a common understanding pertaining to the task-related processes of the team) or team (when members hold similar beliefs with regard to how they should interact with one another) orientations have been proposed (Mathieu, Maynard, Rapp, & Gilson, 2008). Both variations of SMMs have been deemed important to team processes and subsequent performance (e.g., Mathieu, Heffner, Goodwin, Salas, & Cannon-Bowers, 2000). Indeed, the investigation of shared knowledge has been supported and promoted in the sport setting (e.g., Eccles & Tenenbaum, 2004); however, based on our discussions in the previous sections, examining this concept within *and* between the various levels could shed light on the extent to which member knowledge (for both task and team orientations) is consistent throughout the organization. Whereas a coaching staff and an athlete group could demonstrate a shared understanding of pro-social norms within their specific groups (i.e., athletes to athletes, coaches to coaches), neither group may understand the other's position (coaches think athletes should be altruistic whereas athletes think the coaches want them to be aggressive), with the resulting disconnect attenuating group effectiveness.

Strategic consensus

A closely related concept worth noting is strategic consensus (SC), defined as "the shared understanding of strategic priorities among managers at the top, middle, and/or operating levels of the organization" (Kellermanns, Walter, Lechner, & Floyd, 2005, p. 721). One specific difference with respect to the previous section is that SC focuses on the strategic priorities of an organization, thus typically residing within higher-level management teams. The significance of achieving agreement among higher-level beliefs was revealed in a recent meta-analysis, which documented a positive effect of SC on organizational performance (Kellermanns, Walter, Floyd, Lechner, & Shaw, 2011).

In sport, this concept certainly translates to management and coaching groups. These individuals contribute to the establishment of organizational culture and values (e.g., Arnold & Fletcher, 2012). Further, frequent communication and transparency with athletes facilitate collaboration and cohesion (e.g., Andrews, 2015; Gilbert et al., 2001). Take, for example, the situation described in the introduction to this chapter, where the idea of management shedding athletes in the hopes of obtaining a more favorable draft position was presented. If all managerial members are not in agreement with this direction, the information translated to support staff, coaches, and athletes could result in disconnected perceptions throughout the organization. As such, it seems appropriate that SC be at the forefront of organizational priorities, and that they be translated to all members. Research should seek to determine the benefits of such transparency and consensus in sport, for both individual and group level variables.

Empowerment

Researchers typically discuss two elements of organizational empowerment, where structural empowerment is the actual process of delegating authority (e.g., coach or formal athlete leader selection), and psychological empowerment represents team members' beliefs in their collective control of the work environment (Mathieu, Gilson, & Ruddy, 2006). The relevance of this concept to sport is perhaps not surprising given that many theories discussed in the activity setting support the importance of empowerment (e.g., self-determination theory; Deci & Ryan, 2000). In practice, this concept also has been supported in the real world of professional sport. Phil Jackson, one of the most successful coaches in the National Basketball Association, rarely called timeouts, and indicated that he would rather his athletes work through the situation themselves (Jackson & Delehanty, 2013). He believed that this would increase their confidence in themselves, and it also indicated that the coach trusted them to make difficult decisions. As this is an isolated illustration from professional sport, targeted research attempts at supporting the use of empowerment across the various levels of the organization are warranted.

Multi-level analysis

Group-related research in sport psychology has experienced a shift in method of analysis, with the advocacy of multi-level analyses in order to account for between- and within-group differences (e.g., Hox, 2010). To date, much of this work has involved between-group (i.e., teams) variation. However, it would be worthwhile to investigate the issue of further nesting within organizations (i.e., athletes, coaches, and managers are all nested within groups, which are then nested within the larger organization). For example, when assessing cohesion (or any other group level construct), we are often interested in athlete perceptions of the immediate team. It would be interesting to determine whether increased perceptions of cohesion pertaining to the athletes, coaching staff, or that of the management group, would also translate to a more cohesive organization as a whole. As an extension to this point, recent sport research has investigated the nature of subgroups within the team itself (e.g., cliques; Martin, Wilson, Evans, & Spink, 2015), and perhaps also accounting for these subgroups within our group level analyses would increase our understanding of the dynamics present within sport teams.

Social network analysis

Another area worth future investigation pertains to the use of social network analysis (SNA). SNA is a tool that allows researchers to examine networks within an organization, and these networks provide researchers with a way of thinking about social systems that focuses attention on the relationships among the members that make up the organization (Borgatti, Everett, & Johnson, 2013). It also offers a visual representation of the interactions among participants, and can identify influential members within subgroups or smaller entities. Notably, Wölfer, Faber, and Hewstone (2015) promoted SNA as important for properly understanding, predicting, and explaining the behaviors exhibited by individuals. As such, this would be particularly useful in terms of understanding the influential members within the various organizational levels, and also the connections or bridge relations between them (i.e., knowledge and information transfer systems). This form of analysis would also provide organizations with a visual representation of the grouping tendencies within the organization, and this could either support or refute the presence and interconnectedness of the various levels (i.e., the main themes within this chapter).

Practical implications

What are some of the practical implications emanating from this group dynamics focus? The following section discusses (1) the significance of creating an environment where organizations can flourish (proactive vs. reactive behaviors), (2) important considerations for TB and teamwork, (3) a need to work toward increased coordination between organizational levels, and (4) the benefits derived from increasing perceptions of involvement and belonging with organizational members.

Condition-focused approaches

Groups are complex and dynamic systems, which inherently change over time in ways that are rarely predictable and are based largely on past experiences and future objectives (McGrath et al., 2000). As such, often it is difficult to predict group behavior, and we find ourselves reacting to developments within the group, rather than taking proactive measures (e.g., Hackman, 2012). Hackman (2012) discussed the importance of providing fertile conditions that will facilitate the growth and thriving of an organization, and termed this a condition-focused approach. At the managerial level, this means evaluating and laying the groundwork in terms of the types of resources or supportive outlets that need to be in place in order to enable the proper growth of others (i.e., coaches and athletes). Indeed, Hackman (2012) goes as far as suggesting that 60 percent of how well a group eventually performs is based on the condition-setting pre-work. The specific conditions that are pertinent to the current chapter involve bringing in the right people, establishing clear norms, providing a supportive organizational context, and demonstrating team-focused coaching (Hackman, 2011). In terms of the first condition, the selection of athletes is conducted at the management or coaching levels; however, it is the athletes who must interact most consistently with those new members. As such, those selections made by the managerial and coaching levels directly influence the athletes. With respect to the remaining three conditions, the importance of transparency, communication, and support across the organization is stressed. When productive norms are instilled and reinforced by management, coaches and athletes feel supported within the organization. In addition, when process losses are decreased and synergistic gains are increased (i.e., team-focused coaching), all members of the organization benefit. Thus, organizations that take care in laying the groundwork to foster conditions that are conducive to effective group functioning (i.e., by carefully implementing condition-setting pre-work) are likely to experience greater success than those constantly "fighting fires."

Considerations for TB and teamwork

Based on a recent citation analysis involving TB interventions in sport, Bruner, Eys, Beauchamp, and Côté (2013) suggested that efforts to improve team functioning through TB protocols have been somewhat limited in their scope, and future work should target the larger organization (expanding from solely working with athletes and coaches). Coincidently, McEwan and Beauchamp (2014) recently integrated the information from the I/O psychology and sport literature, and proposed a conceptual framework for teamwork and team effectiveness in sport. Based on an input-mediator-outcome model, these authors suggested that a wide range of variables (i.e., inputs) will influence a team's effectiveness, and that these variables can occur at the individual, the team, and external (e.g., organizational) levels. In terms of outcomes, these involve behaviors (e.g., performance), as well as cognitive (e.g., efficacy beliefs) and affective (e.g., satisfaction) states at the team and individual levels. This practical framework provides a possible template from which to work toward organizational integration of objectives, as it clearly articulates the inputs from the various levels of the organization, and also demonstrates that outcomes can be specific to those levels (see McEwan & Beauchamp, 2014). As one practical extension, the inclusion of organizational level outcomes may serve to further consolidate the efforts of all group members. For example, if the individual and team level outcomes are achieved, organizational level outcomes such as increased prestige, identity as a winning culture, or financial gains all will be more likely to occur. In this instance, all organizational members should benefit.

Subgroup coordination

Practically speaking, one of the main messages in this chapter is that there are various groups within an organization, and that understanding and working with the interconnectedness of these groups is an important consideration. As such, those attempting to facilitate the functioning of their sport organizations should certainly focus on increasing the coordination among these groups. The significance of this endeavor cannot be overstated; in fact, Eccles and Tenenbaum (2004) advocated for coordination and communication in sport, and emphasized that an expert team is more than a team of experts. In their conceptual framework of coordination in teams, *teams* require *coordination*, which relies on *shared knowledge*.

This importance of coordination is supported by the classic work of Ivan Steiner (1972), who provided a "law" of group productivity. Steiner believed that a team's eventual productivity was the result of its potential productivity (in sport, this could be resources or athletic skill) minus the team's process losses (in sport, this could be poor communication or coordination). You can imagine that an organization that has a plethora of resources (potential productivity) would expect to be successful; however, based on Steiner's (1972) model, productivity is typically compromised by poor coordination, so further examination of coordinating processes between organizational levels is warranted.

Identification and belonging

At the beginning of this chapter, we highlighted the challenge of distinguishing "we" and "they" within sport organizations. One practical implication that can be taken from the material in this chapter is the importance of delineating and promoting the "we." As was demonstrated, there are numerous opportunities within an organization to belong to a group, whether it be along typical fault lines creating groups of "athletes" or "coaches," or within one of these groups as a subgroup or a clique. Regardless, the importance of feeling included within that group is apparent. Researchers support the need for individuals to belong (e.g., Baumeister & Leary, 1995), the tendency to generate perceptions of identity based on group membership (e.g., social identity theory; Tajfel & Turner, 1979), and more recently, the development of efficacy beliefs based on perceptions from the group (e.g., sociometer theory; Leary & Baumeister, 2000). As such, while establishing objectives and coordinating behaviors are indispensable activities (see previous practical implications), their effect will be attenuated if members do not feel as though they are included in the "we." Establishing a sense of identity and belonging across the organization (regardless of organizational level) is therefore a worthwhile endeavor.

Conclusion

At the beginning of this chapter, we introduced a quote from Carron (1980) in which he suggested that individual behavior occurs in groups and, as such, to properly understand individual behavior we must also understand groups. While it is clear that group research in sport has advanced to a point where we understand a great deal about individuals and groups, it is our hope that the ideas in this chapter will stimulate others to consider the need to examine the influence of groups within groups. We finish by reiterating five key messages for future research within this domain:

- The investigation of shared knowledge within *and* between the various levels of sport organizations could shed light on the extent to which member knowledge (for both task and team orientations) is consistent throughout the organization.
- It seems appropriate that strategic consensus be at the forefront of organizational priorities, and that they be translated to all members. Research should seek to determine the benefits of such transparency and consensus in sport, for both individual and group level variables.
- Targeted research attempts at supporting the use of empowerment across the various levels of the organization are warranted.
- Group-related research in sport psychology has experienced a shift in method of analysis, with the advocacy of multi-level analyses in order to account for between- and within-group differences, but it would be worthwhile to investigate the issue of further nesting within organizations.
- Social network analysis would be particularly useful in terms of understanding the influential members within the various organizational levels, and also the connections or bridge relations between them.

References

Allen, J., & Shaw, S. (2009). Women coaches' perceptions of their sport organizations' social environment: Supporting coaches' psychological needs? *The Sport Psychologist, 23*, 346–366.

Andrews, S. R. (2015). Emotional control and instructional effectiveness: Maximizing a timeout. *Strategies: A Journal for Physical and Sport Educators, 28*, 33–37.

Argote, L., & McGrath, J. E. (1993). Group processes in organizations: Continuity and change. In C. L. Cooper & I. T. Robertson (Eds.), *International review of industrial and organizational psychology* (pp. 383–389). New York: John Wiley & Sons.

Arnold, R., & Fletcher, D. (2012). A research synthesis and taxonomic classification of the organizational stressors encountered by sport performers. *Journal of Sport & Exercise Psychology, 34*, 397–429.

Baumeister, R. F., & Bushman, B. J. (2011). *Social psychology and human nature* (2nd ed.). Belmont, CA: Wadsworth Cengage Learning.

Baumeister, R. F., & Leary, M. R. (1995). The need to belong: Desire for interpersonal attachments as a fundamental human motivation. *Psychological Bulletin, 117*, 497–529.

Beauchamp, M. R., & Eys, M. A. (2014). *Group dynamics in exercise and sport psychology* (2nd ed.). New York: Routledge.

Beauchamp, M. R., Bray, S. R., Eys, M. A., & Carron, A. V. (2003). The effect of role ambiguity on competitive state anxiety. *Journal of Sport & Exercise Psychology, 25*, 77–92.

Borgatti, S. P., Everett, M. G., & Johnson, J. C. (2013). *Analyzing social networks*. Thousand Oaks, CA: Sage Publications.

Brawley, L. R., & Paskevitch, D. M. (1997). Conducting team building research in the context of sport and exercise. *Journal of Applied Sport Psychology, 9*, 11–40.

Bray, S. R., Balaguer, I., & Duda, J. L. (2004). The relationship of task self-efficacy and role efficacy beliefs to role performance in Spanish youth soccer. *Journal of Sports Sciences, 22*, 429–437.

Bruner, M. W., Eys, M. A., Beauchamp, M. R., & Côté, J. (2013). Examining the origins of team building in sport: A citation network and genealogical approach. *Group Dynamics: Theory, Research, and Practice, 17*, 30–42.

Campbell, D. T. (1958). Common fate, similarity, and other indices of the status of aggregates as social entities. *Behavioral Science, 3*, 14–25.

Cannon-Bowers, J. A., Salas, E., & Converse, S. A. (1993). Shared mental models in expert team decision-making. In J. N. J. Castellan (Ed.), *Current issues in individual and group decision making* (pp. 221–246). Hillsdale, NJ: Lawrence Erlbaum.

Carlson, K.B. (2012). No winners: Children still keeping score despite move to end sports competition. *National Post*, September 22. Retrieved from http://news.nationalpost.com/news/canada/no-winners-children-still-keeping-score-despite-move-to-end-sports-competition

Carron, A. V. (1980). *Social psychology of sport*. Ithaca, NY: Movement.

Carron, A. V., & Eys, M. A. (2012). *Group dynamics in sport* (4th ed.). Morgantown, WV: Fitness Information Technology.

Carron, A. V., Colman, M. M., Wheeler, J., & Stevens, D. (2002). Cohesion and performance in sport: A meta-analysis. *Journal of Sport & Exercise Psychology, 24*, 168–188.

Cartwright, D., & Zander, A. (1968). *Group dynamics: Research and theory*. New York: Harper & Row.

Crombie, D., Lombard, C., & Noakes, T. (2009). Emotional intelligence scores predict team sports performance in a national cricket competition. *International Journal of Sports Science and Coaching, 4*, 209–224.

Cunningham, G. B. (2009). Examining the relationships among coaching staff diversity, perceptions of diversity, value congruence, and life satisfaction. *Research Quarterly for Exercise and Sport, 80*, 326–335.

Deci, E. L., & Ryan, R. M. (2000). The "what" and "why" of goal pursuits: Human needs and the self-determination of behavior. *Psychological Inquiry, 11*, 227–268.

Doherty, A. J., & Carron, A. V. (2003). Cohesion in volunteer sport executive committees. *Journal of Sport Management, 17*, 116–141.

Doherty, A. J., & Chelladurai, P. (1999). Managing cultural diversity in sport organizations: A theoretical perspective. *Journal of Sport Management, 13*, 280–297.

Doherty, A. J., Patterson, M., & Van Bussel, M. (2004). What do we expect? An examination of perceived committee norms in non-profit sport organizations. *Sport Management Review, 7*, 109–132.

Duda, J. L. (2001). Achievement goal research in sport: Pushing the boundaries and clarifying some misunderstandings. In C. G. Roberts (Ed.), *Advances in motivation in sport and exercise* (pp. 129–182). Champaign, IL: Human Kinetics.

Eccles, D. W., & Tenenbaum, G. (2004). Why an expert team is more than a team of experts: A social-cognitive conceptualization of team coordination and communication in sport. *Journal of Sport & Exercise Psychology, 26*, 542–560.

Eys, M. A. & Carron, A. V. (2001). Role ambiguity, task cohesion, and task self-efficacy. *Small Group Research, 32*, 356–372.

Eys, M. A., Carron, A. V., Bray, S. R., & Beauchamp, M. R. (2003). Role ambiguity and athlete satisfaction. *Journal of Sports Sciences, 21*, 391–401.

Eys, M. A., Carron, A. V., Bray, S. R., & Beauchamp, M. R. (2005). The relationship between role ambiguity and intention to return. *Journal of Applied Sport Psychology, 17*, 255–261.

Fletcher, D., & Arnold, R. (2011). A qualitative study of performance leadership and management in elite sport. *Journal of Applied Sport Psychology, 23*, 223–242.

Fletcher, D., & Wagstaff, C. R. D. (2009). Organizational psychology in elite sport: Its emergence, application and future. *Psychology of Sport and Exercise, 10*, 427–434.

Fletcher, D., Hanton, S., & Wagstaff, C. R. D. (2012). Performers' responses to stressors encountered in sport organizations. *Journal of Sports Sciences, 30*, 349–358.

Forsyth, D. R., & Burnett, J. L. (2010). Group processes. In E. R. Baumeister and E. Finkel (Eds.), *Advanced social psychology* (pp. 495–534). New York: Cambridge University Press.

Giges, B., Petitpas, A. J., & Vernacchia, R. A. (2004). Helping coaches meet their own needs: Challenges for the sport psychology consultant. *The Sport Psychologist, 18*, 430–444.

Gilbert, W. D., Gilbert, J. N., & Trudel, P. (2001). Coaching strategies for youth sport Part 2: Personal characteristics, parental influence, and team organization. *Journal of Physical Education, Recreation, & Dance, 72*, 41–46.

Gould, D., Guinan, D., Greenleaf, C., & Chung, Y. (2002). A survey of US Olympic coaches: Variables perceived to have influenced athlete performances and coach effectiveness. *The Sport Psychologist, 16*, 229–250.

Hackman, J. R. (2011). *Collaborative intelligence: Using teams to solve hard problems.* San Francisco, CA: Berrett-Koehler Publishers.

Hackman, J. R. (2012). From causes to conditions in group research. *Journal of Organizational Behavior, 33*, 428–444.

Hanton, S., Wagstaff, C. R. D., & Fletcher, D. (2012). Cognitive appraisals of stressors encountered in sport organizations. *International Journal of Sport and Exercise Psychology, 10*, 276–289.

Henriksen, K., Stambulova, N., & Roessler, K. K. (2010a). Holistic approach to athletic talent development environments: A successful sailing milieu. *Psychology of Sport and Exercise, 11*, 212–222.

Henriksen, K., Stambulova, N., & Roessler, K. K. (2010b). Successful talent development in track and field: Considering the role of environment. *Scandinavian Journal of Medicine & Science in Sports, 20*, 122–132.

Hoption, C., Phelan, J., & Barling, J. (2014). Transformational leadership in sport. In M. R. Beauchamp & M. A. Eys (Eds), *Group dynamics in exercise and sport psychology*. 2nd edn, (pp. 55–72). New York: Routledge.

Hox, J. (2010). *Multilevel analysis: Techniques and applications.* New York: Routledge.

Jackson, P., & Delehanty, H. (2013). *Eleven rings: The soul of success.* New York: The Penguin Press.

Jones, R. L., & Wallace, M. (2005). Another bad day at the training ground: Coping with ambiguity in the coaching context. *Sport, Education and Society, 10*, 119–134.

Jowett, S., & Lavallee, D. (2007). *Social psychology in sport.* Champaign, IL: Human Kinetics.

Jowett, S. & Poczwardowski, A. (2007). Understanding the coach-athlete relationship. In S. Jowett & D. Lavallee (Eds.), *Social psychology in sport* (pp. 3–14). Champaign, IL: Human Kinetics.

Kellermanns, F. W., Walter, J., Floyd, S. W., Lechner, C., & Shaw, J. C. (2011). To agree or not to agree? A meta-analytical review of strategic consensus and organizational performance. *Journal of Business Research, 64,* 126–133.

Kellermanns, F. W., Walter, J., Lechner, C., & Floyd, S. W. (2005). The lack of consensus about strategic consensus: Advancing theory and research. *Journal of Management, 31,* 719–737.

Lawrence, B. S. (2006). Organizational reference groups: A missing perspective on social context. *Organization Science, 17,* 80–100.

Lawrence, B. S. (2011). Who is they? Inquiries into how individuals construe social context. *Human Relations, 64,* 749–773.

Leary, M. R. & Baumeister, R. F. (2000). The nature and function of self-esteem: Sociometer theory. *Advances in Experimental Social Psychology, 32,* 1–62.

Locksley, A., Ortiz, V., & Hepburn, C. (1980). Social categorization and discriminatory behavior: Extinguishing the minimal intergroup discrimination effect. *Journal of Personality and Social Psychology, 39,* 773–783.

Loughead, T. M., Munroe-Chandler, K. J., Hoffmann, M. D., & Duquay, A. M. (2014). Athlete leadership in sport. In M. R. Beauchamp & M. A. Eys (Eds), *Group dynamics in exercise and sport psychology* (pp. 110–127, 2nd ed.). New York: Routledge.

Martin, K. A. (2002). Development and validation of the coaching staff cohesion scale. *Measurement in Physical Education and Exercise Science, 6,* 23–42.

Martin, L. J., Carron, A. V., & Burke, S. M. (2009). Team building interventions in sport: A meta-analysis. *International Review of Sport and Exercise Psychology, 5,* 3–18.

Martin, L. J., Wilson, J., Evans, M. B., & Spink, K. S. (2015). Cliques in sport: Perceptions of intercollegiate athletes. *The Sport Psychologist, 29,* 82–95.

Mathieu, J. E., Gilson, L. L., & Ruddy, T. M. (2006). Empowerment and team effectiveness: An empirical test of an integrated model. *Journal of Applied Psychology, 91,* 97–108.

Mathieu, J. E., Heffner, T. S., Goodwin, G. F., Cannon-Bowers, J. A., & Salas, E. (2005). Scaling the quality of teammates' mental models: Equifinality and normative comparisons. *Journal of Organizational Behavior, 26,* 37–56.

Mathieu, J. E., Heffner, T. S., Goodwin, G. F., Salas, E., & Cannon-Bowers, J. A. (2000). The influence of shared mental models on team process and performance. *Journal of Applied Psychology, 85,* 273–283.

Mathieu, J., Maynard, M. T., Rapp, T., & Gilson, L. (2008). Team effectiveness 1997–2007: A review of recent advancements and a glimpse into the future. *Journal of Management, 34,* 410–476.

McEwan, D., & Beauchamp, M. R. (2014). Teamwork in sport: A theoretical and integrative review. *International Review of Sport and Exercise Psychology, 7*(1), 229–250.

McGran, K. (2015). With lottery teams tanking for Connor McDavid, it's time NHL rethinks draft. Retrieved from http://www.thestar.com/sports/breakaway_blog/2015/03/tanking-for-mcdavid-time-for-nhl-to-have-a-playoff-for-draft-order-or-end-the-draft-altogether.html

McGrath, J. E., Arrow, H., & Berdahl, J. L. (2000). The study of groups: Past, present, and future. *Personality and Social Psychology Review, 4*(1), 95–105.

Oxford Dictionaries (2015). "draft". Oxford: Oxford University Press. Retrieved from http://www.oxforddictionaries.com/definition/english/draft

Rapisarda, B. A. (2002). The impact of emotional intelligence on work team cohesiveness and performance. *The International Journal of Organizational Analysis, 10*, 363–379.
Sherif, M., & Sherif, C. (1953). *Groups in harmony and tension: An integration of studies of intergroup relations*. New York: Harper & Brothers.
Spink, K. S., Wilson, K. S., & Odnokon, P. (2010). Examining the relationship between cohesion and return to team in elite athletes. *Psychology of Sport and Exercise, 11*, 6–11.
Spink, K. S., Wilson, K. S., Priebe, C. S. (2010). Groupness and adherence in structured exercise settings. *Group Dynamics: Theory, Research, and Practice, 14*, 163–173.
Steiner, I. D. (1972). *Group processes and productivity*. New York: Academic Press.
Tajfel, H. (1981). *Human groups and social categories*. Cambridge: Cambridge University Press.
Tajfel, H., & Turner, J. (1979). An integrative theory of intergroup conflict. In W. G. W. Austin (Ed.), *The social psychology of intergroup relations* (pp. 33–47). Monterey, CA: Brooks-Cole.
Thelwell, R. C., Lane, A. M., Weston, N. J., & Greenlees, I. A. (2008). Examining relationships between emotional intelligence and coaching efficacy. *International Journal of Sport and Exercise Psychology, 6*(2), 224–235.
van Knippenberg, D., & Schippers, M. C. (2007). Work group diversity. *Annual Review of Psychology, 58*, 515–541.
Wagstaff, C. R. D., Fletcher, D., & Hanton, S. (2012a). Positive organizational psychology in sport. *International Review of Sport and Exercise Psychology, 5*, 87–103.
Wagstaff, C. R. D., Fletcher, D., & Hanton, S. (2012b). Positive organizational psychology in sport: An ethnography of organizational functioning in a national sport organization. *Journal of Applied Sport Psychology, 24*, 26–47.
Wagstaff, C. R. D., Fletcher, D., & Hanton, S. (2012c). Exploring emotion abilities and regulation strategies in sport organizations. *Sport, Exercise, and Performance Psychology, 1*, 268–282.
Wagstaff, C. R. D., Hanton, S., & Fletcher, D. (2013). Developing emotion abilities and regulation strategies in a sport organization: An action research intervention. *Psychology of Sport and Exercise, 14*, 476–487.
Wang, Y. S., & Huang, T. C. (2009). The relationship of transformational leadership with group cohesiveness and emotional intelligence. *Social Behavior and Personality, 37*, 379–392.
Williams, N., Whipp, P. R., Jackson, B., & Dimmock, J. A. (2013). Relatedness support and the retention of young female golfers. *Journal of Applied Sport Psychology, 25*, 412–430.
Wölfer, R., Faber, N. S., & Hewstone, M. (2015). Social network analysis in the science of groups: Cross-sectional and longitudinal applications for studying intra- and intergroup behavior. *Group Dynamics: Theory, Research, and Practice, 19*, 45–61.
Zakrajsek, R. A., Abildso, C. G., Hurst, J. R., & Watson, J. C. (2007). The relationships among coaches' and athletes' perceptions of coaching staff cohesion, team cohesion, and performance. *Athletic Insight, 9*, 1–12.
Zucchermaglio, C. (2005). Who wins and who loses: The rhetorical manipulation of social identities in a soccer team. *Group Dynamics: Theory, Research and Practice, 9*, 219–238.

12
OPTIMAL ENVIRONMENTS FOR TEAM FUNCTIONING IN SPORT ORGANIZATIONS

Katrien Fransen, Filip Boen, Jeroen Stouten, Stewart Cotterill, and Gert Vande Broek

Introduction

Despite its importance in optimizing a team's effectiveness, the application of sport psychology practices often gets overshadowed by the training of physical abilities, technical skills, and tactical insight. Yet, in order to fully realize the physical, technical, and tactical potential of athletes in team sports, the environmental circumstances need to be adequate. The present chapter will outline how the team coach can create optimal environments for team functioning in different facets of the coaching job. We focus on the latest research trends that identify the crucial markers of optimal environments for team functioning in sport organizations.

First, although most research has focused on the coach as the only leader of the team, an emerging trend towards the importance of shared leadership can be observed: leadership is no longer restricted to one person but is shared within the team. Second, Haslam, Reicher, and Platow (2011) pointed to a gap in the extant research in stating that "the causal role played by the social group remains conspicuously absent from most (if not all) previous treatments of leadership" (p. 44). The social identity approach to leadership (Haslam et al., 2011) is the first to transform the group itself from a marginal to a central presence in its leadership focus. Similar to the evolution in organizational research, the trend to put the social group instead of the leader in the center of attention has recently entered the sport literature. In this chapter we build on the social identity approach by illustrating the importance of building a shared identity within the team. Third, creating an optimal team environment is fairly easy when athletes perform at their best and the organization is successful. However, it is also crucial that organizations maintain a positive environment when their performance team faces challenges or setbacks. In this final part of the chapter, we will identify the characteristics of highly resilient teams environments (i.e., teams that are able to effectively withstand stressors). To summarize, the present chapter will outline how the coach can facilitate the team's performance by optimizing the above-mentioned factors: (1) the coach as facilitator of *shared leadership*; (2) the coach as *identity manager*; and (3) the coach as conflict manager to create *highly resilient* teams.

The coach as facilitator of shared leadership

> Talent is important, but the single most important ingredient after you develop talent is internal leadership. It's not the coaches as much as one single person or people on the team who set higher standards than that team would normally set for itself.
> Mike Krzyzewski: coach, 2008 and 2012 Olympic champion USA basketball team
> (Krzyzewski, 2009, p. 85)

When it comes to leadership within sport organizations, one often pictures the coach in the role of leader of the performance team. However, it is important to realize that athletes can fulfill important leadership roles. Several studies have highlighted that higher quality athlete leadership resulted in higher team identification and a stronger task and social cohesion (Fransen, Coffee, et al., 2014; Fransen, Van Puyenbroeck, et al., 2015a; Loughead, Fransen, Van Puyenbroeck, Hoffmann, & Boen, under review; Price & Weiss, 2011). Furthermore, athlete leaders have been shown to be the catalysts in the contagion of team confidence throughout the team. In volleyball, soccer, and basketball, it has been shown that the expression of team confidence by the athlete leaders in the team was one of the most important sources of the players' team confidence (Fransen, Vanbeselaere, De Cuyper, Vande Broek, & Boen, 2015; Fransen et al., 2012). Two experimental studies further confirmed that the team confidence contagion throughout the team emanates from the athlete leader (Fransen, Haslam, et al., 2015; Fransen, Steffens, et al., 2015). More specifically, their findings revealed that team members had greater team confidence when the leader expressed high confidence in the team's success, as a result of which their performance improved. By contrast, Fransen and colleagues observed that when leaders expressed low confidence in their team, team members' confidence dropped and their performance deteriorated.

Recently, the impact of supporting or thwarting players' need for competence by the athlete leaders has been investigated (i.e., by the provision of positive/negative feedback and the expression of high/low confident body language, respectively) (Fransen, Vande Broek, Vansteenkiste, & Boen, 2015). The study findings revealed that athlete leader's support of their teammates' competence enhanced their intrinsic motivation and performance relative to a neutral control group, whereas the athlete leader's thwarting of competence undermined their teammates' intrinsic motivation. Furthermore, structural equation modeling demonstrated that the effect of competence support/thwarting on intrinsic motivation, both at the individual and at the team level, was fully mediated by team members' competence satisfaction. Moreover, a direct positive impact of competence support emerged on performance improvement. Athlete leaders thus seem to have the capacity to influence the team confidence and intrinsic motivation of their teammates (in both positive and negative ways), thereby significantly affecting team members' performance. In conclusion, coaches should use the power of their athlete leaders to establish an optimal team environment. Also in organizational settings, shared leadership has been shown to be more beneficial for team performance than vertical forms of leadership, in which one formal leader is positioned hierarchically above the team (Wang, Waldman, & Zhang, 2014).

Shared leadership between coach and athlete leaders

One of the first studies to compare coach and athlete leadership behaviors was conducted by Loughead and Hardy (2005). Their findings demonstrated that coaches and athlete leaders exhibited different leadership behaviors. More specifically, it was shown that coaches were perceived as exhibiting training and instruction and autocratic behaviors to a greater extent than athlete leaders, while athlete leaders exhibited more social support, positive feedback, and democratic behaviors than their coaches. Recent research further confirmed that the leadership of the coach and the leadership of athlete leaders complemented each other. More specifically, coaches and athlete leaders were seen as equally good leaders when it came to providing task instructions or communicating with the club board, media, or sponsors. Meanwhile, leaders within the performance team (i.e., the athlete leaders) are perceived as taking the lead in motivating their teammates on the field and creating a good team atmosphere off the field (Fransen, Van Puyenbroeck, et al., 2015b).

Not only do coaches and athlete leaders exhibit different leadership behaviors and fulfill different leadership functions, they also have a different influence on important group dynamics constructs. For example, Price and Weiss (2013) revealed that coach leadership was more influential than athlete leadership for predicting individual outcomes and collective efficacy. Athlete leadership, on the other hand, was more strongly related to social cohesion than coach leadership, and both athlete and coach leadership were equally important for task cohesion. Recently, the influence of the coach on team confidence and team cohesion was compared with the impact of athlete leaders in a sample of 343 athletes (eight soccer teams, eight volleyball teams, and eleven handball teams) (Fransen, Decroos, Vande Broek, & Boen, under review). The findings demonstrated that the leadership quality of both coaches and athlete leaders predicted a unique part of the variance of team confidence and team cohesion. That is, coach leadership was more predictive for team members' confidence in obtaining the goal (i.e., team outcome confidence), and athlete leaders had more predictive power for teammates' confidence in the team's abilities to perform the process well (i.e., collective efficacy). Furthermore, coach leadership was more predictive for task cohesion, whereas athlete leadership was more predictive for social cohesion. However, when taking into account the indirect effect through members' team identification, for task cohesion the impact of athlete leaders also outscored the impact of the coach.

Given that coaches and athlete leaders have a unique impact on different important indicators of optimal team functioning, we suggest that a high-quality team environment is characterized by a structure of shared leadership, in which the coach and athlete leaders can complement each other. Alternatively, the athlete leader's impact on the team might be more direct given that athlete leaders have more interaction with team members and are more likely to share common experiences. For example, in an organizational context, Wo, Ambrose, and Schminke (2015) showed that top leaders influence employees only indirectly as this leadership trickles down first from the top to the middle management and only then to employees. Hence, this illustrates that coach leadership sets the environmental tone for athlete leadership, which subsequently reinforces similar attitudes and behavior in team members. The coach here acts as an important role model for the athlete leaders and the team (Mayer, Kuenzi, Greenbaum, Bardes, & Salvador, 2009).

Shared leadership within the team

Based on the empirical evidence mentioned above, it can be recommended that coaches share leadership with the athlete leaders in their organization to create an optimal environment. However, one could wonder whether it is enough to share the leadership with one athlete in the team. To date, the majority of the research on athlete leadership has focused on the team captain, as the formal leader of the team (e.g., Dupuis, Bloom, & Loughead, 2006; Grandzol, Perlis, & Draina, 2010; Voelker, Gould, & Crawford, 2011). The captain of the team is expected to act as a liaison between the coaching staff and the players, to act as a leader during all team activities, and to represent the team at receptions, meetings, and press conferences (Mosher, 1979). Furthermore, the captain is expected to take the lead on task aspects, such as coaching his/her teammates on the field, but also on social aspects, such as providing social support (Voelker et al., 2011). In short, coaches, athletes, fans, and media appear to assume that the team captain takes the lead both on and off the field.

In this regard, Fransen, Vanbeselaere, De Cuyper, Vande Broek, and Boen (2014) distinguished between four leadership roles that athletes can occupy, two leadership roles on the field: (a) the *task leader*, who gives his/her teammates tactical advice and adjusts them when necessary; and (b) the *motivational leader*, who encourages his/her teammates on the field to perform at their best; and two leadership roles off the field: (a) the *social leader*, who develops a good team atmosphere outside of the playing field, and (b) the *external leader*, who handles the communication with club management, media, and sponsors. Given the differences between of each of these leadership roles, it might be disputed whether it is realistic that the team captain has the ability to fulfill such different leadership functions.

Fransen, Vanbeselaere, et al. (2014) identified the four leadership roles in the teams of 4,451 athletes and coaches across nine different team sports in Flanders. Their findings demonstrated that in only 1 percent of the teams, the team captain was perceived as best leader for all of the four leadership roles. Even more noteworthy was that in 44 percent of the teams, the captain was not perceived as best leader for any of the leadership roles. These findings underline the fact that the leadership qualities attributed to the captain as the team's formal leader are overrated. Instead, the informal leaders (i.e., those players who emerge as natural leaders in the team without formal leadership recognition), rather than the captain, take the lead, both on and off the field. Shared leadership in this regard is an emergent team property of mutual influence and shared responsibility among team members, whereby they lead each other toward goal achievement (Wang et al., 2014). The fact that the team captain is not the only leader, but instead leadership is shared throughout the team, was also observed by other studies (e.g., Loughead & Hardy, 2005).

Sharing the lead has been linked to several favorable outcomes. For example, it has been demonstrated that when different individuals fulfill the different leadership roles, team members are more confident in the abilities of their team and identify more strongly with their team. Moreover, a negative, albeit small correlation was observed with the team's place in the ranking (Fransen, Vanbeselaere, et al., 2014): the more leadership was dispersed across the team, the higher the team was ranked. In addition, it was shown that even shared leadership within a single leadership role (e.g., more than one task, motivational, social, or external leader) was beneficial for the task and social cohesion within the team (Fransen, 2014). Shared leadership is especially relevant when teams are truly interdependent (cf. Liden, Wayne, & Bradway, 1997) and have adequate knowledge, information, and individual performance potential (Mumford, Friedrich, Vessey, & Ruark, 2012). If these conditions are not met, sharing responsibilities can be a liability when the degree of sharing is too large. Moreover, by continuous practice, teams are able to create a sense of routine, yet through such routines they limit the potential impact of leadership because they render the team sufficiently competent to deal with challenges. However, when new skills need to be developed or when situations emerge to which routines do not give appropriate answers (e.g., when conflict arises or the team face setbacks), shared leadership is essential to guide the team in the right direction (Morgeson, 2005).

Identifying the leadership structure in the team

Given the positive outcomes highlighted in the previous section, it seems important for a coach to facilitate athlete leadership within sport organizations to optimize the performance team environment. However, before developing athlete leadership, it is crucial to obtain an insight into the existing leadership structure within the team. Who are the right leaders for the right job? The perception of the coach in this regard might differ from the leadership perceptions of the players; nevertheless, the latter is the most important when it comes to effective athlete leadership: if the athlete leaders appointed by the coach are not seen as athlete leaders by their teammates then they will not be followed.

Social network analysis (SNA) (Fransen, Van Puyenbroeck, et al., 2015b) constitutes a novel diagnostic tool that uses the perceptions of individuals to identify the key leaders on the different leadership roles within the team. This network approach also allows the coach to map the evolution of leadership structures over time. By using this network approach, coaches can appoint task, motivational, social, and external athlete leaders that are supported by the team's diagnostics. A clear delineation of the leadership role, followed by feedback from the coach on the fulfillment of their leadership role, will assist the further development of the leadership qualities of the athlete leaders. That athlete leaders realize that teammates support and even expect their leadership will likely further motivate them to accept their role and engage in high-quality athlete leadership behavior (Benson, Eys, Surya, Dawson, & Schneider, 2013).

Athlete leadership development

In line with the previous section, it is important as a coach to not only identify prospective athlete leaders within a team but also to facilitate and develop athlete leadership within a team. An autocratic, controlling coaching style, in which the coach imposes the rules, norms, goals, and way of working to his/her players without permitting any athlete input, will most likely result in a flock of meek sheep (Morrison, 2011). Such an environment offers very limited opportunities to develop effective athlete leadership in a team. By contrast, an autonomy-supportive coaching style provides voice to athletes when deciding team rules, norms, and goals. This participation might lead to accountability and a greater commitment. It can be assumed that a coaching style in which athletes are given autonomy, rather than being controlled nurtures the development of athlete leaders' abilities to lead and cope with challenging situations.

There is an apparent autonomy paradox though. Increased personal autonomy can jeopardize the team's sense of cohesion (Langfred, 2000). That is, team members who employ their autonomy often focus on their individual goals, and risk losing a sense of team needs. As such, individual autonomy may promote a detachment from the team by facilitating individuals' pursuit of their own path rather than focusing on the team goals. However, Langfred (2000) demonstrated that autonomy at the team level (i.e., the level of control and discretion the group is allowed in carrying out tasks assigned by the organization) does have a positive influence on the team's sense of cohesion. Hence, it is important for coaches to find the right balance here by providing autonomy at the team level while fostering a clear joint vision on the team's goals. This is the first step in creating an optimal environment via athlete leadership development. However, before being able to provide high-quality athlete leadership, athlete leaders need adequate competence in their leadership role. Until recently, the area of athlete leadership development in sport had received very little attention within the literature (for a review, see Cotterill & Fransen, 2016).

An example leadership development program has been developed by Gould and Voelker (2010). Their captaincy leadership development program included several one-day leadership training clinics for team captains each fall and spring semester. In these clinics, the major components of leadership are introduced (e.g., positive peer modeling, communication, motivation, and team cohesion). Consequently, the athletes are offered various exercises which help them to improve their skills as a captain in these key leadership areas (e.g., how to approach and talk to their coach about player issues, how to motivate teammates). Furthermore, the captains have the opportunity to identify common team problems and collaborate with peers on how they might handle them as a leader. The team captains are also equipped with a separate self-study guide. This guide includes basic information on the key leadership skills, as well as examples of athletes and coaches who are effective in implementing these leadership skills.

Although Gould and Voelker's leadership program has several positive characteristics, it is unfortunate that the program is only aimed at captains or athletes identified as possessing leadership potential. As noted previously, informal leaders, rather than formal leaders, are often perceived as the real leaders in a given team (Fransen, Vanbeselaere, et al., 2014). Interestingly, a leadership development program that not only aims to develop formal but also informal leaders has recently been developed by Cotterill (under review). His program seeks to develop athlete leadership in elite professional cricketers in three specific domains: captaincy development; leadership skill development; and personal growth and leadership development. It is important to note that the second domain pertains to every player in the squad. Each player is given opportunities to act as a leader and to take on positions of responsibility, as they are assigned specific leadership roles during training and practice games. By developing the leadership skills of multiple athletes in the team, this leadership development program follows the recent trend that leadership is not only provided by the team captain but rather is shared throughout the team.

We have argued here that athlete leaders can occupy four different leadership roles. Therefore, it is important to develop leader's abilities with regard to their specific roles. More specifically, a task leader needs to obtain insight in the game tactics, whereas a motivational leader needs to know how to motivate each of his/her teammates (i.e., knowing which players need to be encouraged, and who would benefit more from being calmed down). Off the field, the athlete leaders also need to learn specific competencies: the social leader needs to learn how to deal with intra-team conflict and how to manage the team atmosphere, while an external leader should be trained in communication skills to represent the team with organizational senior management, media, and sponsors. Consequently, appointing the "right" athlete leaders to the appropriate roles is only the first step toward optimizing the organizational environment through leadership development. That is, athlete leaders need to educated as to the competences that are crucial for their specific leadership role. High-quality leadership in each of these four roles will result in stronger team confidence, higher team identification (Fransen, Coffee, et al., 2014), stronger task and social cohesion (Loughead et al., under review), and, ultimately, improved performance (Fransen, Haslam, et al., 2015; Fransen, Steffens, et al., 2015).

Avoiding the risks of sharing the lead

Despite the benefits of shared leadership for optimal team functioning highlighted here, sharing leadership also carries significant risks. For example, if the appointed task leader has a strongly different view regarding playing strategy than other task leaders or the coach, contrasting messages during the game might lead to confusion and doubt in the team. In order to avoid the risks of shared leadership and to develop an effective shared leadership structure, we suggest two important preconditions that coaches should keep in mind.

First, coaches should aim for role clarity, and avoid role ambiguity. It is essential that coaches work with athletes to clearly delineate the function and responsibilities attached to a given leadership role. Perceptions of role ambiguity (i.e., the lack of clear, consistent information regarding an individual's role) have been associated with decreased task cohesion and lower confidence in their own ability to successfully fulfill the leadership role (Eys & Carron, 2001). On the other hand, if athlete leaders are well-informed of the expectations that are connected to a given leadership role, this is likely to facilitate role satisfaction (Beauchamp, Bray, Eys, & Carron, 2005), overall athlete satisfaction (Eys, Carron, Bray, & Beauchamp, 2003), and better fulfillment of their leadership role (Bray & Brawley, 2002). Clearly then, delineating the function of the different athlete leaders is an important precondition for effective shared leadership and the optimization of the team environment.

Second, and even more importantly, for shared leadership to be effective there must be the development of a shared vision. A shared vision with regard to the team norms, values, and goals is crucial to get all athletes "on the same page". To obtain a shared vision, coaches should provide adequate autonomy support and mutually agree common goals with the athletes, as well the norms and values that are necessary to reach these goals. The more team members internalize the team's goals as their own, the more a shared accountability is likely to be established, as a result of which players are likely to be more strongly committed to reach these aims. That all individuals strive for the same goals will promote coherence between the athlete leaders, coach, and senior management, thereby optimizing team functioning.

The coach as identity manager to develop a shared vision

For a long time, researchers have attempted to explain group phenomena in sports teams based on the motives, attitudes, and actions of the individual athletes. In this regard, sport scientists often used self-determination theory (SDT; Deci & Ryan, 1985) as a framework. SDT postulates that individuals have three basic needs (i.e., autonomy, competence, and relatedness) that need to be fulfilled in order to become intrinsically motivated for their sport activities. Although this theory has provided useful insights regarding the motivation of athletes, it is in essence an individualistic theory, which focuses on the individual athlete. A sports team, however, is more than the sum of its individual parts, and therefore greater insight might be gained from a theory that focuses on group dynamics.

The social identity approach (SIA; Tajfel & Turner, 1979) was one of the first motivational theories to transform the group itself from a side-effect of individual cognitions to a central presence in its analysis. Despite its prominence in organizational settings, the social identity approach has, until relatively recently, been largely overlooked within the domain of sport (Rees, Haslam, Coffee, & Lavallee, 2015). Nevertheless, SIA offers great potential for gaining a deeper insight into the specific team processes required for optimizing team environments within sport organizations.

The social identity approach asserts that the psychology and behavior of team members is shaped by their capacity to not only think, feel, and behave as individuals (in terms of personal identity as "I" and "me"), but also, and often more importantly, as group members (in terms of a shared social identity as "we" and "us"; Haslam, 2001; Turner, Hogg, Oakes, Reicher, & Wetherell, 1987). Group identification, also termed team identification, refers to the extent to which we define ourselves in terms of our group membership. It is this internalized sense of a shared identity (i.e., one's sense of themselves as part of "us") that "makes group behavior possible" (Steffens, Haslam, & Reicher, 2014; Turner, 1982, p. 21). Basketball Hall of Fame coach Phil Jackson illustrated the importance of shared identity by noting, "good teams become great ones when the members trust each other enough to surrender the *Me* for the *We*" (Jackson & Delehanty, 1995, p. 21). In their recent review, Rees, Haslam, Coffee, and Lavallee (2015) pointed out that social identity is not only the basis for sports group behavior, but also for formation and development, support and stress appraisal, and leadership. We next elaborate on each of these components.

First, as mentioned before, individuals are able to define themselves as group members (e.g., as members of the same sport organization) instead of defining themselves as being unique individuals. This shift in self-definition allows people to *act as group members*. Furthermore, the SIA asserts that when people define the self in terms of their social identity, they strive to define the in-group as positively distinct from comparison out-groups. In other words, athletes and fans of a particular team will strive to emphasize how their team is better than the rival teams. If this cannot be achieved in terms of objective performance (i.e., better ranking), other positive comparison dimensions such as best team atmosphere or best fair play might be drawn upon.

Second, the traditional view of group formation and development postulates that individuals become, and remain, group members to the extent that they believe it is in their personal interests to do so (Carron, Widmeyer, & Brawley, 1985). According to this literature, group membership is based on individuals' motivations, and as soon as groups no longer meet the team members' need, they will disband and disintegrate. However, as Rees et al. (2015) pointed out, this approach cannot explain why people make a point of being "die-hard" fans, who stick with their team through thick and thin. Instead, they suggest that the core process that binds group members (i.e., athletes, coaches, senior management, or fans) to each other is *depersonalization*, through which individuals define themselves in terms of a social identity that is shared with others. Not only does social identity form the basis for joining new groups, it is also the basis for ongoing group development. In this regard, Wann and Branscombe (1990) showed that social identification, rather than the satisfaction of personal needs, is the key motivator of continued group support. Along the same lines, Turner, Hogg, Turner, and Smith (1984) observed that the failure to win a game can actually foster team members' commitment to the group, which is in contrast with the traditional approach of individual needs.

Third, it has been shown that we are more likely to offer and receive help from people that (are perceived to) belong to the same in-group, or, in other words, who represent a shared social identity. For example, in their experimental study Levine, Prosser, Evans, and Reicher (2005) investigated the willingness of the participants (all Manchester United fans) to help an injured man, who was dressed with either a Manchester United shirt (i.e., member of the same in-group) or a Liverpool shirt, their rivals (i.e., member of the out-group). The study findings revealed that when the injured man was dressed in a Manchester United shirt, 92 percent of the participants offered help. When dressed in the Liverpool shirt, only 32 percent of the participants were eager to help the injured man. The authors concluded that social identification is thus a strong predictor of support. Along the same lines, Haslam and Reicher (2006) found that when people's sense of a shared identity increased, they provided each other with more social support and effectively resisted the adverse effects of situational stressors. By contrast, when people's sense of shared identity declined, they provided each other with less support and succumbed to stressors. Morgan, Fletcher, and Sarkar (2013) also identified a shared identity as an important characteristic of highly resilient teams (i.e., teams which are able to succesfully withstand stressors).

Fourth, the recent application of SIA to leadership argues that leaders' effectiveness depends on the extent that leaders are able to create and manage a shared identity within a group (Haslam et al., 2011). In other words, effective leaders are able to create a shared sense of "we" and "us" within the team. This is nicely illustrated by chief executive officer Lewis Ergen, who noted that "the ratio of We's to I's is the best indicator of the development of a team" (Quick, 1992, p. 20). Steffens, Haslam, Reicher, et al. (2014) have recently distinguished between four dimensions of effective identity-based leadership. First, leaders need to be *in-group prototypes* (i.e., represent the unique qualities that define the group and what it means to be a member of the group). Second, they need to be *in-group champions* (i.e., advance and promote the core interests of the group). Third, leaders need to be *entrepreneurs of identity* (i.e., bring people together by creating a shared sense of "we" and "us" within the group). Fourth, and finally, leaders need to be *embedders of identity* (i.e., develop structures that facilitate and embed shared understanding, coordination, and success).

Recent research in the sport domain has revealed that high-quality coaches who were able to create a shared sense of "we" and "us" within the team, instigated increased team confidence and stronger task and social cohesion among team members (De Backer et al., 2011; Fransen, Decroos, Vande Broek, et al., under review). Furthermore, not only coaches were able to influence the team identification of the athletes, athlete leaders were also shown to fulfil a key role to create a sense of "us". More specifically, it was demonstrated that high-quality athlete leaders caused their teammates to think, feel, and behave in terms of "we" (as a team), rather than in terms of "I" (as individuals). In turn, this stronger feeling of connection with the team resulted in enhanced team member confidence in the abilities of their team, created a stronger task and social cohesion, and improved the team's performance (Fransen, Coffee, et al., 2014; Fransen, Decroos, Vande Broek, et al., under review; Fransen, Haslam, et al., 2015; Fransen, Steffens, et al., 2015). These findings suggest that not only coaches, but also athlete leaders, are of crucial importance to foster an environment characterized by a sense of "we", and again highlights the importance of creating sport organizations shaped by shared leadership.

The coach as conflict manager to create highly resilient teams

Life is easy when thriving on successes and wins and when everything works out the way it was planned. However, a sports season is characterized by unforeseen circumstances (e.g., injury of a key player) and regular setbacks (e.g., defeats). Furthermore, given the nature of team sports, intra-team conflicts can also be expected. In order to create an optimal team environment it is crucial for sport organizations to effectively withstand stressors and become highly resilient. It is noteworthy that the resilience of a team is more than the sum of the individual players' resilience. Therefore, Morgan et al. (2013) identified four particular team attributes that characterize resilient teams (see Figure 12.1): (1) group structure; (2) task-involving climate; (3) social capital; and (4) team confidence. Even when team members are taking up personal responsibilities and possibly even a leadership role in the team, when it comes to conflict, the coach's leadership is highly valued and expected. Hence, it is important for coaches to foster these resilience characteristics in order to facilitate optimal team environments for

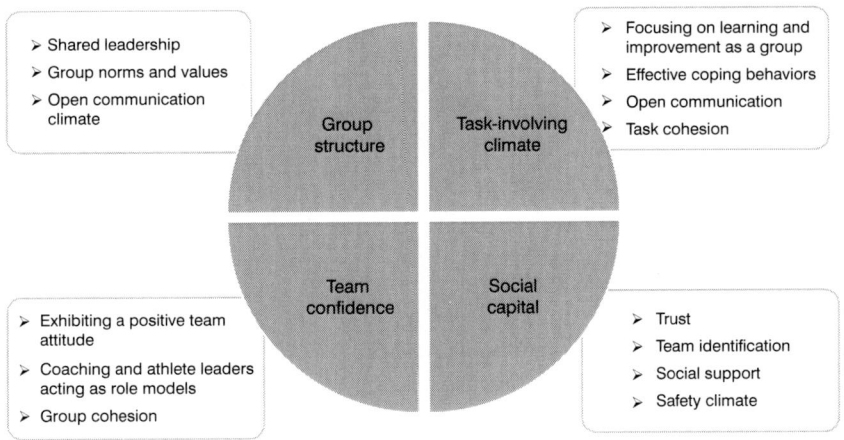

FIGURE 12.1 The four attributes that characterize resilient teams

Source: Based on Morgan et al., 2013.

effectively handling conflict, within-team conflict as well as when the team is confronted with external stressors (e.g., repeatedly losing, injuries, etc.). We will outline each of these team characteristics in detail.

Group structure

The first characteristic of highly resilient teams pertains to the creation of an optimal group structure, characterized by collective group norms and values, shared leadership, and an open communication climate. Such factors are likely to be important at the outset of a given competition period, but also when the team encounters challenges, such as intra-team conflict.

First, if a clear structure of athlete leadership has been established in the team, not only the coaches, but also the athlete leaders have to ensure that all players pursue common team goals. However, if an athlete should deviate from the expected behavior, it is also the task of their teammates to reprimand such individuals and remind them of the team's norms, values, and goals. Pressure from within the team can be more effective than pressure from the coach. At first athlete leaders who dare to stand up for their opinion might cause disagreements within the team, but it is exactly these discussions that can make players stronger and able to work more effectively as a team.

Second, by providing voice to the athletes, they will be more committed to realize their goals and adopt the postulated norms and values. Research in non-sport organizational teams has demonstrated that more empowered teams were also more productive and proactive than less empowered teams (Kirkman & Rosen, 1999). Furthermore, the empowered workers were more satisfied with their job and more committed to their team and organization. In order to empower athletes the role of the coach requires change. More specifically, organizational research on self-managing teams has demonstrated that the most effective leadership behaviors of the external leader (i.e., the coach in sports teams) are those that facilitate the team's self-management through self-observation, self-evaluation, and self-goal-setting (Manz & Sims, 1987). Similarly, it would be beneficial for coaches to encourage their team to monitor, be aware, and to evaluate their level of performance, in order to set appropriate performance goals. Such an open communication environment will also allow coaches and athletes to discuss intra-team conflicts openly. In this way, players are allowed to voice their opinions, resolve their differences, and find a common way of interacting with each other.

Task-involving climate

A second important characteristic of highly resilient teams is a task-involving climate. Such a climate focuses on learning and improvement together as one team, instead of promoting intra-team comparison. Morgan et al. (2013) established that resilient teams are able to focus on both personal and team development because they are able to filter out irrelevant cues and isolate what is important. Furthermore, they revealed how resilient teams exhibited a range of effective behaviors to overcome stressors, thereby increasing the likelihood of team progression. For example, thorough preparation for difficult moments (e.g., having a plan B or C if plan A does not work out during the game) was seen as an important factor that could make the difference when encountering difficult match situations.

When conflict arises or when there have been deviations from goals, norms, or values, communication will be crucial. It is the task of the coach, together with the athlete leaders, to clearly outline each player's responsibility and to remind the players of the common goals, as they were set at the start of the season. Several studies have reported that such open communication, which reflects the shared values and emphasizes the common goal to aim for, is optimal for resolving conflicts, to get everyone back on the same wavelength, and to enhance task cohesion within the team (Smith, Arthur, Hardy, Callow, & Williams, 2013; Sullivan & Feltz, 2003). It is noteworthy that athlete leaders also seem to play a role in creating a task-involving climate given that previous studies demonstrated that teams with high-quality athlete leadership are also characterized by stronger task cohesion (Fransen, Decroos, Vande Broek, et al., under review; Price & Weiss, 2011)

Social capital

The third characteristic of highly resilient teams is the existence of high-quality interactions and caring relationships within the team, also called the social capital of a team (Morgan et al., 2013). Resilient teams develop emotional bonds, because of which players accept their teammates, regardless of individual differences. Furthermore, this strong emotional bond and closeness between team members will give players the feeling that they can rely on each other and that teammates would provide assistance if needed.

This social support and advice of peers is also captured as team-member exchange (TMX; Seers, 1989). TMX is a unidimensional concept that represents an individual's overall perception of exchanges with other members of the team. This exchange can vary in terms of the content and process of exchange. In the case of low TMX, exchanges are limited to what is required for the completion of the task. High TMX on the other hand involves the exchange of resources, assistance, and support that extends beyond what is necessary for task completion (Liden, Wayne, & Sparrowe, 2000). High TMX is related to offering work-related expertise and providing feedback. As such, TMX has been argued to provide the necessary conditions for team members to experience a sense of meaning and impact (Liden et al., 2000).

People often turn to peers for guidance and support, especially if they experience difficult and challenging situations (e.g., Baumeister & Leary, 1995). It has been demonstrated, however, that there is substantial variability in the degree of assistance and support that people receive from peers, as evidenced from research on TMX (Seers, 1989). The social support and cooperation found in high TMX environments are expected to help in maintaining balance and control over challenging circumstances. Indeed, TMX provides task-related and social support to individuals (Murphy, Wayne, Liden, & Erdogan, 2003), which has been shown to buffer the negative effects of several stressors (e.g., Cobb, 1976; House & Wells, 1978).

In order for TMX to fully develop, trust is essential. Mike Herbert, former head coach of the American volleyball team, emphasized the importance of trust in dealing with conflicts as follows:

> As I look back on the conflicts we encountered, it is clear to me that all of us had benefitted from our earlier work together with the concept of trust. They were learning to trust each other when taking on issues. They were freeing themselves of the fear of retaliation that often accompanies such intimate discussions. We were able to arrive at a full awareness of both the problem and a solution without having to waste time tiptoeing around the issue. We trusted each other to refrain from unfairly exposing each other to ridicule. We trusted each other to leave individual agendas behind and to contribute to the dialogue in an open and unselfish fashion. All of this was possible only because sufficient levels of trust were in place. Regardless of how talented your players are, a positive environment that includes a solid mutual trust among everyone involved with the program is vital for your program both on and off the court. When I am asked to reveal the secret to my past success, I could answer that I was an exceptional skill trainer, a tactical genius, a thorough game planner, and a great motivational speaker, but I don't. Instead, I tell them the truth: I spent most of my time trying to get people to learn how to trust. All of the other elements are important, but trust is the one variable without which the entire program-building effort would collapse.
>
> (Herbert, 2014, p. 87)

To develop trusting relationships within sport environments, a *safety climate* needs to be established, characterized by mutual respect and understanding, in which players feel sufficiently safe to freely voice their opinion. Respect and understanding link to an important antecedent of trust, that is, integrity (Mayer, Davis, & Schoorman, 1995). Benevolence (i.e., the extent to which players care for each other's welfare and competence) together with the extent to which players are considered qualified and competent equally contribute to trust development. Players look for these properties to make estimates of how much others can be trusted. Such a climate will emphasize players' feeling of being united and forms a warm environment to positively deal with intra-team conflicts.

Finally, fostering team members' identification with the team has also been found to positively predict team resilience. That is, research has demonstrated that coaches and athlete leaders who were able to strengthen the players' team identification also strengthened their confidence in the team's abilities and in attaining their goals (Fransen, Coffee, et al., 2014; Steffens, Haslam, Reicher, et al., 2014). In turn, this stronger feeling of connection with the team resulted in an improved performance (Fransen, Haslam, et al., 2015; Fransen, Steffens, et al., 2015).

Team confidence

The fourth, and final, characteristic of team environments that effectively withstand stressors is team confidence. When coaches express confidence in their team, the athletes will be inclined to have confidence as well (Fransen, Vanbeselaere, et al., 2015). Not only the coaches, but the athlete leaders also have an important responsibility in being a role model for their team. It has been shown that when athlete leaders expressed high confidence in their team, this confidence spread throughout the team. As a result, their teammates were also highly confident in the abilities of their team and, as a consequence, their performance increased. In contrast, when athlete leaders expressed that they lost confidence in their team's chances, their behavior negatively affected teammates' team confidence and their performance decreased (Fransen, Haslam, et al., 2015; Fransen, Steffens, et al., 2015).

Conclusion

In this chapter, we have outlined how coaches can create a climate of shared leadership, how coaches together with their athlete leaders can instigate a sense of "us" among team members, and how coaches can make their team more resilient when obstacles are encountered. Although these are important tools for coaches to create an optimal team environment, they do not guarantee stability. Instead, in sport organizations conflict is inevitable and may damage the optimal team environment. However, group conflict is not by definition positive or negative for team development. Rather, the way in which the team deals with these conflicts is crucial for the outcome (Martin, Bruner, Eys, & Spink, 2014). In this

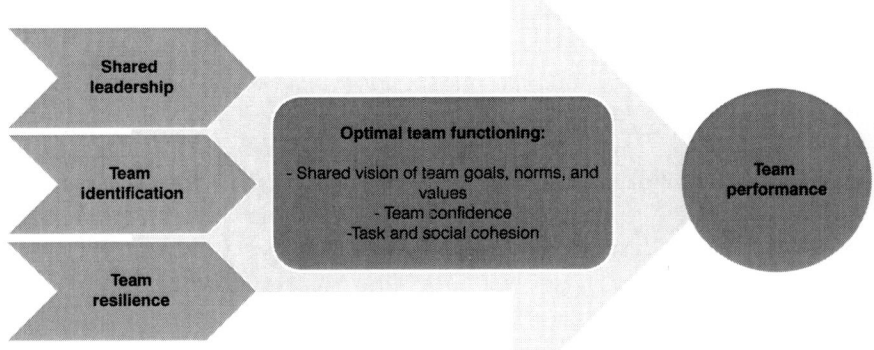

FIGURE 12.2 A model of shared leadership, team identification, and team resilience as predictors of optimal team functioning and performance

regard, the four characteristics of highly resilient teams provide valuable tools for coaches to prevent or effectively handle the conflicts that will arise throughout the development process of a team environment. When conflict is handled well, it might even prove to be valuable for the development of the team.

Highly resilient teams that have a clearly established structure of shared leadership, and in which the players strongly identify with their team are characterized by several strengths, as summarized in Figure 12.2. For example, an effective structure of shared athlete leadership will promote a shared vision with regard to the goals, norms, and values of the team. The associated responsibility will foster athletes' motivation and their commitment to achieve the team goals, thereby enhancing the team performance environment (Nicolaides et al., 2014). In addition, a strong identification with the team will foster players' adherence to these team norms (Spears, Doosje, & Ellemers, 1999), and also players' team confidence (Fransen, Coffee, et al., 2014; Fransen, Decroos, Vanbeselaere, et al., 2015; Fransen, Haslam, et al., 2015), the team's task and social cohesion (De Backer et al., 2011; Fransen, Decroos, Vande Broek, et al., under review), the team's optimal functioning (Martin et al., 2014), and eventually the team performance (Fransen, Haslam, et al., 2015; Fransen, Steffens, et al., 2015; Lembke & Wilson, 1998). To summarize, by facilitating shared leadership, via the creation of a shared sense of "us" within the team and organization by fostering performance team resilience, coaches can establish an optimal environment for team functioning, in good times, but also when facing obstacles or setbacks.

Key messages for future research and practice:

- Although most research has focused on the coach as the only leader of the team, an emerging trend towards the importance of shared leadership can

be observed: leadership is no longer restricted to one person but can be shared within the team.
- It is crucial that organizations maintain a positive environment when the performance of thr team faces challenges or setbacks. Hence, research attention should be dedicated to the development of characteristics associated with highly resilient team environments.
- Coach and athlete leaders have different influences on athletes and teams. Further research is required to establish the effectiveness and efficacy of longitudinal interventions to explore the development of these effects.
- The coach can facilitate the team's performance by optimizing the following factors: (1) the coach as facilitator of shared leadership; (2) the coach as identity manager; and (3) the coach as conflict manager to create highly resilient teams.

References

Baumeister, R. F., & Leary, M. R. (1995). The need to belong: Desire for interpersonal attachments as a fundamental human motivation. *Psychological Bulletin, 117*(3), 497–529. doi: 10.1037/0033-2909.117.3.497.

Beauchamp, M. R., Bray, S. R., Eys, M. A., & Carron, A. V. (2005). Multidimensional role ambiguity and role satisfaction: A prospective examination using interdependent sport teams. *Journal of Applied Social Psychology, 35*(12), 2560–2576. doi: 10.1111/j.1559-1816.2005.tb02114.x.

Benson, A. J., Eys, M., Surya, M., Dawson, K., & Schneider, M. (2013). Athletes' perceptions of role acceptance in interdependent sport teams. *The Sport Psychologist, 27*(3), 269–280.

Bray, S. R., & Brawley, L. R. (2002). Role efficacy, role clarity, and role performance effectiveness. *Small Group Research, 33*(2), 233–253. doi: 10.1177/104649640203300204.

Carron, A. V., Widmeyer, W. N., & Brawley, L. R. (1985). The development of an instrument to assess cohesion in sport teams – The Group Environment Questionnaire. *Journal of Sport Psychology, 7*(3), 244–266.

Cobb, S. (1976). Social support as a moderator of life stress. *Psychosomatic Medicine, 38*(5), 300–314.

Cotterill, S. T. (under review). Developing leadership skills in sport: A case study of elite cricketers. *International Journal of Sport and Exercise Psychology*.

Cotterill, S. T., & Fransen, K. (2016). Athlete leadership in sport teams: Current understanding and future directions. *International Review of Sport and Exercise Psychology, 9*, 116–133.

De Backer, M., Boen, F., Ceux, T., De Cuyper, B., Hoigaard, R., Callens, F., . . . Vande Broek, G. (2011). Do perceived justice and need support of the coach predict team identification and cohesion? Testing their relative importance among top volleyball and handball players in Belgium and Norway. *Psychology of Sport and Exercise, 12*(2), 192–201. doi: 10.1016/j.psychsport.2010.09.009.

Deci, E. L., & Ryan, R. M. (1985). *Intrinsic motivation and self-determination in human behavior*. New York: Plenum.

Dupuis, M., Bloom, G. A., & Loughead, T. M. (2006). Team captains' perceptions of athlete leadership. *Journal of Sport Behavior, 29*(1), 60–78.

Eys, M. A., & Carron, A. V. (2001). Role ambiguity, task cohesion, and task self-efficacy. *Small Group Research, 32*(3), 356–373. doi: 10.1177/104649640103200305.

Eys, M. A., Carron, A. V., Bray, S. R., & Beauchamp, M. R. (2003). Role ambiguity and athlete satisfaction. *Journal of Sports Sciences, 21*(5), 391–401. doi: 10.1080/0264041031000071137.

Fransen, K. (2014). Athlete leaders as key figures for optimal team functioning: The mediating role of players' team confidence and their team identification. Doctoral dissertation, KU Leuven, Leuven.

Fransen, K., Coffee, P., Vanbeselaere, N., Slater, M., De Cuyper, B., & Boen, F. (2014). The impact of athlete leaders on team members' team outcome confidence: A test of mediation by team identification and collective efficacy. *The Sport Psychologist, 28*(4), 347–360. doi: 10.1123/tsp.2013-0141.

Fransen, K., Decroos, S., Vande Broek, G., & Boen, F. (2015). Leading from the top or leading from within? A comparison between coaches' and athletes' leadership as predictors of team identification, team confidence, and team cohesion. *International Journal of Sports Science and Coaching*.

Fransen, K., Haslam, S. A., Steffens, N. K., Vanbeselaere, N., De Cuyper, B., & Boen, F. (2015). Believing in us: Exploring leaders' capacity to enhance team confidence and performance by building a sense of shared social identity. *Journal of Experimental Psychology: Applied, 21*(1), 89–100. doi: 10.1037/xap0000033.

Fransen, K., Steffens, N. K., Haslam, S. A., Vanbeselaere, N., Vande Broek, G., & Boen, F. (2015). We will be champions: Leaders' confidence in "us" inspires team members' team confidence and performance. *Scandinavian Journal of Medicine & Science in Sports*. Published ahead of print. doi: 10.1111/sms.12603.

Fransen, K., Van Puyenbroeck, S., Loughead, T. M., Vanbeselaere, N., De Cuyper, B., Vande Broek, G., & Boen, F. (2015a). The art of athlete leadership: Identifying high-quality leadership at the individual and team level through social network analysis. *Journal of Sport & Exercise Psychology, 37*(3), 274–290. doi: 10.1123/jsep.2014-0259.

Fransen, K., Van Puyenbroeck, S., Loughead, T. M., Vanbeselaere, N., De Cuyper, B., Vande Broek, G., & Boen, F. (2015b). Who takes the lead? Social network analysis as pioneering tool to investigate shared leadership within sports teams. *Social Networks, 43*, 28–38. doi: 10.1016/j.socnet.2015.04.003.

Fransen, K., Vanbeselaere, N., De Cuyper, B., Vande Broek, G., & Boen, F. (2014). The myth of the team captain as principal leader: Extending the athlete leadership classification within sport teams. *Journal of Sports Sciences, 32*(14), 1389–1397. doi: 10.1080/02640414.2014.891291.

Fransen, K., Vanbeselaere, N., De Cuyper, B., Vande Broek, G., & Boen, F. (2015). Perceived sources of team confidence in soccer and basketball. *Medicine & Science in Sports & Exercise, 47*(7), 1470–1484. doi: 10.1249/MSS.0000000000000561.

Fransen, K., Vanbeselaere, N., Exadaktylos, V., Vande Broek, G., De Cuyper, B., Berckmans, D. … Boen, F. (2012). "Yes, we can!": Perceptions of collective efficacy sources in volleyball. *Journal of Sports Sciences, 30*(7), 641–649. doi: 10.1080/02640414.2011.653579.

Fransen, K., Vande Broek, G., Vansteenkiste, M., & Boen, F. (2015). *The crucial role of competence support by athlete leaders: An experimental test in a soccer context*. Manuscript submitted for publication.

Fransen, K., Decroos, S., Vande Broek, G., Boen, F. (in press). Leading from the top or leading from within? A comparison between coaches' and athletes' leadership as predictors of team identification, team confidence, and team cohesion. *International Journal of Sports Science and Coaching*.

Gould, D., & Voelker, D. K. (2010). Youth sport leadership development: Leveraging the sports captaincy experience. *Journal of Sport Psychology in Action, 1*(1), 1–14. doi: 10.1080/21520704.2010.497695.

Grandzol, C., Perlis, S., & Draina, L. (2010). Leadership development of team captains in collegiate varsity athletics. *Journal of College Student Development, 51*(4), 403–418.

Haslam, S. A. (2001). *Psychology in organizations: The social identity approach*. London: Sage.

Haslam, S. A., & Reicher, S. (2006). Stressing the group: Social identity and the unfolding dynamics of responses to stress. *Journal of Applied Psychology, 91*(5), 1037–1052. doi: 10.1037/0021-9010.91.5.1037.

Haslam, S. A., Reicher, S. D., & Platow, M. J. (2011). *The new psychology of leadership: Identity, influence and power*. New York: Psychology Press.

Herbert, M. (2014). *Thinking volleyball*. Champaign, IL: Human Kinetics.

House, J. S., & Wells, J. A. (1978). Occupational stress, social support, and health. In A. McLean, G. Black & M. Colligan (Eds.), *Reducing occupational stress: Proceedings of a conference* (pp. 78–140). Washington, DC: HEW (NIOSH) Publication.

Kirkman, B. L., & Rosen, B. (1999). Beyond self-management: Antecedents and consequences of team empowerment. *The Academy of Management Journal, 42*(1), 58–74. doi: 10.2307/256874.

Krzyzewski, M. (2009). *The gold standard: Building a world-class team*. New York: Buisness Plus.

Langfred, C. W. (2000). The paradox of self-management: Individual and group autonomy in work groups. *Journal of Organizational Behavior, 21*(5), 563–585.

Lembke, S., & Wilson, M. (1998). Putting the "team" into teamwork: Alternative theoretical contributions for contemporary management practice. *Human Relations, 51*(7), 927–944. doi: 10.1023/a:1016951611667.

Levine, M., Prosser, A., Evans, D., & Reicher, S. (2005). Identity and emergency intervention: How social group membership and inclusiveness of group boundaries shape helping behavior. *Personality and Social Psychology Bulletin, 31*(4), 443–453. doi: 10.1177/0146167204271651.

Liden, R. C., Wayne, S. J., & Bradway, L. K. (1997). Task interdependence as a moderator of the relation between group control and performance. *Human Relations, 50*(2), 169–181. doi: 10.1023/A:1016921920501.

Liden, R. C., Wayne, S. J., & Sparrowe, R. T. (2000). An examination of the mediating role of psychological empowerment on the relations between the job, interpersonal relationships, and work outcomes. *Journal of Applied Psychology, 85*(3), 407–416. doi: 10.1037/0021-9010.85.3.407.

Loughead, T. M., Fransen, K., Van Puyenbroeck, S., Hoffmann, M. D., & Boen, F. (under review). *An examination of the relationship between athlete leadership and cohesion using social network analysis*. Manuscript submitted for publication.

Loughead, T. M., & Hardy, J. (2005). An examination of coach and peer leader behaviors in sport. *Psychology of Sport and Exercise, 6*(3), 303–312. doi: 10.1016/j.psychsport.2004.02.001.

Manz, C. C., & Sims, H. P., Jr. (1987). Leading workers to lead themselves: The external leadership of self-managing work teams. *Administrative Science Quarterly, 32*(1), 106–129. doi: 10.2307/2392745.

Martin, L., Bruner, M., Eys, M., & Spink, K. (2014). The social environment in sport: Selected topics. *International Review of Sport and Exercise Psychology, 7*(1), 87–105. doi: 10.1080/1750984x.2014.885553.

Mayer, D. M., Kuenzi, M., Greenbaum, R., Bardes, M., & Salvador, R. (2009). How low does ethical leadership flow? Test of a trickle-down model. *Organizational Behavior and Human Decision Processes, 108*(1), 1–13. doi: 10.1016/j.obhdp.2008.04.002.

Mayer, R. C., Davis, J. H., & Schoorman, F. D. (1995). An integrative model of organizational trust. *The Academy of Management Review, 20*(3), 709–734. doi: 10.2307/258792.

Morgan, P. B. C., Fletcher, D., & Sarkar, M. (2013). Defining and characterizing team resilience in elite sport. *Psychology of Sport and Exercise, 14*(4), 549–559. doi: 10.1016/j.psychsport.2013.01.004.

Morgeson, F. P. (2005). The external leadership of self-managing teams: Intervening in the context of novel and disruptive events. *Journal of Applied Psychology, 90*(3), 497–508. doi: 10.1037/0021-9010.90.3.497.

Morrison, E. W. (2011). Employee voice behavior: Integration and directions for future research. *The Academy of Management Annals, 5*(1), 373–412. doi: 10.1080/19416520.2011.574506.

Mosher, M. (1979). The team captain. *Volleyball Technical Journal, 4,* 7–8.

Mumford, M. D., Friedrich, T. L., Vessey, W. B., & Ruark, G. A. (2012). Collective leadership: Thinking about issues vis-à-vis others. *Industrial and Organizational Psychology, 5*(4), 408–411. doi: 10.1111/j.1754-9434.2012.01469.x.

Murphy, S. M., Wayne, S. J., Liden, R. C., & Erdogan, B. (2003). Understanding social loafing: The role of justice perceptions and exchange relationships. *Human Relations, 56*(1), 61–84. doi: 10.1177/0018726703056001450.

Nicolaides, V. C., LaPort, K. A., Chen, T. R., Tomassetti, A. J., Weis, E. J., Zaccaro, S. J., & Cortina, J. M. (2014). The shared leadership of teams: A meta-analysis of proximal, distal, and moderating relationships. *The Leadership Quarterly, 25*(5), 923–942. doi: 10.1016/j.leaqua.2014.06.006.

Price, M. S., & Weiss, M. R. (2011). Peer leadership in sport: Relationships among personal characteristics, leader behaviors, and team outcomes. *Journal of Applied Sport Psychology, 23*(1), 49–64. doi: 10.1080/10413200.2010.520300.

Price, M. S., & Weiss, M. R. (2013). Relationships among coach leadership, peer leadership, and adolescent athletes' psychosocial and team outcomes: A test of transformational leadership theory. *Journal of Applied Sport Psychology, 25*(2), 265–279. doi: 10.1080/10413200.2012.725703.

Quick, T., L. (1992). *Successful team building.* New York: AMACOM American Management Association.

Rees, T., Haslam, S. A., Coffee, P., & Lavallee, D. (2015). A social identity approach to sport psychology: Principles, practice, and prospects. *Sports Medecine, 45*(8), 1083–1096. doi: 10.1007/s40279-015-0345-4.

Seers, A. (1989). Team-member exchange quality: A new construct for role-making research. *Organizational Behavior and Human Decision Processes, 43*(1), 118–135. doi: 10.1016/0749-5978(89)90060-5.

Smith, M. J., Arthur, C. A., Hardy, J., Callow, N., & Williams, D. (2013). Transformational leadership and task cohesion in sport: The mediating role of intrateam communication. *Psychology of Sport and Exercise, 14*(2), 249–257. doi: 10.1016/j.psychsport.2012.10.002.

Spears, R., Doosje, B., & Ellemers, N. (1999). Commitment and the context of social perception. In N. Ellemers, R. Spears, & B. Doosje (Eds.), *Social identity: Context, commitment, content* (pp. 59–83). Oxford: Blackwell.

Steffens, N. K., Haslam, S. A., & Reicher, S. D. (2014). Up close and personal: Evidence that shared social identity is a basis for the "special" relationship that binds followers to leaders. *The Leadership Quarterly, 25,* 296–313. doi: 10.1016/j.leaqua.2013.08.008.

Steffens, N. K., Haslam, S. A., Reicher, S. D., Platow, M. J., Fransen, K., Yang, J., . . . Boen, F. (2014). Leadership as social identity management: Introducing the Identity

Leadership Inventory (ILI) to assess and validate a four-dimensional model. *The Leadership Quarterly, 25*, 1001–1024. doi: 10.1016/j.leaqua.2014.05.002.

Sullivan, P. J., & Feltz, D. L. (2003). The preliminary development of the scale for effective communication in team sports (SECTS). *Journal of Applied Social Psychology, 33*(8), 1693–1715. doi: 10.1111/j.1559-1816.2003.tb01970.x.

Tajfel, H., & Turner, J. C. (1979). An integrative theory of intergroup conflict. In W. G. Austin & S. Worchel (Eds.), *The social psychology of intergroup relations* (pp. 33–47). Monterey, CA: Brooks-Cole.

Turner, J. C. (1982). Towards a redefinition of the social group. In H. Tajfel (Ed.), *Social identity and intergroup relations* (pp. 15–40). Cambridge: Cambridge University Press.

Turner, J. C., Hogg, M. A., Oakes, P. J., Reicher, S. D., & Wetherell, M. S. (1987). *Rediscovering the social group: A self-categorization theory*. Oxford: Blackwell.

Turner, J. C., Hogg, M. A., Turner, P. J., & Smith, P. M. (1984). Failure and defeat as determinants of group cohesiveness. *British Journal of Social Psychology, 23*(2), 97–111. doi: 10.1111/j.2044-8309.1984.tb00619.x.

Voelker, D. K., Gould, D., & Crawford, M. J. (2011). Understanding the experience of high school sport captains. *The Sport Psychologist, 25*(1), 47–66.

Wang, D., Waldman, D. A., & Zhang, Z. (2014). A meta-analysis of shared leadership and team effectiveness. *Journal of Applied Psychology, 99*(2), 181–198. doi: 10.1037/a0034531.

Wann, D. L., & Branscombe, N. R. (1990). Die-hard and fair-weather fans: Effects of identification on BIRGing and CORFing tendencies. *Journal of Sport & Social Issues, 14*(2), 103–117. doi: 10.1177/019372359001400203.

Wo, D., Ambrose, M., & Schminke, M. (2015). What drives trickle-down effects? A test of multiple mediation processes. *Academy of Management Journal, 58*(6), 1848–1868. doi: 10.5465/amj.2013.0670

13

"WE ARE IN THIS TOGETHER"

A social identity perspective on change and conflict management

Matthew J. Slater, Jamie B. Barker, and Stephen D. Mellalieu

Introduction

Change and conflict are influential across individual, intra-group, inter-group, and organizational levels. In this chapter we draw on one of the most prominent psychosocial paradigms of intra- and inter-group relations to emanate from organizational psychology to develop our understanding of change and conflict management. That is, the social identity approach. Theoretically and practically, the social identity approach has much to contribute to the continually changing landscape of elite sport (see, for an example, Slater, Coffee, Barker, & Evans, 2014). Prior to reviewing social identity literature we first introduce the growing salience of change and conflict management in elite sport.

Change and conflict management

Change is inherent in elite sport as organizations strive for continued improvement and, ultimately, success (Wagstaff, Gilmore, & Thelwell, 2015). In addition, the structures and layers within organizations themselves are becoming more complex due to, for example, innovations in sport science and medicine. It follows that there is much work to be done, first, to mitigate the negative effect of change on individuals (e.g., to protect against the brittle psychological contract that staff perceive can be created by change; Wagstaff et al. 2015) and, second, to optimize group functioning by harnessing the energies (e.g., mobilization of effort, cooperation) of organizations to allow them to thrive during change (see, for a broader review, Wagstaff, Fletcher, & Hanton, 2012). Indeed, the immediate, frequent, and unambiguous feedback in elite sport may be a key influence in why change occurs so often, bringing positive organizational change into sharp focus.

Preliminary investigations of organizational change in elite sport (e.g., Gilmore, 2009; Wagstaff et al., 2015) have broadly reported the negative impact of change on sporting organizations. Nevertheless, growing research in elite sport indicates that adversity can be a catalyst for team resilience if managed appropriately (e.g., Morgan, Fletcher, & Sarkar, 2015). By providing a social identity perspective on change at the organizational level, this chapter aims to provide some steps to reverse the negative perceptions of organizational change. Although the primary focus of this chapter is on managing change from a social identity perspective, we also discuss the topic of conflict as an inevitable consequence of organizational change and offer a discussion of ways in which it can be managed.

The social identity approach

The social identity approach is a term used to encapsulate both social identity (Tajfel & Turner, 1979) and self-categorization theories (Turner, Hogg, Oakes, Reicher, & Wetherell, 1987). Originating from "minimal group" studies (e.g., Tajfel, 1970) that sought to better understand inter-group discrimination, the social identity approach posits that in addition to one's personal identity – an individual's distinct and unique personality (i.e., "I" and "me") – individuals define themselves through a range of social identities (i.e., "we" and "us"). Defined, social identity refers to an "individual's knowledge that he [or she] belongs to certain social groups together with some emotional value and significance to him [or her] of this group membership" (Tajfel, 1972, p. 292). In other words, social identities reflect individuals' internalized group memberships (e.g., a university employee, an athlete in a sports team, or a member of a walking group). Further, Cameron (2004) proposed social identity to be a multidimensional construct comprised of three elements: cognitive centrality; in-group affect; and in-group ties. Cognitive centrality refers to the relative importance placed by the individual on their group membership (e.g., the university employee may indicate that their affiliation with the university is extremely important to them). In-group affect refers to the positive emotions experienced by an individual in correspondence with one's group membership (e.g., the athlete emotes joy and pride when their sports team wins). In-group ties refer to the strength of connection and belonging felt by the individual with others in the group (e.g., the walking club member feels strong connections with their peers and this facilitates high levels of social support; Haslam & Reicher, 2006). As alluded to here, a high level of social identification has been reported to have positive ramifications (e.g., increased social support). Social identity scholars (e.g., Haslam, 2004) posit that this occurs because individuals derive a sense of who they are (e.g., self-concept) from their social identities (e.g., "we" are a successful team). Accordingly, those that psychologically connect with a group will be motivated to enhance their group in a way that places the group as positive, unique, and long-lasting. In sum, social identities help individuals increase their self-esteem, invest in group-orientated behaviors, have meaning in their lives, feel a sense of belonging, and raise their aspirations (Mael & Ashforth, 2001).

According to the social identity approach, the group and contextual processes outlined above reflect primary principles that are pertinent for scholars and practitioners to understand to enhance individual and group cognition, functioning, and performance (Haslam, 2014). It is along similar lines that scholars in sport and exercise psychology have noted the "myth of individualism" (Wagstaff & Larner, 2015). As Wagstaff and Larner explain, the myth of individualism refers to the misconception that sport performance is determined in its entirety by individual talent and effort. The shortcomings of this individualistic approach have been echoed too by prominent social identity theorists. Specifically, over a decade ago, in his text *Psychology in organizations: The social identity approach,* Alexander Haslam (2004) stated "in order to fully understand perception and interaction in organizational contexts, we must do more than study the psychology of individuals *as individuals*. Instead, we need to understand how social interaction is bound up within individuals' *social identities*" (p. 17, emphasis in original). Fortunately, empirical examination of individuals' social identities, including associated individual- and group-level ramifications, have been subject to over four decades of scholarly activity within the social identity tradition. It is beyond the scope of the current chapter to cover all this body of literature but it is hoped that what is presented will stimulate perusals into further scholarly work as well as future research endeavors in sport settings.

The role of social identities has been examined across clinical, health, and organizational domains (see, for reviews, Haslam, 2004; 2014). Broadly, evidence within the social identity tradition has led to an enhanced understanding of the social psychological processes that provide the foundation for individual and team functioning. Typically, high levels of social identification have been found to predict a positive and adaptive psychological approach (e.g., buffer against stress; Haslam, O'Brien, Jetten, Vormedal, & Penna, 2005, and reduce burnout; Haslam, Jetten, & Waghorn, 2009). For instance, social identity has been claimed to be crucial in the development and resolution of clinical depression (Cruwys, Haslam, Dingle, Haslam, & Jetten, 2014). In a review of the burgeoning literature, Cruwys and colleagues (2014) concluded identification with meaningful groups predicts lower levels of depression. At a group level, high levels of social identity typically have a positive effect on indicators known to be crucial for team functioning, including cohesion (e.g., Anastasio, Bachman, Gaertner, & Dovidio, 1997) and collective efficacy (e.g., Fransen et al., 2014). Accordingly in sport psychology literature, there is growing attention from researchers regarding the contribution of the social identity perspective, particularly speaking to the point of building upon individualistic approaches and focusing on the internalized group memberships within which athletes (e.g., Bruner, Broadley, & Côté, 2014) and performance directors (e.g., Slater, Barker, Coffee, & Jones, 2015) operate.

Organizationally, social identity principles are of interest because individuals connect with groups across a range of levels from discipline teams (e.g., the sport scientists and medics within a sport organization), through department teams (e.g., the science and medicine team within a sport organization), to the organization themselves (e.g., the holistic sports club or body). Understanding, integrating, and enhancing these multi-level social identities is a key ingredient for effective change management. Indeed, Slater, Evans, and Turner (2016) propose that change is likely to disrupt internalized group memberships in a manner that has individual-, group-, and organizational-level implications.

Individually, losing internalized group memberships can have deleterious effects. In addition to reducing the pertinent group functioning variables discussed thus far (e.g., social support, cohesion, and collective efficacy), researchers have reported that threatening group memberships (or simply imagining losing a social identity) leads individuals to report reduced clarity in their self-concept and an associated decrease in self-esteem (Slotter, Winger, & Soto, 2015). Taken together with data indicating that strong team identification leads to maintained well-being following adversity (Inoue, Wann, Funk, Yoshida, & Nakazawa, 2015) and is a characteristic of resilient teams (Morgan et al., 2015), it is clear disruptions to social identities may have negative implications for organizational performance through not only reduced team functioning and resilience, but also via individuals' mental health in those employees affected by change. To alleviate such concerns, Slater et al. (2016) suggested that to implement change effectively key stakeholders could seek to understand and work with the social identities of the affected employees. This is because, based on social identity theorizing, individuals intrinsically invest in their group memberships and see the fate of the group as their own. Therefore, working with (as opposed to working hierarchically over, or neglecting) group identities, where the vision of change is to invest in and empower the collective organization to mobilize their resources, is more likely to facilitate effective change. Evidence has indicated such a "power through", rather than "power over", approach (see, for a review, Turner, 2005) is a more beneficial and sustainable option for leadership generally and following repeated group failure (Slater, Coffee, Barker, Haslam, & Steffens, under review). Thus, individuals in positions of power and influence must act with caution given the dynamics of change and conflict management. For instance, splitting apart groups where members derive a strong sense of themselves (e.g., by being part of a particular sport organization) could be expected to cause conflict and, in turn, may direct individuals to act as *individuals* (i.e., for their own personal gain rather than the sport organization's).

In sum, though perceptions of stakeholders in elite sport may suggest the opposite (Wagstaff et al., 2015), change does have the potential to be seen positively (Wagstaff, Gilmore, & Thelwell, 2016). In particular, change is an opportunity to reflect, and sequentially develop further, the psychological belonging between individuals.

Mechanisms to promote social identities

> The power of groups is unlocked by working with social identities not across or against them.
>
> (Haslam, 2014, p. 8)

Having observed that social identities are meaningful and matter in organizations it is perhaps no surprise that promoting social identities may be a valuable mechanism through which to implement change and deal with conflict. The quote at the start of this section is taken from Haslam's (2014) landmark article centered on making good theory practical. Haslam (2014) noted that despite four decades of social identity research surrounding the importance of internalized group memberships, it is only more recently that the application and utility of the social identity approach has gained attention from scholars and practitioners. Accordingly, and building on the discussion to this point, in this section we identify and explain mechanisms through which effective change management may be facilitated with a view to optimize organizational functioning. To this end, the discussion first introduces the broad framework of the 4Rs (reflecting, representing, realizing, and reappraisal; Slater et al., 2016), before delineating the ASPIRe model (actualizing social and personal identity resources; Haslam, Eggins, & Reynolds, 2003) as a specific organizational-level intervention.

The 4Rs: reflecting, representing, realizing, and reappraisal

Initially, Haslam, Reicher, and Platow (2011) conceptualized the 3Rs framework of reflection, representation, and realization, as a sequential leadership development program. Building on this, Slater et al. (2016) proposed the 3Rs approach could be a valuable developmental framework to create unique and distinctive social identities during change. Further, as an extension of the 3Rs, the authors suggested a fourth R (reappraisal) with the view of optimizing group and individual responses to the ubiquitous stress experienced during change. Consistent with social identity principles discussed thus far, Slater et al. highlighted the contribution of the 4R framework through the underpinning tenet that "the creation of a unified collective entity can be best nurtured by working *through* the group, rather than imposing broad changes or specific new values *over* the group" (p. 12).

For detailed processes within the 4R's, readers are directed to Slater et al. (2016), but in brief there are four objectives. First, the purpose of reflection is to involve all members of the organization to identify what identities matter to individuals within the organizational context. Second, the purpose of representation is to establish shared characteristics (i.e., values) of the collective identity that can be championed. Third, the purpose of realization is to collectively plan and engage with activities and strategy for the organization to live out its identity in reality. Finally, it is proposed the creation of a distinctive and shared social identity, through reflecting, representing, and realizing, facilitates group members' cognitive reappraisal of the inherent stress during change. Aligned with the 4Rs as a broad developmental framework, the ASPIRe model (Haslam et al., 2003) provides a specific intervention that has been proposed to facilitate organizational practices.

The ASPIRe model

In 2003, based the on social identity approach, Haslam and colleagues conceptualized the ASPIRe model for use in organizations. The purpose of the ASPIRe model is to harness individuals' personal and social identity resources to, in turn, generate optimal employee satisfaction, performance, and well-being (Haslam et al., 2003). The program passes through sequential processes; first, promoting employees' personal identities, through subgroup identities, to an organizational identity. It is argued that the incremental nature of the process allows for diversity to be acknowledged and embraced as nuanced contributions to "our" distinct group identity (and subsequent organizational identity). In sum, employees move or transition from their unique personal identity, which they do not share, to a group and organizational identity, which they do.

In brief, the ASPIRe model incorporates four phases: ascertaining identity resources (AIRing); subgroup caucusing (Sub-Casing); superordinate concensualizing (Super-Casing); and organic goal setting (ORGanizing). Readers are referred to Haslam and colleagues' (2003) seminal article for a detailed discussion of the ASPIRe model process, but what follows is a brief overview applied to sport. In the AIRing stage all individuals (i.e., staff and athletes) associated with the sport organization identify the identities that are relevant (i.e., psychologically salient) for them within the context of the organization. This may include elements of one's personal identity in addition to salient social identities with a view to establishing the social identities that are relevant for work practices. For example, the head coach may define themselves within the coaching group (along with other coaches, e.g., goalkeeping coach), the staffing group (along with other staff, e.g., physiotherapists), and the organization (along with all athletes and staff within the organization). Accordingly, following the AIRing stage, the organization can be divided by these meaningful subgroups that incorporate everyone at the club, with a view to: (a) maximize the differences between groups; and (b) minimize the differences within groups. This foundational phase is often overlooked during times of change management, particularly within inherent time constraints; however, it is arguably the most important phase. It lays the foundations for work to come. Evidence pertaining to this point has been reported by Eggins, O'Brien, Reynolds, Haslam, and Crocker (2008) indicating that when individuals are given the opportunity to specify the groups with which they identify (as they do during the AIRing phase), the groups reported by employees often diverge from how managers cluster employees together (e.g., via the employee role or responsibility). Further, personal-disclosure mutual-sharing (PDMS; Dunn & Holt, 2004), a team-orientated intervention familiar to the applied sport psychology literature, may have utility as a vehicle within the AIRing phase.

The next stage, of Sub-Casing, involves internal discussions within the identified subgroups to agree on collective goals, identify potential barriers to these goals, and, ultimately, begin the development of a shared identity to be carried forward. Continuing with the example of a head coach, a subgroup of coaches would consider, what is "our" identity as coaches in this sport organization? Importantly, individuals are empowered to do this in a bottom-up manner, allowing them to intertwine salient personal identity differences within their subgroup identity if desired. Still operating within the rubric of the organization, the subgroup identity created is likely to have prior meaning; nevertheless creativity in the development of values and emphasizing differences between subgroups is encouraged (Haslam et al., 2003) and may be in sharp focus during change. Third, Super-Casing brings these subgroup identities together to establish shared goals and develop an organizational identity. For example, the subgroup of coaches would come together with other staff and athlete subgroups to understand the overarching organizational identity and goals emanating from these subgroups. It is proposed, and recent evidence supports the hypothesis, that individuals are more likely to internalize the organizational identity and goals because they incorporate subgroup differences (Peters, Haslam, Ryan, & Fonseca, 2012). The final stage, ORGanizing, involves making decisions regarding which goals that were established during Super-Casing should be taken forward. Once agreed, plans and structures are developed to progress "us" towards the fulfillment of the organizational identity. Leadership processes particularly come to the fore in the final stage where decision makers evaluate the appropriateness of the organizational goals set, but given the preceding phases, leaders are well-positioned to make decisions in the collective interests – a key principle in creating psychological bonds between leaders and followers (see, for a review in sport, Slater et al., 2014). Practically, the ORGanizing process is a collaborative one, and may include representatives from each subgroup. For example, the performance director may lead a discussion that includes a representative from each subgroup to plan activities to fulfill the prominent organizational goals.

In short, the ASPIRe model may create two inextricably linked social identities for each individual: a subgroup identity (e.g., "us" coaches), and an organizational identity (e.g., "us" as a club). Importantly though, as Haslam and colleagues (2003) stated, "this social identity should *differ* from that which informed the initial AIRing phase in so far as it *builds upon and explicitly recognizes the subgroup identities that emerged during Sub-Casing*" (p. 94, original emphasis). In other words, the ASPIRe model aims to create an organization in which athletes and staff define themselves in terms of a relatively complex organizational-level identity (as members of the focal organizational unit), but are simultaneously aware of the subgroup memberships (e.g., as a coaching team) from which that identity has been forged.

Herein lies one of the main potential contributions of the ASPIRe model. It has been suggested that, "a range of positive organizational outcomes flow from a superordinate organizational identity that recognizes, accommodates, and encourages subgroup identities that reflect the shared self-determined interests and aspirations of employees" (Haslam et al., 2003, p. 101). Indeed, in an investigation with military medics, data suggested that implementing the ASPIRe model increased employees' identification with the subgroup and organization, together with increasing employees' support of organizational strategy (Peters et al., 2012). Such a bottom-up approach is in contrast to other researchers, who have suggested that organizations are more effective when there is a single, top-down, status quo organizational or team identity (e.g., Gaertner, Dovido, Anastasio, Bachman, & Rast, 1993). However, the ASPIRe model is practical and pragmatic in so far as suggesting subgroup identities should be embraced as different and underpinning features of, and functions, within the organizational identity. And yet currently, despite this intervention framework, sport organizations may not have heeded the opportunities. Or, to rearrange the quote with which we started this section (Haslam, 2014), sporting organizations may be yet to fully "unlock the power of groups".

Preparing for a bumpy ride! Managing conflict through change

Changing the social identity of an organization is a challenging process. Indeed, when seeking to foster superordinate organizational and subgroup identities a degree of conflict will occur, both within and across groups. Conflict is itself therefore an inevitable consequence of change within any group of individuals or organization, particularly in sports contexts (Martin, Bruner, Eys, & Spink, 2014). Identifying strategies to manage the conflicts that occur through these periods of change can subsequently offer insight for those individuals tasked with overseeing change within their organization or group.

Conflict is defined as a dynamic process that occurs between interdependent parties as they experience negative emotional reactions to perceived disagreements and interference with the attainment of their goals (Barki & Hartwick, 2004, p. 234), and has been widely reported in a variety of settings (e.g., Deutsch, 1990; Jehn, 1995), including sports teams and organizations (see e.g., Holt, Knight, & Zukiwski, 2012; Mellalieu, Shearer, & Shearer, 2013; Paradis, Carron, & Martin, 2014). The content of the conflict can take many forms including task, relationship, and process (cf. Jehn, 1997). Task conflict exists when disagreements among group members occur in relation to the content of tasks being performed and includes differences in viewpoints, ideas, and opinions. Relationship conflict exists when interpersonal incompatibilities are present among group members. Last, process conflict is present when disagreements arise regarding the manner in which tasks should be delegated and performed. The three forms of conflict can be viewed from an inter- or intra-perspective at both the group and individual level and comprise vertical and horizontal structures (Schermerhorn, Hunt, & Osborn, 2003). Vertical conflict occurs between hierarchical levels in organizations with disagreements often occurring between supervisors and subordinates over a range of issues (e.g., performance, deadlines, goals). Horizontal conflict occurs between persons or groups at the same hierarchical level within an organization and commonly involves goal incompatibilities, interpersonal factors, or scarce resources (Schermerhorn et al., 2003).

When attempting to deal with conflict it is important to first distinguish between the terms "management" and "resolution". Conflict management occurs when the parties in the conflict find a way to contain the conflict, in terms of its frequency, intensity, duration, or other ways (Maoz, Mintz, Morgan, Palmer, & Stoll, 2004). In contrast, conflict resolution occurs when all the participants accept a permanent solution to the problem that is the source of the conflict (Maoz et al., 2004). The subtle difference between the two constructs is the acceptance of the individuals involved of a long-term solution, as opposed to a "firefighting" strategy that may merely contain or control the conflict episode at hand. Resolution therefore deals with *both* the issues and the conflictual behavior, whilst management deals more with the resulting outward behavior and subsequent actions (Maoz et al., 204).

While a limited body of knowledge exists that has considered conflict management and resolution in sport (see Mellalieu et al., 2013), a wealth of literature can be sourced from organizational psychology. However, we present a note of caution here when attempting to transfer the principles of organizational psychology research into sport. While such research provides potential insight into the principles of conflict and its consequences in sport, care should be taken before suggesting the value of such principles without consideration of its context, and ultimately the undertaking of sport-specific investigations to substantiate those principles.

When considering literature from the organizational domain, research into conflict strategies has been conceptualized to differ across two dimensions (cf. Blake & Mouton, 1964; Rahim & Buntzman, 1990), comprising concern for self (satisfying own needs) and concern for others (satisfying the needs of others). When these two dimensions are combined, five main strategies are identified: (1) problem-solving – indicative of those who have a high concern for self and the other. Here, common interests are identified via open exchanges of information in order to create integrative solutions that meet both parties' needs; (2) obliging (accommodating, yielding) – indicating a low concern for self but high concern for the other through downplaying differences and stressing commonalties; (3) dominating (competing) – representing a high concern for self and low concern for others, seeking to fulfill one's own interests at the expense of the other; (4) avoiding (withdrawing) – representing a low concern for self and other, with the aim to not acknowledge or enter into the conflict situation; and (5) compromising – a midpoint concern for self and other that seeks to achieve outcomes that meet somewhere in the middle, with both parties gaining some, but not complete, satisfaction.

The large body of literature in organizational psychology suggests that successful individuals are flexible in their approach to conflict management and resolution by assessing the various personal and situational constraints present in the conflict episode (Rahim, 2001). It is also noteworthy to consider that the conflict management process adapted will generally leave a legacy, often termed "sticky" conflict residue, which will, in turn, influence the attitudes of the individuals/groups involved and their subsequent future relations (cf. Rahim, 2001).

A central principle of many conceptual approaches to conflict is that it is prone to escalate (i.e., become more intense, hostile, and competitive). To facilitate thinking regarding how to resolve or manage such conflict, many theorists (e.g., Fisher & Keashly, 1990) "package" conflict into distinct yet related stages in the escalation course, defining each stage by changes in overt behavior, patterns of interaction, perceptions, and attitudes (cf. Fisher, 1990; Glasl, 1982), termed *discussion*, *polarization*, *segregation*, and *destruction*. These stages form the basis of the contingency approach to conflict intervention (see e.g., Fisher & Keashly, 1990) whereby different management or intervention strategies are viewed as appropriate and effective at different points in time. Fisher and Keashly's four-stage model describes four types of intervention strategies in response to these stages, stipulating that interventions should be sequenced and coordinated in order to de-escalate and resolve the conflict.

At the *destructive* stage, the primary intent of the parties involved in the conflict is to destroy, or at least control, the other by force. Here, third parties function as peacemakers by forcefully setting norms, defining unacceptable behavior, and isolating parties when necessary to keep the hostility under control. In work environments, these types of activities may comprise zero-tolerance policies, moving parties to separate departments and behavioral contracts handled through the human resources (HR) or personnel department. If the relationship can be stabilized and a commitment to joint effort is made, the way is then cleared for using other strategies depending on the parties' receptivity and sense of the critical issues involved in the conflict (e.g., whether it is substantive or relational in nature). In the *segregation* stage, competition and hostility predominate, and the conflict is perceived as threatening basic identity and security needs. An immediate form of control is therefore necessary in order to halt escalation and show that agreement is still possible on substantive issues. Here, strategies such as arbitration or power mediation can be utilized, indicative of a "providing impetus" intervention style, whereby a leader/manager informs their employees to either resolve the situation themselves or it will be resolved for them (Fisher & Keashly, 1990).

Once hostility is under control, consultation can be offered to assist parties in examining the dynamics of their conflict and the setting of "ground rules" for enhancing the relations towards one of trust and mutual respect. Such a form of intervention is often alien in sport organizations due to its clear and direct focus on relational issues. However, the introduction of teams as a critical element of organizational functioning may be suggestive of the capacity among some organizational members to deal with these more sensitive yet critical issues. Employee assistance programs (for sport examples, see e.g., Hawkins, Blann, Zaichkowsky, & Kane, 1994) as well as process-minded management may be able to provide this expertise, assuming the focus is on the relationship level as opposed to that of the person.

When a conflict reaches the *polarization* stage, relationship issues are central, as trust and respect are threatened and distorted perceptions and stereotypes emerge. At this stage, the key activity is consultation as it deals directly with relationship issues. Once a problem-solving orientation is established, work on the substantive issues can be handled by mediation, and the parties can be moved towards negotiating on their own. Finally, in the *discussion* stage, the key goal is to guarantee that communication between parties is accurate and perceptions of each other and the conflict of interests are grounded in reality. When needed, a third party can take a conciliation approach to facilitate clear and open communication on interests so that the parties can begin negotiating directly themselves. Within organizations, this type of intervention is typically reflected in the numerous informal processes and skills that employees and co-workers use with each other on a daily basis during formal and informal interactions in the working environment.

In seeking to develop social identity among sport organizations, practitioners should be cognizant of the content (task, relational), structure (horizontal, vertical), and stage of the occurrence of any conflict that may arise when enacting such a change management process. For example, a common source of vertical conflict that may occur in sport organizations is one between a coach/manager and their athlete. Often the conflict has origins of a task nature (i.e., de-selection due to poor or incorrect technical/tactical performance), indicative of a *discussion* stage for required management or resolution. However, if not addressed, this situation may escalate into one of a more relational-based nature (i.e., "my coach is not giving me the opportunity to prove what I can do. They don't like me, they no longer speak to me, so I'll never get picked so why should I bother with them?"), typified by *polarization* between the parties in conflict, with the further potential for escalation into stages requiring *segregation* and *destruction*-focused intervention.

A critical element in the development of effective change management systems is that an organization must consider the process in which its structures and methods of operations may lead to, or support, the proliferation of conflict among its members. For example, flatter power structures, such as those of high-performance environments (i.e., support staff performance working under a sole performance director), do not reduce the amount of conflict and may in fact increase it due to the fact that equal power relationships encourage individuals to engage in open communication (Kabanoff, 1991). This can lead to a greater exchange of information and consequently offer greater possibility for opposing ideas to be expressed. However, it should be noted that such forms of conflict tend to be cognitive in nature and hence facilitate cohesion and solidarity among workers (Kabanoff, 1991). In contrast, hierarchical structures with large power disparities tend to result in more hidden forms of conflict that manifest themselves in more covert and potentially counterproductive ways (Kolb, Bartunek, & Putnam, 1992).

Finally, the contingency approach to the escalation of conflict and the consideration of the sticky residues of conflict further emphasize the importance of preventive individual skill development for managers and subordinates (such as communication, perspective taking, and negotiation). Indeed, a focus on developing these relevant skills and competencies of the workforce is considered one of the primary strategies for resolution of potential "hot spot" situations or tensions in groups/individuals resistant to change (Fisher & Keashly, 1990).

Limitations and future research directions

Aligned with Fletcher and Wagstaff's (2009) seminal proposal that organizational psychology has much to contribute to the changing face of elite sport, it appears that the social identity approach too has value to elite sport both theoretically and practically. Notwithstanding this opportunity, there are limitations particularly centered on the lack of attention paid by researchers and practitioners to social identity principles within sport settings, which are highlighted with the purpose of stimulating future endeavors.

Haslam (2014, p. 13) asserted "there is now a colossal literature that speaks to the importance of internalized group memberships for peoples' sense of self, for their psychology more generally, and for their behavior". The evidence consistently spans health, clinical, and organizational domains and thus, on the one hand, one would not expect different results in elite sport settings. Most significantly because the social identity approach places the context and group dynamics, within which phenomena are being studied, at the heart of empirical investigations (Haslam, 2004). That being said, studying social identity principles in elite sport provides an opportunity to deepen our understanding of the psychosocial influences at the heart of numerous topics, including intra- and inter-group relations, leadership, and change (to name but a few). In addition, the discussion thus far speaks to the point that *applied* social identity literature is in comparative infancy, but perhaps is the realm within which elite sport has most to gain (i.e., from taking theory to practice).

Despite Haslam and colleagues' (2003) proposal of the ASPIRe model over a decade ago, it has taken time for the model to be empirically investigated. Indeed, there are relatively few applied articles that have examined its efficacy and effect on organizational outcomes (see, for an exception, Peters et al., 2012). Herein lies an opportunity for a systematic program of applied research examining the efficacy of social identity-informed organizational interventions (i.e., the ASPIRe model) to facilitate, for example, change and conflict management. Currently, it is unclear to what extent the specific ASPIRe model, or more generally, the 4R framework, will be successful in achieving the vision of facilitating organizational practices in elite sport. The contextual sensitivity of social identity approaches is a strength; nevertheless it's applicability, although advocated in sport psychology literature (see Slater et al., 2014; 2015), is – at least empirically – in its infancy. This is particularly so from an applied perspective. For example, each English Premier League (EPL) Club has a high number of groups (or subgroups) organized differently to business organizations. Anecdotally, there are examples of leaders such as Sir Clive Woodward who have successfully transitioned from business settings to elite sport (see Woodward, 2003). Indeed, despite a raft of synergies between business and elite sport there are contextual differences. For example, each EPL Club has an academy to develop the next generation of talent. It is not known, for instance, whether the ASPIRe model would be best implemented with the holistic club (which it is assumed would be preferable for the development of shared values across the organization), or whether the context dictates that the academy and first team practices are kept separate.

Further, at an applied level, team-building interventions from sport psychology literature may provide fruitful lines of inquiry (e.g., PDMS). PDMS (Dunn & Holt, 2004) involves individuals publically disclosing previously unknown stories about the self. Typically, PDMS has been adopted as a short-term, athlete-focused intervention aiming to improve athletic team functioning (e.g., Barker, Evans, Coffee, Slater, & McCarthy, 2014). Indeed, evidence from Barker et al. (2014) indicated that PDMS increases levels of social identity, together with promoting particular values athletes' ascribe to their team identity (e.g., to focus on supportive relationships), and associated outcomes (e.g., collective efficacy; Barker et al., 2014). It is unknown whether PDMS may have utility at an organizational level, but based on social identity theorizing and the specific phases of the ASPIRe model (Haslam et al., 2003) it may be hypothesized that PDMS would be an effective vehicle within the AIRing stage. Similarly, in change contexts, it has been posited that PDMS will help organizations to reflect (Slater et al., 2016). Nevertheless, empirical investigations are needed.

A final consideration for future research is an examination of the consequences of attempting to change the social identity of an organization and subgroups within it. Akin to the dearth of research into social identity in sport organizations, there has been a lack of consideration of conflict experiences in sport, particularly those which seek to understand conflict management and resolution. To date, the existing literature has been descriptive in nature and focused on the characteristics of the conflict episode itself within organizational settings in sport (see e.g., Mellalieu et al. 2013), as opposed to exploring how groups and organizations actually deal with the conflict experienced. It is also noteworthy that the organizational behavior literature suggests that while conflict management and resolution styles share a degree of overlap with an individual's personality traits, they are also related to a person's culture and gender (Solomon & Theiss, 2013). This association provides a wealth of opportunities for researchers to consider the influence of such personal and situational factors on conflict episodes within sport organizations, and the overall quality of the change management process adopted.

Conclusion

In elite sport there is a changing landscape where organizations continually strive for excellence and improvement. As a result, experiences of change and conflict are ubiquitous and inherently provide opportunities for improvement in so far as they are embraced. The social identity approach has much to contribute to elite sport broadly, and to change and conflict specifically, both theoretically and in the applied realm. In particular, adopting a social identity lens aids understanding of the psychosocial mechanisms (i.e., individuals' social identities) underpinning cognitions and behaviors in organizations and relevant subgroups. In sum, empirical evidence within the social identity tradition is beginning to translate into applied models. The research presented in this chapter has begun to provide insights into how, organizationally, elite sport can understand and promote stakeholders' social identities and facilitate successful change, minimizing potential negative consequences from phenomena such as intergroup conflict. Indeed, there remains much to be understood regarding social identities in sport and it is hoped this chapter stimulates systematic programs of research both broadly within elite sport and within specific contexts (e.g., during a change of manager/coach). We finish by reiterating the key messages for future research and applied practice.

Key messages for future research

- Individuals do not define themselves solely in a vacuum. Individuals define themselves in terms of the groups to which they belong (i.e., "us" and "we").
- Social identities matter and need to be understood to fully explain peoples' cognitions and behaviors across intra- and inter-group settings within sport organizations. There are clear implications of such observations for managing change and conflict as well as broader organizational issues.
- Strong social identification gives rise to positive individual-, group-, and organizational-level outcomes because individuals see the fate of the group as their own and strive to enhance "our" distinctiveness.
- It is time for scholars to direct their research activity to the applied realm. In other words, it is time to go from theory to practice (Haslam, 2014).
- Despite the wealth of literature in organizational psychology, only a limited body of knowledge has considered conflict management and resolution in sport. Before transferring the findings of organizational psychology research, investigation is first needed in sport-specific contexts to consider the value of such principles.

Key messages for applied practice

- There is opportunity for elite sport to work with and promote social identities to facilitate change management and organizational functioning more broadly.
- Change will disrupt internalized group memberships in a way that has individual-, group-, and organizational-level consequences. Such a challenge brings opportunity for reflection and the harnessing of social identities across organizations.
- Practitioners should embrace evidence-based models (e.g., the 4Rs) to underpin their practice to develop group and organizational identities.
- Conflict is an inevitable consequence of change in organizations, characterized by several forms (vertical, horizontal), origins (task, relation, process), and stages of severity (discussion, polarization, segregation and destruction).

- Individuals responsible for change should plan for and develop skills and strategies to manage and resolve conflict accordingly. These include being aware of the stage of the conflict escalation and developing relevant competencies among the workforce (e.g., communication, perspective taking, and negotiation) to prevent escalation of new and existing episodes.

References

Anastasio, P. A., Bachman, B. A., Gaertner, S. L., & Dovidio, J. F. (1997). Categorization, recategorization, and common ingroup identity. In R. Spears, P. J., Oakes, N. Ellemers, & S. A. Haslam (Eds.), *The social psychology of stereotyping and group life* (pp. 236–256). Oxford: Basil Blackwell.

Barker, J. B., Evans, A. L., Coffee, P., Slater, M. J., & McCarthy, P. J. (2014). Consulting on tour: A multiple-phase personal-disclosure mutual-sharing intervention and group functioning in elite youth cricket. *The Sport Psychologist, 28*(2), 186–197.

Barki, H., & Hartwick, J. (2004). Conceptualizing the construct of interpersonal conflict. *International Journal of Conflict Management, 15*(3), 216–244.

Blake, R. R., & Mouton, J. S. (1964). *Managerial grid*. Houston, TX: Gulf.

Bruner, M. W., Broadley, I. D., & Côté, J. (2014). Social identity and prosocial and antisocial behavior in youth sport. *Psychology of Sport and Exercise, 15*, 56–64.

Cameron, J. E. (2004). A three-factor model of social identity. *Self and Identity, 3*, 239–262.

Cruwys, T., Haslam, S. A., Dingle, G. A., Haslam, C., & Jetten, J. (2014). Depression and social identity: An integrative review. *Personality and Social Psychology Review, 18*, 215–238. doi:10.1177/1088868314523839.

Deutsch, M. (1990). Sixty years of conflict. *International Journal of Conflict Management, 1*, 237–263.

Dunn, J. G. H., & Holt, N. L. (2004). A qualitative investigation of a personal-disclosure mutual-sharing team building activity. *The Sport Psychologist, 18*(4), 363–380.

Eggins, R. A., O'Brien, A. T., Reynolds, K. J., Haslam, S. A., & Crocker, A. S. (2008). Refocusing the focus group: AIRing as a basis for effective workplace planning. *British Journal of Management, 19*, 277–292. doi:10.1111/j.1467-8551.2007.00541.x.

Fletcher, D., & Wagstaff, C. R. D. (2009). Organizational psychology in elite sport: Its emergence, application and future. *Psychology of Sport and Exercise, 10*, 427–434.

Fisher, R. J. (1990). *The social psychology of intergroup and international conflict resolution*. New York: Springer-Verlag.

Fisher, R. J., & Keashly, L. (1990). Third party consultation as a method of intergroup and international conflict resolution. In R. J. Fisher (Ed.), *The social psychology of intergroup and international conflict resolution* (pp. 211–238). New York: Springer.

Fransen, K., Coffee, P., Vanbeselaere, N., Slater, M. J., De Cuyper, B., & Boen, F. (2014). The role of athlete leaders in affecting the team confidence of their teammates and coaches: The mediating role of team identification and collective efficacy. *The Sport Psychologist, 28*(4), 347–360.

Gaertner, S. I., Dovido, J. F., Anastasio, P. A., Bachman, B. A., & Rast, M. C. (1993). The common ingroup identity model: Recategorization and the reduction of intergroup bias. *European Review of Social Psychology, 4*, 1–26.

Gilmore, S. (2009). The importance of asset maximisation in football: Towards the long-term gestation and maintenance of sustained high performance. *International Journal of Sports Sciences and Coaching, 4*(4), 465–488.

Glasl, F. (1982). The process of conflict escalation and roles of third parties. In G. B. J. Bomers & R. B. Peterson (Eds.), *Conflict management and industrial relations* (pp. 119–140). Boston, MA: Kluwer-Nijhof Publishing.

Haslam, S. A. (2004). *Psychology in organizations: The social identity approach.* (2nd ed.). Thousand Oaks, CA: Sage Publications.

Haslam, S. A. (2014). Making good theory practical: Five lessons for an applied social identity approach to challenges of organizational, health, and clinical psychology. *British Journal of Social Psychology, 53*(1), 1–20.

Haslam, S. A., & Reicher, S. D. (2006). Stressing the group: Social identity and the unfolding dynamics of responses to stress. *Journal of Applied Psychology, 91*(5), 1037–1052.

Haslam, S. A., Eggins, R. A., & Reynolds, K. J. (2003). The ASPIRe model: Actualizing social and personal identity resources to enhance organizational outcomes. *Journal of Occupational and Organizational Psychology, 76,* 83–113.

Haslam, S. A., O'Brien, A., Jetten, J., Vormedal, K., & Penna, S. (2005). Taking the strain: Social identity, social support, and the experience of stress. *British Journal Social Psychology, 44*(3), 355–370. doi:10.1348/014466605X37468.

Haslam, S. A., Jetten, J., & Waghorn, C. (2009). Social identification, stress and citizenship in teams: a five phase longitudinal study. *Stress and Health, 25*(1), 21-30.

Haslam, S. A., Reicher, S. D., & Platow, M. J. (2011). *The new psychology of leadership: Identity, influence and power.* Hove: Psychology Press.

Hawkins, K., Blann, W., Zaichkowsky, L., & Kane, M. A. (1994). *Athlete/coach career development and transition.* Canberra: Australian Sports Commission.

Holt, N. L., Knight, C. J., & Zukiwski, P. (2012). Female athletes' perceptions of teammate conflict in sport: Implications for sport psychology consultants. *The Sport Psychologist, 26,* 135–154.

Inoue, Y., Wann, D. L., Funk, D. C., Yoshida, M., & Nakazawa, M. (2015). Team identification and postdisaster social well-being: The mediating role of social support. *Group Dynamics: Theory, Research, and Practice, 19*(1), 31–44. doi:10.1037/gdn0000019.

Jehn, K. A. (1995). A multimethod examination of the benefits and detriments of intragroup conflict. *Administrative science quarterly, 40*(2), 256–282.

Jehn, K. A. (1997). Affective and cognitive conflict in work groups: Increasing performance through value-based intragroup conflict. In C. de Dreu & E. van De Vliert (Eds.), *Using conflict in organizations* (pp. 87–100). Thousand Oaks, CA: Sage.

Kabanoff, B. (1991). Equity, equality, power, and conflict. *Academy of Management Review, 16*(2), 416–441.

Kolb, D. M., Bartunek, J. M. and Putnam, L. L. (1992). *Hidden conflict in organizations.* Thousand Oaks, CA: Sage.

Mael, F. A., & Ashforth, B. E. (2001). Identification in work, war, sports, and religion: Contrasting the benefits and risks. *Journal for the Theory of Social Behaviour, 31,* 197–222. doi:10.1111/ 1468-5914.00154.

Martin, L. J., Bruner, M., Eys, M. A., & Spink, K. (2014). The social environment in sport: Selected topics. *International Review of Sport and Exercise Psychology, 7,* 87–105. doi: 10.1080/1750984X.2014.885553.

Mellalieu, S., Shearer, D. A., & Shearer, C. (2013). A preliminary survey of interpersonal conflict at major games and championships. *The Sport Psychologist, 27,* 120–129.

Morgan, P. B. C., Fletcher, D., & Sarkar, M. (2015). Understanding team resilience in the world's best athletes: A case study of a rugby union World Cup winning team. *Psychology of Sport and Exercise, 16*(1), 91–100. doi: 10.1016/j.psychsport.2014.08.007.

Paradis, K. F., Carron, A. V., & Martin, L. J. (2014). Athlete perceptions of intra-group conflict in sport teams. *Sport and Exercise Psychology Review, 10*(3), 4–18.

Peters, K. O., Haslam, S. A., Ryan, M. K., & Fonseca, M. (2012). Working with subgroup identities to build organizational identification and support for organizational strategy: A test of the ASPIRe model. *Group and Organization Management, 38*, 128–144. doi: 10.1177/1059601112472368.

Rahim, M. A. (2001). Managing organizational conflict: Challenges for organization development and change. *Public Administration and Public Policy, 87*, 365–388.

Rahim, M. A., & Buntzman, G. F. (1990). Supervisory power bases, styles of handling conflict with subordinates, and subordinate compliance and satisfaction. *Journal of Psychology, 123*(2), 195–210.

Schermerhorn, J. R., Hunt, J., & Osborn, R. N. (2003). *Organizational behavior.* (8th ed.) Chichester: Wiley.

Slater, M. J., Barker, J. B., Coffee, P., & Jones, M. V. (2015). Leading for gold: Social identity leadership processes at the London 2012 Olympic Games. *Qualitative Research in Sport, Exercise, and Health, 7*(2), 192–209. doi:10.1080/2159676X.2014.936030.

Slater, M. J., Coffee, P., Barker, J. B., & Evans, A. L. (2014). Promoting shared meanings in group memberships: A social identity approach to leadership in sport. *Reflective Practice: International and Multidisciplinary Perspectives, 15*(5), 672–685.

Slater, M. J., Coffee, P., Barker, J. B., Haslam, S. A., & Steffens, N. (under review). Leaders mobilize followers by cultivating a sense of shared social identity content. *British Journal of Social Psychology.*

Slater, M. J., Evans, A. L., & Turner, M. J. (2016). Implementing a social identity approach for effective change management. *Journal of Change Management, 16*(1), 18–37.

Slater, M. J., Evans, A. L., & Turner, M. J. (2016). Implementing a social identity approach for effective change management. *Journal of Change Management.* doi:10.1080/1469701 7.2015.1103774. Published ahead of print.

Slotter, E. B., Winger, L., & Soto, N. (2015). Lost without each other: The influence of group identity loss on the self-concept. *Group Dynamics: Theory, Research, and Practice, 19*(1), 15–30.

Solomon, D., & Theiss, J. (2013). *Interpersonal communication: Putting theory into practice.* New York: Routledge.

Tajfel, H. (1970). Experiments in intergroup discrimination. *Scientific American, 223*, 96–102.

Tajfel, H. (1972). Social categorisation. English manuscript of "La categorisation sociale". In S. Moscovici (Ed.), *Introduction à la Psychologie Sociale* (Vol. 1, pp. 272–302). Paris: Larosse.

Tajfel, H., & Turner, J. C. (1979). An integrative theory of intergroup conflict. In S. Worchel & W. G. Austin (Eds.), *The psychology of intergroup relations* (pp. 33–47). Monterey, CA: Brooks-Cole.

Turner, J. C. (2005). Explaining the nature of power: A three-process theory. *European Journal of Social Psychology, 35*, 1–22.

Turner, J. C., Hogg, M. A., Oakes, P. J., Reicher, S., & Wetherell, M. S. (1987). *Rediscovering the social group: A self-categorisation theory.* Oxford: Basil Blackwell.

Wagstaff, C. R. D., Fletcher, D., & Hanton, S. (2012). Positive organizational psychology in sport. *International Review of Sport and Exercise Psychology, 5*, 87–103.

Wagstaff, C. R. D., & Larner, R. J. (2015). Organizational psychology in sport: Recent developments and a research agenda. In S. D. Mellalieu and S. Hanton (Eds.), *Contemporary advances in sport psychology: A review* (pp. 91–119). London: Routledge.

Wagstaff, C. R. D., Gilmore, S., & Thelwell, R. (2015). Sport medicine and sport science practitioners' experiences of organizational change. *Scandinavian Journal of Medicine & Science in Sports, 25*(5), 685–698. doi:10.1111/sms.12340.

Wagstaff, C. R. D., Gilmore, S., & Thelwell, R. (2016). When the show must go on: Investigating repeated organizational change in elite sport. *Journal of Change Management, 16*(1), 38–54. doi:10.1080/14697017.2015.1062793.

Woodward, C. (2003). *Winning!* London: Hodder & Straughton.

INDEX

absenteeism 2, 17, 71
achievement goal theory 179, 184–6, 204, 206
affective events theory (AET) 39, 46
ASPIRe model 260–3

board of directors: *see* executive board
burnout 12, 14, 20–1, 39, 66, 71, 91, 102, 104, 109, 127–8, 188, 258

change 256–69; attitudinal responses to change 67; consequences of change 66; managerial change 65–6, 130; organizational change 5, 50–1, 63, 65, 92–3, 107, 113, 133–4
Chief Executive Officer (CEO) 72–3, 76, 156, 161, 188, 224, 244
climate: climate of sensitivity 67; emotional climate 35; motivational climate 44, 52, 107–8, 112, 127, 154, 169, 185, 188, 204, 221, 245, 247; organizational climate; 5, 71, 84, 88, 92, 105, 133, 169–70
coaching type behaviors 165–7
commitment in sport 11–28, 39, 45, 63, 68, 72, 93, 177, 188, 240, 244, 253, 265; affective commitment 15–16; antecedents of commitment 18; continuance commitment 15–16; correlates and outcomes of commitment 17; normative commitment 15–16; occupational commitment 17, 64; organizational commitment 23, 64, 72; three–component model of commitment 16
conflict 17–19, 46, 49, 63, 72, 108, 183, 193, 197, 203, 206, 221, 236, 239; management of conflict 241, 245–50, 257–269
Construal-Level Theory (CLT) 158–9, 169; construal fit 168
culture 121, 123, 131, 268; cultural stress 89–90, 92; high performance culture 73; organizational culture 5, 35, 45, 52; 73, 75, 133, 135, 223–4, 226; working culture 68

emotional contagion 42, 47, 95
emotional intelligence 40–1, 50, 53, 74, 105, 109, 224
emotional labor 39, 48, 69, 75, 77, 94
emotion regulation 38, 44–5, 48–50, 53, 138
Emotions as social information (EASI) model 42–4
empathy 181–2
empowerment 64, 166, 226, 230
engagement 4, 27, 39, 44, 49, 63–4, 73–4, 102, 105, 162
eudemonic well-being 102–5
executive board 63, 93, 156
exit, loyalty, voice, and cynicism 69–71

Four (4)Rs model 260, 269
functioning 4, 6, 40, 49, 52, 92, 130–3, 187, 260, 265, 269

Index **275**

group structure 129, 222, 245–6

hedonic well-being 102–5
human engineering 2–5

identity 23, 39, 158, 229, 235; identity manager 243–5; moral identity 179, 182–3; professional identity 63, 109; social identity 47, 129, 229, 256–270; team identification 236, 238, 242–5, 249–50
instructing type behavior 167–9
integrated model for emotion research in sport organizations 36

leadership: effective leadership 113, 158; leadership development 260; leader distance 156, 158–60, 167–9; leadership/inspirational type behaviors 162–5; leadership issues 87–8; leadership *in* organizations 156; leadership *of* organizations 156

management personnel 34, 63, 67, 71, 74, 76, 93, 105, 161, 203, 208, 218–20, 222–8, 238, 241, 244
media stress 194–6, 199, 202
meta–model of stress, emotion, and performance 37, 87
moral atmosphere 183–4
moral disengagement 180–1
moral emotion 179–80
moral identity 182–3
multi-level analysis 52, 226–7, 230, 259
myth of individualism 3–4, 258

National Governing Bodies (NGBs) 65, 157
National Sport Organization (NSO) 49, 128, 133

occupational stress 2, 17, 72
organizational citizenship behavior 4, 17, 64, 68, 73, 132, 177, 187
organizational dynamics 5, 120–1, 130–1, 133, 188
organizational strain 86
organizational stress 4, 84–6, 132, 194; coping 91; interventions 91–3, 112; outcomes 91; responses 90, 125
organizational stressors 4, 39, 84, 87–90, 122, 125, 224; stressor appraisals 90, 223; withstanding stressors 223–4, 236, 244, 249
organizational support 18–19, 64, 156

Performance Director 2, 14, 34, 44, 63, 66, 72–5, 93, 111, 120, 154, 156, 161, 186, 188, 222, 224, 258, 262, 266
personal disclosure and mutual sharing (PDMS) 27, 46, 261, 268
personnel psychology 2–5
personal stress 20, 27
politics (also political) 88, 93, 113, 130, 194
positive organizational psychology in sport (POPS) 3, 5, 133
psychological contract 49, 63, 68–70, 74, 256
psychosocial capital 49

research design 6, 51, 85, 93, 126, 140
research methods 93, 111–12; cluster analysis 27; diary 53; ecological momentary analysis 53; ecologically valid 44; and experience sampling methods 53; latent profile analysis 27; qualitative 93; quantitative 93; quasi–experimental 38
resilience 41, 50, 92, 120–142, 245, 249–50, 257, 259; organizational resilience 132–3, 134–7, 139–40, 14; team resilience 128–30, 139–40, 236, 244–50, 257, 259

satisfaction 4, 17–18, 21–2, 39, 64, 69, 90–1, 102–4, 112, 154, 159–60, 221, 261, 264
self-determination theory (SDT) 23, 104–5, 166, 184, 185–6, 226, 243
shared knowledge 225, 229
shared leadership 129, 225, 235–44, 246, 249–50
social capital 129, 135–36, 245, 247–9
social environment 3, 35, 179, 183, 185, 188, 217–30
social media 193–9, 203, 208–9
sociocultural 49, 52, 88, 121–25, 128, 130–32, 138, 142
strategic consensus, 225, 230
stress 83, 112, 120–42, 194, 195; buffers against stress 258; stress inherent in sport 260; *see also* organizational stress, personal stress
subgroup 12, 26, 44, 218–29, 261–3, 268–9
support staff 26, 53, 88, 93, 111–12, 114, 178, 180, 188, 194, 197, 208, 226, 266

team building 221, 227–8, 268
team confidence 236–7, 242, 245, 249
teamwork 196, 222, 225, 227–8
transformational leadership 18–19, 27, 129, 153–71, 221
tripartite model of leadership (TML) 160–3
turnover 2, 17, 20–1, 26, 39, 63–73

Taylor & Francis eBooks

Helping you to choose the right eBooks for your Library

Add Routledge titles to your library's digital collection today. Taylor and Francis ebooks contains over 50,000 titles in the Humanities, Social Sciences, Behavioural Sciences, Built Environment and Law.

Choose from a range of subject packages or create your own!

Benefits for you
- Free MARC records
- COUNTER-compliant usage statistics
- Flexible purchase and pricing options
- All titles DRM-free.

Benefits for your user
- Off-site, anytime access via Athens or referring URL
- Print or copy pages or chapters
- Full content search
- Bookmark, highlight and annotate text
- Access to thousands of pages of quality research at the click of a button.

REQUEST YOUR FREE INSTITUTIONAL TRIAL TODAY

Free Trials Available
We offer free trials to qualifying academic, corporate and government customers.

eCollections – Choose from over 30 subject eCollections, including:

Archaeology	Language Learning
Architecture	Law
Asian Studies	Literature
Business & Management	Media & Communication
Classical Studies	Middle East Studies
Construction	Music
Creative & Media Arts	Philosophy
Criminology & Criminal Justice	Planning
Economics	Politics
Education	Psychology & Mental Health
Energy	Religion
Engineering	Security
English Language & Linguistics	Social Work
Environment & Sustainability	Sociology
Geography	Sport
Health Studies	Theatre & Performance
History	Tourism, Hospitality & Events

For more information, pricing enquiries or to order a free trial, please contact your local sales team:
www.tandfebooks.com/page/sales

Routledge
Taylor & Francis Group

The home of Routledge books

www.tandfebooks.com